What people are saying about

He Was Our Man in Washington

Owen Symes is a rising young star who has created a masterful social history of the Obama years. This book clarifies the underlying contradictions of the Obama administration, linked to global capitalism. The clarification of Obamacare and other policies for health and human services is especially helpful. As we move forward, Symes's analysis helps us shed our illusions so we can avoid making the same mistakes all over again.

Howard Waitzkin, Distinguished Professor Emeritus of Sociology, University of New Mexico; Adjunct Professor of Internal Medicine, University of Illinois; author and coordinator, *Health Care Under the Knife: Moving Beyond Capitalism for Our Health*

Here is a comprehensively researched, well-argued, and balanced evaluation of Obama's presidency. Given the hostile caricatures promoted by the Trump regime and its spokespersons, Owen Symes has produced a valuable assessment of hopes and promises, strengths and failures of an important chapter in US history.

Richard D. Wolff, Professor of Economics Emeritus, University of Massachusetts, Amherst; coauthor of *Contending Economic Theories: Neoclassical, Keynesian, and Marxian*

He Was Our Man in Washington

A History of the Obama Years

He Was Our Man in Washington

A History of the Obama Years

Owen Symes

Winchester, UK
Washington, USA

JOHN HUNT PUBLISHING

First published by Zero Books, 2021
Zero Books is an imprint of John Hunt Publishing Ltd., No. 3 East St., Alresford,
Hampshire SO24 9EE, UK
office@jhpbooks.com
www.johnhuntpublishing.com
www.zero-books.net

For distributor details and how to order please visit the 'Ordering' section on our website.

ISBN: 978 1 78904 331 0
978 1 78904 332 7 (ebook)
Library of Congress Control Number: 2020931784

A CIP catalogue record for this book is available from the British Library.

Design: Stuart Davies

UK: Printed and bound by CPI Group (UK) Ltd, Croydon, CR0 4YY
Printed in North America by CPI GPS partners

We operate a distinctive and ethical publishing philosophy in
all areas of our business, from our global network of authors to
production and worldwide distribution.

Contents

Acknowledgments

History is a collaborative effort that would be impossible without the cooperation of many myriads of people. Acknowledging those with whom I have cooperated is, then, not just polite but imperative.

Foremost among those I must acknowledge is my Dad, through whose parenting and by whose example I have come to seek Truth and Justice. He and my wife, to whom I owe a great deal of my maturity and empathy, were gracious enough to wade through this work in an effort to edit it into some kind of coherence.

Many others deserve acknowledgment as well, including my hospitable in-laws who supported me with shelter and kindness; the journalists, historians, and memoirists upon whom I relied for information; the US taxpayer for funding the archives, government printing offices, and libraries (here's to you, Clarkson Independence District Library!) upon which I drew quite heavily; and my college professors who taught me to criticize and investigate with, I hope, some semblance of success.

Finally, I should like to acknowledge the labors imbedded within this work: more than 1200 hours of research and 300-plus hours of writing; perhaps 135 books read, yielding a collection of notes totaling a million words; and an additional 150 or more articles, books, and websites consulted. Any mistakes found did not result from lack of trying.

Introduction

The Obama Legacy

Barack Obama first garnered national attention after his 2004 speech to the Democratic National Convention. In that speech senator Obama lauded America as a place where "simple dreams" found fruition: "we can say what we think, write what we think, without hearing a sudden knock on the door...we can have an idea and start our own business without paying a bribe," a place where people "don't expect the government to solve all their problems," but do understand that "with just a slight change in priorities, we can make sure that every child in America has a decent shot at life, and that the doors of opportunity remain open to all."[1]

During 2008 he built upon these themes of individualism balanced with the conscientious (but necessary) use of government power, coupling them to the legacy of the civil rights movement and a defense of Free Market Capitalism. In March 2008 he spoke in Philadelphia, stating the goal of his campaign was: "to continue the long march of those who came before us, a march for a more just, more equal, more free, more caring, and more prosperous America...I believe deeply that we cannot solve the challenges of our time unless we solve them together, unless we perfect our union by understanding that we may have different stories, but we hold common hopes..."[2] In speaking to the people of Berlin in July of 2008, he touted the combined defense of Europe against communist aggression, the opening of markets after the Cold War and the consequent "spread of information and technology" that "reduced barriers to opportunity and prosperity." He spoke of the world as "more intertwined than at any time in human history."[3]

What struck a chord with many listeners, however, was not Obama's defense of capitalism or entrepreneurship; rather, they appreciated his recognition of their everyday hardships and his promise to use the power of the federal government to alleviate the many injustices that so unfairly weighed upon the working people of this country. In April 2008, speaking in Pennsylvania before that state's primary election, he said:

> We're here because there are families all across this country who are sitting around the kitchen table right now trying to figure out how to pay their insurance premiums, and their kids' tuition, and still make the mortgage so they're not the next ones in the neighborhood to put a For Sale sign in the front yard; who will lay awake tonight wondering if next week's paycheck will cover next month's bills.
>
> We're not here to talk about change for change's sake, but because our families, our communities, and our country desperately need it. We're here because we can't afford to keep doing what we've been doing for another four years. We can't afford to play the same Washington games with the same Washington players and expect a different result. Not this time. Not now...
>
> It is now our turn to follow in the footsteps of all those generations who sacrificed and struggled and faced down the greatest odds to perfect our improbable union. And if we're willing to do what they did; if we're willing to shed our cynicism and our doubts and our fears; if we're willing to believe in what's possible again; then I believe that we won't just win this primary election, we won't just win this election in November, we will change this country, and keep this country's promise alive in the twenty-first century.[4]

These rousing words combined with a general distaste of the failures of Republican government – the war, the environmental destruction, the prioritization of business over people – to propel this young senator into the Oval Office, where he spent the better part of the next decade grappling with affairs both foreign and domestic. Now that his administration has come to an end, what are we to make of him, his policies, his global impact as leader of the Free World™? Opinions differ.

Conservatives were nearly universal in a dismal opinion of Obama's time in office. *National Review*'s Andrew C. McCarthy painted Obama's history of community organizing in Chicago as "gussied-up...rabble-rousing," his political views as radically left, and in 2014 wrote a book-length case for impeaching the president, asserting Obama had been "violating his oath to preserve the Constitution, shredding the separation of powers, using the vast bureaucracy to repress his political opponents, and misleading the public about both his objectives and his failures" throughout his tenure as chief executive.[5]

Robert Ehrlich at the *Washington Examiner* admitted Obama's charisma and charm, but characterized Obama as "hyper-partisan and ultra-liberal." Ehrlich criticized the president for overseeing explosive spending and a sluggish economic recovery, for pushing "market-bending" policies in pursuance of one social justice cause after another, like the president's attempts at reinvigorating subprime lending in the hope of inflating rates of American homeownership, despite the inability of these subprime buyers properly to afford this piece of the American Dream. He further asserted that Obama had damaged American healthcare with a "one-size-fits-all" top-down federal diktat, while simultaneously dragging the federal government into imposing climate change belief onto good-faith skeptics when, in fact, "the science reflects constant temperature change on earth"; this policy resulted, wrote Ehrlich, from Obama's "anti-growth, limited horizon" left-wing politics.[6]

On the liberal side, assessments were mixed to positive. Ross Douthat at the *New York Times* looked forward to Obama's legislative achievements standing the test of time. While admitting the deep imperfections in Obama's chief domestic accomplishments, he pointed out that the economy *did* recover thanks in part to the Recovery and Reinvestment Act, and that the predictions of doom from his rightward opponents (hyperinflation and the debt crisis, for instance) never materialized. Healthcare costs had not ballooned, employers had not dumped people in droves, and "the insurance expansion [inaugurated by the Affordable Care Act] was large enough to matter." He saw Obama's foreign policy record as far more mixed – too hawkish in Libya, too dovish in Syria – but ultimately Obama's policy of "don't do stupid shit" kept America out of any Bush-style disasters. Even so, wrote Douthat, "a lot of small failures, no less than one major one, can leave the world less safe – and there were enough failures that Obama very clearly did."[7]

The Atlantic's Ta-Nehisi Coates emphasized that the symbol of America electing a black man to the presidency was not a symbol *merely*, but carried weight as all symbols do: "there is nothing 'mere' about symbols. The power embedded in the word *nigger* is also symbolic. Burning crosses do not literally raise the black poverty rate, and the Confederate flag does not directly expand the wealth gap."[8] He praised Obama's ability to cross America's racial divide through his "ability to emote a deep and sincere connection to the hearts of black people, while never doubting the hearts of white people."[9] And even with his faults and in the face of severe conservative resistance, Obama managed accomplishments: he "remade" American healthcare, "revitalized" the Justice Department's anti-discrimination wing, and "began" dismantling the federal private prison system; he supported marriage equality, ended Don't Ask Don't Tell, and committed the presidency to ending the War on Drugs via presidential commutation – 944 commutations in all, more than the past 11 presidents combined.[10]

Farther to the Left, opinions turned back against Obama. Cornel West encapsulated this view, writing that while Obama paid lip service to many progressive issues, he ultimately preferred an unjust compromise over a just conflict. "Unfortunately, Obama thrives on being in the middle. He has no backbone to fight for justice. He likes to be above the fray. But for those of us who are *in* the fray, there is a different sensibility. You have to choose which side you're on, and he doesn't want to do that." West elaborated: "Obama's attitude is that of a neo-liberal, and they rarely have solidarity with poor and working people. Whatever solidarity he does offer is just lip-service to suffering but he never makes it a priority to end that suffering."[11]

Who does a better job of approximating reality? In order to make some sense of a president of such immediate vintage, I have elected to view his 8 years in office through a series of topical focal points that taken together give some approximation of how his administration grappled with many of the various issues and crises that dotted his White House tenure. Despite the heated partisan rhetoric, what comes out of this analysis is a president who more than anything else desired to give America more of the same. He was not the radical revolutionary many conservatives feared and many leftists wanted. He found comfort in the liberal tradition of faith in a market with some government oversight (but not too much!), of an interventionist foreign policy, of the myth of American Exceptionalism.

He entered office wanting to distance himself from what he considered the maladaptations of the Bush II years – most especially the unrealistic grandiosity of the War on Terror. But, as his presidency got under way, he abandoned any pretense to progressive change. He would continue to fight terrorists, just with a little more circumspection. Invasion and occupation were phased out in favor of drone strikes and a reliance on local allies and proxies. Civil liberties continued to be violated at home, although with a more robust legal justification. The tactics would change, the strategic vision amended, but the underlying need for war would never seriously be questioned.

In economic terms the Obama administration continued the

bipartisan consensus of neoliberalism, a form of liberalism that views markets as naturally efficient and the best method of structuring practically all human activity, economic or otherwise. He admitted that the market was sometimes imperfect, and thus his administration did make tweaks to the existing system that improved the lives of some and held the rich to some modicum of account. The Dodd-Frank Act thus created the Consumer Financial Protection Bureau, among other reforms. Tellingly, however, the fundamentals of the economic system – especially the all-encompassing drive for private profit at public expense – was not addressed.

The acceptance of neoliberal orthodoxy (that markets can solve anything) affected Democratic efforts at overhauling American healthcare as well. The Affordable Care Act proved to be a bandage for some, stemming the bleeding of the body politic to one degree or another, but the disease – the false assumption that private greed would yield public good – persisted. Health insurance coverage expanded considerably, the quality of coverage continued to be ruled by the profit motive, and so insurance, drug, and hospital corporations made billions in profits while most Americans continued to be frustrated with their slapdash constellation of healthcare. And even with expanded insurance coverage, the underlying material causes of so much illness – lack of housing, poor living conditions, unsafe work environments, overwork and lack of leisure time, stagnant wages – and the flawed emphasis on specialists over general practitioners in American medicine were never addressed.

On the margins of American society some legal improvements resulted from the Obama years. Obama's racial track record with regards to African Americans proved especially mixed. He offered no major legislative initiatives to address black economic hardship or the War on Drugs that gutted so many black communities. He talked about racial issues rarely until his second term, when police violence against minorities became a nationally publicized issue, but when he did so the Right was quick to vilify him as pandering to minority voters and needlessly dividing the nation. During his second term he did work more diligently within the confines of the executive branch to offer some meager amelioration to black Americans.

Obama's 2008 campaign and the first few years of his term were not energetically supportive of gay rights, at least not to the extent that many in the gay community had hoped for. Indeed, his desire to compromise at all costs often put him on friendly terms with conservatives that saw non-normative sexual mores as sinful, diseased, or otherwise socially harmful. Still, he did eventually push for the repeal of Don't Ask, Don't Tell (DADT) that brought gay people fully into the ranks of the armed forces. By the 2012 election he had come around to support the right of homosexuals to marry. Once pushed, Obama and his administration put rhetorical muscle and executive verve into supporting this marginalized group – at least within the narrow confines of the establishment – by refusing to defend the Defense of Marriage Act (DOMA) and penning several executive orders aimed at defending gay rights.

The gains made for trans Americans under Obama's watch were real, they were narrowly confined, and they were dangerously ephemeral. Transpeople found some degree of representation within the administration – no meager thing; several executive orders made their lives appreciably easier in the labor market and the military. These gains, however, did nothing to chip away at the broader fundamental assumptions in the very areas that trans identity focused: personhood and its relation to the self and the broader social fabric. Instead, the mainstream narrative of trans identity as a disease in need of a cure was generally accepted, the binaries of the status quo affirmed.

In the fight against climate change Obama made some effort to promote the adoption of clean and renewable energy. At the same time, however, he continued his predecessor's policy of promoting domestic fossil fuel production. Not only was natural gas included among the ranks of "clean" power within administration policy, but oil production continued its drastic expansion under Obama's presidency. While congressional combativeness prevented significant climate-oriented legislation from passing, the legislation championed by the president, relying as it did upon the very "market forces" that had caused global warming in the first place, could not have solved the problem in any case.

Obama's energy policy contradicted not only his attempts at fighting climate change but also set his administration squarely against the interests of America's Indigenous Peoples. Rhetorically, the president pledged to defend their ancient rights and traditions against further encroachment, but in practice he only exercised his powers in their defense after immense pressure was exerted upon him from below. His default rested with the extractivist industries eager to fill their hungry maws at the expense of the First Nations.

A Note on Method and Ideology

History concerns the thoughts and actions of humans, which being social creatures act and think in relation to one another in a complex series of interconnected families, clans, municipalities, social clubs, corporations, nation states. These various groupings possess more or less power to act based upon the structures that constitute the economics and politics of a given society, which we might think of as the overarching connective web. Individual success depends upon their relationship with other people – their standing within a given association, that group's relative influence and power among other groups, and the society's position relative to its neighbors. No one is an island; we are all continental.[12]

Since individual success is a result of how one copes within group and structure, history written with a focus on the atomized individual and their "self-made" success, severed as it is from the relational truth of human existence, caters to the tastes of those already possessed of power who would prefer to consider themselves as the masters of their universe. Such history does not account for group dynamics or hierarchies of power, meaning that an individual's success is often falsely attributed purely to their attitude, talent, or essential character. Little or no mention is made of the opportunities they had access to on account of their rank, caste, socio-economic status, location, etc. Or, if they be one of the precious few exceptional individuals who rise "from rags to riches," they are then held up as an exemplar to which the multitude looks in frustrated longing.

I am no court historian committed to the empty chronicling of kings and potentiates, happy to pen books whose gilded pages seek through their shimmer to mask oppression and exploitation and misery. I am not interested in writing history for the powerful, but rather in critiquing power and holding it to account. To that end I have stuck to analyzing groups and structures, using individual actors as exemplars of a given trend, tendency, movement. My aim in this has been to understand the structures that undergird the various groups competing or cooperating among one another, thus to make sense of the choices individuals made under the social circumstances in which they found themselves, and in so doing call into question the prevailing narrative of radical individualism (or Great-Manism) weighing down the eyes of contemporary commentary and popular scholarship.[13]

Facts are infinite and human comprehension somewhat less so; no one is able to compass all the data around them. We filter this infinity through our sensory perceptions, our temperaments, our beliefs, our passions. We call this filtering process *ideology*, that mental framework through which we discern those facts we consider important. Looking into the past is no exception to this, as the inquirer must by necessity pick and choose the facts, statistics, examples, topics that are allowed a place within the historical narrative. The relationship between information and ideology should be a reciprocal one; mental structure guides the search for facts and the facts shape further the mental structure.[14]

I approached this history from the perspective of socialism, a view I arrived at about the time I finished preliminary research on the War on Terror and the Great Recession. By socialism I do not mean the authoritarian state ownership of the economy (as in the USSR), but rather a belief that economic and political democracy go hand in hand. Voting for our leaders means little when we spend most of our waking lives working in places run like dictatorships. Markets fail as a solution to this problem because they tend to favor the rich and are therefore undemocratic in nature. As much as possible I have worked to ensure that my ideology has not unduly twisted reality too much out of proportion. The facts may never speak for themselves, but I did my best to listen to what I thought they had to say.[15]

Chapter 1

The Forever War

1.1 The War for the Greater Middle East Begins

The United States emerged from World War Two with a level of dominance unseen in recorded history. The old powers of Britain, France, and Germany lay in ruins, as did more recent claimants to global preeminence like Japan and the USSR. Of all the industrialized nations, only the United States exited that second world conflagration more vigorous than it had entered. Over the course of the war, American products – trucks, weapons, food, oil – had flooded across the world, American bases (over 2000 of them) had dotted the globe, and Americans had filled the skies and the seas and the fields of battle. Now, with the guns all but silent, the Truman administration found itself not only possessed of its pre-war holdings (the various colonies and territories and "apportionments" in Puerto Rico, Guam, Hawaii, Alaska, the Philippines, etc.), but also occupying Japan, portions of Germany and Austria, along with former colonial possessions like the southern tip of Korea. All told, the 132 million people of the continental United States now administered some 135 million people all over the world.[1]

At first Truman's administration contemplated occupation and direct government. To that end, the War Department estimated the US would need perhaps 2.5 million men to remain under arms for 1946 alone. Americans, however, jubilant in their overwhelming victory but tired of a martial existence, revolted at this prospect in a wave of protest never before seen in American history. Domestically, Truman's office received some 60,000 postcards in a single day demanding the troops come home; and congresspeople were inundated with baby shoes all reading "bring daddy home." More troubling still, from Truman's perspective, troopers mutinied. A total of 20,000 GIs in Manila, not interested in garrisoning any colony anywhere, mutinied, with many declaring solidarity with the Filipino guerrillas; responding to these demonstrations, 20,000 more soldiers protested in Honolulu, 3000 in Korea, 5000 in Calcutta, with 3000 more sailors in Guam staging a hunger strike and further demonstrations breaking out in China, Burma, Japan, France, Germany, Britain, and Austria – with additional supporters staging protests in Washington DC, Chicago, and New York. American leadership did its best to brush the incidents under the rug, but they did ultimately acquiesce. Truman's administration reduced a force of 8 million in May 1945 down to 1 million by the end of 1946. Lamented the president: "...our influence throughout the world, as well as China, waned as the millions of American soldiers were processed through the discharge centers."[2]

This trend towards demobilization did not last long. The perceived threat of communism revitalized the case for American interventionism, and Truman did his level best to whip the American people into a frenzy so that never again would Americans retreat as thoroughly as they had after the First World War from the responsibilities of the world stage. The Berlin Air Lift of 1948, the 1949 communist victory in China, the USSR's spreading influence in Eastern Europe, rising communist political power in Italy and elsewhere, all these and more primed the American people for more thoroughgoing intervention, which came when communist North Korea threw its tanks across the border into the South (then-governed by a dictator friendly to the West). Many of these "aggressive" actions had been provoked – Stalin's blockade of Berlin that necessitated the Berlin Airlift, for example, being a reaction to the US introducing the Deutschmark into Berlin, which Stalin considered an encroachment on the USSR's economic prerogatives in its zone of occupation, or North Korea's attack upon the South being the climax of a mutual conflict waged by both countries, but the American government did not paint things that way, and the American people, ignorant of the complex grays of geopolitics, embarked upon an anti-red crusade.[3]

The focus of American power and activity was Europe, center of the nineteenth-century world, the world wars that resulted from that "glorious" century, and now the epicenter of the standoff between Russia and the United States. Other areas of the world, however, soon came to play their own special roles. Proxy wars were fought in the post-colonial regions, as emerging peoples and nations sought Soviet help against their former oppressors (and the governments those oppressors left behind), and American aid poured in to counteract these "communist" offensives. Hence our involvement in Greece and Turkey, the Korean War, our interventions in Indonesia, Cuba, Chile, and Vietnam; the prerequisite of preeminence, i.e. the exertion of power so as to dominate events to your advantage, constantly pushed US interests all around the globe. The Manifest Destiny of the previous century redefined itself in the twentieth as a crusade of liberty (capitalism) against tyranny (communism).

The Middle East fit into this new global order by a mere quirk of geology. Its nations sat atop vast quantities of oil. Since hegemony in an industrial world requires energy, this was a fact of singular importance to the West. Britain had sought control over Iranian oil fields since the early twentieth century, pursuing energy security so as to keep its fleet and therefore its empire afloat. France did the same in Algeria. America, by 1945, had taken an interest in the recently solidified kingdom of Saudi Arabia, promising support for the new king in return for favorable terms should oil be found there in noteworthy quantity.

After the Second World War, England and to a lesser degree France attempted to reassert themselves in the region but could not rekindle past glory. England's primary contribution to local politics was the haphazard creation of the Jewish state, which was to have profound ripples across the politics of the region. Renewed European dominance of the region did not last a decade. In 1956, Britain and France in tandem with Israel attempted, by independently attacking an upstart Egypt (then attempting to nationalize the Suez Canal and at that time friendly to the USSR), to act outside the wishes of American policymakers. This precipitated the Suez Crisis, at the conclusion of which the Old World withdrew from its direct role in the area, content to sell arms to the new Arab countries and their Israeli rival and let the US maintain the oil supply to the West.[4] With America now predominant in the region, it needed local allies to act as a counterweight to a hostile Egypt. President Eisenhower turned to Saudi Arabia, saying he wanted to "[build] up King Saud as a major figure in the Middle Eastern area…[to] restore Middle East oil markets in Western Europe."[5]

US involvement escalated in the 1970s with the falling off of domestic oil production and our increasing reliance on imported supplies. The policy of supporting local proxies, begun under Eisenhower, grew to match this mounting involvement. In addition to Saudi Arabia, Israel was added to counterbalance Syria, Iran to tip the scales against Iraq. Weapons poured into the region, with Iran being the world's largest arms importer through the end of the decade.[6]

The use of regional proxies continued through the duration of the Cold War, but cracks in the strategy showed themselves with the fall of the Iranian Shah's government and its replacement by the Islamic Republic of Iran, a government hostile to the United States (and its undue influence in the country). President Jimmy Carter and his defense team, fearful that the Soviets would take advantage of the instability and thus threaten Western oil access, responded to the Iranian Revolution by declaring that the Persian Gulf now fell directly within the US sphere of interest, and that America would use any means at its disposal to defend the region. This declaration was coupled with our contemporaneous response to the hostage crisis in Tehran: in 1980, president Carter ordered US special forces to liberate the Americans held captive by Iranian students. Although the mission ended in fiasco, it opened the doors to military intervention and inaugurated what has been an ongoing and gradually escalating US war in the region.[7]

Increasingly in the 1980s, the US preference of relying upon proxy forces met with local frustration and the renewed desire in government circles to use American military force directly. With the defeat in Vietnam of so recent vintage, however, this desire was not at first universal. The Reagan administration had to proceed in a somewhat piecemeal fashion in its use of military intervention. It began by declaring the (first) "War on Terror," responding to perceived provocations from Libya and the spate of terrorist attacks perpetrated by the Palestinian Liberation Organization and other Islamist groups popping up in the region. American efforts to engage in this struggle were uninspired. A total of 1200 marines were deployed in Beirut (the primary result of which was a devastating bombing of a marine base and the ignominious withdrawal of US forces); air strikes were launched against Libya; and much was said against the evils of using terror as a political tool. Defeating "terror," however, was not the priority.[8]

Stabilization of the Middle East, so as to allow the free flow of oil into the West, remained the chief concern of US policy makers. To that end, the US and its allies sold weapons to an embattled Iraq, trying its Baathist best to win a quick war against revolutionary Iran but finding itself enmeshed in a barbed wire jellyfish from which there seemed no escape. Iranian revolutionary ardor and their existing stock of US weapons from the days of the Shah proved more than capable of matching Iraqi ambition, and it was only with foreign military aid (the US provided Iraq with, among other things, military intelligence, computer equipment, helicopters, and trucks) that Saddam Hussein was able to exterminate his way through an 8-year stalemate to an exhausted peace. This war, the most destructive since 1945, allowed the US to play both sides, as it publicly sold equipment to Iraq (while encouraging its allies to sell them weapons) and privately provided arms to Iran. All the while, fearing a Soviet push into a vulnerable and still oil rich Iran, US planners kept their nuclear arsenal at the ready, preferring to annihilate Iran rather than see it fall to Soviet occupation.[9]

At the same time, the US ramped up arms shipments to the Afghan resistance to the Soviets, who had sent soldiers into Afghanistan in order to bolster the communist government there against Islamist rebels. Aid had originally been sent under the Carter administration, although it was limited in its extent to medical supplies with some obsolete weapons thrown in as well. Republicans subsequently increased US support, including anti-aircraft missiles, with the objective of trapping the Soviets in their own Vietnamesque quagmire. This we achieved and after nearly a decade of fighting against jihadists of many nations, the USSR finally agreed to pull out of Afghanistan – leaving the urban-centered communist government vulnerable to eventual takeover by the conservative Taliban. Not for the last time would jihadist resolve couple with Western hardware to give a superpower a bad time.

The fall of the Soviet Union brought the renewed confidence of the Reagan years to a fever pitch, and any reliance on local proxies was discarded out of hand. Now, as the unrivaled global power, US policymakers felt they could take direct action wherever they saw fit – and Saddam Hussein soon proved the first test of this direct approach. Responding to the Iraqi invasion of Kuwait, a coalition led almost exclusively by US forces invaded from Saudi Arabia and drove Iraq out. To facilitate military operations, the US established bases in Saudi Arabia that it continued to maintain after the war ended. After the fighting the US also imposed economic sanctions upon Iraq that crippled its economy without actually toppling Saddam Hussein (he was still begrudgingly needed as a counterweight to Iran). These sanctions were enforced via "No-Fly Zones," and resulted in a decade-long air war against Iraq that amounted to something only slightly less than genuine occupation of that country. Between 1991 and 1996, Operation Provide Comfort II (over Kurdish regions) resulted in 42,000 sorties flown over Iraq. Operation Southern Launch, establishing a No-Fly Zone in southern Iraq, amassed 150,000 sorties between 1992 and 2003.[10] To give a sense of the effect this air war had upon the Iraqi economy, note that between 1991 and 1996 Iraq's per capita GDP never rose above $507, compared to $2304 in 1989.[11]

From the US perspective, thanks to quick and direct intervention, Iraq was kept from acquiring undue influence on the region (and its oil reserves) and the status quo in all its inky shimmer was maintained – all while finally shaking off the military malaise of Vietnam and proving the dawn of the twenty-first century would be one glowing with successful US interventions abroad. Nary a thought was paid to the growing discontent (among people flush with our cash and armed with our weapons) US policies continued to prompt.

This air occupation of Iraq continued despite a change in the political party occupying the White House. Indeed, Clinton's policies in the Middle East remained steadfast in their devotion to the status quo. Israel continued to receive regular defense subsidies, a policy commitment dating back decades. Between 1976 and 2004, Israel was the largest annual recipient of US foreign assistance. By the early twenty-first century, annual Foreign Military Financing grants from the US to Israel represented about one-fourth of the overall Israeli defense budget.[12] Tyrannies like Egypt (an ally since the late 1970s when it abandoned the Soviet sphere) and Saudi Arabia received lavish support as well. US forces remained deployed in Saudi Arabia throughout the Clinton presidency.

Clinton did not use ground troops in the Middle East as had been done by his two Republican predecessors, but he was more than eager to use air power and long-range missiles in the pursuit of US interests, as the bombing campaigns in the Balkans and the cruise missile strikes in the Sudan and Afghanistan show. So while the details might have differed, the overarching policy objectives remained just as Carter had established – with the key innovation that the extent of territory within which the US thought it necessary to act in order to maintain its vital interests in the region expanded over time, encompassing not just the countries surrounding the Persian Gulf but places like Libya, Afghanistan, and the Balkans.

1.2 Global War on Terror

Muslims eager to resist US hegemony in the Middle East sometimes turned to the power of the nation state (as was the case in Iran), sometimes turned to the machinery of the UN, sometimes turned to the recourse of terrorism. That some Muslims would employ terrorist tactics is neither intrinsic to Islam (religious terrorism traces its roots to the Jewish zealots of the first century CE and can also be found among the Thugi of India and Evangelical anti-abortionists in America), nor all that surprising. Local states and the UN were either too weak or too beholden to American subsidies to be able to resist effectively and no group of Muslims was capable of waging a conventional war against overwhelming American forces.[13] Terrorism, on the other hand, seemed like a possibly effective alternative for three reasons. (1) The Iranian Revolution proved that US proxies were not invulnerable to Indigenous pressure; (2) Reagan's withdrawal of US marines from Lebanon after terror attacks there had killed more than 100 Americans in 1983 made terrorism look effective against direct American intervention; (3) the defeat of the Soviet Union in Afghanistan (and its subsequent political collapse) gave men like Osama bin Laden a concrete sense of self-importance, as they considered the resistance of the Mujahideen central to that victory.[14]

Responding to decades of US aid to Israel – in the form of weapons sales and UN security council vetoes that favored Israeli interests over Arab; responding to a strong US military presence in Saudi Arabia, the site of Islam's two holiest cities; responding to what they saw as the successor to the imperial regimes of Europe, a new network of jihadists fighting under the name al Qaeda committed itself to redressing grievances with how the US chose to exert itself in the Muslim World. America's legacy in the Middle East fostered al Qaeda in more ways than one, however. The group's funding came often directly from American coffers. After World War Two, the United States operated military installations in Saudi Arabia that were built by a fledgling construction firm owned by the bin Laden family – and these were not the only American contracts the bin Laden firm received at the time. These American ties helped catapult the bin Laden firm into economic success and it soon became the preferred construction firm of the Saudi government. The money obtained from American customers and others served to educate a young Osama bin Laden, and also gave him the fortune he needed to fund his military aspirations – first against the Soviets and later against the Americans.[15]

During the 1990s bin Laden struck at the periphery of American power, attacking a pair of US embassies in Africa and also a US airbase at Dhahran that killed 19 Americans. The air force responded to this attack by building a new base in the remote desert of Saudi Arabia at the cost of $150 million, and remarkably, the contractor the Saudi government hired to make this new American installation a reality was the bin Laden firm.[16] In 1998 bin Laden issued a fatwa against "Jews and Crusaders," listing three items – American occupation of Saudi Arabia, American sanctions against Iraq, and American support for Israel – as clear signs that the US had declared war against Allah. Bin Laden and his followers vowed to rise to His defense.

Given this context, we Americans must understand that the 9/11 attack did not, except in the most literal sense, come out of the clear blue. They were perfectly rational attacks upon *the* global interloper, the political actor responsible for overthrowing democratic government (Iran, 1953), torpedoing the Israeli-Palestinian peace process by bankrolling and turning a blind eye to much Israeli aggression, providing Iraq with the WMD later used to exterminate the Kurds (then invading that same country and bombing it for a decade), propping up the dreadful monarchy in Saudi Arabia, and waging a decades-long covert war against revolutionary Iran. 9/11 was thus a response to our attempts to "stabilize" the politics of the Muslim World for our benefit. It should not be controversial to admit that it was reasonable that some of the inhabitants of the region did not see things done for US interests as good for *their* interests, whatever tactics they chose to use in an attempt to change their situation.

Since this conflict for the Greater Middle East had hitherto been waged, with a few notable exceptions, without the use of American troops, the US population was only vaguely aware of this fight. Sustained coverage of our billions in funding to Israeli colonizers, Egyptian generals, and Saudi royals over the course of a generation does not make for a profitable news cycle. This was why the American people reacted so forcefully after the 9/11 attack, rallying behind a government that, less than a year earlier, had been steeped in controversy surroundings its very electoral legitimacy. Most Americans did not realize (indeed, they were never told) that the fight had been going on for a generation. Popular US reaction assumed that the attacks were completely unprovoked, and the US government took full advantage of this ignorance to pursue an even more aggressive and direct form of Middle Eastern stabilization.

President George W. Bush immediately framed the aftermath

of 9/11 in terms of a war between freedom and fascism, good and evil. He said in September 2001: "Americans are asking, why do they hate us? They hate what we see right here in this chamber – a democratically elected government. Their leaders are self-appointed. They hate our freedom – our freedom of religion, our freedom of speech, our freedom to vote and assemble and disagree with each other."[17] Comparing al Qaeda with twentieth-century fascism,[18] Bush II showed his ignorance of Middle Eastern history: he equated al Qaeda (an Islamist organization seeking a break with the West, the destruction of contemporary nation states, and the return of the caliphate) with Western ideologies and movements that assumed the primacy of the nation state and subsumed religion under the banner of nationhood.[19] This made for a good sound bite, but grievously inept public policy.

It should be noted, however, that despite Bush II's black and white mindset, he never framed the conflict as a war between Islam and Christianity per se, or as a clash of civilizations; in universalizing fascism and applying it as a descriptor to al Qaeda, he saw the fight purely in Western terms of liberal democracy and enlightenment against dictatorship and the hindrance of personal freedom. Even so, his Christianity tinged his view of the Middle East, and he saw it as a special region of the world. During a phone conversation with French president Chirac, Bush II said: "Gog and Magog are at work in the Middle East. Biblical prophesies are being fulfilled. This confrontation is willed by God, who wants us to use this conflict to erase His people's enemies before a new age begins."[20] His attitude, coupled with the influence of Dick Cheney and his neo-conservative foreign policy mindset that viewed military assertiveness as the foundation of American global leadership, produced a redeclared War on Terror.[21]

The Taliban that controlled Afghanistan (where al Qaeda had been based) was given an ultimatum to either give up all those the US *suspected* of being involved in the attacks, or face deadly retribution.[22] Let us pause for a moment to consider this chain of events. Within weeks of the terrorist attack, the US government claims it knows who carried out the strike (not unreasonable, but certainly a conclusion reached in great haste); it demands of the sovereign nation in which the suspects are based extradition of those suspects; it makes these demands without providing any evidence to the government of Afghanistan; and it bolsters them with the threat of deadly force. The rapidity of these events, the cavalier handling by Bush II's administration of a foreign power, should indicate to us that, as far as the United States government was concerned, sovereignty was just a word and meant little in the face of national vengeance. If this seems an unfair analysis, consider if the reverse had occurred: members of the KKK (or some other white nationalist group) are implicated in bombing Kabul, the capital of Afghanistan, destroying the Pul-e Khishti mosque. In response, the Afghans quickly demand those they think *might* have done it be extradited to them for trial and judgment. If we refuse to comply, they bellow, we should expect a nationwide bombing campaign to commence forthwith. We are then given a few weeks to think it over. Would that satisfy our national honor, our expectation for fair dealing, mutual respect, and national sovereignty? No.[23]

At any rate, the Afghans did not acquiesce to US demands, and bombing (of a country, mind, that had never attacked us) began in October 2001, followed swiftly by invasion. US special forces, supporting local Afghans already fighting against the Taliban, waged a lightning campaign that led to the downfall of Taliban rule, without completely crushing their organization. As the administration turned its attention elsewhere, the new government of Afghanistan, backed by a few thousand US and allied troops, would endeavor to bring order and governance to a vast and unstable country. Sometimes herculean efforts by locals and coalition forces made significant progress in some areas, like education for women (curtailed under the Taliban), but the Taliban was allowed to metastasize across the poorly-guarded border in Pakistan; and by 2007 a resurgence saw fighting escalate across the country, most especially in the east. Bush II left office with Afghanistan very much in trouble.

It is interesting to note bin Laden's response to the US invasion of Afghanistan. In November 2001, bin Laden said: "The entire West, with the exception of a few countries, supports this unfair, barbaric campaign, although there is no evidence of the involvement of the people of Afghanistan in what happened in America. The people of Afghanistan had nothing to do with this matter. The campaign, however, continues to unjustly annihilate the villagers and civilians, children, women and innocent people."[24]

In December 2001, after the brunt of the US air campaign, he commented further:

America bears an unspeakable crusader grudge against Islam. Those who lived these months under continuous bombardment by the various kinds of US aircraft are well aware of this. Many villages were wiped out without any guilt. Millions of people were made homeless during this very cold weather. Those oppressed men, women, and children now live in tents in Pakistan. They committed no [crime].[25]

Domestically the federal government gave itself vastly augmented authority to surveil citizens and foreigners alike. This was not a fundamental shift, for in the wake of the 1995 Oklahoma City Bombing Congress passed (with broad bipartisan support) and president Clinton signed the Antiterrorism and Effective Death Penalty Act of 1996, and in 1999 Clinton also signed the Intelligence Authorization Act for Fiscal Year 1999, which expanded the scope of roving wiretaps. Still, the new surveillance powers created after 9/11 were far reaching. On October 26, 2001

Bush II signed the USA PATRIOT Act into law – again passed with overwhelming bipartisan support. The law expanded the ability of the government to conduct roving wiretaps (tracing multiple phones without multiple subpoenas), to monitor email and business records, to have more authority over undocumented immigrants (including holding them indefinitely without trial), to make it harder to appeal detention, and also to expand the working definition of a terrorist.[26] Among the many provisions, Section 215 gave the government broad power to ask businesses for records relating to someone suspected of terrorist or terrorist adjacent activities. This would come under severe criticism during the Obama years but very little materialized at the time.[27]

Of the litany of surveillance programs created or expanded under Bush II's tenure, some had generally understood legal backing – like the activities authorized under the USA PATRIOT Act – while others stood on muddier ground. Stellarwind, for instance, was a program under the National Security Administration (NSA) whereby phone and email records of American citizens were collected without any kind of warrant. This program sought to target Americans communicating with foreigners, so as to establish possible links to terrorist activity, but since it did not go through the established FISA (Foreign Intelligence Surveillance Act) court for approval via warrant, it may have been illegal. Even putting aside congressional statutes, Stellarwind violated existing executive orders detailing aspects of executive branch surveillance activities, which the administration neglected to update as circumstances and processes evolved. To both charges of illegality, Bush II's legal team fell back on their interpretation of presidential wartime powers, which – they asserted – trumped both congressional oversight and existing executive orders. After some of these activities were brought to light during his second term, and amid internal administration tensions that nearly led to the resignation of most of his Justice Department's leadership, Bush II acquiesced to some congressional involvement, thus continuing the surveillance, limiting it more specifically to al-Qaeda-related targets, and placing it on a more solid legal foundation.[28]

Some "reform" came in 2008 with the passage of the FISA Amendments Act. It explicitly permitted the NSA and the FBI to collect the messages of noncitizens both abroad and on American soil, without individual court orders, even when those targets were communicating with Americans. This new authorization worked in parallel to the executive branch's traditional workaround for FISA: transit authority, whereby those information streams the government claims do not begin and end with an American citizen or on American soil could be surveilled without FISA involvement. For those streams where foreigners may be communicating with other foreigners but also the occasional American, the government would use the FISA Amendments Act, limiting it to the collection of content from specific targets. At base, when Congress made it easier for the NSA to pick up its foreign targets' messages without getting individualized warrants for each target, Congress also decided to let the government pick up international messages to and from Americans – incidentally but inevitably – without a warrant, as well.[29]

In addition to these efforts, Bush II's administration drastically increased the size and scope of the federal government, establishing the Department of Homeland Security, the Transportation Security Administration, and the Immigration and Customs Enforcement agency, broadening the security apparatus of the state in ways that seemed somewhat contrary to the Small Government mantra of the Republican Party. With all this government activity, Bush II's administration refused to countenance the repeal of their recently passed tax cuts or to find ways other than deficit spending to fund their war and the string of new or expanded government agencies that arose in its conflicted wake. The ballooning of the federal budget deficit was the predictable outcome of this lack of funding foresight.[30]

The swiftness and ease with which Afghanistan was apparently won convinced Bush II's defense team that they could apply quick and decisive US military pressure anywhere they chose. The target they chose next was Iraq, a member of what Bush called the "Axis of Evil." In early 2002, before the Taliban was even routed in Afghanistan, the administration consulted with Central Command (CENTCOM, the US military's administrative delineation for the Greater Middle East) on how an invasion of Iraq might proceed. Thus, while Bush II later regretted his inability properly to secure and stabilize Afghanistan, that failure rests most prominently on his shoulders; he made the call to turn American attention elsewhere before the work in Afghanistan had been brought to a stable conclusion.[31]

He pushed for the invasion of Iraq for three reasons, none of which the administration discussed forthrightly with the American public at the time. (1) His administration was eager to prove the efficacy of preventative war by taking out a "threat" to the United States before it struck. (2) Bush and his team wanted to assert the unique prerogative of the US to remove regimes it saw as odious. (3) They sought to reverse the practice of exempting the Islamic world from neoliberal standards, that is to say electoral democracy and limited government (friendly to US interests), market economics (that favored American businesses), and a modicum of respect for human (especially woman's) rights. This was to put the words of defense secretary Rumsfeld, spoken a week after 9/11, to the test: "We have a choice, either to change the way we live...or to change the way that they live, and we...chose the latter."[32]

The administration's public campaign to convince the American people that an invasion of Iraq was necessary relied on altogether different arguments. (1) Iraq was a historic enemy of the US, possessed of one of the world's largest armies, and led by a man of the same ilk as Hitler or Stalin. (2) Iraq had violated

UN resolutions and treaties and had either already reacquired WMD or was in the process of regaining them. (3) They had funded terrorism in the past and were very likely involved with al Qaeda.

As it turned out, none of these lines were true. The yellow cake uranium officials claimed Iraq had bought in order to build weapons turned out to be a hoax, the aluminum tubes were not for WMDs, the purported drone armada was laughably ineffective, and no evidence was ever found of any mobile weapons labs.[33] After the invasion, 34 million pages of documents were seized and translated from Hussein's Iraq and nothing surfaced to substantiate a partnership between Hussein and al Qaeda.[34] Each time one line was debunked the administration turned to another, willfully disregarding intelligence that called their fundamental drive to attack Iraq into question and massaging the paltry evidence there was into a coherent narrative.

Unhelpfully, Saddam Hussein, fearing domestic troubles, behaved as if he possessed such weapons (to make himself look powerful in the eyes of the Iraqi people), never being as transparent with the UN and the US as he could have been. He calculated, reasonably but in the end wrongly, that hinting at his possession of WMD in public while allowing UN weapons inspectors unhindered access across his economically devastated country would defuse the situation. He therefore allowed the return of UN inspectors in 2003 and hundreds of investigators visited more than 500 sites (all without advanced notice and with prompt access provided to the facilities) and found no WMD.[35] Hussein, however, had not counted on the unilateral resolve of Bush II's administration to invade, heedless of the facts on the ground. Said one senior administration advisor in the summer of 2002, "We're an empire now, and when we act, we create our own reality. And while you're studying that reality – judiciously, as you will – we'll act again, creating other new realities, which you can study too, and that's how things will sort out. We're history's actors, and you, all of you [journalists] will be left to study what we do."[36]

After secretary of state Colin Powell, one of the most respected members of the Bush team, gave a presentation at the United Nations throwing his support behind the need to invade Iraq for its possession of Weapons of Mass Destruction, enough people fell in line behind the administration that war became politically possible. The invasion began on March 19, 2003, and the Hussein regime proved an easy topple (so much for the vaunted power of the fourth largest army in the world!). The collapse of Iraqi resistance was so swift that on May 1, 2003 president Bush II felt confident enough to speechify aboard the *USS Abraham Lincoln*, declaring major combat operations in Iraq over (against the backdrop of a banner proclaiming "mission accomplished").[37] Ominously, in 2004 bin Laden echoed Bush II's optimism concerning events in Iraq: "Be glad of the good news: America is mired in the swamps of the Tigris and Euphrates. Here [Bush II] is now, thank God, in an embarrassing situation and here is America today being ruined before the eyes of the whole world."[38]

Under the leadership of Paul Bremer, appointed by Bush II, the Coalition Provisional Authority busied itself with organizing the aftermath of the invasion. Two of Bremer's decisions stand out as the twin pillars upon which subsequent US failure rested: (1) the removal of Baathists from the national bureaucracy and (2) the disbanding of the Iraqi army.

On May 16, Brenner issued Order Number 1. Taking the denazification of Germany after World War Two as his unexamined example, Bremer decided to exclude Baathists from the new Iraqi state apparatus. Students of Iraqi history will remember that Saddam Hussein had been a Baathist; indeed, his was the only political party in the country. People joined the state-backed party not so much out of ideological ardor but to further their careers. Removing Baathists from the scene, therefore, denuded the country of the vast majority of its experienced administrators, teachers, bureaucrats. The decision threw almost the entirety of the "coordinator class" out of the post-war vision – the city of Fallujah, for example, had not a single teacher left employable as a consequence of this order.[39]

Brenner promulgated Order Number 2, disbanding the Iraqi army, on May 23. Recall that Iraq had been a creation of post WW1 European imperialism, cobbled together by the French and the British from former Ottoman provinces so as to promote European interests in the region. The result was a country with little in the way of unity. Ethnic and religious rifts crisscrossed the Fertile Crescent. The army stood as perhaps the only institution of any national significance. Moreover, the disbanded (but not disarmed) soldiery, now jobless, would not simply disappear into the ether. Many would reemerge to resist what they came to see as an American occupation.[40]

The debaathification of the bureaucracy and disbanding of the army had the added consequence of ending centuries of Sunni dominance in the region. Early in the history of Islam, and barely a generation after the death of Muhammad, Muslims quarreled over who rightfully should lead the Muslim community (*ummah*): the Sunni and the Shia emerged from this disagreement, the former now encompassing perhaps 90 percent of Muslims, the latter 10 percent.[41] Within the boundaries of Iraq itself, however, the Shia outnumbered the Sunni, so a Sunni-dominated government was one constituted of a religious minority. In dismantling the existing institutions of power, therefore, the Americans allowed the Shia, suppressed and repressed under a more secular Baathist rule that happened to favor Sunnis, to emerge as the chief political force in Iraq, one with a decidedly religious edge. This relegated the Sunnis (mostly former bureaucrats and soldiers) to a position of relative political weakness.

Given these twin errors, and the 2 million people (possessing weapons, respect, and built-in communications networks) they disempowered and alienated, it is fair to say that US mishandling of the immediate aftermath of the invasion produced the anti-American insurgency. This resistance picked up steam in 2004 and 2005, as Sunni Iraqis combated the Americans and their Shiite allies. It then erupted into sectarian civil war as Sunnis more deliberately targeted Shiites and Shiites responded in kind. Unprepared for the stiffening resistance, US troops engaged in careless, clumsy raids against mostly Sunni Iraqis, imprisoning thousands and provoking an ever angrier public outcry. Many ended up at a refurbished Saddam-era site called Abu Ghraib. The torture of Iraqi prisoners at the hands of American guards there, once made public, spawned a wave of Iraqi resistance and galvanized international support for the growing insurgency.[42]

Al Qaeda, its leadership driven into the mountains of Pakistan, found new membership in Iraq, as people were drawn to the presence of American troops and the myriad opportunities to find eternal glory fighting the American empire. Among them was one al Zarqawi, who pledged fealty to al Qaeda and formed an Iraqi franchise operation, al Qaeda in Iraq (AQI). It was this organization that demolished the Golden Mosque in 2006, igniting the full fires of sectarian warfare.[43] Their campaign throughout the country was a self-conscious "management of savagery" and deliberately brutal. Starting from the premise that even a brutal state was better than one led by *kuffar* (apostates), these sectarian fighters sought to vex and exhaust their enemies through atomized acts of terror that would stretch US and "Zionist" resources to their limits. It was hoped by AQI leaders like al Zarqawi that the very public defeat of the US and its surrogates in Iraq would inspire the toppling of other Middle Eastern client states.[44]

By 2007, Sunnis in Iraq's Anbar province, initially receptive to AQI owing to their shared religious denomination, rose up against the organized butchery to repulse the insurgents. Thirty tribes joined forces, forming militias to combat the jihadists. This coincided with a determined push by president Bush II to "surge" the number of US troops in the country with the goal of "clear, hold, build," a doctrinal mantra popularized by the man chosen to lead the surge, general David Petraeus. This increase in US troop levels came more than 3 years after Bush II had declared combat operations in the country over; 3 years after his administration had assured the American people that the transition of Iraq from authoritarian dictatorship to functioning liberal democracy would take a few years at most; 3 years after the Department of Defense found itself scrambling to implement neoliberal notions of capitalist economic organization and bourgeois notions of representative democracy in a country it had originally expected to shock, awe, and leave in short order.[45]

The troop surge, taking advantage of the Indigenous "Anbar Awakening" against AQI, managed to bring the insurgency to a temporary end. Bush II thus left office content that he had stabilized the country for his successor. His confidence was such that his administration negotiated the eventual withdrawal of US troops with the Iraqi government, setting the ultimate date as 2011. It was the opinion of the departing administration that, the insurgent hump having been surmounted, there remained only the cleanup of the refuse and the organizing of the peaceful mechanisms of the state. Thus for the second time would Bush II prematurely make assurances that combat in Iraq was winding down.

The reality of the surge was that it bought a little time. It did nothing to mend the ancient rift between Sunni and Shia, nothing to bridge the divisions between the various sections of an artificial country, nothing to redress Sunni political grievances, and nothing to address the long-standing grievances the jihadists harbored against American imperialism. Thus, the war had been brought down to a state of glowing embers; kindling was still

31

ready at hand.

Among the domestic surveillance, bombing campaign, and foreign invasion, Bush II's administration, keen on preventing another 9/11 heedless of the moral cost, inaugurated a regime of torture. CIA agents engaged in "enhanced interrogation" of suspects captured in relation to the Global War on Terror, most infamously the practice of water boarding but also sleep deprivation for days on end leading to hallucinations, keeping prisoners in stress positions for long durations, etc. Alternatively, terror suspects were held at black sites, foreign locations outside even the meager restrictions placed upon personnel on US-controlled territory, where less "civilized" methods were brought to bear upon detainees. Domestic controversy ultimately led to legislation banning torture, although in acquiescing to overwhelming congressional pressure and signing the bill, Bush II issued a signing statement (his interpretation of the law) that left open the possibility of ignoring the statute should the president need to exercise his inherent warfighting powers.[46]

Republicans defended these interrogation methods as necessary and effective tools in the fight against terror. The most compelling success story cited was the waterboarding of several captured al Qaeda members which led to the intelligence breakthroughs that culminated in the execution of Osama bin Laden (a claim echoed in the movie Zero Dark Thirty, which received direct input and assistance from a happily cooperative CIA). Contemporaneous CIA cables and memos unearthed by later Senate investigators, however, contradicted this narrative: in fact the information the CIA did obtain had been given to them by cooperative detainees who had not been tortured. Only later were these men subjected to enhanced interrogation, just in case they had anything else to divulge.[47]

1.3 War on Terror: Interminable

1.3.1 Guantanamo and Torture

Immediately after winning the 2008 presidential election, Obama tapped Robert Gates – Bush II's outgoing secretary of defense – to stay on into the new administration. Gates accepted the position and remained secretary well into 2011. Keeping Bush II's secretary of defense, in hindsight, signaled what would become Obama's *modus operandi* with regards to the War on Terror: reform the methods but keep fighting it. Indeed, those waiting with bated breath for Obama to end unilaterally the indefinite detentions at Guantanamo, pull US troops from across the world and bring them home, or investigate the full length and breadth of Bush II's many crimes against humanity had misread their man. Obama had been critical of Bush II for some time, but always from the perspective of method, not goal. For instance, he questioned national surveillance practices not because they intrinsically violated civil liberties but because the way Bush II's team had implemented them violated the rule of law. In 2006, then senator Obama had said: "There is no one in Congress who does not want president Bush to have every tool at his disposal to prevent terrorist attacks – including the use of a surveillance program...We do not expect the president to give the American people every detail about a classified surveillance program, but we do expect him to place such a program within the rule of law and to allow members of the other two coequal branches of government – Congress and the judiciary – to have the ability to monitor and oversee such a program."[48]

Before sinking his teeth into combat operations, troop numbers, or air strikes, president Obama signed executive orders seeking to remedy two of the more damaging wounds done to American international standing by Bush II's administration: (1) the use of torture and (2) the indefinite detention of terrorism suspects at Guantanamo Bay. The optimism with which these initial moves were greeted soured, however, as the administration ran up against political resistance and the limits inherent in Obama's critique of his predecessor's policies.

He banned the use of torture, a commendable act when compared to his predecessor, surely, although his new CIA chief – Leon Panetta – said contemporaneously that the agency would continue the practice of extraordinary rendition, whereby suspects were transferred to the custody of a third country for questioning. This, and the fact that Obama's Justice Department, promises for greater transparency notwithstanding, had already used the "states secrets" privilege to block a pending lawsuit regarding CIA torture practices, did not bode well.[49]

Early in 2009 Obama also ordered the closing of Guantanamo Bay. His Justice Department, under Eric Holder, began preparations for trying detainees there in civilian court (rather than the military tribunals favored by Bush II's administration). Serious problems emerged almost immediately, however. Closing Guantanamo meant moving its 242 prisoners somewhere else, either to another prison or liberating them to another country, depending on the individual circumstances of each inmate. Complexity permeated this task: many inmates were lower-level detainees, often with only a tangential connection to terrorist activity but from countries like Yemen that had weak central government – suppose one of these individuals, once freed to their home country, decided to take up arms and ultimately killed an American? No one inside the administration relished taking on the prospect of such responsibility.[50]

As 2009 came to a close and the Obama administration still grappled with what to do, an attempted terrorist attack on US soil profoundly shook the administration's confidence. On December 25, Umar Farout Abdulmutallab tried to detonate an underwear bomb aboard Northwest Airlines Flight 253 before it left the ground. Abdulmutallab saw his attack as "retaliation," in his words, for the United States' support of

Israel, which continued in its "killing of innocent and civilian Muslim populations in Palestine," as well as for America's "killing of innocent and civilian Muslim populations in Yemen, Iraq, Somalia, Afghanistan, and beyond, most of them women, children, and noncombatants."[51] His bomb failed to detonate properly and he was apprehended with severe burns.

After initially receiving medical treatment and talking cooperatively with federal investigators, Abdulmutallab then went silent. Obama had come to office intent on closing Guantanamo Bay and reviewing the Bush II era practice of trying suspected terrorists via military tribunals rather than civilian courts. After Abdulmutallab's sudden silence, Republicans went on the political attack, claiming the terrorist had only stopped talking after he had been read his Miranda rights by the FBI, who told him he had a right to remain silent. This, said the GOP, was the perfect example of why it was foolhardy for the administration to use civilian processes in dealing with enemy combatants – and American lives were now in danger as a result of Obama's softness. Surely, they said, Abdulmutallab would have continued to cooperate, providing valuable intelligence, if only the Obama administration had not been driven by liberal ideology to inform him of his rights. While this narrative did not have the facts on its side – Abdulmutallab had *already stopped talking* before he was read the Miranda warning, and the decision to do so had been made by a senior career FBI agent, following consultations with other career agents and not by a political appointee under Obama's umbrella – the political fallout had profound consequences, hardening the position of the Obama administration. Henceforth it championed the use of civilian courts over military ones with less fervor, deciding instead to reform the military commissions and use them for certain cases. The attack, combined with robust congressional resistance, also destroyed Obama's hopes of closing Guantanamo. Subsequent legislation forbade detainee transfers onto US soil, and rather than fight that political battle Obama settled for a compromise: no new Guantanamo detainees. The population might not shrink, but, he reasoned, at least it certainly would not grow.[52]

Prison hunger strikes and other forms of resistance brought Guantanamo back to the administration's attention during Obama's second term. One inmate went so far as to hoard his medication and deliberately overdosed on it, killing himself. These desperate acts reignited the administration's desire to do something. While Obama refused to exercise the same level of presidential authority as his predecessor and claim a war-related reason for circumventing Congress, which would have allowed him to transfer detainees onto American soil, his administration did work diligently to audit the prisoner population, increase the number of those deemed low-level or not dangerous, and negotiate with other countries to achieve their successful liberation abroad. Ultimately, while the prison remained open, its population was reduced from 242 to 41. Of those that remained, ten were being charged or convicted in the military commissions system and 31 were still being held in indefinite detention without being either charged with a crime or allowed a trial.[53]

1.3.2 Afghanistan

A shift in focus toward a deteriorating Afghanistan proved to be one of the primary drifts in tactics for the Obama administration. Weeks into his presidency, Obama approved reinforcements to the tune of 17,000 soldiers and appointed a new commander to the battlespace, general Stanley McChrystal, to lead this augmented force to victory. McChrystal had made a reputation for himself commanding the special operations forces in Iraq. Now elevated to a much more public command, there were high hopes that this was the man to bring the military situation back from the brink. Defense secretary Gates made it clear to the new general that the victory conditions were to be narrowed considerably from the days of George W. Bush: stability defined as a protracted lull in the carnage came to replace a stability defined by democracy and a complete absence of Taliban activity.[54]

At the behest of an offhand remark from Gates, McChrystal set about evaluating the situation before him, producing a report that startled the president and sent his administration into a bitter and divisive debate. The general, considering the situation on the ground to be far worse than his predecessor had thought, asserted that he would require 40,000 troops (instead of the 17,000 Obama had originally agreed to send) if victory were to be achieved. Obama, aware of the potential political costs of such a surge, balked at the massive request, as did many in his administration. What followed was several months of acrimonious debate between those in the administration who wanted a lighter troop footprint and those who favored a larger troop number and McChrystal's recommendations.[55]

By the winter of 2009, Obama agreed to a compromise of 30,000 troops, with the understanding that the surge would be evaluated for effectiveness the following year, and the troops withdrawn from Afghanistan in 2011. The military was not happy with the prospect of a known withdrawal – nor were Obama's political opponents – but it seems that within the context of the Iraq War and the antiwar feeling that generated, such considerations were necessary in order to gain the votes required to pass this troop surge through the Democrat controlled Congress (many of whom were elected on antiwar platforms).[56]

These political fights seemed far away indeed from the happenings in Afghanistan itself. With additional troops inbound and his combat numbers growing, McChrystal initiated counter insurgency operations in Halmar province with the objective of clearing it of Taliban insurgents and stabilizing the situation for the remaining population. He initiated new combat rules stating that troops were to engage in "courageous restraint," firing only when fired upon. The objective was to limit civilian casualties and stop the creation of new terrorists while also gaining the trust of the population.[57]

McChrystal's "courageous restraint" was put to the test early in 2010 with Operation Moshtarak (meaning "together"), an assault on the city of Marja by US Marines and British allies. The plan called for Afghan auxiliaries to hold positions taken by their NATO shock troops, followed in turn by Afghan government officials ready to provide essential services to the local population – so-called "government in a box." It was hoped that this operation would serve as the model for future operations. The operation disappointed McChrystal's expectations. The "clearing" performed by NATO troops proved all too reversible; the Afghans assigned to "hold" the reconquered territory often lacked the resolve necessary to do so; and the essential government services failed to materialize.[58] McChrystal, recognizing that he had not analyzed the situation as well as he might have, went back to the drawing board, only to be yanked from command after a *Rolling Stone* article written by a reporter embedded with him quoted some less than complimentary comments the general and/or his staff had made about the administration, notably vice president Biden. McChrystal never offered his bosses an explanation or defense for the remarks, leaving Obama with little choice other than termination.[59]

General Petraeus, popular hero of the 2007 Iraq Surge, succeeded to command in Afghanistan late in 2010. From the administration's perspective, he had the knowledge, experience, and clout to hit the ground at a run. Indeed, he sprinted through a year of command, rolling back the "courageous restraint" of McChrystal, ramping up night raids and offensive operations. Rather than concentrate on counterinsurgency, as he had done in Iraq, Petraeus threw his troops – whose numbers now reached an all-time high of 100,000 – into hunter-killer missions, the objective being to "get to a point of some transient stability and the appearance of success." This push for even momentary stability fell in line with secretary Gates' narrowing of objectives in Afghanistan.[60]

By the summer of 2011 Petraeus had stepped down from his Afghan post to succeed Leon Panetta as director of the CIA (Panetta was taking over from Gates as secretary of defense). In June, Obama declared the surge in Afghanistan to be a success: peace was in sight, much of the country was under the control of Afghan security forces, and the Taliban (although it would perhaps never be totally destroyed) was severely weakened. This view was a little too rosy. If the objective was to shatter Taliban resistance and force them to the negotiating table, then the surge failed. If the objective was momentary stability, however, then it had a modicum of success, although it was incomplete stability. The most that can be said of the Afghan surge was that it bought the government of prime minister Karzai and its NATO backers time – but time for what? As in Iraq, that remained an open question. Further training, further purchases of military equipment, further shoring up of the Afghan security forces was the default answer, but that answer dodged some very serious problems that did not have a military solution.

Even fighting against Afghan government forces with better equipment and more thorough training, the Taliban refused to go away. But putting them to one side for a moment, there were other issues that would keep the situation in Afghanistan from developing as the West desired. First, the Karzai government was too corrupt to unify the country. Officials accepted bribes as if it were part of their job description. Public works money disappeared into a thousand private coffers. President Karzai often circumvented the legal system and released prisoners before their scheduled trial dates.[61] Afghanistan's 2009 presidential election, fraudulent in many respects, saw Karzai remain for a second term, while leaving the central government held in even lower esteem by the provincial population. His days in power ended in 2014, when he was succeeded by Ashraf Ghani, yet the corruption was endemic and could not be fixed by the replacement of a single man. The second issue was the Janus-faced policy of our nominal ally Pakistan, discussed in the next section.

With the apparent success of the surge, and the administration's initiatives in Pakistan and elsewhere pummeling the leadership of the Taliban and al Qaeda, government officials declared an official end to the war in Afghanistan on October 26, 2014. Around 10,000 American soldiers remained to continue supporting the Afghan government; half this number remained after 2015. Subsequent Western oversight would continue under America's Operation Freedom's Sentinel and NATO's Operation Resolute Support. Obama called this a "responsible conclusion" to the conflict.[62] Over the next several years, however, amid continued Afghan corruption and ineptitude, the Taliban regained lost ground and support, and the conflict looked far from over as the next president took office in 2017.

1.3.3 Drone Warfare in AfPak and Beyond

The troop surge in Afghanistan was but one aspect of a larger plan by the defense team of Obama's administration to stabilize the situation. In addition to using ground troops to shore up hostile areas, kill terrorists, and bring about the security necessary to achieve political stability, Obama's administration sought a closer working relationship with Pakistan.

The US-Pakistan relationship had been poor since America all but abandoned the region after the defeat of the Soviet Union in Afghanistan. The Pakistanis were convinced that the US would abandon the region again, and thus saw little reason to put their full weight behind a conflict between a fickle America and a Taliban with much local support.[63] There were also those in the Pakistani government, that is to say the military, who thought the US coveted their nuclear arms.[64] During the years of Bush II, much treasure had been spent in an effort to buy Pakistan's support in the War on Terror. Their support was initially recognized as necessary because the main US supply route into Afghanistan ran through Pakistani territory. As the war in Afghanistan intensified toward the end of Bush's time in office, Americans came to realize that the amount of effort the Pakistanis put into policing their border with Afghanistan mattered as well, for Afghan fighters made use of Pakistan's remote hinterlands to hide, regroup, and continue the fight.

Obama took office and soon recognized the necessity of closer cooperation with Pakistan, especially in directly confronting a Taliban that now operated as a legitimate military force in both Pakistan and Afghanistan. Obama's national security team, recognizing the importance of Pakistan in terms of the US effort in Afghanistan, rechristened the theater of operations AfPak (Afghanistan-Pakistan) and broadened US strategic vision to include both countries.[65] Despite US efforts, however, the Pakistanis remained aloof; doubts concerning the American commitment to the region remained, and some Pakistani leaders were not eager to destroy the Taliban completely, as they pondered the future possibility of using the Taliban as a local proxy in their ongoing feud with India.[66]

It was an offensive into Pakistan's hinterland regions, more than perhaps anything else, that Obama sought from this reticent ally. While his diplomatic efforts failed to achieve this, Pakistan did eventually act. The Pakistani Taliban, engaging in an ever-increasing number of suicide strikes within Pakistan, could not be ignored forever. In June 2014 the Pakistani army finally invaded North Waziristan (Operation Zarb e Azb) which saw some limited success.[67] Nevertheless, American diplomats were never able to garner a great degree of Pakistani cooperation, forcing the administration to turn to other options.

It was in this context – heightened troop numbers seeking to rein in a disintegrating Afghanistan, diplomatic efforts to recommit Pakistan to our fight having but limited success, and the continued ability of enemy combatants to slip away from US firepower – that drones appeared as a possible solution. As in many foreign policy endeavors, Obama's drone initiatives got their start during the previous presidency. In 2008, Bush II's administration first decided to augment the drone campaign in Pakistan, leading to 30 known drone strikes that year.[68] Bush II also decided it was no longer necessary to inform the Pakistanis of impending strikes over their territory. Operationally, this was justified by Bush II's administration because the Pakistanis were thought to have tipped off targets after receiving notification of an impending strike from the US. Diplomatically, this only soured US-Pakistani relations further.

Obama, although he had campaigned for a recalibration toward Afghanistan and had agreed to surge the troop levels there, saw the fiasco in Iraq and was understandably reticent about troop deployments as an effective tactic in the Global War on Terror. He signaled early on his preference for covert and unconventional methods when he told his head of the CIA, "The CIA gets what it wants."[69] Given this preference and the Pakistani's lack of cooperation in assaulting the Taliban from their side, Obama took quickly to the use of drones as a more flexible alternative. With each passing year more strikes were authorized and carried out. During Bush II's presidency, 48 drone strikes were known to have been authorized; yet between 2009 and October 2015 the Obama administration was known to have authorized 353, and the casualties from these strikes reached several thousand.[70]

These strikes, moreover, occurred across multiple countries and beyond US-declared combat zones. Not only Afghanistan but Pakistan, Yemen, and Somalia were all recipients. US intelligence indicated to the incoming president that Yemeni tribal lands had come under the control of al Qaeda, which warranted a US response.[71] Obama signed off on the first strike over Yemen in 2009, which killed an estimated 40 people, mostly women and children; as of August 2015, 490 people were known to have been killed in Yemen as a result of the drone campaign.[72] Much of the intelligence for these operations was gathered via an NSA geolocation system used by JSOC (Joint Strike Operations Command) called Gilgamesh, which operated as a fake cell tower that forced the mobile phones of targeted individuals to connect to it so that their location could be pinpointed.[73] This reliance upon Signal Intelligence was commonplace. A similar program employed by the CIA known as Shenanigans used pods deployed on aircraft that inhaled massive amounts of data from any wireless device (routers, computers, smartphones, etc.) within range. During Operation Victory Dance, operators managed over the course of 6 months to map the wifi fingerprints of nearly every major town in Yemen.[74] The limitations of this methodology were made plain during the army's Operation Haymaker, which took place in Afghanistan during 2012, in which drone strikes relied upon this intelligence gathering to provide support to ground forces. Over the course of a 4-month period, nearly 90 percent of the people killed in drone strikes related to that operation were *not* the intended targets.[75]

Debate raged about the moral implications and political ramifications of these tactics. Obama, for instance, was the first president since the Civil War to authorize the assassination of another American. Anwar al Awlaki, an imam of a mosque in Fall Church Virginia in 2002 and rhetorical inspiration for a number of terror attacks – including (alleged the administration) the 2009 shooting at Fort Hood – was killed in a drone strike in Yemen toward the end of 2011, after having been shadowed for weeks beforehand. No court order was sought in the taking of his life. No attempt was made to apprehend him and bring him to trial. In keeping with the logic of Bush II's administration, Obama's team pointed to the necessities of global warfare when dismissing the civil rights of an American and insisted that they did their due diligence. Attorney general Eric Holder defended the administration in 2013, writing that long-standing legal precedent had established that citizenship did not make one immune from targeting so long as the government takes "special care [to consider] all relevant constitutional considerations, the laws of war, and other law with respect to US citizens." Furthermore, lethal force against an American living abroad who is "actively engaged in planning to kill Americans" was justified given three criteria: (1) the government has determined the individual to be an imminent threat; (2) capture is not feasible; and (3) the operation will be carried out according to "applicable law of war principles."[76]

The crusade against evil that had left Bush II's administration so little room for the kind of due process any US citizen should expect and demand of their government was downgraded by Obama into a more pedestrian kind of war, but the violation of civil liberty remained persistently justifiable. The government easily could muster the resources to track and kill a citizen over the course of weeks but could not be bothered to capture and bring them to trial. The Bush-Cheney template of endless war against *terror suspects* who had no due process rights of any kind continued unhindered.[77]

The president did not see things that way; he took pride in the "due process" provided within the executive branch to potential drone strike targets, ensuring to the best of his ability that military operations were held to some sort of civilian account. He took personal responsibility for these attacks, making it a point to authorize each individual use of force (which initiated the process of acquiring and eliminating a target). While his attempts to create a standardized process through which drone strikes had to be authorized indicate the seriousness with which he took this responsibility, the lack of transparency baked into these workflows ensured that any successor uninterested in ethics or accountability would not be kept in check by anyone outside the executive branch of government.[78]

Although Obama's efforts in the AfPak theater would continue right up to the end of his second term, the climax, at least from the perspective of the American public, certainly came with the assassination of Osama bin Laden. This most wanted man had been in hiding in Pakistan for some time, of that much US intelligence was all but certain. It took a determined effort by the CIA, however, to track down one of his old drivers, then the compound the man frequented, then the little details that seemed to indicate first that the owner of the compound did not want to be found, then perhaps that he was the man they sought. At no point did the preponderance of evidence support the thesis that this mystery man was bin Laden. Always there was plenty of reason to doubt – and yet enough reason to hope that they had their man.

As the administration grew more confident that they had found bin Laden, five options emerged for how to proceed: (1) a bomber strike to wipe out the compound and all inside, (2) an assault by helicopter to capture/kill the target, (3) a raid by CIA officers, (4) a joint raid with Pakistan, or (5) alerting Pakistan to US suspicions and hoping they would act to apprehend the suspects.[79] After allowing all the principals to voice their opinions, Obama decided to green light a SEAL raid by helicopter.[80] Memories of Operation Eagle Claw (the botched attempt by the Carter administration to rescue Americans held by Iranian revolutionaries) haunted the Situation Room, but in the event things went well from the American perspective.[81] At the cost of several unintended deaths, a blatant violation of Pakistani sovereignty, and the prospect of nuclear war (what if the nuclear-armed Pakistanis had thought the US raid to be an invasion by their bitter enemy India?), bin Laden was killed.

Obama would continue to use these tactics – drones, covert operations, air strikes – in other operations beyond Afghanistan, Pakistan, and the fight against al Qaeda. By 2014, the US Special

Operations Command (SOCOM) operated in 150 countries and by 2015 dwarfed the British military in size. When he assumed command of SOCOM in 2014, General Votel opined that it was indeed a golden age for US special operations forces. And where SOCOM was not, there were American Unmanned Arial Vehicles doing reconnaissance, bugging the electronics of foreigners, and striking ground targets.[82]

1.3.4 The Islamic State

Iraq and its environs took a back seat during Obama's first term. While troops flooded into Afghanistan, while diplomatic efforts in Pakistan went nowhere, while drones reconnoitered and bombed more with each passing month, the military quietly carried out the Status of Forces Agreement signed by Bush II and wound down the American presence in Iraq. All US troops were set to leave the country by the end of 2011. Obama's defense team thought it prudent to keep a few thousand Americans behind as an insurance policy against future discord, and while individual Iraqi politicians might have agreed with this in theory (and in private), publicly their electorate would not countenance a continued American presence: unwilling to be subjected to further US occupation, Iraqis demanded that if American troops were to stay in their country they be subject to Iraqi law rather than extradited to face US justice unaccountable to the Iraqi people. In this case, American pride and Iraqi independence left no room for compromise, and Iraq was left with American money and American arms but not American soldiers.[83]

After the situation deteriorated in Iraq in 2014, a common talking point of administration critics would be how the presence of US troops, even in limited numbers, could have stiffened Iraqi resolve, helped in training their soldiers, or otherwise assisted in halting their future military defeats to some significant degree. Obama's final secretary of defense, Ash Carter, voiced this position in its most reasonable form, asserting that a small residual force, advising and assisting the Iraqis, "could have provided some ballast" to the Iraqis; in his estimation, the lack of US troops did not necessitate the troubles to come, but made their coming more likely.[84] Even if Obama could have forced the issue and pressed an agreement past vigorous Iraqi resistance, in all likelihood it would not have made a decisive difference. Regardless of a handful of American troops, the Iraqi political situation would have deteriorated along sectarian lines as it did in actual fact. Perhaps Iraqi prime minister Maliki would not have been quite as brazen, thinking that US troops meant a keener US eye watching his machinations, but his authoritarianism was present even while the US still had a direct military involvement in Iraq. He had already shown his preference for Shiite over Sunni. Moreover, the corruption rife within the Iraqi army, with units at half strength or less and generals collecting pay for full rosters, would not have changed with the presence of a few American soldiers.

At any rate, the paper strength of Iraq did not seem to necessitate a physical American presence. Its nominal GDP had risen from $36.6 billion in 2004 (after the invasion had all but halted economic activity) to $180.6 billion in 2011, with per capita GDP rising from $1352 to $5529 in the same period. Profits from oil were increasing ($17.2 billion in 2004 up to $82.9 billion in 2011). This more stable economic situation paid for a substantial military. Iraq's security forces could count on perhaps 670,000 servicepeople.[85] These forces were by no means supposed to be ill equipped. The Iraqi government spent billions acquiring US arms with which they would complete the rebuilding of their armed forces begun during US occupation.[86] Some of these shipments reached their destination in time for the coming fight. By September 2011, for example, the Iraqi army could boast a force of at least 140 M1A1 Abrams tanks, some of the best in the world.[87]

With the tactical success of the 2007 surge, the improvement in economic indicators, and the steadily reequipping Iraqi military, stability for the embattled nation seemed at long last to be coalescing into a solid reality. There were still issues, of course: prime minister Maliki enflamed sectarian tensions by willfully favoring Shiites over Sunnis, Iran remained a powerful influence on Iraqi politics, and the country's political institutions were still fundamentally fragile. To the Obama administration these issues seemed, though real, not critical in any immediate sense. Iraq, the thinking went, had weathered the worst of things and was now heading in the right direction; it could safely be placed on the back burner.

By December 2011, the withdrawal of US forces now complete, prime minister Maliki reneged on promises of better cooperation with his rivals and cracked down on his political and religious opponents. The day after the last American soldiers left he issued an arrest warrant for the vice president of Iraq – a Sunni – whose bodyguards had been accused of plotting to attack Shiite politicians. As 2012 progressed, he began arresting mostly Sunni Baathists, took direct control of the army, fired Sunni commanders and replaced them with Shiites from his political party, purged the intelligence service of Sunnis, and arrested Sunni critics. Most notably, in December 2012 he had Rafe el Esawa, the finance minister, along with 16 of his guards, thrown in jail. Reacting to these efforts at centralizing power, protests erupted in Ramadi and Fallujah in early 2013. On April 9, Iraqi troops attacked protestors in Hawija. Sunni militias responded by attacking army checkpoints, and the fighting soon spread to the Sunni-majority city of Mosul. Further clashes, arrests, and protests followed before Maliki made a belated attempt at compromise by ordering troops to withdraw from Ramadi and Fallujah, leaving a vacuum of Sunni resentment.[88]

In the meantime, by mid-2011 the Arab Spring (a wave of anti-government protests spreading across the Greater Middle East) had bloomed into full vigor. Protests in Syria had grown into open rebellion against the government of Bashar al Assad. An important faction of these resistance fighters were conservative Muslims disdainful of the Western-backed dictators ruling so many Middle Eastern countries and eager to return to theocratic rule of one sort or another. Not all the rebel groups agreed with this political end goal, and the resulting disagreements over the details of what victory might look like led to infighting among the rebels and a deepening of the Syrian chaos.[89]

It was into this mounting disarray that members of al Qaeda in Iraq (aka the Islamic State of Iraq, or ISI) descended, led by al Baghdadi, a veteran jihadist who had been fighting in Iraq since at least 2006. After the assassination of bin Laden, Baghdadi vowed a wave of revenge killings. In an effort to make good on this promise, as well as spread his specific brand of militant Islam, he targeted first Christian Iraqis around Baghdad and then, during the second half of 2011, moved his attention to Syria. Over the course of the next 2 years, taking advantage of the intra-rebel conflicts, Baghdadi gained leadership over an ever-growing coalition of anti-government forces. The most important of these acquisitions was Baghdadi's incorporation of the rebel group Nusra into his ranks, as they had taken the city of Raqqa from Assad. The manpower and territory that resulted from this combination of Islamic State in Iraq and Nusra gave Baghdadi the confidence to declare the creation of ISIS, the Islamic State of Iraq and Syria (sometimes referred to by the Obama administration as ISIL, the Islamic State of Iraq and the Levant).[90]

Assad, fighting multiple rebel groups and somewhat hampered by hostile US policy, proved unable to stamp out ISIS, and by 2013 they had become a regional power in their own right, using their considerable resources (personnel, land, and money) to commit thousands of attacks and hundreds of suicide bombings. They paid for this vast outlay of violence by several means: extorting funds from local Christians and

Shiites, stealing money from drivers at checkpoints, engaging in protection rackets. They stole more than $400 million from a bank in Mosul; they gained control of several oil fields and worked to sell the oil illicitly; and they received foreign funding, possibly from Qatar, Turkey, or Saudi Arabia.[91]

By early 2014, the political situation in Iraq had deteriorated considerably while the forces of al Baghdadi had gained considerable strength. Sensing an opportunity, ISIS began probing Iraqi defenses. At first these were but the raids of an insurgent force. Baghdadi, surely, remembered the power of American ordinance and sought to circumvent such conventional Goliaths with the many Davids of guerilla warfare. In June 2014, during one such incursion, his forces came to the realization that the Iraqi army defending nearby Mosul hardly existed at all. In fact, it was a literal paper tiger – the commanding general doctored records to make it appear as though far more troops were deployed in the area than actually were, then pocketed the money sent to him to be distributed to these soldiers.[92] The Iraqi defenders present, mostly Shiites, made little effort to defend the Sunni town and retreated in defeat. Thus did a few hundred insurgents, driven on the winds of uninterrupted victory and religious zeal, capture the second most populous city in Iraq.[93]

The ISIS capture of Mosul proved a disaster. It threw the governments of Iraq, Iran, and the United States into a thrombosis of painful damage control. The Iraqi parliament met to form a government but failed amid political deadlock. The country's most important Shiite cleric declared a fatwa urging all Iraqis to fight ISIS. In Iran the leader of the Quds Force deployed two battalions of the Revolutionary Guard into Iraq specifically to fight ISIS.[94] Reluctant to deploy troops back into the country in large numbers (and balancing the desire to see Assad fall against wanting to defeat ISIS), Obama called for political reforms within Iraq and pledged increased US material support, including air strikes, to bolster the efforts against ISIS. He said: "Our objective is clear: we will degrade, and ultimately destroy, ISIL through a comprehensive and sustained counter-terrorism strategy. First, we will conduct a systematic campaign of airstrikes against these terrorists...Second, we will increase our support to forces fighting these terrorists on the ground."[95]

US airstrikes against ISIS began in September 2014. In October, this effort officially became Operation Inherent Resolve. These American efforts were augmented by other nations, as France, Holland, the UK, Australia, and Canada (among others) contributed air forces and struck ISIS targets toward the end of 2014. They proved unable to stem the wave of ISIS conquests, however. Local forces remained either too disjointed or too battered to offer decisive resistance. Palmyra in Syria and Ramadi in Iraq soon fell to ISIS forces.[96]

The reach of ISIS then spread beyond Syria and Iraq. By 2016, affiliates were fighting Western forces or their native proxies in Nigeria, Somalia, Egypt, Libya, Yemen, and Afghanistan. Islamic terrorism, it seemed, was multiplying in the face of Western violence rather than succumbing to it. Recognizing his own success, al Baghdadi renamed ISIS to simply the Islamic State, hoping to reflect the broader nature of what he thought would become a universal caliphate for all Muslims. He exhorted other Muslims (in his eyes, Sunnis) to migrate to the Islamic State or "fight in his land wherever that may be." He also said, "O Muslims, Islam was never for a day the religion of peace. Islam is the religion of war. Your Prophet was dispatched with the sword."[97]

Some Muslims obliged. As of early 2018, 143 attacks have occurred in 29 counties killing 2043 people (mostly civilians but some soldiers and police as well). Some examples: an attack on the Bardo Museum in Tunisia killed 23 and hospitalized 36, ending in a bloody siege and security forces killing two of the three attackers. ISIS claimed responsibility for one gunman killing 38 and wounding 40 at a seaside resort in Tunisia. Amedy

Coulibaly – a French Muslim – killed four hostages at a kosher deli before being killed by police (two associates of his, Said and Cherif Kouachi, assaulted the office of the inflammatory (often Islamophobic) paper *Charlie Hebdo*, killing 12 and injuring 11, but they claimed affiliation with al Qaeda in Iraq rather than ISIS). Omar Mateen, an American Muslim, opened fire on the Pulse night club (a known gay club) killing 49 – the most deadly terror attack on US soil since 9/11.[98]

Toward the end of Obama's second term, coalition forces did rack up some important victories. Tikrit fell to US-backed forces by April 2015, Ramadi in December 2015, Fallujah in June 2016. Still, the going was slow and the criticism against the administration was unrelenting. By the end of Obama's second term Assad continued his war in Syria, using chemical weapons against his opponents in defiance of Obama's "red line." Amid the almost universal condemnation heaped upon Assad for his brutal handling of the Syrian Civil War, he and his supporters (including an expeditionary force from Putin's Russia) pushed Islamic State out of Raqqa (the origin of their most powerful campaigns), and by November 2017 their last major Syrian stronghold had been cracked and emptied of any pretentions to universal governance of the *Ummat al-Islam*. In Iraq, the once startling borders of the universal caliphate receded. The victories of 2015-2017 culminated in Iraqi prime minister Abadi formally declaring victory over the caliphate in the wake of his forces' retaking of Mosul in July 2017.[99]

Alternatives to Obama's strategy of air strikes and equipping local proxies made for dramatic rhetoric but little practical sense given the political realities imposed by the failures of Operation Iraqi Freedom (2003-2011). Some conservatives called for the deployment of 10,000 US troops back into Iraq, others 20,000, and one general wanted the US to invade Syria directly. Ultimately, however, there was more agreement among Obama and his critics than the sound bites let on. Both sides saw ISIS – a force of perhaps 10,000 soldiers responsible by 2015 for governing millions of people and defending a large chunk of territory – as some sort of existential threat to America. All within the political mainstream were committed to continued US military involvement in the region – bombings, raids, arms sales to dictators, autocrats, and corrupt regimes – as if such tactics could do anything more than provide another thin veneer of stability to be pierced later on by another group of angry, disenfranchised, alienated locals sick of the corruption and the tyranny bankrolled by US "strategic interests."[100]

1.3.5 AFRICOM

The campaigns of Bush II's administration began in Afghanistan and gravitated around Iraq. Ancillary attention was paid to terrorism elsewhere in the world. With little fanfare a new military command came into being toward the end of Bush II's presidency: Africa Command (AFRICOM), which took direct responsibility for the US military presence on the African continent. Although begun under the auspices of a strictly non-combat role, taking on a mission of support and assistance, training, and humanitarian aid, the soldiers of AFRICOM would, under Obama's presidency, be called upon to wash their spears in battle.

The first great test of this new command came as a result of the Arab Spring, that wave of popular protest which began in Tunisia circa 2010, toppling the dictator there, then spreading its way into Egypt, Libya, Syria, and elsewhere. In Egypt, popular unrest eventually unseated the longtime US ally, generalissimo Mubarak. By early 2011 Gaddafi's Libya buckled against the rising tide of protest. Gaddafi considered the protestors to be agents of al Qaeda and attempted to quell the clamor with force.[101]

The Obama administration, for the first time in its tenure, found itself faced with a problem that hadn't been a direct inheritance of Bush II's administration. Obama's reaction to this novel situation thus illuminates his own proclivities and beliefs all the better. Despite campaign rhetoric denouncing US military intervention abroad, Obama had mainly critiqued recent US activities as foolhardy and lacking the bolster of international law, not immoral or imperialist in and of themselves. Moreover, Obama had never been a dove on national security matters. As far back as 2002, while a state senator in Illinois, Obama said: "...I stand before you as someone who is not opposed to war in all circumstances. After September 11, after witnessing the carnage and destruction, the dust and the tears, I supported this administration's pledge to hunt down and root out those who would slaughter innocents in the name of intolerance, and I would willingly take up arms myself to prevent such a tragedy from happening again. I don't oppose all wars."[102]

The Obama team agreed that something had to be done in Libya. But what? A direct military intervention with ground troops seemed out of the question, that option having been removed from the realm of the politically possible by a decade of bloodletting in Iraq and Afghanistan. That left some sort of limited intervention – air strikes came immediately to mind, reminiscent of Clinton in Sudan (bombed in 1998) and Reagan in Libya (bombed in 1986). Obama did not want to be seen as acting unilaterally as Bush II had done during the buildup to the 2003 invasion of Iraq. Thus, he secured the support of NATO and the Arab League – his ambassador even obtained approval from the United Nations in the form of Security Council Resolution 1973 – for an international intervention. The resolution cited the deteriorating situation, escalating violence, and heavy civilian casualties; gross human rights violations and the violence of the Libyan government; and resolved to use force in order to protect Libyan civilians.[103]

President Obama echoed the language of the UN, and articulated the just cause animating the NATO-led intervention in the following terms:

> I'm also proud that we are acting as part of a coalition that includes close allies and partners who are prepared to meet their responsibility to protect the people of Libya and uphold the mandate of the international community...Today, we are part of a broad coalition. We are answering the calls of a threatened people. And we are acting in the interests of the United States and the world.[104]

So, a limited intervention of an international character, made up primarily of air strikes against Gaddafi's forces coalesced and by March 2011 planes from the United States, with additional strikes by the UK and France, bombed targets in Libya. Subsequently, anti-Gaddafi forces went on the offensive and captured much territory, land which then fell to a Gaddafi counter attack before being taken once more by rebel forces; this continued, with additional air strikes by NATO planes, until by August 2011 the combined might of rebel ground forces and NATO air superiority had driven Gaddafi from power.

The Obama administration quickly claimed victory. In several speeches throughout 2011 and 2012 he lauded the triumph of liberty over tyranny, looked forward to the fruits of the Libyan revolution, and emphasized American support for the democracy that was sure to take root in a now free Libya. Take, for instance, his speech in response to the death of Gaddafi himself (October 21, 2011):

> So this has been a remarkable year. The Qadhafi [sic] regime is over...Usama bin Laden is gone, and the idea that change could only come through violence has been buried with him. Something's happening in our world. The way things have been is not the way that they will be. The humiliating grip of corruption and tyranny is being pried open. Dictators

are on notice. Technology is putting power into the hands of the people. The youth are delivering a powerful rebuke to dictatorship and rejecting the lie that some races, some peoples, some religions, some ethnicities do not desire democracy. The promise written down on paper, "All human beings are born free and equal in dignity and rights," is closer at hand.[105]

Indeed, it appeared that such collective action as President George W. Bush had seemed so unwilling to take, coupled with a more nimble military approach that eschewed the commitment of US ground troops, had produced much to be proud of, optimistic even. The Libyan rebels had been more or less unified in their efforts to oust Gaddafi; the country had fewer people than Iraq but more wealth than Afghanistan – including oil to sell to European neighbors across the Mediterranean Sea; and at the time democratic institutions in Egypt and Tunisia seemed to offer blueprints for Libya's transition.[106] In the context of a more stable Afghanistan, an Iraq that was – at least in 2011-2012 – out of the headlines, and the May 2011 announcement of Osama bin Laden's assassination, Obama had much to celebrate on the counter-terrorism front. Like Bush II circa 2004, however, victory did not guarantee progress, stability, or peace.

The various groups fighting against Gaddafi, now free of the gravitational force of a common enemy around which they could orbit, came into conflict with each other. The new government, seeking control and unity, pushed for the militias to register under the aegis of the ministry of defense or be disarmed, thus (it was hoped) at least putting these armed groups under some degree of government influence. The remaining Libyan bureaucracy, however, was not up to this task, and various militias were often not willing to work under these terms. Consequently, Libyan politics emerged from the fall of Gaddafi surrounded by armed groups ready and willing to agitate in pursuit of their own self-interest.[107]

Violence subsided for a time, but a rise in jihadist attacks in Tripoli and Benghazi kept Libyans on edge and inflamed tensions among various groups. The US only took notice of this failing political situation after its consulate in Benghazi was attacked by groups allied with al Qaeda. The fledgling Libyan government reacted to this deteriorating situation by cracking down on non-sanctioned militias on a large scale, but their attempts to disarm these armed myriads failed. In 2014 parliamentary elections were held in which the nationalists faced off against the Islamists. The newly elected Council of Deputies came to be dominated by the nationalists, causing the Islamists to claim the election fraudulent and form their own rival government, the Islamist National Salvation Government. The two sides spent a year contesting Libya before agreeing "in principle" to unite under a Government of National Accord, the authority of which was, despite a December 2015 ceasefire and some diplomatic success by UN agents to bring the various factions into accord, still precarious.[108]

Internal Libyan conflicts were made all the worse by meddling by other regional powers. The United Arab Emirates backed the nationalists while Qatar backed the Islamists.[109] A lack of Western peacekeepers did not help either. The reasons for a lack of peacekeepers were several: (1) The NATO campaign had been predominantly carried out by airpower with little direct involvement from Western ground forces; (2) Britain and France took the lead in these operations and bore proportionally more of the costs than in similar operations elsewhere (something Obama insisted on); (3) the intervention was controversial within NATO ranks, with only half the alliance making military contributions and less than a third committing to strike operations; (4) disagreements about the implementation of the UN resolution (protecting civilians vs. regime change) stymied after-conflict action by that body; (5) Western countries were already exhausted by more than a decade mucking around in Afghanistan and Iraq; (6) and the Libyans themselves, in the form of the interim authority, objected to a foreign presence that would call their legitimacy into question.[110]

The predictions made after Gaddafi's death proved to be, even within the immediate context of Libya itself, tragically optimistic. The reality, one of fratricidal bloodletting, still has yet fully to play itself out. Alas, the violence did not stop at the national border. As a direct result of the turmoil wrought by the fall of one regime, another country, this one a staunch US ally, nearly collapsed.

In northern Mali, a landlocked country west of Libya, the historically nomadic Tuaregs had long sought independence from the central governments of the regional powers (principally Mali and Niger). Groups of these Tuaregs had spent years under the employ of Gaddafi, fighting in his Islamic Legion. When the Gaddafi government fell, these mercenaries returned to northern Mali. Once home, they fomented rebellion against the Malian government. The Indigenous Tuaregs benefited from their military training and equipment, and the rebellion spread.[111]

In March of 2012, amid the growing political chaos inaugurated by the Tuareg rebellion, a US-trained officer in the Malian military named Amadou Haya Sanogo overthrew the civilian government, proclaiming a new regime (the National Committee for Recovering Democracy and Restoring the State or CNRDRE, as if the acronym had even brevity to recommend its use). His government then promptly faced the dual crises of (1) independent Tuaregs (having by this point declared the Malian province of Azawad to be a free and independent nation), who apparently received assistance from a local al Qaeda affiliate, and (2) external sanctions from both the United Nations and the African Union. Desperate, the military relinquished control of the Malian government within a month of the coup and new elections were held in 2013.

At its height, the Tuareg rebellion controlled two-thirds of Mali, but the chaos and political instability the rebellion inaugurated allowed jihadists to swarm the countryside, co-opting much of the Tuareg's momentum and giving the existing government yet another opponent with which to grapple. Much of the north soon fell into the hands of Islamist groups. At this point the desperate government invited the French to assist them in putting down the rebellion in the north, which brought some 2500 French soldiers into the country, along with contingents from other African nations. This campaign resulted in thousands of deaths and displaced 200,000 civilians internally, 144,000 abroad.[112]

In 2015, peace talks in Algiers yielded an agreement between three main parties: the Malian government, Arab and Tuareg pro-independence armed groups under the aegis of the Coordination of Azawad Movements (CMA), and pro-government militia auxiliaries. The agreement envisioned the use of two main tools to bring the conflict to an end: disarmament and transitional justice. The disarmament process began with the creation of a special unit called the Operational Mechanism of Cooperation, known by its French acronym MOC, which was to be composed of three battalions: one in Timbuktu, one in Gao, and one in Kidal. According to the original plan, these battalions would help secure the re-establishment of the state's presence in the north as well as the rest of the disarmament process, in which other combatants would be integrated into the regular army.

In late 2016, the first MOC battalion was formed in Gao. A total of 200 soldiers from the Malian army and nearly 600 fighters from other armed groups composed this unit. But in early January 2017, as members of the battalion were on standby awaiting their first deployment as a joint patrol, jihadists blew up their barracks, killing 77 people in the deadliest terror attack in Malian history. The attack, which was claimed by the al Qaeda linked group al-Mourabitoun, highlighted perhaps the biggest local obstacle to stability: the fact that jihadist groups, responsible for so much of the violence in Mali, were not part of the formal peace process. The country remains in a precarious state.[113]

As conflicts such as those in Libya and Mali intensified, the Obama administration funded more missions in more countries, increased the use of local proxies and allies, and authorized the construction of countless supply depots and little airfields up and down the continent. New rapid reaction and quick response forces were formed, specialized teams working directly on counter-terrorism missions. One, for instance, was a contingent of AFRICOM personnel and officials drawn from various government agencies formed to help secure hundreds of Nigerian schoolgirls kidnapped by members of Boko Haram. Another was Special Warfare Unit 10, whose mission includes, said its commander, "building critical host nation security capacity; enabling, advising, and assisting our African CT [Counter-Terrorism] partner forces, so they can swiftly counter and destroy al-Shabab, AQIM, and Boko Haram [local jihadist groups]."[114]

Obama's policy in Libya was the loudest example of a typically quiet approach. Across the African continent, AFRICOM spent the two terms of the first black president dotting the landscape with outposts, bases, forward supply positions. Local airfields allowed US spy drones to operate, local troops made use of US equipment and training to hunt down their enemies (or topple their government, as was the case with Mali), and US special forces spread themselves across Africa, engaging in some 546 "activities" over the course of 2013 alone, a 217 percent increase from 2008.[115] The sustained expansion of this battlespace over the course of Obama's presidency, occurring as it did almost entirely out of the public's view, bodes ill for the future.

1.3.6 The War at Home

At home, Obama continued to sustain gigantic military budgets. He also supported the perpetuation of the US government's pervasive surveillance programs. In both cases he sought some reforms – perhaps a greater degree of transparency or a more rational bureaucratic process – but he did not question the underlying validity of either. His administration also continued to allow the panoply of terror fighting to be applied by law enforcement against American civilians (see also section 4.1.5.3)

Obama's presidency began promisingly when it came to the defense budget. Overall national security spending decreased from about 20 percent of the federal budget in 2010 to less than 16 percent in 2015. This happened because (1) the Obama administration succeeded in reducing the number of American soldiers deployed abroad, and (2) the partisan budget fights that occurred in 2011 resulted in mandatory cuts ("sequestration") to the defense budget in lieu of congressional compromise.[116] By the end of Obama's second term, however, and in the face of threats from the likes of ISIS, Obama championed increases in defense spending. In 2015 about $736 billion was spent on the US military; that sum had risen to $818 billion by 2017.[117]

The Obama administration happily defended or extended the existing surveillance infrastructure. For example, on May 26, 2011 Obama signed the PATRIOT Sunsets Extension Act of 2011, extending by another 4 years those aspects of the PATRIOT Act that were set to expire. It was only with the 2013 leaking of government documents by Edward Snowden – a contractor working with the NSA – that the full weight of these surveillance initiatives began to bear on the public mind, pressuring Obama into initiating some reform measures.

One of the more substantial programs disclosed under Snowden's leaks was Prism. Instituted between 2007 and 2008 as a replacement for the controversial Terrorist Surveillance Program, Prism – under the auspices of the FISA Amendments

Act of 2008 – could demand internet communications data from private companies, most of which ended up coming from Google, Yahoo, and Microsoft.[118] Thanks to the 2008 FISA Amendments Act, these companies were granted retroactive immunity (meaning they could not be prosecuted for participating in the previous, dubiously legal Bush-era surveillance) on the condition that they cooperate with the US government in the gathering of intelligence going forward. While this program did not collect phone data (that was collected under a separate program but under the same legal authorization) or information based on keywords or names, and purported to forgo the indiscriminate collection of bulk data, in Prism's efforts to collect the emails, Skype calls, instant messages, file transfers, and social media details of "targeted selectors," it also amassed a wealth of information concerning Americans with no clear connection to any malfeasance, malevolence, or malice. Moreover, once collected, both the data and metadata could be accessed by the FBI, CIA, and NSA, meaning that over time great swaths of the US intelligence community gained access to an almost incomprehensible amount of private information.[119]

In addition to the raw collection of intelligence data, the NSA harvested millions of messaging contacts lists, searched email content, tracked and mapped cell phone location data, and undermined local encryption attempts. It used cookies to piggyback onto online advertisers' tools in order to pinpoint targets and augment surveillance capabilities, accessed Yahoo and Microsoft data centers to collect user information from a worldwide population, spied on those using the Xbox Live service, or playing Second Life and World of Warcraft – even going so far as to recruit some of the users of these games and platforms to be NSA informants.[120] Reminiscent of the FBI's attempts to defame Martin Luther King Jr. by tapping his phones and collecting information on his sexual dalliances, the NSA kept abreast of the sexual activity of those it deemed "radical"

Muslims (who held uncomfortable political views but were not suspected of any crime), hoping to use such information against them in the future.[121]

Further disclosures revealed the NSA's far reaching foreign surveillance practices. Under a program called Black Pearl, the NSA targeted Petrobras (Brazil's largest company), UNICEF, the European Commissioner, and the Israeli prime minister, along with targets in France, Britain, Germany, Mexico, Spain, and China. America's allies among that list grew understandably alarmed that the US would violate national sovereignty in such a systematic and penumbral way. In toto, perhaps 122 high ranking leaders and officials were targeted by the NSA.[122]

This invasive constellation of camera-eyes boasts only the meagerest of oversight, public or otherwise. While a warrant must be obtained for telephone surveillance requests, the procedure is classified and few warrants are denied: 212 FISA warrant requests were made in 2012 and none were denied. A total of 564 were approved between 2012 and 2014.[123] Congress receives classified reports on these procedures, but the public can access only some basic statistics. Under section 702 of the 2008 FISA Amendments Act, which undergirds Prism, the government need only establish before the FISA court that procedures are in place to ensure that foreign intelligence is gathered from only non-US persons "reasonably believed" to be outside US borders, prohibiting the targeting of those believed to be within US borders at the time when the government wants the data. In addition, "minimization procedures" need to be demonstrated to the FISA court to guard against accidental collection, retention, and dissemination of information about US persons. In practice, however, the FISA courts have no ongoing authority to oversee Prism's activities, and no mechanisms are in place to ensure FISA-approved procedures are indeed being followed. The NSA has adhered to a 51 percent certainty protocol, meaning that so long as they are at least 51 percent sure that a target is outside the US and not a US citizen, they consider themselves able to go ahead with surveillance; this has resulted in the collection of vast quantities of US data.[124]

Edward Snowden fled the United States before issuing his disclosures to journalists – and real questions remain concerning his motivations. After all, most of the documents he obtained did not have to do with the surveillance of US citizens and were not disclosed to journalists at the time, and the timing of his journey (first to Hong Kong and then to Russia) remains suspect. Whether an idealistic quest to right a wrong, a narcissistic drive to obtain personal recognition, a plan to weaken the foundations of the surveillance infrastructure (perhaps a combination of some or all), by the time Snowden arrived in Moscow, his adventure had evolved, by his intent or not, into a mission of disclosing key national secrets to a foreign power.[125] He was helped by others with interests that differed from those of the United States – and that fact alone branded him a traitor, at least in the mainstream. Secretary of defense Ash Carter summed up the consensus of the administration regarding Snowden:

> He revealed that the United States tries to collect information on potential antagonists and criminals, and that it does so using cyber-tools as well as other means. Of course it does. We would be derelict in our duties if we did not, and it's ridiculous to think that this came as a surprise to any serious observer of world affairs. An ethical whistle-blower might question aspects of how this is done without publicly exposing any and all of our methods.
>
> Furthermore, a true whistle-blower who is concerned about potentially illegal or unethical behaviors would first have attempted to call attention to them through legitimate channels, seeking correction of the problems. There's no record that Snowden ever made any such effort...
>
> The result was real harm to national security, to US

international diplomacy, and to US companies. By every test, Snowden fails the standard for ethical whistle-blowing.[126]

Snowden was only the most high-profile case in an unprecedented conflict between government officials and whistleblowers and/ or leakers of classified information. Through most of America's recent history, the leaking of classified information was not prosecuted so draconianly. US law does not recognize the disclosure of classified information, in and of itself, to be a crime; rather, Congress delineated over time several specific kinds of data – the identity of covert agents, specifics about surveillance techniques – that if publicized without authorization could constitute a crime. The primary legislative mechanism through which Congress accomplished this delineation was the Espionage Act passed during World War One, which made it a felony to communicate potentially harmful information about "national defense" to an unauthorized recipient. Given its ambiguous language and the wide-ranging (and possibly unconstitutional) circumstances in which this act could be used, it has for the most part been applied only in cases regarding actual spies. Indeed, during the Cold War the government only attempted to prosecute three leakers (who passed classified information to journalists, for instance, rather than directly to hostile governments) under the Espionage Act (in 1957, 1971, and 1983), only the last of which resulted in a successful conviction.[127]

During Obama's two terms in office, his administration cracked down on leakers as no administration had done before, ultimately charging seven individuals for violation of the Espionage Act, more than double the combined total from Eisenhower to Bush II. Some of this additional effort resulted from congressional pressure to contain national-security related leaking, which was perceived to be on the rise. Much of it resulted from changes in technology. While the ability to copy and disseminate information across a wide area has led to the possibility of bulk leaks such as the cache of documents made public by Snowden, such technological innovations have also made the investigation of leaks by government officials more fruitful as well. This has resulted in more referrals leading to viable cases, prosecutions, and convictions.[128]

In the wake of Snowden's revelations, and the national conversation that would only have occurred in light of the documents he revealed to the public, lawmakers offered some meager reform, but refused to countenance a true reversal of policy. No branch of government seemed eager to hobble America's Intelligence Community from gathering information – any information, all information – so long as the slightest chance existed that such data might one day stop a terrorist attack. Senate debate led by Republican Rand Paul in 2015 saw Section 215 of the USA PATRIOT Act fail its renewal effort, although the USA Freedom Act (which Obama signed into law on June 2, 2015, one day after the expirations) renewed that and other sections of the PATRIOT Act that had been allowed to expire, with the caveat that the NSA stop its mass collection of phone data. In lieu of the NSA's efforts, phone companies are now required to retain phone data which the NSA can then obtain so long as a targeted individual is specified and permission granted by a federal court. In addition to this congressional reskin of existing surveillance, the Obama administration did tweak some standard operating procedures via Presidential Policy Directive 28, which ended "about collection" by the NSA in favor of looking for traffic between specific persons of interest, dealing a slight blow to the bloated surveillance complex of the NSA.[129]

What did all of this surveillance accomplish? Most of the surveillance apparatus that came to public attention during Obama's presidency had been constructed under his predecessor. Toward the end of Bush II's administration, in seeking to audit the government's vast intelligence gathering, the FBI's general counsel, Valerie Caproni, sampled the leads generated under the Bush II era program "Stellarwind" for the years 2001-2003: defining "useful" to be that which made a substantive contribution to identifying a terrorist or identifying a potential confidential informant, she found that 1.2 percent of leads were useful to American national security. In 2006 she conducted a more comprehensive review of Stellarwind leads between March 2004 and January 2006, finding that none had proved useful.[130] Audits such as this one inject some skepticism into consistent pronouncements by government officials that their sweeping surveillance powers are justified on pragmatic grounds – and sidestep altogether the stickier moral problem of living under a government with the kind of access to our private lives as we usually find in dystopian novels like *1984* or *A Scanner Darkly* (see also section 2.6.1).

The Obama administration certainly considered invasive programs like Prism to be integral in waging the War on Terror. Members of the administration dismissed concerns that the US spied on the world in the mold of Big Brother. Said deputy national security advisor for strategic communications Ben Rhodes: "I had to spend my days explaining to our liberal base that Obama wasn't running a surveillance state because of the activities of the NSA, which we couldn't really talk about."[131] Granted, no second 9/11 occurred, although the Obama years did see an uptick in small-scale, lone wolf style attacks, the kind that are very difficult to detect ahead of time due to the limited networking – and thus the amount of SIGINT (signals intelligence) available to gather – required to pull off such an attack. Between 2001 and 2008, some 166 terror attacks were recorded, 6 percent of which were carried out by attackers linked to Jihadism or Islam – although the vast majority of the 3000 killed by such terrorists died on 9/11; white supremacists, fascists, and Christian fundamentalists constituted about 21 percent of the attacks with two known fatalities. Between 2009 and 2016, 202 attacks occurred domestically, with 17 percent showing links to

Jihadism – and 30 percent linked to white supremacists, fascists, and Christian fundamentalists; the former killed 103 (half at the Pulse night club shooting), the latter 61 people.[132]

What the Obama years saw, therefore, despite the totalitarian efforts of the Intelligence Community, was a proliferation and dissemination of terror – and a diversification as well. Hitherto, most fatal terror had been committed against Americans in the name of Allah; to that deadly pantheon we can now add idols of the reactionary Right. Radicalized and extremist Islam remains a threat to Americans, but through Obama's two terms and beyond, the specter of radicalized white terror is, once again, unfurling its pall across the land – and thus far there has been no federal reaction to this resurgent home-grown menace.

1.3.7 What is Stability?

The War on Terror expanded from Afghanistan into Iraq and Pakistan during Bush II's presidency, then to Syria, Yemen, Libya, Mali, and beyond under Obama. It spread as the American military (and to a lesser extent the militaries of its NATO allies) spread themselves further afield, with armed groups of Muslims emerging to do battle. Indeed, the correlation between US efforts at counter-terrorism and the creation of new terror groups is quite startling. Before September 11, 2001 the US State Department had designated 21 groups as terrorist organizations (many having no affiliation with Islam). After that paradigm shifting attack and through 2016, 39 jihadist groups had been added to the list, 25 of which were designated so under president Obama.[133]

This expansion was baked into the essence of this conflict. Recall that George W. Bush was quick to declare the new War on Terror a conflict of global reach and Manichean stakes. Little wonder that suspicious and angry Muslims would take his words at face value, add to them an implied threat to Muslim sovereignty the world over, and take up the AK-47 in response. Now, nearly 20 years after its start, we Americans find ourselves fighting not the Taliban or al Qaeda merely, but a hundred al Qaeda or ISIS affiliates (in Iraq, Somalia, the Islamic Maghreb, the Caucuses, Bangladesh, the Philippines, and the Arabian Peninsula, to name but a few), along with ISIS-inspired lone wolves.

Political protests against the Western-backed regimes that dotted the Middle East, and maintained the local stability so desired by Western leaders, added to the chaos and strife brought about by the War on Terror. Beginning in Tunisia, this "Arab Spring" toppled the regime there but left the country in a state of bedlam from which many chose to flee. As the Arab Spring and the War on Terror spread – to Libya, Syria, Egypt, Bahrain – so too did the violence and sometimes chaos of more tumbling regimes, civil wars, or state repressions. Countries convulsed and people fled. Tunisians escaped to Libya, then when that country crumbled under Western bombs they braved the Mediterranean in search of shelter. Syrians fled their endless civil war. Iraqis fled deteriorating security in the face of ISIS invasion. Despite the wealth of Europe, these destitute and shellshocked people were met not with charity but hostility, leading to a resurgence of nationalist and far-right political parties in countries like Germany, the UK, and France.[134]

As of 2018, the Muslim World can lay claim to tens of millions of displaced persons, wars raging in Syria, Afghanistan, and Yemen, with other conflicts still simmering in Libya, Mali, Nigeria, and Iraq. Crisis after crisis arrives on the scene: the landscape fills with the charred buildings, dilapidated vehicles, desiccated corpses, and haunted gazes of a Muslim World wracked by endless violence and constant socio-political upheaval. Reliable and agreed upon estimates for the total casualty figures of the War on Terror are difficult to come by, since they depend on how the war's battlefields are defined, what count as casualties tied to the various conflicts, and the degree of reliability of the data itself. A partial reckoning (including deaths directly related to military operations and those indirect deaths resulting from subsequent political instability and additional conflict) is as follows: 1,000,000 dead in Iraq, 220,000 in Afghanistan, 80,000 in Pakistan;[135] 500,000 in Syria;[136] at least 91,000 in Yemen;[137] 16,000 in Libya;[138] 17,800 Americans (3000 on 9/11, 7000 soldiers, and 7800 American mercenaries in subsequent combat).[139] This puts the total (which does not include deaths in Mali, Somalia, Nigeria, Lebanon, etc.) at 1,924,800 people, of which 0.009 percent were Americans. For some perspective, an average of 37,900 Americans per year died in car crashes between 2001 and 2017, so over the course of that period perhaps 645,000 Americans died in that way, 37 times the number dead through our fight against terrorism.[140] (Compare these to the deaths related to the Opioid Crisis, section 3.2.1.)

North Africa and the Middle East have been volatile for practically all of the twentieth century. Colonization, oil extraction, and proxy Cold War fights made sure of that. In the twenty-first century, the dictators and oligarchs who rule these countries, most either installed at the behest of a Western power or supported by the West, have had to deal with the discontent of those they have tyrannized. Moreover, the West has had to contend with a violent reaction (in the form of Muslim terrorism) to its century-old policy of economic extraction and political domination in service of National Profit. The Global War on Terror is a Western reaction to this Muslim reaction to the Western endeavor to control the Middle East. That all the dictators, military aid programs, embargoes, air strikes, and invasions of the past 50 years have failed to provide the stability policy makers in the US, UK, France, etc. have so earnestly sought should give us pause to consider that perhaps it is the goal, and not the methods, that should be questioned.

Critics of Bush II and Obama sometimes point to their half measures as the reason for our continued lack of Final Victory – this criticism bringing with it such strategic wisdom as "bomb them back to the Stone Age." The solution, from this point of view, would seem to be obvious: commit to commitment. If you're going to fight a war, fight a war! But such a total war would be no small task. Fighting two limited wars over the course of a generation has been trouble enough already. We would have to commit perhaps our entire economic output to fight a counter insurgency and guerilla war across half the world, from the Philippines to the Eurasian step, the Cradle of Civilization and the southern Mediterranean to Central Africa – and maybe even beyond that, into the West itself, in order to even come close to achieving victory. If, however, we had no hope of winning the Vietnam War, a comparatively little struggle in a geographically concentrated area, then what hope would we have fighting the most sprawling military campaign in world history? And even if victory in this hypothetical Third World War *could* be achieved, recall what committing to commitment had cost Rome.

For a hundred years the Republics of Rome and Carthage warred for control of the western Mediterranean world. Rome eventually vanquished Carthage but at stupendous cost. Rome was only able to best Carthage when that infant empire brought to bear against its more mature foe everything it could muster. This was not some distant colonial war of the nineteenth century, not a UN peacekeeping mission of the twentieth, and certainly no twenty-first century counterinsurgency program out of General Petraeus' playbook. It was a death-struggle and both sides crossed the river Styx. The city of Carthage fell to Roman flames, but the conflict wrecked the political institutions of Rome by sending them careening down the path of conquest and plunder on a scale with which their institutions could not cope. The century after Rome's triumph over Carthage witnessed its conquests of practically the entire Mediterranean world – and more territory besides – but with this string of subsequent victories came the seeds of decline: soldiers returned from war fat with spoils, the influx of money into the Roman economy created a new class of elites who vied with each other for political power, far-off generals, busy conquering or governing foreign territory, commanded their armies with ever-increasing independence from senators hundreds of miles away in Rome itself, the Roman people became more dependent on government outlays (funded by conquests), and before the birth of Christ the Republic had traveled down the fiery road of civil war, emerging on the other side a despotism.[141]

If so many Muslims are willing to attack us in part or in total as a reaction against Western meddling in their affairs, then it stands to reason that the surest way to end the struggle would be to stop meddling in their affairs. In his 1998 fatwa against "Jews and Crusaders," bin Laden listed three items – (1) American occupation of Saudi Arabia, (2) American sanctions against Iraq, and (3) American support for Israel – as a clear US declaration of war against Allah, and thus cause enough for Muslims to fight. When pressed in a later interview, however, on whether he would stop fighting if the US reversed these policies, bin Laden waffled, saying he would continue to fight the US until it had ceased its aggression against all Muslims everywhere, a suspiciously broad declaration. While we can play it safe and assume bin Laden was as dedicated as he claimed, and therefore implacably committed to continued warfare, it stands to reason that many of his soldiers, supporters, and those who give him their tacit approval are somewhat less fanatical and would very likely cease their struggles against America if such concrete changes in US policy became a reality.[142]

Difficult as this transition would be – in the short-term many terrorists would probably continue the fight in some way, shape, or form – in the long run the fire would surely die out in the hearts of our enemies. The cessation of bombing campaigns, drone assassinations, night abductions, wholesale invasions, military equipment sales to local tyrants (most especially Saudi Arabia), and economic sanctions that cripple the people and leave the ruling oligarchy untouched would denude the propagandist of their subject matter, the recruiter of their most potent tools.

Additionally, we in the West need to come to grips with the bitter reality that, not only are we directly creating terrorists with every bomb we drop and every battalion we send, we are also funding the terrorists and their ideology. Wahhabism, the especially militant strand of Islam found in Saudi Arabia – where bin Laden and a majority of the 9/11 hijackers originated – has been bankrolled by Western oil money and protected by a monarchy wielding US, German, French weapons. The Saudi government has, since the 1970s, spent some $100 billion exporting its austere and intolerant version of Islam abroad, certainly more than what the Soviet Union spent on propaganda over a similar length of time.[143] Saudi money has funded the building of thousands of mosques and schools and the production of a plethora of literature and audio/video propaganda in countries with large Muslim populations like Indonesia, Malaysia, Pakistan, India, but also places like America and the United Kingdom, all tinged with the Wahhabist doctrine of Islam. And this money has had a real effect, turning more moderate communities increasingly toward Wahhabism. If we truly wish to stop jihadist terror, we will need to grapple with our role in the spread of this most militant and uncompromising form of Islam, the nation state that promotes it, and the energy dependence that funds their tyranny.[144] The Obama administration did work to reduce American dependence on foreign oil, but as we shall see in section 5.2.2, this did not mean a reduction in our general reliance on fossil fuels.

The United States under the 8 years of the Obama administration continued the fight against global terrorism vigorously. At the beginning of his presidency, Obama told defense secretary Gates in an interview, "I'm no peacenik" and indeed, that is a fair characterization.[145] Although Obama was criticized by many for his lax handling of terrorism – for instance by touring the Middle East in 2009, seen by many on the Right as needlessly "apologizing for America" – although he was criticized even by members of his own defense team,[146] Obama did, in fact, preside over an *expanding* War on Terror. Tactical changes, like the shift away from troop deployments and toward drones, special operations, and local auxiliaries mask an assumption common to both presidents: *that the War on Terror needed to be fought*. The forty-third president's doctrine of "preventative war" transitioned smoothly into the forty-fourth's "responsibility to protect."

Chapter 2

Economy in Crisis

2.1 Intro to American Economics

2.1.1 Three Economic Theories

Economics is essentially the study of the production and distribution of goods and services, with the various modes of organizing this human activity denoted by generalizing terms that seek to capture the dominant characteristics of a given system of production and distribution. In our contemporary capitalist system, for instance, we see the predomination of both private ownership of enterprises that produce things and private markets that distribute those things. Three basic theories currently encapsulate the field of economics: neoclassical, Keynesian, and Marxian. Each theory – and its variants – have sought to understand capitalistic economic organization, its strengths and weaknesses, how best to harness its energies for human betterment. These theories have real world implications and effects, for politicians will adopt the theory that aligns with their understanding of the economy, and push policy and legislation based upon that intellectual foundation.

Neoclassical economics (embodied in the works of men like Wilfredo Pareto) concresced at the end of the nineteenth century and begins its analysis from the standpoint of the individual, assuming people have a rationally working mind, the ability to labor, and the desire to consume things. From this vantage point, economics thus becomes the intermingling of rational individuals all vying for their desires via the use of their labor energy, a competition of each against all. The price and distribution of goods, jobs, and wage levels, all are understood as being based on individual preference and desire to work toward a goal.[1] This competition occurs in the marketplace, naturally dominated by the laws of supply and demand, i.e. if people want something, they will work harder for it, pay more for it, and find ways to provide more of it. So long as this market process is left to its own devices, the theory goes, the most optimum economic distribution will result.[2]

Keynesian analysis, named after the economist John Keynes, resulted from the worldwide depression of the 1930s, the socialist challenge to an economic status quo that seemed so incapable of properly distributing the fruits of human labor, and the inability of neoclassical economists to provide adequate explanation for such a severe and lasting economic downturn. Keynes attempted to reassess things so as to save capitalism from itself, to rein in its excesses while still keeping as much of the existing order as possible. Rather than the individualistic theorizing of neoclassicalism, Keynes attempted to analyze the economy structurally, to understand the overarching economic rules that govern individual behavior (how much things cost, how much people consume, etc.). In so doing, he replaced individual preferences as the driving force of most economic behavior with mass psychology and habit. He also sought to understand wages not through the neoclassical lens of labor power and individual desire to work but instead through institutional power and group psychology. Individualism still held pride of place in understanding the behavior of investors, because individual investor confidence had a decisive influence on where money was invested. This fact left a degree of uncertainty in the economic system that Keynesians thought required government intervention to balance. Left on its own, the market might eventually come to some sort of equilibrium between supply of labor and demand for labor, but the delay involved was socially unacceptable and so government would need to take on the role of investor (or even employer) of last resort, ensuring full employment, the rigorous movement of money throughout the economy, and the avoidance of sustained economic depression.[3]

Radical criticism of capitalist economic organization sunk deep roots in the middle of the nineteenth century and gained further momentum during the Great Depression, based predominantly on the works of Karl Marx. While neoclassicalism starts from the individual, and Keynesianism from the inner laws of capitalism, Marxian economics begins from an analysis of the historical development of capitalism. In so doing, it rejects the idea that the negative behaviors found within capitalist societies (greed, selfishness, rapacity) are the fundamental essence of "human nature" (something neoclassicalism asserts) and instead posits (1) the capitalist system promotes certain behaviors to the detriment of others; and (2) because it is a historically-developed phenomenon, capitalism is neither inevitable nor insurmountable – it is not "the end of history," merely one more phase in human development.

The Marxian analysis of capitalism itself centers on the concept of economic class. From the Marxian standpoint, your class is determined by your relation to the economic *surplus*, that is to say the excess of output that is not consumed in the production process.[4] The Marxian critique of capitalism is based on the observation that this surplus is hoarded by the few who, in keeping that which is given value by the work of others, exploit the labor of the many. Politically, then, and unlike either neoclassicalism or Keynesianism, policies based on Marxian theory seek to overturn this state of affairs and deliver to laborers control over the use and distribution of the surplus.[5] The contradictory interests of the surplus owners (the few) and the surplus producers (the many) are what dominate Marxian economic analysis, although it is important to note that contemporary Marxian theory does not fall into the deterministic trap of assuming only one underlying cause for all human thought and action. In focusing specifically on class conflict,

Marxian theory consciously "overdetermines" a particular causal factor so as to highlight it, while acknowledging that the world is a holistic complex wherein all influences all, to one degree or another (see also section 6.1.2).[6]

With the economic slowdown of the late 1960s, and the accompanying revelation of government corruption, abuse of power, and ineptitude, Keynesian analysis fell out of favor, replaced by neoliberalism, a reenergized neoclassicalism that still sought the perfect efficiency of a totally free marketplace. Thinkers like Milton Friedman and Friedrich von Hayek responded to the criticism of the previous decades, offering some new insights into both individual human nature and market imperfections that they thought addressed both the Keynesians and Marxians. To resolve market imperfections, neoliberals typically turned to private negotiations between affected parties. Since most neoliberals were especially wary of government regulators attempting to grapple with the infinite complexities of economic life, they asserted that, rather than involving the dead hand of government regulators (for example) to tax companies and redistribute wealth to pay for publicly-felt costs ("externalities") like illness resulting for unsafe working conditions or environmental degradation resulting from industrial waste, a better solution would be to allow the affected parties to negotiate privately and come to some sort of agreement. In the neoliberal's perfectly organized society, government would defend the importance of property rights above all else, ensuring transaction costs remain low and that not too many parties are involved in dispute resolution, lest things devolve into chaos. This limited government role would, they theorized, facilitate such individually handled negotiation and compromise. Their emphasis on private encounters permeates neoliberal public policy, which seeks the privatization of as much of human interaction as possible, assuming that with the basics of law and order maintained, the private sphere will tend naturally toward an optimum organization.[7]

Economic reality never fits perfectly into theoretical models of any stripe, but the divergence between neoliberalism and reality remains vast. While neoliberals often paint markets as natural entities that are later modified by government intervention, they are in fact created by political processes and thus inseparable from them. Laws and regulations favor some groups over others, meaning market competition is never "perfect," but always skewed a certain way. Even where markets are somewhat level, success breeds resources accumulation, political clout, and friendlier government regulations for some over others. Political clout combines with the tendency under capitalism toward monopoly to yield large corporations with an extreme concentration of power. The rich and powerful then concern themselves less with innovation and more with making money off what they already have or what already exists in the economy – a phenomena known as rent seeking.[8] This was what happened to the US economy after the 1970s, as more and more growth resulted not from the creation of new goods and services useful to everyday life, but rather in the "financialization" of the economy, to be discussed later on. Neoliberalism also could not resolve the capitalist cycle of boom and bust, its inherent instability.[9]

While neoliberals preached that free markets would yield free lives, the tendencies of neoliberal capitalism did much to make the crises and sufferings endemic to capitalism more broadly that much worse, all while shunting reams of money to the wealthy. The top 1 percent of Americans received more than 80 percent of the total increase in the nation's income between 1980 and 2005, almost doubling their overall share of the wealth. CEO wages relative to those of their workers soared: in 1965, the average CEO made 24 times as much as an average worker; 35 times as much in 1978; 71 times as much by 1989; 300 times as much by the end of the 1990s.[10] While people at or below the median income saw their wages rise about 1 percent yearly between 1980 and 2014, the top 1 percent (those receiving more than $1.3 million per year) witnessed yearly income increases of between 3 and 6 percent, reversing the trend in the 1950s which saw more income growth among the bottom and middle of the income ladder than among the rich.[11]

In reading the likes of Friedman or Hayek, who promised so much even in the face of the devastation their ideas actively caused, I am reminded of the words of eighteenth-century philosopher Jean Jacques Rousseau, comparing the promises made by the defenders of "civilization" with its bloody, brutal, oppressive reality:

> I open the books on right and on ethics, I listen to the scholars and jurisconsultants and, moved by their ingratiating discourses, I deplore the miseries of nature, I admire the peace and justice established by the civil order, I bless the wisdom of public institutions...Fully instructed about my duties and happiness, I close the book, leave the class-room, and look around me; I see unfortunate peoples groaning under an iron yoke, mankind crushed by a handful of oppressors, starving masses overwhelmed by pain and hunger, whose blood and tears the rich drink in peace, and everywhere the strong armed against the weak with the frightful power of the laws...So this is the fruit of peaceful institutions! Pity, indignation swell up in the depths of my heart. Ah barbarous philosopher! read us your book on a battlefield![12]

This reality of wealth concentration and corporate greed, of individuals desperately trying (by means fair or foul) to get ahead or just survive within the American economy, and of government acquiescence in this state of affairs, maintained a fragile semblance of prosperity into the first years of the twenty-first century. The coming crash, however, would prove that the busts inherent in the capitalist system had not been eliminated, and the cost of repeating this lesson yet again, after so many prior crises, was high indeed.

2.1.2 Prior Crises in the American Economy

In tracing the history of the Great Crash, we must keep in mind the difference between immediate and ultimate causes. The economic crisis of 2007-2008 traces its immediate roots to the vicissitudes of the post-World War II period of growth and stagnation, the subsequent policy decisions, and the business practices that resulted from these new policies. This period, in turn, originated from the pre-war Great Depression, which originated from the previous period of rampant speculation and uneven growth, which came out of an earlier period of boom and bust as the US industrialized and capitalized during the latter nineteenth century. Given this economic interconnectedness, a brief look at the major crises that preceded 2007 will assist in our understanding of the immediate facts of the matter. This historical record shows that capitalist economies are naturally subject to periods of boom and bust; equilibrium eternally eludes them. It is this structural reality that fundamentally caused the crisis of 2007, undergirding the myriad of policy decisions, risky business practices, and outright fraud that precipitated the Great Recession. Economic bubbles (and all the unreasonable confidence, frenzied speculation, and rapacity that come with them) are inevitable in a system that organizes society into competing parties, that prioritizes individual success over group survival. Private greed does not yield public good.

Panic of 1837

Britain had invested heavily in the westward expansion of white Americans, meaning that much British capital was tied up in land, cotton, and/or slaves. When the Bank of England began raising its interest rates in 1836, American banks followed suit.

This forced down the price of American securities (any proof of ownership or debt that has been assigned a cash value), which along with falling cotton prices and federal policies that drove specie (gold and silver) from eastern cities westward, curtailed loans from the larger eastern banks and precipitated a panic in the US financial system. Mercantile districts in the northeast were hit hard, but it was the Cotton Belt of the South that took the brunt of the damage. First in Mississippi, Alabama, and Louisiana – where several successful planters had overinvested in future success and thus did not have the necessary capital to meet a crisis – then later in Georgia and even Florida, citizens found themselves defaulting on payments, causing bank failures. Despite a brief recovery in 1838, the depression lasted well into the 1840s. Many individual states (mostly southern ones) defaulted on their debts, angering British investors and making future investment in those states, say for economic diversification or internal improvement, more difficult and costly.[13]

Panic of 1857

Fueled in part by gold deposits discovered in California, the economic prosperity of the 1850s brought with it confidence and therefore increasingly risky investment and speculation. The primary area of speculation was railroads, where legitimate infrastructure projects competed with phantom "paper railroads" for investment dollars. A bubble in railroad stock resulted from this frenzy of speculation. Uncertainties appeared as the supply of California gold slowed, the *Dred Scott* Supreme Court decision shattered the Missouri Compromise and put the future of US territories (and therefore railroad expansion) in doubt, and banks became more wary of loaning their money westward. Railroad stocks saw their peak in July; N.H. Wolfe and Company failed in August, shaking investor confidence, with some selling off their railroad concerns. At the end of August the failure of the Ohio Life Insurance and Trust Company, brought about by rampant fraud, further highlighted the precarious health of many railroad investments. Confidence exploded amid a now quite public financial panic. Government remedy focused on replacing paper bank notes with hard specie currency, promising that the ultimate stabilization of the currency would work better in the long run than any immediate relief of personal hardship.[14] Unlike the panic of 1837, the 1857 panic mostly affected the more urban and industrialized northern states. This popularized the notion in the South that the North required southern help to keep the US economy stabilized. Southern calls for secession abated for a time, as some hoped the panic would make the North more amenable to southern interests.[15]

Great Depression I: 1873

The decades after the Civil War were with derision referred to as the "Gilded Age" by the American satirist and grouch Mark Twain. By this he sought to point out that while the rich got ever richer, beneath the gold veneer languished a population both poor and unhappy. There is, as in every historical age, truth in this simple analysis. The Haves constantly take advantage of the Have-nots, the Clever of the Simple, the Rich of the Poor. Adam Smith recognized as much: "All for ourselves, and nothing for other people, seems, in every age of the world, to have been the vile maxim of the masters of mankind."[16] Still, those in control of the factories and the credit (the means of production and distribution) seemed to grow ever richer on the backs of an increasingly sick, poor, and desperate workforce (those who actually create value out of raw stuff) – the small and slowly growing numbers of the middle class (bureaucrats, middle managers, educated professionals) notwithstanding.

This trend had existed before the Civil War (slavery being the prime example) but it accelerated with increasing pace thereafter. The laboring class noticed this widening disparity, understood that the status quo only served to crush them under a pile of someone else's money, and organized various forms of resistance. While many eighteenth-century thinkers had considered it axiomatic that the economic freedom necessary for political freedom could be obtained by the exercise of free-market principles, more and more farmers, laborers, factory workers, writers, and politicians on the American scene were questioning that logic. They considered the increase in *big* business (a necessity of capitalist development, since competition always has winners that then seek to maintain their power),[17] and its dominance of policy on a state and national level, to be an impediment to the exercise of their political rights. Therefore, attempting to redress this economic imbalance between individual workers and those associations of businessmen we refer to as corporations, workers united in unions and began refusing to work under poor conditions and poor pay.[18]

With the rise of labor unions came much violence and upheaval. Strikes were initiated as a response to wage decreases or poor working conditions or "unfair" competition by immigrant or convict labor; and resisted by management with the help of police, privately hired "detectives," so-called scab workers brought in to replace unionized workers, political denouncements of labor resistance, and laws limiting or seeking to prevent the organization of the poor. The Great Railroad Strike of 1877, for instance, saw a 45-day strike by several hundred thousand loosely organized railroad workers, resulted in the death or injury of hundreds, and was brought to an end only when president Hayes intervened with federal troops, a good example of how necessary direct government involvement has been to the success of capitalist enterprises.[19]

This struggle is the historical context within which the depression of 1873 occurred. The specifics of the crisis involved speculation. This period saw the rapid development of new technologies and the building of additional railroads. Drastic outlays in investment brought stock prices around the world to a fever pitch by 1873. Amid another boom in railroads, the US and Germany ceased the production of silver coinage, with the US changing over to an exclusively gold standard of specie. This reduced the domestic supply of money, raising interest rates and hurting those who carried large loads of debt (e.g. farmers). The ensuing public outcry scared investors, who then shied away from long-term investments. By September 1873, the US economy had hit a crisis as Jay Cooke & Company – a major banking establishment – found itself unable to unload millions of railroad bonds, which it had hitherto sold to raise money it could then loan to others. Without the ability to raise additional capital, confidence in the firm's credit plummeted and bankruptcy followed soon thereafter. This scared investors and depositors, who worried that their own money might not be safe in their banks either, setting off a chain reaction of bank failures as banks lacked the financial reserves to allow so many of their customers to withdraw funds at the same time. Factories then began to lay off workers in the face of scarce credit (the banks that survived being too lacking in confidence to lend money in such a panicked environment) and a slowing economy. Railroad construction, which had constituted so much of the preceding investment and therefore employment, decreased sharply, throwing a receding economy into depression. Upwards of 30 percent unemployment resulted during this 5-year downturn.[20]

As the depression deepened, workers drew together in stronger associations, seeking through mutual aid to weather the economic storms. The most successful of these laborious institutions sought to unify the white, male, skilled workers, which gave some industries increased bargaining power but left millions of unskilled, migrant, female, and/or black workers to fend for themselves. So, while business interests were more often than not knit together to one degree or another, Labor found itself split along lines of profession, race, and sex. Government action made union organizing far more difficult by nakedly supporting the interests of the business class. In 1884, for instance, President Cleveland, a man with a reputation for inaction, roused himself to battle in response to a strike comprised of some 150,000 railroad workers, citing the strike's interference in the transportation of US mail as *casus belli* for the army to end the strike by force.[21] The power of Labor would be broken temporarily in the nationalist furor and subsequent communist scaremongering that followed World War One before rising once more in the wake of the Great Depression.

Great Depression II: 1929

The 1920s saw much apparent prosperity fueled by unthinking speculation and the exploitation of labor. More people had access to more amenities, but the vast majority remained impoverished and discontent. A total of 42 percent of families subsisted on less than $1000 per year (one-third the average salary for 1920).[22] The prosperity of the minority of the well-to-do was in its own way illusory, subject as capitalist economies are to periods of boom and bust, something made more extreme by the loosened energies of unregulated and arrogant businessmen seeking short-term profit heedless of long-term disaster. The real estate bubble that wracked Florida in this period, the careless farming practices that brought on the Dust Bowl, the rampant speculation in the stock market bespeak a level of economic navel gazing that, with the benefit of hindsight, could only have ended in disaster. As with so many human endeavors, however, the immediate purview of many people was limited by what they wanted to see and what they were allowed to see. Those of the middle and upper class inhabited a society organized around an economy that assumed eternal growth, ruled by business-friendly politicians, beautified by giddy advertisements promising happiness-from-purchasing-stuff, and blinded by the preeminence of an America practically unharmed by the Great War. Little wonder that so many found it so difficult to see the hard truth waiting for them at the end of the decade.[23]

The stock market crash of 1929 ruptured this state of affairs, slowing the economy and precipitating a collapse. As Panic spread at the swiftness of the downturn, confidence plummeted to new lows, economic activity slowed in an environment starved (in part by federal monetary policy) of loans and credit, and a recession turned into a depression.[24] With investment collapsed, credit unavailable, and companies shedding jobs, unemployment reached 25 percent in places by 1932-33. Localities attempted to fill the gap in labor demand with public works, but with less employment and production came a shrinking tax base and thus few resources to devote to such relief efforts. Although president Hoover, belatedly, attempted to step in with federally funded public works projects, it was Franklin D. Roosevelt, winning a landslide Democratic victory in 1932, who really put some energy into federally-backed employment.

FDR had done the politically astute thing and promised everything to everyone during the electoral campaign. Upon his election, it did not seem at all clear what his actual policy would be. He started with the banks. Due to loan defaults and prior overconfidence (and thus undercapitalization), banks found themselves unable to keep up with mounting depositor demand for cash withdrawals. With depositors unable to withdraw their cash, and banks unable or unwilling to lend credit, the overall supply of money shrank, further forcing banks to liquidate assets or short sell real estate in order to stay afloat. Many buckled under the pressure and a rash of bank closures followed. News of closures only fueled the demand for cash withdrawals (people wanted their money before *their* bank closed), and billions of dollars left bank vaults in short order. Many, finding their bank moneyless, lost their deposits altogether, since many of the failing banks had been utterly unregulated and thus did not provide any protection or insurance against possible failure.

Responding to calls for the government to do *something*, FDR thus called for a bank holiday that paused events long enough for the Panic to subside for a moment.

Having promised during the campaign to balance the federal budget, FDR's first year budget plan called for an 8 percent reduction in defense spending and $125 million in reductions of federal wages, $105 million of which would come from the reduction of WWI veterans' pensions.[25] Soon, however, he changed gears in response to immense public pressure for federal assistance and continued the interventionist policies begun by his beleaguered and outmatched predecessor, spearheading a series of acts, work programs, laws, and projects designed to do anything but keep the government still. He used government funding to electrify rural areas, build dams, roads, and other public works, paid artists, painters, and photographers to chronicle and beautify American culture, established social security and welfare, and in so doing began racking up a federal deficit that had already started to inch upwards under Hoover's administration. The New Deal, as his hodgepodge of public works, financial regulation, and labor law reform came to be called, pumped billions into federal jobs and, for a time, drastically expanded the employing role of the national government. Despite legal controversy – including many programs being declared unconstitutional by a hostile Supreme Court – the economy slowly improved, with GDP rising by 50 percent and unemployment declining to 14 percent by 1937.[26]

For the financial sector of the economy, the most important piece of New Deal legislation was the Glass-Steagall Act passed in 1933 that sought to regulate commercial and investment banks. Commercial banking involves the typical depositing of money in a checking or savings account, which banks then use to make loans to consumers or small businesses. Investment banking refers to the kind of banking activity found on Wall Street, for instance when publicly traded companies issue stocks or bonds in order to fund themselves, or when people trade securities (any proof of ownership or debt that has been assigned a cash value) hoping to make a profit. A common interpretation of the Great Depression at the time pinned much of the blame on the intertwining of these two types of banking, as problems on Wall Street ripped through the national financial system, denuding regular depositors of their money and banks of the confidence to lend. The new law required that commercial banking and securities activities be separated, so that a problem in one sector would henceforth be insulated from the other.[27]

The success of various aspects of the New Deal, however limited, coupled with his decisive reelection in 1936, led Roosevelt to a disastrous overconfidence. As his second term began, and thinking that the economy was back on track, he pursued a balanced federal budget for 1936-37, scaling back federal spending; at the same time, the Federal Reserve was tightening monetary policy (reducing the amount of money in circulation and therefore the availability of credit). The combined result was a recession in 1937-38.[28] At the same time, in an attempt to make the Supreme Court less hostile to the New Deal, Roosevelt had pushed unsuccessfully for Supreme Court reform in 1937.The failure of his effort (which made Roosevelt appear nakedly power hungry to many observers) destroyed much of his political capital and severely curtailed any response to the recession that he might otherwise have been able to push through Congress.

By 1940, the economic downturn coupled with the increasingly hostile international situation prompted FDR to push for more federal spending once again – this time with an emphasis on defense. These federal outlays would increase with each fascist victory.[29] The government directly employed 4 million people by war's end, a 400 percent increase from 1940; that coupled with massive government contracts to private firms fulfilling wartime production demands brought unemployment down from 14 percent in 1940 to 2 percent in 1943; gross national product rose from $91 billion before the war to $214 billion by war's end; all of this economic activity pushed federal expenditures beyond all previous precedent, with the government spending twice during the war what had been spent in the previous 150 years combined.[30]

1970s Stagflation and Early 1980s Recession

While the 1950s and 1960s were decades of incredible prosperity for the United States, its economy humming with activity, its cities and farmland untouched by the devastation of war, and its international commercial competition reduced to heaps of ash and agony, such unrivaled supremacy could not last forever. As western Europe recovered from the war, as the USSR's economy continued to grow (often faster than the United States, in fact),[31] as Japan and South Korea developed and bolstered their economies, American firms found themselves facing stiffer competition. Moreover, the Johnson administration, already adding to an expanding defense budget by trying to spend its way to victory in Vietnam, increased federal spending still further with a series of domestic programs collectively called the Great Society. This uptick in federal spending, coupled with steep tax cuts, swelled the supply of money, resting largely on government deficits, which in turn inflated prices. By the 1970s, energy prices began to rise as well, with oil spiking from $4 per barrel in 1973 to $30 in 1979, further chipping away at the underpinnings of the post-war prosperity by raising costs generally and slowing economic growth.[32] This duel phenomenon of increased inflation and decreased economic growth combined into "stagflation," and it brought about a rise in unemployment to 7.5 percent by 1975.[33]

By way of a response, in 1971 president Nixon took the US off the gold standard, devaluing the US dollar, stimulating demand for now cheaper US exports, but also making the importation of goods more expensive. In response to rising unemployment, Nixon also implemented a freeze on prices and wages, although this was soon replaced by a more relaxed monetary policy, allowing inflation to resume. This was the extent of presidential involvement in economic affairs, as Nixon was preoccupied with foreign policy (and later the Watergate Scandal).

The inflation that continued to plague the US for the remainder of the decade influenced a generation of economic thinking. Rather than combating recession (with tax cuts or increased federal spending), inflation became the key focal point of federal economic concern. Responding to the unfocused and simplistic labors of the Nixon administration, libertarians took the reins of national discourse and sought to cut welfare outlays and taxes more broadly.[34]

The federal response of this new neoliberal consensus and focus on inflation above all else began under president Carter when he appointed as chairperson of the Federal Reserve Paul Volcker in 1979. Volcker set the expectation of things to come when he told Congress that year that in order to bring inflation under control, "The standard of living of the average American has to decline."[35] Throughout the 1980s Volcker battled inflation via increases to interest rates (lowering the supply of money in the economy, thus increasing its value and therefore counteracting its inflation), which resulted in an economic recession that lasted until 1983.

Reagan, after defeating Carter and winning the presidency in 1980, championed a legislative counterpart to the policy of the Federal Reserve. His economic policy, referred to as "Reaganomics" or "trickle-down economics," took legislative form in the Economic Recovery Tax Act of 1981. This was the first large-scale attempt to implement neoliberal economic policy and did so via large tax breaks for the richest Americans and their corporations.[36] It was sold to the American people as liberating business from the onerous weight of taxation, which would allow investment into the economy, more job opportunities, and (miraculously) would still give the government sufficient tax revenues by taxing a larger and more vibrant economy at lower rates. By 1983, the recession ended and a return of economic growth characterized the remainder of the decade, much of it fueled not by robust job growth and a generally rising standard of living but by a risk-taking financial sector and an increasing reliance upon the trading and acquisition of debt.

Savings and Loan Crisis (1986-1995)

While the stock market momentarily crashed on "Black Monday" in 1987, the overall US economy seemed to have returned to a prosperous path. The Savings and Loan industry, however, did not share in the recovery. After World War Two, these "thrifts," i.e. financial firms that typically dealt in home mortgages, saw their profits suffer under the weight of federal regulations capping the rates they could charge. Looking for other profit avenues, thrifts began experimenting with checking accounts and alternative mortgage instruments, which kept many thrifts profitable through the stagflation of the 1970s despite the dearth in home construction. By 1980, thrifts constituted $600 billion in assets, $480 billion of which was mortgage loans, or about 50 percent of the US home mortgage market.[37]

Two deregulatory laws were passed in the early 1980s that changed the context within which these thrifts operated. In 1980, president Carter signed the Depository Institutions Deregulation and Monetary Control Act (DIDMCA). This law forced all banks to abide by the rules of the Federal Reserve, allowed banks the ability to merge together, stripped Glass-Steagall of Regulation Q (which set maximum interest rates for any deposit account other than demand deposits), and allowed institutions to charge any loan interest rate they chose. It set the stage for the growth of massive bank holding companies that were Too Big to Fail and opened the door for more predatory lending practices. It also began the process of stripping Glass-Steagall of its efficacy. Then in 1982, president Reagan signed the Garn-St. Germain Depository Institutions Act. This deregulated Savings and Loan associations, allowing banks to provide "adjustable rate mortgages," and other such flexible financial "products." The lending authority of the associations was expanded while the regulatory oversight under which they were permitted to lend was drastically reduced.[38]

Within the context of deregulated activity, Savings and Loans also found themselves pressured by asset-liability mismatch. As the Federal Reserve fought inflation, it raised the short-term interest rates. These rate increases made it so that the short-term costs of funding became higher than the return to be gained on mortgage loans, since many such loans had fixed-rate mortgages and thus could not adjust to the now increased short-term rates. Savings and Loans were thus pressured to focus more on high-interest rate transactions. Losses on fixed-rate mortgages mounted, causing some Savings and Loans to become insolvent. Regulators responded to this with forbearance, allowing the institutions to remain open, while also reducing capital standards (the amount of money they had to keep on hand) for those associations that remained solvent. These insolvent institutions, far from remedying their problems while they remained open, only saw their financial predicament worsen over time.

All of this – deregulation, less profit from traditional sources, increasingly risky lending, financial loss – combined with fraud within Savings and Loan firms to produce a crisis in the industry. Savings and Loans in Ohio and Maryland almost collapsed in 1985 and were only saved by their state governments draining their Federal Deposit Insurance Corporation funds in order to allow the firms to survive runs by their depositors. Lincoln Savings and Loan collapsed in 1989, losing $3.4 billion and implicating five sitting US senators – the "Keating Five" – in political scandal (including Republican senator John McCain). Midwest Federal Savings and Loan collapsed in 1990, referred to at the time as the largest financial disaster in Minnesota history.[39] Responsible for insuring these hemorrhaging institutions, the Federal Savings and Loan Insurance Corporation could not keep up with the mounting losses and faced bankruptcy.

By 1989 the federal government responded with the Financial Institutions Reform, Recovery, and Enforcement Act. It abolished the now-bankrupt Federal Home Loan Bank Board, to be replaced by the Savings Association Insurance Fund; it abolished the Federal Savings and Loan Insurance Corporation, replacing it with the Office of Thrift Supervision to charter, regulate, examine, and supervise savings institutions (which it failed adequately to do in the lead up to the 2007 crash). The bill also created the Federal Housing Finance Board to oversee the 12 Federal Home Loan Banks ("district banks"), created the Resolution Trust Corporation to dispose of failed thrift institutions taken over by regulators after January 1, 1989, and gave both Fannie Mae and Freddie Mac (government-sponsored entities that backed many US mortgages) additional responsibility to support mortgages for low- and moderate-income families.[40] By the time the crisis came to a resolution, the Savings and Loan industry had received a taxpayer bailout totaling $250 billion.[41]

Early 2000s Recession

With US manufacturing sluggish from a decade of expensive US exports, job outsourcing, and international competition, the economic growth and prosperity (such as it was) of the 1990s rested on speculation upon ever more vapid sectors of the economy. Whereas land speculation, then slave speculation, then railroad speculation, then mortgage speculation had tickled investor fancies in the past, the advent of the world wide web in 1993 (via the publicly developed web browser Mosaic) and the increasing digital connectivity of the 1990s allowed a new kind of speculation to emerge as the new millennium approached: internet-based companies. While government-funded innovations had made the basic technology of the internet a reality, its use was privatized under the Clinton presidency via the Telecommunications Act of 1996, which deregulated much of broadcasting and communication in the United States, gave away licenses to broadcast signals on public airways, and prompted the consolidation of telecommunications into several major firms.[42] Private firms chomped at the bit to invest in this new sector of the economy.

Into this climate of new technology and increasing interest in telecommunications investment came new companies like Netscape Communications, Lycos, and Excite – which excited investor interest – and slightly more seasoned companies like Microsoft and Apple. Many uninformed investors became eager to invest in anything internet related, anything with a ".com" affixed to it. Investment banks, which profited from the initial public offerings made by new dotcom companies, stoked already eager investors, and the fervor with which many speculated resulted in a bubble. Companies did not have to make a product or turn a profit for investors to flock to them – much in the same way that 1920s land speculators reaped huge dividends on useless Florida swampland that, because it all looked the same on a piece of paper, appealed to many an engorged prospector.[43]

Many new companies engaged in a "growth over profits" mode of operation, incurring net losses after spending on advertising trying to build market share and spread good word of mouth. If they offered a product or service, it might be provided at a severe discount or even for free, since the future brand recognition was considered more important than any immediate profit. While not erroneous in itself, many of the dotcom companies spent lavishly on utter frivolity. Meanwhile government investment in communication infrastructure, expecting a drastic increase in the need for ubiquitous broadband access, saddled the public sector with much debt.[44]

News of a Japanese recession, increased awareness of the cashless nature of many internet companies, a ruling by a federal judge that found Microsoft in violation of the Sherman Antitrust Act through its monopolistic business practices all served to shake investor confidence. On November 9, 2000, Pets.com, a mere 9 months after its initial public offering, went out of business. It collapsed amid an overall decline in most internet stocks, with perhaps $1.755 trillion erased from existence.[45] The 9/11 attacks further accelerated the decline in the stock market, and several accounting scandals – most notably ENRON in October 2001 and Worldcom in June 2002 – further eroded investor confidence. Those companies that survived this thrashing often did so at much lower valuations.[46] Subsequent economic recovery would rely upon the rise of yet another bubble – that of the housing market.

2.2 The Crisis of 2007

The philosophical admonitions of neoliberalism succeeded in convincing politicians and much of the public that "deregulation" was necessary to repair the American economy. Business-friendly legislation resulted from this new consensus, which allowed the financialization of the economy and an increasing reliance on creative accounting practices rather than real productive enterprises to yield economic growth. This rise in new financial "products," poorly regulated by any government entity, produced in turn a bubble in American homes which, when it burst, repercussed across the world, precipitating the worst economic downturn since the 1930s.

Two deregulatory measures have already been mentioned. The 1980 DIDMCA stripped Glass-Steagall of Regulation Q (which had set maximum interest rates for most deposit accounts), and allowed institutions to charge any loan interest rate they chose. The 1982 Garn-St. Germain Depository Institutions Act deregulated Savings and Loan associations, allowing them to provide "adjustable rate mortgages." St. Germain, coupled with a general relaxation of regulatory oversight, helped spur on the Savings and Loan Crisis of the late 1980s. The government bailout of the surviving Savings and Loan institutions gave the impression that the financial sector, at base, would be protected should another such crisis occur.[47]

In 1999, the Gramm–Leach–Bliley Act was signed by president Clinton and completed the process of denuding Glass-Steagall of its efficacy. The Act repealed substantial sections of the Glass-Steagall Act, including the removal of barriers prohibiting any one institution from acting as an investment bank, commercial bank, and insurance company at the same time. The removal of this barrier allowed further consolidation of the financial industry, risking the creation of institutions that, in their length and breadth, were "Too Big to Fail," that is to say, so large that their failure would cause a domino effect and collapse the entire financial sector.[48]

In 2000, the Commodities Futures Modernization Act was also signed into law by president Clinton. This legislation allowed those who dealt with Over The Counter Derivatives (contracts that are traded and negotiated privately between two parties, without going through an exchange or other intermediary) to be regulated under general "safety and soundness" standards, rather than by specific federal securities laws (the purview of the Securities and Exchange Commission) or by the Commodity Futures Trading Commission. With no specific agency overseeing this portion of American finance, such derivatives grew unsupervised in worth and ominence.[49]

The takeover of the US economy by the financial sector came as a direct result of these bipartisan measures at deregulation, as commercial, investment, and new "shadow banking" institutions grew immensely in size and complexity. The shadow banking entities rivaled the traditional commercial banks in their ability to provide credit to the US economy but resided within institutions like the insurance giant AIG's financial services division that fell outside the purview of existing financial regulations and regulators. Competition between these new financial institutions and the old guard pushed general lending standards down across the entire financial industry.[50] As often occurs during capitalistic competition, it was a race to the bottom – who could issue the cheapest, shoddiest product for the most short-term profit.

The financial sector's share of GDP doubled from 4 to 8.3 percent between the 1970s and 2006, its debts increasing from $3 trillion to $36 trillion, its profits constituting 27 percent of all corporate profits in 2006 (up from 15 percent in 1980).[51] Much of this growth could only have happened as a result of deregulation. And with the growth of the financial sector came a slew of "financial innovations" – new ways of eking out a living by making money self-replicate. Much of this innovation came out of attempts to make money not with equity (the raising of capital, presumably for investment in some productive enterprise) but with existing debt, specifically debt incurred for a fixed, often short, term originating from various corporations, mutual funds, governments, agencies, and banks. This market of debt, the "wholesale money market," was most easily accessed by large banks with diversified business interests and internal controls that (they claimed) would allow them to take on the risk of investing in debt.

Large financial institutions used their resources to perfect the process of debt securitization, whereby debts (first mortgages, later other forms as well) were moved off the balance sheets of the parent organization and bundled together to create a new "product" that could be sold (for a sizable fee) to others who could then participate in the financial profit chain.[52] Thus was the Mortgage-Backed Security born. These bundles of debt were advertised as low-risk: they were initiated by large entities thought to be systematically significant and therefore under some degree of government protection should things go wrong and, moreover, were based on mortgages. It was thought most people would pay back their mortgage debt, so financiers considered them relatively safe bets. The assumption became, therefore, that if a "product" was somehow based on mortgages, it was likely to be profitable and reliable. Little consideration was given to the health of the individual mortgages upon which such "products" were based.[53]

Further assurance of profitability was provided via the Credit Default Swap, a financial contract whereby a buyer of debt attempts to eliminate possible loss arising from default by the debt issuer by having the issuer of the debt insure the buyer's potential losses as part of the transaction. These Credit Default Swaps, based on sophisticated computer models that indicated only a Great Depression level of simultaneous defaults could crack this contractual armor, seemed foolproof. AIG's financial branch issued them in droves, accepting sizable premiums for their efforts. "It was like free money," recalled AIG's primary proponent of the practice.[54]

A related financial innovation, again allowed to come about as a result of deregulation, was subprime lending. In the 1970s, the housing industry started to run out of investment capital. This was met with foreign investment in the US housing market, which allowed continued expansion. At the same time, lenders started to look to poor and minority communities as possible sources of profit. Some lent under the federal mandate of the Community Reinvestment Act of 1977 (CRA), which encouraged lending to such risky places. Most, however, sought to lend outside the apparatus of this federal mandate and began issuing so-called Sub-Prime Mortgages, that is to say loans to borrowers who did not meet the standards set forth by Fannie Mae or Freddie Mac, the Government Sponsored Entities that underwrote the majority of US mortgages. Black communities were especially targeted by these high-interest loans, which yielded high returns to investors. Soon, such mortgages crept into securitized "products" like mortgage-backed securities, meaning that such "products" that seemed to be safe, based as they were on rock-solid mortgages, were in actuality underpinned by increasingly risky financing. Additionally, many of these Sub-Prime Mortgages were themselves bundled and sold to the Government Sponsored Entities, infecting their balance sheets with riskier-than-advertised debt.

Conservatives would later lay much of the blame for the crash upon the federal government and its insistence, via the Community Reinvestment Act and the policies of the Department of Housing and Urban Development, that banks lend to lower-income buyers regardless of what the market might dictate.[55] Timing exonerates the CRA from responsibility, however. It was passed in 1977 and subprime lending only became an issue more than 20 years later – after further banking deregulation; moreover, only 6 percent of subprime loans were CRA loans. Conservatives also put the blame on the Government Sponsored Entities (Fannie Mae and Freddie Mac), but blaming them misses the mark as well. The subprime loans that infected so many securities did not adhere to the lending standards of either entity, and even when they did lower their underwriting standards, did not correspond to the fevering of the subprime market.[56]

By the early 2000s the demand for US houses (fueled by foreign interest, government policy, the financialized economy's thirst for debt in which to invest, and the American consumers' need to indebt themselves in order to maintain their standard of living) had hit fever pitch, and mortgage originators clamored to meet this demand by hook or by crook. In addition to a constant expansion of home construction and a pervasive trend of mortgage refinancing, further financial innovation like NINJA (No Income No Job (no) Asset) loans, and Adjustable Rate

Mortgages (that began with low interest rates but spiked after a few years) had, over the course of the recent past, targeted poor and historically underbanked populations, as predatory lenders saddled these new home buyers with copious amounts of debt.

This drastic expansion of the home market caused a steady rise in the price of homes, which resulted in the housing bubble. Within this bubble, construction firms, home renovators, and homebuyers all acted as though housing prices would increase interminably, driving new homes to be built, bought, sold, renovated, and sold again in a constant cycle of ever-expanding profits. When necessary, each and all resorted to accumulating more debt (for instance a homeowner using their existing mortgage as collateral, called "refinancing") to facilitate the build-buy-sell-renovate-sell cycle. This exacerbated already rising US debt levels incurred as people attempted to maintain socially-acceptable levels of consumption and retain existing living standards in the face of stagnant wages and an economy that catered with increasing exclusivity to the rich.[57]

Like all historical economic bubbles, this one eventually popped, but because it was a bubble within the American housing market, it had a worldwide impact. Recall, much individual and family wealth was tied to mortgages, many investors (foreign and domestic) had sunk money into American mortgage debt, financial institutions big and small traded and profited from debt whose insurance and foundation rested on mortgage debt, and Government Backed Entities underwrote huge swathes of American mortgage debt. Any tremors in the mortgage world, therefore, would quake across world finance as well.[58]

The bubble burst when too many people failed to make good on their mortgage payments. By 2006, delinquency rates were drastically increasing, and with them home foreclosures. This led to a devaluing of financial assets like mortgage-backed securities, founded as they were upon mortgage debt. Buyers of these assets then left the market, leaving banks with a lot of now valueless securities assets. Those most heavily invested in these securities then experienced a liquidity crisis, meaning they were overleveraged, taking on too much risk with too little ability to pay if depositors came asking for their funds back.

Regulators, their efforts disjointed, underfunded, or captured by financial interests, failed to head off the crisis. New financial "products" often lacked a specific regulator – and even when they did, regulators like Federal Reserve chair Alan Greenspan specifically resisted new rules that might cover new financial innovations, arguing instead that, "The self-interest of market participants generates private market regulation."[59] With congressional approval, existing rules were scaled back or done away with entirely, and those regulations that remained in place were enforced by an increasingly threadbare coalition of federal agents.

The War on Terror exacerbated this state of affairs, as for instance when the FBI chose after 9/11 to prioritize antiterrorism over mortgage fraud investigations. Money and resources were made available for the former and kept from the latter. Bush II's last attorney general, Alberto Gonzales, defended this set of priorities: "I don't think anyone can credibly argue that [mortgage fraud] is more important than the war on terror. Mortgage fraud doesn't involve taking loss of life so it doesn't rank above the priority of protecting neighborhoods from dangerous gangs or predators attacking our children."[60] Perhaps he was correct (although we should recall that financial speculation has ruined far more American lives than have terrorists of all persuasions). At any rate, this is a telling example of the government finding the resources for activities it is willing to prioritize. In the coming legislative battle over bailouts, economic stimulus, and the need for stronger regulations, opponents constantly sang the refrain of *How will we pay for this?* The money existed, or could be raised, but somehow it made its way to the military and the financial sector more than it did to America's working class.

2.3 Response and Recession

2.3.1 Restoring Confidence

American Libertarianism withers under scrutiny. The twin suns of historical research and lived reality scorch it to ash. George W. Bush admitted as much after no private buyer could be found for Lehman Brothers and it was forced on September 15, 2008 to declare a chaotic bankruptcy. At that point he turned away from his economic dogma and spearheaded legislation meant to bulwark against further financial freefall, admitting, "these are not ordinary circumstances."[61] The government's first priority was repairing the financial sector, America's economic circulatory system. The financial system was critical if capital was to be allowed to flow, investments to be made, workers to be hired, labor to be compensated, and goods to be bought and sold. The clotting crises forming within and around the Systemically Important Institutions of the financial system threatened, so the administration thought, to infarct the entire economy along with it, spreading inactivity and therefore economic death.

The legislative battle for bailout funds split the Republican Party from its sitting president, and it took multiple attempts before legislation passed Congress and became law. Enacted on October 3, 2008, the Emergency Economic Stabilization Act received the support of 74 percent of House Democrats but only 46 percent of Republicans.[62] The bill authorized the US Treasury to spend up to $700 billion purchasing distressed assets, especially mortgage-backed securities (the so-called TARP or Troubled Asset Relief Program). It also authorized the Treasury to supply cash directly to ailing banks. Most of the funds were directed toward injecting capital into banks and other institutions, since the Treasury was still assessing how effective the direct purchase of specific assets would be. Criteria for which institutions got funding were based on the likelihood of survival, meaning the bigger banks received most of the assistance. It was hoped that such infusions of capital would allow banks to lend with more adventurousness, but in actuality banks used the funds to pay down their debts, acquire other businesses, or invest for the future, rather than issue loans. Thus, while the legislation saved certain institutions from collapse, it did little to stave off a general recession or the continued threat of other large entities collapsing.[63]

Head of the New York Federal Reserve during the initial crisis and later Treasury secretary once Obama took office, Timothy Geithner characterized the crisis most often in military terms, referring to the problematic entities as the five "bombs": the two government-sponsored enterprises (GSEs, Fannie Mae and Freddie Mac), the insurance company AIG, Citigroup, and Bank of America.[64] By November 2008, all had already received loads of public assistance, and yet all were affected by some degree of undercapitalization. The GSEs, Citigroup, and Bank of America would be defused before Obama took office, leaving AIG on the precipice. The Obama administration would then make the decision that, in order to defuse this fifth economic bomb and maintain the financial system so necessary to the US economy, the federal government would stand behind the firm, further reinstilling confidence into a panicked situation and allowing all involved a chance to calm their nerves and restart the lending and spending and buying necessary to basic economic life.

Fannie Mae (the Federal National Mortgage Association) had been chartered in 1934 to buy mortgages insured by the Federal Housing Administration (FHA). It had been authorized to purchase mortgages that adhered to the FHA's underwriting standards, thereby virtually guaranteeing the supply of mortgage credit that banks and thrifts could extend to homebuyers. Fannie Mae either held the mortgages in its portfolio or, less often, resold them to thrifts, insurance companies, or other investors. By 1968, Fannie's mortgage portfolio had grown to $7.2 billion, a debt from which the federal government wished to be released.

The Johnson administration and Congress thus reorganized it as a publicly traded corporation, creating a hybrid, a "government-sponsored enterprise."[65] Two years later, in 1970, the thrifts persuaded Congress to charter a second GSE, Freddie Mac (the Federal Home Loan Mortgage Corporation), to help the thrifts sell their mortgages.

Fannie and Freddie had dual missions, reflecting their private/public hybrid status: (1) support the mortgage market and (2) maximize returns for shareholders. They did not originate mortgages, but purchased them. These were either held in their portfolios or securitized and guaranteed by them – a process innovated by them and which the rest of the financial sector would come to emulate. Government regulation heavily favored these semi-private, for-profit institutions. Congress granted both enterprises special privileges, such as exemptions from state and local taxes. The Federal Reserve provided services such as electronically clearing payments for GSE debt and securities as if they were Treasury bonds. This allowed Fannie and Freddie to borrow at rates almost as low as the Treasury paid. Federal laws allowed banks, thrifts, and investment funds to invest in GSE securities with relatively favorable capital requirements and without limits. In addition, unlike banks and thrifts, the GSEs were required to hold very little capital to protect against losses.[66]

By 2006 Fannie Mae had begun consciously increasing its "penetration into subprime" mortgages. While not necessary to fulfill its government-mandated mission of broadening home ownership, this move was seen by Fannie's leadership as necessary to maintain its profitability. In 2007 Freddie Mac made similar moves, purchasing riskier loans lest it fall "below our return aspirations."[67] When the financial crisis gained steam, federal regulators thought that by buying up troubled assets, the Government Sponsored Enterprises would return a sense of confidence to the market, unaware of the extent to which the GSEs had willfully infected themselves. These increased purchases worsened the financial precarity of both Fannie and Freddie, necessitating the government to place them in a state of conservatorship in September 2008 in order to avert disaster, which as of 2011 had cost taxpayers some $151 billion.[68]

With Citigroup, Bush II's administration was painfully aware of the precariousness of their financial situation – of their dire need, despite already receiving $45 billion in TARP funds before the end of 2008, for additional capital – but wanted to do everything possible to make nationalization of the firm unnecessary. To that end, the Treasury developed a solution whereby the federal government would assume responsibility for the next $15 billion in the company's losses with the Federal Reserve backstopping any remaining hemorrhaging. In return for this protection, the government received about a third of the company's stock; this arrangement gave the government a degree of operational control over Citigroup's policies and procedures but fell short of outright nationalization.[69]

Despite these energetic government reactions to the crisis, the financial sector still quivered at the prospect of risk. Obama thus took office to preside over a weakened and defensive financial sector that, though saved from death, still did not prioritize lending. With credit drying up the economic slowdown gained momentum, prompting cutbacks in family spending as well as business outlays. As families cut back on personal spending businesses sought to cut employees and consolidate assets. The crippled financial system was making the recession worse, while the deepening recession was worsening the financial system. How would the new administration deal with this vicious cycle?

Treasury secretary Geithner, unable simply to lower interest rates that were already essentially zero (which under normal circumstances increases the availability of credit and helps push the economy out of a recession), devised a program of "stress tests" by which federal regulators would delve into the books of major firms, calculate the amount of additional capital needed to survive a catastrophic downturn, and then require the firms to raise that capital. If an unhealthy firm could not raise the capital, the government would forcibly inject the missing funds into the firm. These tests would help ensure that, "banks would have the resources to promote rather than prevent growth."[70]

Whether the stress test method would work, the tests first had to be devised. In the meantime, stopgap measures had to be effected before catastrophe did indeed explode the five bombs. Fannie and Freddie had been largely defused in the turmoil of 2008. Citigroup averted disaster by finding safe harbor behind government bulwarks. Bank of America stabilized thanks to $20 billion in TARP funds.[71] That left the insurance giant AIG.

AIG, its financial products division hitherto immensely profitable but now a cancerous growth that threatened the insurance obligations of this globally-spanning megacorporation, ultimately received $150 billion from the American taxpayer. To give this number some context, it surpassed by $10 billion that which had been spent on federal welfare outlays between 1990 and 2006.[72] When news broke that AIG had used some of its bailout funds to pay executive bonuses, the public roused itself to piques of rage. From the administration perspective, however, while the outrage was morally justified, maintaining the inviolability of contract law was more important.[73]

Meanwhile, the ticking of a sixth bomb garnered national attention in the form of the US auto industry. In the face of the looming collapse of an entire sector of the US economy and the millions of jobs that resided therein, the Obama administration agreed to issue additional TARP loans to keep GM and Chrysler afloat. This announcement came on March 30, 2009 and included aggressive deadlines for the companies to propose viable restructuring plans or else face government-facilitated bankruptcies. Both firms reached bankruptcy by the spring of 2010. The auto bailouts were not popular. They were seen by some as handouts to mismanaged firms that deserved to fail; by others as overly harsh and stringent, especially compared to the loose terms given to the financial industry. It seemed the administration policy pleased no one. But it did, for better or worse, salvage the automotive sector of the economy.[74]

2.3.2 Stimulating the Economy

By early 2010 the stress tests were working their way through the ten largest firms, which ultimately between them raised $66 billion in common equity in an effort to recapitalize. This left a shortfall, in the government's estimation, of $9 billion, and all but one of the firms were seen by the Treasury as having viable plans to fill the remaining capital requirements via private markets. Happily from the perspective of the Treasury, there seemed no need to agonize further over dwindling TARP funds or the specter of nationalization. Whether some problems had been papered over or not, as critics alleged, the stress tests seemed at least a far better indicator of financial health than FDR's bank holiday in 1933, which claimed to have audited the nation's ailing banking sector in a matter of mere weeks. In the end private investors regained their confidence in the wake of the stress tests. Bank of America's stock price went up 63 percent in one week, Citigroup's 35 percent. The equity market's "Fear Index" dropped to its lowest level since the collapse of Lehman Brothers in late 2008. Banks finally began shedding some of their lending reluctance.[75]

The recession seemed to be slowing its rampage as well. Job losses for May through August 2009 stood at about 300,000 – less than half the rate of job loss for the previous 6-month period. Indeed, subsequent economic analysis pegged the technical end of the recession to June 2009. The financial system, while still cut and bruised, no longer hemorrhaged itself upon the larger economy. Perhaps now recovery truly could begin. That is what the administration hoped, but the public outlook was not optimistic. "Things could be worse" or "the downward spiral has slowed" were not comforting slogans. While job losses slowed, unemployment still hit an official figure of 9.6 percent by the summer of 2009, less than the Great Depression's 25 percent but still quite substantial.[76]

With conservative voters recalcitrant, Republicans in Congress opted for a thoroughly anti-Obama legislative strategy. As a rule, if it came from the Obama administration it would be voted down by the majority of the Republican Party, whether it technically agreed with their party platform or not. This stalwart opposition made naked stimulus spending a nonstarter in Congress. Instead, the Obama administration, trying to do what it could to fill the gap in the demand for labor with government-subsidized employment, championed a more modest stimulus bill, the American Recovery and Reinvestment Act, that ultimately would be offset by future spending cuts. This bill, in true neoliberal fashion, was composed of one-third tax cuts (hoping against empirical evidence to give businesspeople more money with which to invest into the American economy) and two-thirds funding provisions. Ultimately, $212 billion of the stimulus went into tax cuts and $296 billion toward improving mandatory programs like Medicaid and unemployment relief. A total of $279 billion remained for discretionary spending that prioritized infrastructure projects.[77]

As a result of this federal stimulus some 42,000 miles of road and 2700 bridges were repaired, replaced, or patched up. A total of $27 billion was invested in green energy and $7 billion in improvements to the nation's broadband infrastructure. Private economic activity picked up thanks to this government stimulus over and above the initial government contribution, yielding a smaller government share in the overall economy.[78] Furthermore, Recovery Act funding bolstered the revenues of localities across the country, allowing many state and local government employees (teachers, police officers, firefighters) to keep their jobs. Given the slow nature of infrastructure projects and the almost invisible effect subsidies had on local and state government operations (things people just assumed would continue to function), the Recovery Act did not provide the promised plethora of "shovel ready" jobs. This lack of pizzazz doomed the stimulus in the battle of public opinion as the administration lacked anything *substantial* that it could point to as an unequivocal stimulus-based success story; this allowed conservatives to lambaste its effect as negligible even as many conservative state politicians – now under less pressure to cut popular state programs – benefited tremendously (if silently) from the federal funds.[79]

For the housing sector, the administration had three objectives: (1) arrest the dizzying drop in home prices, (2) keep mortgage rates as low as possible, and (3) help vulnerable families stay in their homes. To arrest housing prices, Fannie and Freddie were stabilized so that mortgage credit could keep flowing in the face of private capital's retreat. To keep mortgage rates low, Fannie and Freddie were again key, since they were the chief drivers of mortgage credit. To augment their efforts, the Federal Reserve purchased mortgage-backed securities in order to help rates stay low. The HARP Program also purchased securities while streamlining the refinance processes for Fannie and Freddie.

The administration determined that there was little it could do directly to keep people in their homes. According to Geithner, the best help for those upon whom banks had foreclosed was indirect: economic stimulus via tax cuts, unemployment insurance, and safety net spending, all of which would keep people above water while they weathered hard times. Alternatively, the administration pointed to government funding that saved existing jobs (e.g. state-funded teachers) or created new ones via massive infrastructure projects as having the added benefit of allowing people to continue paying their mortgages.[80] These indirect efforts were far less effective than the direct funding of financial institutions. While bailouts went to large corporations and other institutions deemed Too Big to Fail, more than 9 million families –11 percent of the total – lost their homes.[81]

Thus, to the extent that the administration made any effort to keep people in their homes, it did so only through indirect means – through credit availability, mortgage rates, and whatever economic stimulus it could manage to guide through Congress. It assumed without question that housing, while it needed to be affordable, was not a basic right and necessity but rather a product to be exchanged via market mechanisms. Like its approach to healthcare, neoliberal ideology that commodified all and sundry permeated government policy.

2.4 Reforming the System

With the financial storm weathered and recovery slowly but (it was hoped) surely proceeding, the administration seemed tasked next with the question of economic reform. Recall that while the New Deal had not solved the Great Depression (its economic programs had merely alleviated it to a greater or lesser degree), its far reaching reforms – including the Glass-Steagall Act and the Wagner Act which, respectively, overhauled the nation's financial and labor laws – had profoundly affected American economic life. Surely with a popular mandate, the moral high ground, and a Congress controlled by the same party, president Obama and his administration would seize the day and enact similar legislation against the present day's financial malefactors.

Despite some of his rhetoric – and despite what many of his conservative opponents claimed – Obama believed in the system. He believed in capitalism. Wall Street, hedging their electoral bets, ignored his campaign rhetoric and donated generously to his 2008 presidential campaign: of the $298 million received from various industrial sectors by Obama's campaign in 2008, 15 percent came from the finance, insurance, and real estate industries.[82]After succeeding to the presidency, Obama made it clear that he would side with the existing state of affairs, modified to some slight degree. Speaking at the swearing-in ceremony for Treasury secretary Geithner, Obama never mentioned fundamental systemic rot, but rather said that: "[Our] system is now in serious jeopardy. It has been badly weakened by an era of irresponsibility, a series of imprudent and dangerous decisions on Wall Street, and an unrelenting quest for profit with too little regard for risk, too little regulatory scrutiny, and too little accountability. The result's been a devastating loss of trust and confidence..."[83]

Speaking on February 25, 2009, Obama sketched out seven principles that he hoped would guide reform in the direction his administration desired: (1) serious oversight of systemic financial institutions; (2) a regulatory system strong enough to withstand system-wide stress; (3) a rebuilt trust in markets fostered through openness and transparency; (4) the uniform supervision of financial products; (5) strict accountability, including at the executive level of the financial sector; (6) comprehensive regulations that appropriately match regulator to financial institution, and (7) globally-minded financial rules that take into account the worldwide nature of the financial industry and work with other nations to ensure global financial stability.[84] These principles evinced a decidedly conservative kind of reform, seeking stability over justice.

If his view of the American economic structure had not been apparent from his campaign donations, his early presidential pronouncements, or the makeup of his economic team, it became readily apparent in March 2009. At the peak of the financial crisis, and as the automakers were scrambling for life, Obama convened a White House meeting with the country's top 13 financial executives. The bankers, fully aware of the popular ire that had helped catapult Obama to the Oval Office, dreaded the meeting. Even if he had hitherto been friendly to them, might he not – as FDR had done – take advantage of popular outrage for his own personal political advantage and support drastic financial reform? In that atmosphere of general uncertainty, they did not know what to expect.

When Obama received them, he said flatly, "My administration is the only thing standing between you and the pitchforks. You guys have an acute public relations problem that's turning into a political problem. And I want to help...I'm not here to go after you. I'm protecting you...I'm going to shield you from congressional and public anger."

One of the bankers in attendance later said, "The sense of everyone after the big meeting was relief. The president had us at a moment of real vulnerability. At that point, he could have ordered us to do just about anything, and we would have rolled over...He was our man in Washington."[85]

Geithner echoed this fundamental faith in the capitalist system, putting the blame for the recession not on the behavioral incentives and government support of rapacity the capitalist system engenders, but on a general sense of mania:

> The fundamental causes of this crisis were familiar and straightforward. It began with a mania – the widespread belief that devastating financial crises were a thing of the past, that future recessions would be mild, that gravity-defying home prices would never crash to earth...This mania of overconfidence fueled an explosion of credit in the economy and leverage in the financial system. And much of that leverage was financed by uninsured short-term liabilities that could run at any time.[86]

The fundamental problem, for Geithner as well as the administration, was not capitalist economic organization itself, but rather a manic confidence (an interpretation that showed a resurgence in Keynesian-inspired economic analysis in the wake of another capitalist crisis). Geithner, in his analysis of confidence, admitted that the cycle of boom and bust seemed an inescapable fact of capitalism. He never asks, however, how we might organize our economic lives so as to move beyond this system altogether. For him, and for the Obama administration, capitalism was akin to reality itself. It was fundamental.

The very success of the financial stabilization efforts provided just enough breathing room for the system to wheeze onwards unbroken. This success, limited though it was, took the wind out of the sails of those seeking radical reform, taking pressure off the Obama administration to address more fundamental concerns.[87] Without the pressure for drastic reforms, the administration was able to concentrate on saving the existing structures via a technocratic, depoliticized set of solutions: more vigilant regulators, better financial "shock absorbers," and the like – preferably outside the purview of Congress altogether.[88]

Obama's pronouncements did not turn into executive leadership in the creation of reform legislation, however. In discussing reform possibilities, Obama allowed a great degree of "relitigation" among his primary advisors, who then proceeded to debate the time away. From 2009 to 2010, while the stress tests were being drawn up and enacted, and while the economy groped for a sense of confidence, the Obama team argued and debated and dallied. The president, admirably seeking council concerning an issue of great complexity, ultimately let his team get away from him, and as a consequence the executive branch relinquished decisive leadership over the creation of reform legislation.[89]

Congress did not wait to act. In the House of Representatives Barney Frank led a bill through a morass of opposition. Republicans marched united against anything within the same airspace as president Obama; Democrats argued among themselves, as the internal divisions of the party in power made themselves public; regulators pushed back against infringements on their bureaucratic turf; and lobbyists did their level best to protect their little piece of the economic pie, as for instance auto dealers successfully lobbying to be exempt from oversight from the proposed consumer protection agency.[90]

Frank's House bill passed with nary a Republican aye in December of 2009 and moved to the Senate. There, Democrat Chris Dodd pursued reform. Dodd worked tirelessly to form a bipartisan legislation that would pick up at least a few GOP votes. In so doing, he worked to bring conservative Democrats onboard as well. In one instance, he agreed to scrap a stipulation for new fiduciary requirements on brokers and investors (making them less able to scam people out of their money) in order to gain the vote of South Dakota Democrat Tim Johnson. Later negotiations put the stipulation back into the bill.[91]

After a Senate version was passed, it returned to the House for reconciliation. Using the more conservative Senate version as their base, the House passed a final version in June 2010 with three Republicans voting for it; the Senate followed suit with three GOP senators also voting for the legislation; and Obama signed the Dodd-Frank Wall Street Reform and Consumer Protection Act into law on July 21, 2010.

President Obama said of the bill upon signing it into law:

The fact is, the financial industry is central to our nation's ability to grow, to prosper, to compete and to innovate. There are a lot of banks that understand and fulfill this vital role, and there are a whole lot of bankers who want to do right – and do right – by their customers. This reform...is designed to make sure that everybody follows the same set of rules, so that firms compete on price and quality, not on tricks and not on traps...So, all told, these reforms represent the strongest consumer financial protections in history. In history. And these protections will be enforced by a new consumer watchdog with just one job: looking out for people – not big banks, not lenders, not investment houses – looking out for people as they interact with the financial system.[92]

Rather than offering a single, coherent thesis, the resulting legislation grasped at solutions like the Hundred-Handed-Ones of Greek myth. It thus incorporated some of what the Obama team had wanted but also ideas that acted against their wishes. Part of the bill honed in on the mass predation of poorly informed borrowers, which yielded Elizabeth Warren's Consumer Financial Protection Bureau (Title X). Another piece focused on explosive and opaque over-the-counter derivatives trading, yielding a push for a more transparent, market-based trading of derivatives (Title VII). Focusing on the breakdown of responsibility in the extended chains of mortgage securitization yielded reforms seeking to ensure securitizers who would be required to have skin in the game (Title IX). Focusing on the sheer size of banks yielded reforms restricting bailouts and making the industry pay for them (Title II), while also capping banks' further growth (Title VI, Sections 622 and 623). Focusing on banks gambling with client money yielded the reinstatement of divisions between commercial and investment banking via the "Volcker Rule" banning "proprietary trading" (Title VI, Volcker Rule).[93]

Unhappily from the administration's perspective, the Dodd-Frank Act embodied a severe rejection of the 2008 crisis fighters under both Bush II and Obama. There would be no more taxpayer-funded bailouts. Under Dodd-Frank, the Federal Reserve could offer general liquidity support but could not offer individualized solutions for specific banks. In consultation with the president and the Federal Reserve, the Treasury was now required to place failing institutions under the control of the Federal Deposit Insurance Corporation (FDIC), which would operate the bank with a view to breaking it up and selling off its various parts. The Treasury preserved its ability to fund the FDIC's resolution capacity, and these costs would later be recouped via a levy on the financial industry. The Federal Reserve and Ben Bernanke (its chair) thought they could live with this compromise. Bernanke had always been unhappy with the ad hoc interventions he had had to make during the initial phase of the crash, so this new arrangement was at least something of an improvement. Geithner, who viewed himself as the financial equivalent of a soldier meeting an explosive crisis, recoiled at these legislative restrictions, preferring instead the kind of undemocratic (but fast-acting) powers the executive exercises when meeting other national emergencies – like war. He argued: "The president is entrusted with extraordinary powers to protect the country from threats to our national security. These powers come with carefully designed constraints, but they allow the president to act quickly in extremis. Congress should give the president and the financial first responders the powers necessary to protect the country from the devastation of financial crises."[94]

All of these various theories about the crisis of 2007-2009 had major political resonance. All of them made their way into the meandering text of Dodd-Frank. Many of them were sensible and worthwhile measures that redressed some of the grosser imbalances in the financial services industry. A general solution to the fundamental flaws of capitalist economic organization, however, remained elusive.

It is not surprising that a bill sprawling with theories of the reasons for the crisis, a multitude of responses, and all the attendant legislative compromises a lack of cohesive vision necessitated, has had mixed effects. The Consumer Financial Protection Bureau (CFPB), as one of the only federal entities directly tasked with holding businesses accountable for malfeasance, remains the bill's most progressive reform measure – which has also made it a constant target of Republican ire. Since it began operation, the CFPB has received millions of complaints from Americans claiming they have been scammed, harassed, intimidated by financial predators. Between its creation in 2011 and 2017 the Bureau extracted $12 billion from corporations, returning that sum (in refunds and cancelled debts) to 29 million defrauded Americans. As an example, $79 million came in 2015 when Encore Capital Group and Portfolio Recovery Associates were forced to repay tens of thousands of their victims. In addition to returning money to the public, the Bureau instituted new rules in 2013 for mortgage lenders and new guidelines in 2016 for payday lenders, attempting to stop lenders from fleecing victims with loans they know cannot be repaid.[95]

Aside from the CFPB, much of the Dodd-Frank reforms came in the form of proposed rules, regulations, and guidelines. Congress stipulated what it would like to see happen, leaving the details to later efforts – and these efforts took time. In July 2016, after 6 years of labor, 70.3 percent of total rulemaking requirements had been finalized, 9.2 percent had proposed rules yet to be finalized, and 20.5 percent lacked even proposed rules.[96] Critically, the rules and guidelines proposed and enacted often received heavy input from industry lobbyists who, freed from the immediate political backlash that accompanied the law's passage, could massage the implementation to suit their own particular interests.

2.5 Economic Recovery

The Great Recession was declared officially over by the second quarter of 2009, and the damage had been severe. Nearly 9 million jobs had been lost. Unemployment peaked at 10 percent. Nine million American families were foreclosed on. Some $10 trillion in household wealth was erased from existence.[97] The percentage of Americans living in poverty peaked at 16 percent in 2010.[98] But, as the Obama administration remained at pains to point out, without the emergency measures they put in place, things could have been a lot worse – there had not, after all, been another Great Depression.

The recovery from the recession, however, proved slow and arduous. The financial crisis and recession produced an extended de-leveraging of highly indebted households, focused on paying down debt rather than consuming. Lending institutions were acting in a similar manner, which meant that credit was often hard to come by, preventing the proliferation of the loans necessary for economic growth. Uniquely, the housing sector did not, as it had after previous recessions, rebound, since it had been at the epicenter of the economic damage. Foreclosures caused a surplus in properties and, again, consumers were too busy paying off debt to bother with purchasing homes. This weakness in the private sector could have been buffered by additional federal stimulus, but the conservatives (Republican and Democrat) in Congress ensured that that would not happen. Obama, for all his rhetorical emphasis on stimulus in 2009 and 2010, also (much like FDR) found himself enthralled by the siren's call of reducing the national debt, and in working through those two contradictory impulses, he found he could compromise with conservative demands to lower the debt without undue disturbance to his conscience.

The results of the bailouts and stimulus programs were myriad. In raw financial terms, by 2018 bailout funds had been fully recovered, when including interest on loans: $633 billion had been invested, loaned, or granted, with $390 billion returned to the Treasury, $359 billion earned by the Treasury in interest on loans granted (this does not include the trillions pumped into the financial sector by the Federal Reserve, which remains difficult to tabulate). While the stimulus made few splashes in the headlines after its initial congressional career, it did provide states and localities with the funds necessary to keep many public servants employed, albeit without any room for expanding existing services that had already seen severe cuts in the previous decades of neoliberal austerity and privatization. We can sum up the results as a damaged but still functioning status quo. The financial sector, while saddled with some additional regulation, rebounded quickly; no other Too Big to Fail institutions collapsed, and by 2010 the US economy began to grow again.[99]

The administration touted several statistics to show that the recovery was, indeed, a reality. They pointed out that, by 2017, some 15 million private sector jobs had been created (compared to the 9 million lost), putting the unemployment level at about 5 percent. Nominal household net worth had grown by $30 trillion, exceeding pre-crisis levels. Business lending had increased by 60 percent. And the federal deficit had dropped from 10 percent of GDP in 2009 to an average of less than 3 percent since 2014.[100]

These numbers, however, deserve some fleshing out in order for us to obtain a truer picture. In terms of unemployment it is true that the number is half of its recession-era peak, but this is partly because many otherwise able workers dropped out of the job market altogether. Indeed, the labor participation rate (the percentage of adults working or looking for work) toward the end of the Obama presidency was at its lowest point since the 1970s, although a portion of this is doubtless the result of an aging population.[101] More importantly, the jobs created were often of dubious quality: wage growth for all but the highest positions remained stagnant, the number of part time positions rose substantially, and an increasing share of the workforce found itself laboring within so-called alternative work arrangements (on-call, contract workers, freelancers) rather than the direct, full-time employment of the past.[102] Therefore, even those in the US who managed to find jobs during the economic recovery often had to settle for low wages, few benefits, and/or inconsistent hours. Tellingly, despite the steep decline in unemployment, the US poverty rate as of 2017 hovered around 13.9 percent (44.8 million people), a real but woefully inadequate drop from its recession-induced peak.[103]

Ominously, with mild economic recovery came the return of

financial "products" and a resurgent housing market. During the housing crisis and subsequent recession, the Federal Reserve was so desperate to create an economic recovery and a vibrant stock market that it cut interest rates to record low levels and injected trillions of dollars worth of liquidity into the financial system (a policy known as quantitative easing or QE). These tactics succeeded in creating an immense asset boom that caused the S&P 500 to soar by over 300 percent. After nearly a decade of this Federal Reserve-backed asset inflation, the US stock market is now as overpriced relative to its fundamentals as it was at major historic peaks. The US stock market is now more overvalued than it was on the eve of the Great Depression.[104]

Furthermore, by cutting interest rates and buying Treasury bonds and mortgage-backed securities, the Federal Reserve depressed mortgage rates to record low levels. Since 2012, 30-year mortgage rates have averaged about 4 percent, two-thirds the average during the mid-2000s housing bubble. This has resulted in another bubble in the housing market, evinced by the very statistics the Obama administration pointed to as a sign of economic recovery. US housing prices now exceed their housing bubble peak and are up 50 percent since their low point in 2012. Like they did during the housing bubble, US housing prices are rising at a much faster rate than both consumer price inflation and rent inflation, which is a sign of unsustainability.[105] Like clockwork, the signs of economic recovery in a capitalist system also augur another downturn.

According to the Obama administration, however, their efforts were more success than failure. Officials touted some of the following among the accomplishments of reform: (1) a strengthened banking system better able to withstand times of stress; (2) more transparency for mortgage buyers; (3) a government agency devoted to working directly to protect consumers; (4) more transparency in student loans allowing for more informed borrowers; (5) the protection of veterans and active military personnel against predatory lending; (6) greater transparency in financial markets more generally, benefiting retirees, pensioners, and investors alike. They also recognized that more work needed to be done, for instance (1) continuing to give more areas of the financial system greater transparency, (2) ensuring the orderly liquidation authority of the reform bill remains in place (to prevent future bailouts), (3) strengthening the protections already put in place by the CFPB, and (4) adequately funding regulators so as to allow them to keep pace with innovations in the financial sector.[106]

There is some truth to these claims – the Obama administration did make tweaks to the existing system that improved the lives of some and held some sectors of the elite economy to stiffer regulations. The fundamentals remained unchanged, and so the recovery favored those with power and ignored those without. The resources of the state were put one-sidedly at the service of management and shareholders, which resulted in larger, stronger firms that commanded an even greater share of the financial sector. By 2013 J.P. Morgan, Goldman Sachs, Bank of America, Citigroup, Wells Fargo, and Morgan Stanley were all larger than they had been before the Crash – and more financially stable as well. Meanwhile, community banks, already disproportionately affected by the crash itself, have found life increasingly difficult under stricter capital requirements and additional financial regulations.[107]

Contrariwise, the massive bailouts of "systemically necessary" institutions left smaller entities prey to the Invisible Hand, for when smaller banks asked for government help it was often denied. For example, when the Chicago-based Shorebank asked for $70 million in TARP funds in 2010, conservatives claimed this was a "politically connected bank" and the Obama administration backed off, refusing their request; the bank failed that year, denuding many black Chicagoans of a source of credit. So while big business was saved, smaller entities across the country shuttered their doors – or were bought out by larger competitors. 450 banks failed between 2008 and 2011, 85 percent of which possessed fewer than $1 billion in assets.[108]

The bipartisan response to the financial crisis continued the trend toward corporate consolidation, pooling larger sectors of the economy into fewer hands.[109] The economic recovery that followed the crash, moreover, benefited the rich far more than any other class of people. The pre-crisis trend of neoliberal economics continued, and fortunes of the rich continued to grow as wages for the remainder stagnated. The wealthiest fifth of Americans increased their portion of the slowly growing American economic pie, owning 88 percent of the country's wealth by 2016.[110] In 2017 the ratio of CEO pay compared to that of the rank-and-file stood at 361:1 (up from 300:1 during the 1990s).[111]

2.6 Popular Reaction and Resistance

2.6.1 On the Left: Occupy Wall Street

Many Americans on the leftward section of the political spectrum asked why the rich were allowed to hoard so much amid so much scarcity and misery and want, and scorned a Democratic administration they felt had betrayed the working mass of the American people. Frustration at the lack of fundamental reform and the one-sided economic recovery coalesced around a series of protests inside New York City's Wall Street financial district beginning in the fall of 2011. While protestors there were evicted by November, protests spread across the country and ultimately the world. In that year alone, hundreds of protests took place from Alaska to Massachusetts, with 12 events numbering a thousand protestors or more. New York City, the epicenter, peaked at some 30,000 protestors.[112] The Movement lost momentum and spotlight after 2011, and while criticized for lacking concrete goals, solutions, or organization, it gave a voice to a frustrated multitude, initiated a new generation into the vicissitudes of organizing and struggle, and, in highlighting the stark differences between the superrich and everyone else, popularized a crude but powerful rendition of the reality of class conflict: *We Are the 99%.*[113]

Whatever the movement's faults, the government certainly took the protestors seriously and the resources built up over the previous decade to fight "terrorism" were turned against domestic protestors. The Department of Homeland Security (DHS), for instance, turned its attention away from terrorism to surveil protestors, seeing them as *potential* threats to law, order, and the financial sector.[114] The FBI, cooperating with DHS and others, kept tabs on the Occupy movement as far back as August 2011, when the protests were still in the planning stages; and antiterrorism officials from Syracuse, New York to Anchorage, Alaska, Jacksonville, and Tampa, Florida to Richmond, Virginia all discussed possible security threats posed by the growing protest movement.[115]

2.6.2 On the Right: the Tea Party

On the other end of the political spectrum, the Tea Party movement emerged. Rooted in existing strands of American Libertarianism – which emphasizes Small Government, fiscal responsibility, and Free Market Capitalism – the Tea Party emerged in 2009 in the wake of drastic increases to the national debt and the bailouts of Bush II and Obama. Protests began as early as January 2009, but the movement did not coalesce around the legacy of the Boston Tea Party until February, when CNBC business news editor Rick Santelli, responding to the Homeowners Affordability and Stability Plan, lambasted the administration for supporting economic "losers" and called for a modern-day tea party. The first nationwide wave of protests followed later that month across some 40 cities, and by April 15 (federal income tax day) groups had held 750 protests around the country. Protests gained further steam reacting to Democratic efforts at healthcare reform, which Tea Partiers viewed as a federal intrusion into the private sphere and therefore a step down the road to tyranny.[116]

The Tea Party movement combined two long-standing strands of American politics: economic inequality and racial animosity (see also section 4.1.5.4), often intermixing the two. This produced a movement of intense energy that moved quickly to achieve its ends. Seeking legislative recourse, the Tea Party shifted its focus from protest to electoral politics, and in so doing changed the face of the Republican Party. In 2010 alone, some 138 candidates (129 in the House and nine in the Senate) ran with strong Tea Party backing; about a third won their race, depending on how the candidates are categorized.[117] After electing some 60 members to the Republican side of the House, members coalesced into a newly-formed Tea Party Caucus; after defeats in 2012 (mostly by Republican challengers), the caucus went inactive after that year's election cycle. Rhetoric railing against federal deficits (so strong in 2010 and still of real political heft into 2013, when Tea Party Republicans led the efforts to shut down the federal government for a short period) faded into the distance by the time Obama's second term expired, with other issues (like immigration) receiving the lion's share of the conservative electorate's attention. While their stays were sometimes short-lived and their political inexperience hobbled much of their legislative efforts, the Tea Party wing of the Republican Party did much to poison relations between the Republicans in Congress and their Democratic counterparts both in that chamber and at the White House.[118]

Ultimately, while the Tea Party had some real effect, while the frustrated anger it gave some voice to remains an active force in American politics, the movement itself succumbed to the vampirism of professional (for-profit) electoral campaigning. Entrepreneurs, seeking to profit from campaign contributions, fed over the course of several election cycles upon the donations of millions of Americans. The Tea Party Leadership fund, for instance, collected $6.7 million between 2013 and mid-2015, spending only $910,000 to support political candidates; Tea Party Patriots spent only 10 percent of the $14.4 million collected in 2014 on candidates – the remainder went to consultants, vendors, and the founder's salary.[119] As has so often been the case in American politics, energies spent on elections were frustrated and dissipated, leaving those already possessed of power largely unscathed.

Despite these varied protests from the Left and Right, the economic trend of wealth accumulation at the top continued apace. That so much could be hoarded by so few while millions faced homelessness, rationed insulin, braved crumbling bridges, and toiled at multiple jobs brings to mind the words of the thirteenth-century French poet Heldris of Cornwall, who while introducing his romance about a girl named Silence, who was raised as a boy and became a knight, said of the wealthy:

[Rich fools are] *intoxicated with Avarice,*
Their sovereign lady and wet nurse.
Honor is so scarce with them
that they haven't a fistful of it...
What good does it do one to pile up wealth
if no good or honor issues from it?
Assets are worth much less than manure:
at least dung enriches the soil,
but the wealth that is locked away
is a disgrace to the man who hoards it.[120]

Chapter 3

Healthcare Reform

American healthcare is a case study in the weaknesses of the capitalist mode of production, of gearing the economy toward the private accumulation of wealth heedless of public expense, of coupling political influence to economic success, of desiring that which is rightful to be, at best, merely affordable. In detailing the lobbying of a specific medical industry, the greed of a specific subset of doctors, or the inadequacies of our government's attempts at ameliorating these issues, we must bear in mind that this all stems, predominantly, from the set of incentives we have built into our economy: greed is good. We should, therefore, direct our solutions not at a particular individual or corporation, but rather at the system undergirding their actions and incentivizing their behavior.

3.1 A Brief History of Healthcare in the United States

Like in Europe, American healthcare first developed from a mix of charitable hospitals, private doctors, and folk medicine; as the nineteenth century wore on – and especially after the Civil War – reformers and practitioners drove to organize healthcare, rationalize it along *scientific* grounds, put things in order. Folk medicine was driven off and or appropriated, superseded by more regimented care: hospitals, wards, doctors with state-backed certificates.[1] A sovereign profession developed, organized around various professional unions – the American Medical Association, the American Psychiatric Association, etc. – who lobbied state governments to protect them from the encroachment of charlatans, interlopers – and competitors.

The desire to make medical care more standardized and more effective, although it gave doctors a lot of social and political clout and power, was also a legitimate response to the ailments of the Second Industrial Revolution and the advent of Industrial Capitalism on the American scene. Marx chronicled in gruesome detail the unsafe, unhealthy, unsustainable working conditions of England's poor and laboring people, and things were little different when factory-based production moved to the New World. Between 1800 and 1850, as Americans got their first taste of industrialized existence, life expectancy dropped.[2] Even as labor agitation and liberal reform improved conditions somewhat in the decades after the Civil War, conditions remained horrific. People often worked 60-hour weeks with no weekends. Between 1880 and 1900 an average of 35,000 American workers died each year in factory and mine accidents, the highest rate in the industrialized world at the time.[3] The 200,000 workers of US Steel Corporation were forced to work 12 hour days at barely subsistence pay.[4] Transit workers worked 7 days a week, 14 hours a day. Girls in the laundry industry worked 16 to 20 hours a day in poorly ventilated, poorly heated, damp conditions. Andrew Carnegie's mill at Homestead had its workers put in 12-hour days every day except Christmas and the Fourth of July.[5]

In order to keep the number of available wage earners high (and thus keep wages low), US immigration policy promoted a vast influx of immigrants into the country. Transplanted from their native lands, often unable to speak English fluently, and thus less confident than their native neighbors, these immigrant laborers were more easily controlled, worked for less money, and so made for ideal strikebreakers. Moreover, their children entered the workforce, augmenting the millions of little workers drudging their childhoods away on the factory floor: by 1880 one-sixth of American children under 16 had been put to work.[6] Long hours and universal work estranged many families, as attested by the poem of one pants presser:

I have a little boy at home
A pretty little son;
I think sometimes the world is mine
In him, my only one...

'Ere dawn my labor drives me forth
Tis night when I am free;
A stranger am I to my only child;
And stranger my child to me...[7]

The middle class responded to these horrendous conditions – and the infectious diseases they fostered and spread – with reform efforts. The working class responded with strikes and direct action against their managerial tormentors. These forces combined to yield palpable, if incomplete, change. Pressure from workers at the bottom pushed the politicians at the top to act, and reformers in the middle provided policy initiatives that both sides could more or less live with. The American Federation of Labor threw itself behind the emerging workplace safety movement. In one year, the cloak makers union alone called 28 successful strikes over safety concerns in New York. Bakers walked off the job, demanding better ventilation to combat high rates of tuberculosis. Between 1900 and 1910 state governments created or expanded factory inspections, health departments began investigating tanneries, bakeries, and foundries. Factory codes were introduced requiring the removal of dust, and a prohibitive tax was placed on white phosphorus matches to stop the poisoning of workers.[8] These struggles to make working conditions more sanitary and increase pay did the lion's share of the work to combat the effects of infectious diseases like tuberculosis and typhoid that thrived in such wretched conditions, yielding a twentieth century that was far cleaner and healthier.

Twin movements in healthcare at the turn of the century

reinforced this healthier trend: scientific medicine and professionalization. The former studied disease etiology, systematizing and standardizing medical knowledge; the latter standardized the education and training of medical staff, notably doctors and nurses. The stunning successes garnered by medical professionals in fields like bacteriology, the cures and treatments that came to be used on a wide scale thanks to a more universal standard of care, saved the lives of many ill people. So real was this success, and so well was it advertised by medical practitioners seeking to expand their scope of care (and often their customer base), that these improvements in medical care came to dominate the popular understanding of how health improved, relegating the role played by the improvement of social life (living and working conditions) to a mere footnote.[9]

This shift away from public health (or social medicine) and toward individualized medicine took place within the context of American industrialization, and thus the profit motive entered into medicine – a historically nonprofit sector of activity. This can be seen most readily with the evolution of the hospital. Hospitals began in the Middle Ages as religious institutions. In the early modern period they increasingly came under state control, though they retained their ecclesiastical character. Hospitals only began to shed their communal and charitable nature as they shifted toward providing active care under professional supervision within a dynamic and competitive market environment. The care became more effective, the hospital administration more standardized, but hospital services also grew less accessible to those not rich or part of what a particular hospital considered a member of the "desirable" poor. The great mass of people were forced to seek care in overcrowded and underfunded public institutions.[10]

At the same time as doctors and hospitals started to see the economic gains to be had in the increasingly effective treatments now available, progressive-minded public health officials began lobbying for publicly-subsidized treatment of the sick. Private practitioners – organized into guilds like the American Medical Association (AMA) – resisted these efforts, since their revenues came from a private fee-for-service model. Private medical practitioners proved too well organized, socialist agitators too politically weak, and so while European governments (even conservative ones) enacted the first series of public health provisions before and after World War One – seeking to co-opt the appeal socialists were making in those countries – politicians in America thought their interests better served by heeding the wishes of organized medicine rather than organized labor.[11]

The issue arose again during the tumults of the Great Depression, but again organized medicine – now augmented by the first inklings of drug manufacturers and insurance companies but still dominated by the conservative members of the AMA – made Franklin Roosevelt and the Democrats in Congress think twice about spending political capital on a national healthcare structure. Given this resistance, Democratic reformers tackled other aspects of the depression in the early 1930s, notably labor reforms and social security. During his second term FDR found little time to champion much of anything amid political battles relating to a recession and the Supreme Court. World War Two dominated his third term. Death precluded him from achieving reform in his fourth term of office.

Truman made further mention of healthcare, taking his cue from FDR's 1944 campaign promises, but shouts of "socialized medicine" defeated his meager efforts as well.[12] Instead, the years during and immediately following World War Two saw the enactment of major federal healthcare policies that, while not providing basic or essential healthcare to Americans in service of a government obligation to fulfill one's right to health, did begin the trend of covering *just enough people* so as to preclude omnibus reform. Two major policy initiatives stand out.

First: during World War Two wages were by and large

frozen, so companies (needing workers to fulfill the deluge of government contracts) began offering health insurance as a way to entice increasingly scarce workers into their factories. The federal government allowed this practice, and instances of employer-based health insurance grew rapidly during the war years.[13] After the war ended, the federal government solidified employer-based insurance into American healthcare by exempting this insurance from taxes. The Eisenhower administration proposed a blanket exclusion for all employer contributions, and an expanded medical expense deduction to boot. Little concern over the cost or its possible disruptive impact surfaced at the time. Indeed, when one senator at a hearing asked how much the exclusion might cost, an Eisenhower representative responded, "We haven't any figures at all on that."[14] Such an exclusion, while not framed in this way, actually favored people with higher incomes. The higher an employee's income, the more likely they were to receive health insurance, the better those benefits would likely be, and the more valuable any exclusion or exemption would be. Healthcare interest groups and conservative journals argued for the tax exclusion partly on the grounds that it would help thwart a government program. Labor leaders, now thoroughly tied to the status quo, backed the exclusion (oblivious to its fundamental inequity or its likely long-term political effects in weakening the movement for national health insurance).

Second: Congress opted to subsidize in a major way the building of hospitals across the country. In most other developed nations, national health insurance came before the constructing of new, modern hospitals and other healthcare structures; in America the reverse occurred. With still less than half of Americans covered by any kind of health insurance, the federal government funneled great quantities of money into building a modern medical infrastructure of hospitals, research institutes, clinics, etc.[15] Subsidized hospital construction had the additional effect of funneling much American medical energy into new technologies. Medical innovation thus took off in the post-war period. The new hospitals were to be filled with new devices and miracle cures and all the amenities of a bold and shimmering future. This new context of care shifted American medical focus decisively toward specialty care and away from general practice.

This private-insurance based state of affairs afforded a majority with medical coverage: perhaps 60 percent of Americans had private, employer-based health insurance by the early 1960s.[16] Still, it became increasingly apparent – even to liberals – that American healthcare had left too many behind. As Kennedy squeaked past Nixon to win the presidential election, many elderly people (no longer working) and poor people (whose jobs did not afford them the option of health insurance) found themselves unable to pay the rising costs for service in these new hospitals. Under president Johnson's leadership, and with compromises with conservatives in Congress and in the face of severe challenge from the AMA, Medicare and Medicaid passed into law in 1965 seeking to address these issues.

These programs were structured as follows. Medicare, federally run and covering the elderly, split into two parts: Medicare Part A, a mandatory program of hospital insurance funded through payroll taxes; and Medicare Part B, an optional program of physician insurance funded through general taxes, monthly premiums, patient deductibles, and co-payments. Part A had more impact, as it was a form of socialized insurance that underwrote the majority of healthcare risk among elderly Americans. Medicaid, on the other hand, covered the poor and was designed as a federal mandate to be directed on the operational level by the individual states. This resulted, over time, in substantial differences in coverage from state to state.[17]

American healthcare now appeared far more comprehensive. Employer-based coverage covered the majority of workers; Medicare covered hospital and doctors' visits for the elderly; and

Medicaid covered the same for the "deserving" poor (however defined by a particular state government). A significant minority, however, remained uncovered, and even within the expanded system serious flaws soon emerged. Trying to placate the AMA, legislators had established that Medicare fees were to be paid based on long-established or "customary" amounts. Practitioners found they could define "customary" however they chose and the federal government seemed only too happy to pay out.[18] Medicare almost single-handedly doubled the portion of healthcare paid for by government, which rose from 13 percent in 1966 to 26 percent in 1972.[19] Medicaid costs grew rapidly as well. It too was almost designed to inflate medical prices. The legislation required that states continually expand their poverty medical programs to cover every medically indigent resident by 1975. Thus, by 1969, state and federal poverty care programs across the country were spending almost four times what they had spent in 1965.[20] This massive government expenditure made some degree of sense at the time: more sick people became eligible for coverage and thus sought out treatment. Over time, however, as the healthcare industry sought out more and more government dollars, medical costs would rise far out of proportion to the social good being accomplished, and spending skyrocketed. The mountains of federal money would initially come to seduce doctors and other medical practitioners, but over time others would come to climb these greenbacked peaks as well – notably those from the corporate world.

Yet even with Medicare and Medicaid, many – particularly those too poor to buy insurance but too rich to be on Medicaid and too young to be on Medicare – remained in medical purgatory; seeking to cover this large minority as well, the push for universal coverage continued. Nixon, trying to co-opt the liberals of one of their key issues, twice introduced legislation to this effect. His 1971 National Health Strategy rested on an employer mandate: all employers would, under his program, be compelled to pay three-fourths of the premiums for health insurance for their workers and dependents (although significant deductables, co-payments, and annual limits to care did apply). It also sought to reduce costs via the "health maintenance organization." HMOs would pay healthcare providers for comprehensive services per person (a method of payment known as "capitation") rather than on an individual fee-for-service structure. This idea had been floating around since the 1930s (and was called "socialized medicine" by the AMA, like most things they did not like), but the Nixon administration now saw it as a way to curtail costs.[21] In 1974 Nixon doubled down: his plan still relied on an employer mandate, but this time coupled with generous benefits and only limited cost-sharing for the patient; anyone unable to obtain employer-based coverage could enroll in a government program instead. Despite Nixon's 1974 proclamation that comprehensive health coverage was "an idea whose time has come," congressional liberals, confident that they could wait out Nixon and pass legislation after Watergate settled down, refused to go along with Nixon's proposals, and subsequent efforts stalled.[22] Indeed, from then on the notion of a top-down, national coverage program was dropped even by liberals like senator Ted Kennedy. Instead, liberals adopted a more incremental approach whereby portions of the uncovered would be added to the existing programs.

Reagan and the conservative wave upon which he rode tried to rein in Medicare and Medicaid, but made little headway. In fact, congressional Democrats managed to expand federal coverage, while also enacting budget reforms in Medicare that began to control spending. At the same time, however, a disturbing trend in medicine, gaining ground in the 1970s, finally made itself felt by all: corporatization. Private money from employer-based insurance had got the ball rolling in the 1950s and 60s, but billions in federal dollars prompted a rush of private investment into the healthcare sector in the 1970s. Hospital administrators took over the running of hospitals from doctors; drug companies looked less to curing and more to managing disease; all and sundry fought federal regulation or twisted it so as to make as much profit for as little work as possible. Insurance companies, competing with each other for healthy clients to offset the costs of the sick, shook off any vestige of nonprofit status and delved full bore into the cigar smoke of the Conservative Revolution.[23]

By the 1990s, healthcare had become big business – and that business ensured that Clinton's meager healthcare reform initiative failed in 1994. For the remainder of the decade and through the first years of the post-9/11 world, profits soared, costs rose, and deindustrialization robbed even the formerly content of their employer-based healthcare. Hitherto, a policy trap had made American healthcare reform difficult. A majority of people recognized that healthcare needed reform, but simultaneously were satisfied with their own care. Meanwhile, those conglomerates, corporations, firms who viewed healthcare as a business rather than a social good arrayed themselves against reforms that would cut into their bottom line and their base of power. Milquetoast calls for reform, therefore, were met with adamantine resistance.[24] With the election of Barack Obama the healthcare trap seemed set to be broken: the onset of the Great Recession brought into full view the trends of the previous decades, and enough people seemed denuded of their coverage as to make the push for fundamental reform a reality.

3.2 Health and Reform in the Obama Years

3.2.1 Is US Healthcare Broken?

Deciding if something is broken requires an understanding of what its purpose was in the first place. If the purpose of American healthcare is to provide the best coverage to the most people as efficiently as possible, then what passes for a system in this country is inarguably broken. If, however, the purpose of healthcare, like any other sector of a market-oriented economy, is to make as much money as possible by satisfying the demands of those able to pay, then American healthcare is working more or less as intended.

Consider American healthcare before the Affordable Care Act passed through Congress in 2010 and before the ACA reached maturity in 2014. Hospital stays, physician services, medical devices, prescription drugs – all cost more in the United States than in any other developed nation. In 2009, per capita health spending in Japan was $2578, in Britain $2760, in Germany $3371, in Canada $3678, in the US $6714. Despite these substantially higher costs, US healthcare was not appreciably better than in these countries: preventable deaths for the same year were 71 per 100,000 (Japan), 103 (Britain), 90 (Germany), 77 (Canada), compared to the US at 110 per 100,000; infant deaths were 2.8 per 1000 births (Japan), 5 (Britain), 4.1 (Germany), 5.3 (Canada), compared to 6.8 per 1000 births in America.[25] Devoid of context these numbers tell us little, but the fact that our healthcare spending is nearly double that of comparably developed nations without outcomes that are at least on par with them should be cause for concern.

The cost of hospital services has grown faster than costs in other parts of our healthcare constellation. From 1997 to 2012, the cost of hospital services grew 149 percent, while the cost of physician services grew 55 percent. The average hospital cost per day in the United States was $4300 in 2013, more than three times the cost in Australia and about ten times the cost in Spain.[26] Upcoding accounts for some of this discrepancy: doctors are both encouraged and coerced by hospital policies to categorize illnesses such that they maximize the money billable to insurance providers. Moreover, hospitals cloak their billing procedures in darkness or post their prices written in the contemporary equivalent of hieroglyphs: prices are either impossible to find or utterly indecipherable.[27]

"Good business" has replaced "good care" as the mantra of the contemporary American hospital. Nonprofit hospitals shirk their social responsibility to serve the community and instead shovel money into advertising, new gadgets, new specialty wards, and executive salaries. Venture capitalists, observing the profits to be made from expensive medical machines (e.g. MRIs or Proton Therapy devices), invested heavily in hospitals starting in the 1980s. Bankers saw hospitals as a safe investment and offered their own financing resources as well. Companies sprang up to help smaller hospitals broker, build, and install specialty equipment that made for good promotional material but did little in assisting most of the patients they were likely to encounter. This is why, for example, Canada contains a single proton beam therapy machine (which is very expensive but of limited and narrow therapeutic value), but in the United States, three are in Washington DC, four in Florida, and two in Oklahoma City as of 2018.[28]

With all this investment came consolidation, as hospitals bought up their competitors. This resulted in massive price increases because hospital conglomerates that have driven out competition can raise prices without fear that "customers" will go elsewhere. The existence of one dominant healthcare system in a region can result in price increases as high as 40 to 50 percent. One California investigation estimated that premiums were 9 percent higher in San Francisco (where the Sutter Health conglomerate dominates) compared with those in Los Angeles. LA contains several large hospitals (e.g. Cedars-Sinai and Ronald Reagan UCLA Medical Center), and this competition reduces to some degree the pricing of medical services. Another investigation noted the connection between hospital mergers and an increase in both cardiac procedures and inpatient deaths, suggesting that the patients had been subjected to both "suboptimal care" and "overtreatment." These conglomerated hospitals, having monopolized medical care and determined to increase their profits, could concentrate on the most profitable procedures without fretting too much over patient outcomes.[29]

The profit drive explains the marked differences in price that have been noted even within the same hospital for the same service. If a large insurer or government provider refuses an excessive cost, it is passed on to those using smaller insurers or lacking insurance altogether. Only large insurers (representing large potential patient populations) have the bargaining power to rein in what hospitals wish to charge.[30]

Chief executives, even at nonprofit hospitals, have been well compensated for their aggressive business practices. Nonprofits constitute more than two-thirds of American hospitals, and IRS rules state that nonprofit CEOs should receive only "reasonable compensation," determined by considering salaries at similar organizations, but this meager stipulation has not stopped executive pay from increasing tremendously. In most cities, the CEO of the local hospital makes more than other local nonprofit executives. A few examples: in 2012 Jeffrey Romoff of the University of Pittsburgh Medical Center earned nearly $6.1 million (more than the university's president, in fact); Delos Cosgrove of the Cleveland Clinic earned $3.17 million; Thomas Priselac at Cedars-Sinai earned $3.85 million.[31] These earnings put all three nonprofit leaders squarely in the 1 percent.

Though rising more slowly than hospital fees, the cost for physician services is often prohibitively expensive and is determined more by the profit drive than the charitable instinct. Physicians earn the most money in specialty fields rather than general practice. US doctors on average make about 40 percent more than their peers in Germany, for instance, but American orthopedic surgeons make more than 100 percent as much as their German counterparts.[32] We might think, on the theory that economic success is based predominantly on individual preference for work over leisure and the talents one is endowed with, that this compensation scales up proportionally to the training needed or the hours worked, but this is not the case. The highest-paid American doctors are the ones who are best at the business of healthcare – being able to discern the most profitable subdisciplines, the trendiest technologies, the current tendencies in government billing practices. While the median income for primary care doctors stood at $223,000 in 2018, specialists earned $329,000 (plastic surgeons topped the list at $501,000, orthopedists next at $497,000, cardiologists third at $423,000).[33]

The way the market has rewarded certain kinds of doctors over others, regardless of actual public health needs, explains the imbalance in the United States between general practitioners and specialists.[34] The market does not allocate based on medical need; it allocates based on ability to pay – and plenty of those able to pay for healthcare are happy to spend it on specialty care, leaving the demands of the poor and marginalized (who benefit disproportionately from the services of general practitioners) unsupplied. Hence we see the US in possession of 50 percent more MRI machines than the United Kingdom, and 400 percent more than Canada; a greater prevalence of artery bypass procedures, coronary angioplasty procedures, and patients undergoing dialysis in the US than in either Canada, the United Kingdom, or Germany.[35] Our healthcare system emphasizes these expensive specialty procedures rather than the basic fundamentals of healthcare: general practitioners that can monitor patients, alert them to possible problems before they occur, and thus keep people healthier longer, consuming less specialty medicine.

Doctors ensure they are well compensated through a variety of means. They might lobby Medicare to pay out more for their specialty than for others. Since Medicare payments declined somewhat in the wake of late-twentieth century reforms, doctors might instead invest in treatment centers: orthopedists might open an arthroscopy center, or gastroenterologists a colonoscopy center. Being owners of these facilities, doctors are able to charge in ways similar to hospitals (tacking "facilities fees" onto bills, for instance, which charge the patient for the physical space in which they are treated). Doctors might contract their services with hospitals, billing patients separately from services administered directly by hospital staff. They might hire "physician extenders" i.e. nurse practitioners or physician's assistants to make rounds for them, thus increasing the number of patients seen – and the services billed for. Doctors might also take advantage of new intravenous or injectable drugs that could be administered in a doctor's office for a fee (and a markup). For instance, when Takeda developed a monthly version of the prostate cancer drug Lupron (it had a longer needle than the old version and therefore needed to be administered in a doctor's office rather than self-administered at home) urologists suddenly flocked to the hitherto less popular medicine (gynecologists did as well, prescribing it for endometriosis). In the face of cheaper substitutes for Lupron, its manufacturer provided it to doctors at a discount or in the form of free samples, which were then administered and billed at full price.[36]

Pharmaceutical companies have come to see the United States as the promised land, spending upwards of 82 percent of their money within our borders. They claim to spend much of their hard-earned money on research and development, but this is a deliberate obfuscation. In point of fact, US taxpayers pay for most of the research for new drugs, especially in the realm of basic research. Taxes provide the entire budget for the National Institute of Health, devoted to basic research, which hovers between $25 and $30 billion every year, as well as most of the training and research infrastructure upon which the industry draws. Taxpayers also subsidize much of corporate R&D through deductions and tax credits. Overall, drug companies spend perhaps 10 percent of their domestic sales income on R&D, and only 18 percent of that on basic research. This means that only 1.8 percent of sales income is spent on discovering new breakthrough drugs.[37]

Instead, the pharmaceutical industry spends money to lobby Congress for easier regulations, to pay doctors to promote and prescribe certain drugs, to manipulate the patent system so as to retool older drugs for newer uses or reskin existing drugs functionally to extend the lives of existing patents, and to advertise directly to consumers (a practice rarely found outside the US).

One of the most egregious examples of the healthcare industry's massaging of regulations for their benefit and our detriment is within the oligopoly of device manufacturers. Most medical devices are made by only a handful of companies – most knee and hip implants in the US, for instance, are made by just four. These companies have, since the 1970s, worked arduously to ensure that the regulations affecting them are as weak as possible. Medical devices are assigned one of three categories: (1) Class 1, things like tongue depressors that require very little FDA scrutiny; (2) Class 2, those intermediate devices that are more complex but not life-threatening or life-sustaining; (3) Class 3, critical devices (like pacemakers) that sustain life and, when they malfunction, threaten life – these devices require extensive testing to ensure their safety and reliability. In the 1990s device manufacturers discovered that, while the FDA spent thousands of hours reviewing applications for Class 3 devices before they could be sold to the public, Class 2 devices received on average perhaps 20 hours of scrutiny. Armed with this knowledge, device manufacturers slithered their way around the regulations by arguing (to a receptive audience of neoliberal regulators) that many devices one might usually consider to be Class 3 actually possessed "substantial equivalence" to Class 2 devices and therefore required only some modest regulatory review. Subsequent legislation tried to address this issue in 1997 but manufacturer lobbying denuded the bill of any effectiveness.[38]

By 2011 Class 2 submissions numbered between three and four thousand, while Class 3 applications numbered less than

50. As an example of the kind of devices manufacturers have successfully argued do not need to be heavily scrutinized for their safety and effectiveness, consider the Rejuvenate hip implant. It had been touted as a new, more durable device, composed of chromium, cobalt, titanium and thus worth its hefty price. Device manufacturers convinced the FDA that it was "substantially equivalent" to other existing implants and it entered the marketplace in 2008 under the Class 2 category. Recipients of the new device, however, soon complained of issues, and subsequent investigation discovered that when the implant's components ground against each other, the metals leached into the surrounding muscle and into the blood, resulting in joint failure, local tissue and bone death, and, potentially, other internal damage as well. It was recalled soon thereafter.[39]

Lacking new blockbuster drugs to put on the market, and fearing competition from generic alternatives, drug companies have gotten increasingly creative in their efforts to squeeze more profit out of existing formulas, drugs, and patents, another example of rentier capitalism (see sections 2.1.1 and 2.2). Since 2000, US availability of generics has plummeted. For instance, GlaxoSmithKline make a drug called Zofran, which had been approved by the FDA in 1991 to treat nausea during chemotherapy. While Zofran revolutionized cancer care, around 2005 the manufacturer began to encourage its use in other situations. At that point, attests one doctor, "our two best generic injectable antiemetics for emergency use suddenly became unavailable within months of each other...A lot of us felt it was suspicious." One drug of choice, prochlorperazine, became impossible to find, forcing doctors in the ER to prescribe the much more expensive Zofran. Compazine, too, was suddenly in short supply. Prochlorperazine shortages have plagued the United States ever since, although the drug is plentiful in other countries.[40]

In another example, drug companies responded to the

Montreal Protocol, which sought to eliminate the production of CFC propellants that caused a hole in the ozone layer (used in hairsprays, spray paints, asthma inhalers, etc.) in an interesting way (see also section 5.2.1).While the manufacturers of most affected products turned to alternative propellants which did not affect the prices of hairspray or spray paint much at all, drug manufacturers seized on the opportunity to get new patents for asthma inhalers with new propellants, removing from the market long available generic inhaler alternatives. As a result, the price of Albuterol (a common inhaled asthma medicine) rose from about $10 to over $100; it costs $7 to $9 in Australia (also a signatory of the Montreal Protocol and yet somehow unaffected by this price increase). The US price of some inhalers can now reach $300.[41]

In 1997 the FDA relaxed its guidelines for drug advertising, at which point spending for direct-to-consumer drug advertising surged, from $166 million in 1993 to $4.2 billion in 2005. For some drugs, the majority of promotional spending was for direct-to-consumer advertising. In 2000 the drug company Merck spent $160 million advertising its new painkiller Vioxx (double the advertising budget of Nike for the same year). Drug sales for Vioxx amounted to $1.5 billion that year, reaching 25 million people. Vioxx exemplifies both the trend in drug advertising and the consequences of FDA oversight that has been captured by the drug industry. Before the FDA approved the drug, concerns had been raised about it increasing the likelihood of heart attack; these were dismissed by business-friendly regulators within the FDA and the drug went to market. Subsequent research confirmed the connection and ultimately tied Vioxx to some 88,000 heart attacks (about half of which were fatal). For killing 44,000 people, Merck was compelled to pay a fine of $950 million – pricing each human life to be about $21,590.[42]

Perhaps the most egregious example of the brutality endemic to profit-driven medicine to occur in and around the

Obama years was what came to be called the "Opioid Crisis," though really it was simply one more aspect of the crisis of for-profit medicine. Multiple pharmaceutical companies ultimately involved themselves in this fiasco, but we may take Purdue as exemplary. Purdue launched the blockbuster painkiller OxyContin in 1996. Over the course of the next decade the company, helmed by the Sackler family, misled regulators, doctors, and patients as to OxyContin's addictive properties, marketing the drug not just for severe instances of pain but more mundane levels as well (something the Sackler family admitted to in a 2007 lawsuit).[43]

While Purdue's profits soared during this time, the Sackler family grew fabulously wealthy as well: between 1995 and 2007 they received some $1.32 billion from Purdue; after legal pressures relating to opioid deaths mounted (the kind of economic "externalities" companies refuse as a matter of course to consider in their cost/benefit analyses), the family increased its share of company dividends and over the next decade received an additional $10.7 billion from Purdue.[44] When the addictive nature of the drug finally came to widespread public attention, doctors and hospitals became more reticent to prescribe it, leading to the emergence of heroin and then the synthetic opioid fentanyl as black market alternatives.[45]

Lawsuits have now inundated Purdue and the Sackler family, with some two thousand brought to court by states, cities, and counties that have had to foot the immense medical bills related to the healthcare costs incurred in treating the victims of the crisis. Desperate to extirpate themselves from this legal butcher's table, Purdue has offered to settle them all for about $10 billion. Said the company: "The people and communities affected by the opioid crisis need help now. Purdue believes a constructive global resolution is the best path forward, and the company is actively working with the state attorneys general and other plaintiffs to achieve this outcome." This sum amounts to about $25,000 for each of the 400,000 people killed by opioids between 1997 and 2017. A total of $3 billion would come from the Sackler family directly (worth $13 billion and ranked the nineteenth richest family in America); while this is a substantial sum in relation to the $35 billion earned by Purdue from the sale of OxyContin, it pales in comparison to the $500 billion spent in dealing with the fallout across the country.[46]

As the examples cited above show, "deregulation" – as was the case with banking and finance – was really just a clever way of saying "regulations that favor private profit," and this has always been the case. The AMA campaigned vigorously to keep medicine "deregulated," claiming a single-payer healthcare system was "socialized medicine." Yet they were all too happy to accept Eisenhower-era regulations institutionalizing vast federal subsidies for hospital construction. In the 1980s, while the FDA became less stringent when it came to what drugs firms could introduce into the market, the US Patent Office became far more accommodating in allowing extensions on existing patents. Hospitals were allowed to combine and conglomerate – giving them massive market power – but federal lawmakers would countenance no such power be given to the representatives of the body politic via some form of national health insurance program. Individuals, powerless in the face of giant insurance companies, hospitals, drug makers, or even organized physicianry, could but hope they were enrolled in a sturdy employer-based insurance plan. Deindustrialization and wage stagnation, alas, made that less and less of a consolation.

3.2.2 The Affordable Care Act

By the time president Obama took office in 2009, the push for healthcare reform was already well underway. The Senate Finance Committee, led by Max Baucus, officially began looking into the possibilities of healthcare legislation on May 6, 2008. These hearings underscored the current consensus: American healthcare had become utterly unmanageable and the piecemeal solutions of the past several decades had not resolved things. The solutions contemplated, however, hardly smacked of fundamental change. Senator Chuck Grassley stressed at the time that reform required using the private health insurance system as the foundation upon which to build:

> As you all know, people are used to their employer providing health benefits. They like their employers' work and they do not want us to disturb that. They like that their employers take care of their billing, and by and large they are satisfied... So health reform should not up-end the system and do harm while trying to help folks without insurance.[47]

Although the stage was set for an attempt at reform, why, with the War on Terror raging and the economy in crisis, did Obama choose to put his political muscle behind healthcare so early on in his presidency? The readiness of congressional leaders, receptivity to reform of key interest groups, and broad consensus about the architecture of reform likely pushed Obama into believing health reform to be eminently achievable and thus worth pursuing. He thought it to be a goal both worth accomplishing and politically possible.[48]

Agreeing with most congressional Democrats, the Obama administration had no interest in "up-end[ing] the system." With few exceptions, "socialized medicine" was not on the table. To a degree this was unavoidable. The American healthcare policy trap was still somewhat in effect: too many people were just satisfied enough with their coverage that the clarion call for reform was, at best, muddled and unfocused. Many more people than hitherto wanted reform – but many still did not want *their* healthcare molested. This reality meant that the Obama administration and congressional allies would either have to cooperate with at least some of the pillars of the medical status quo to achieve reforms acceptable to them, or organize a sustained grassroots campaign of national scope to pressure the medical Special Interests into acquiescing to more fundamental change. Democrats chose the former.

Recognizing that some kind of reform was inevitable, interest groups including the pharmaceutical, hospital, and insurance industries lobbied for the least invasive, most beneficial reforms they could get, working hard with congressional and executive representatives to negotiate compromises all could live with.[49] Most of the special interests could live with expanded insurance coverage, since that meant more (government-subsidized) customers and revenues, so that is what reformers focused on primarily. Negotiations between congressional Democrats and healthcare lobbyists produced two deals behind closed doors, one with drug manufacturers and the other with hospital associations.

Big Pharma wanted government to subsidize insurance coverage, but recoiled in horror at the prospect of direct federal negotiation over drug prices, since that would set general price ceilings and eat into their profit margins. In the end they got what they wanted. Democrats promised that future reform legislation would not include direct negotiations over Medicare prices, importation of cheap drugs from abroad, or other measures that might eat into pharmaceutical profits. In return, Big Pharma would provide some $80 billion of cost savings on drugs and pay for an advertising campaign supporting reform legislation. The cost savings would come via rebates on drugs purchased under the Medicaid program and discounts on drugs that seniors purchased out of pocket when they entered the gap (i.e. the "doughnut hole") in Medicare prescription drug coverage. This deal came with political cost when it came to light later in 2009: Obama's political reputation was sullied by this example of politics-as-usual sausage making.

The second deal, this one with the hospital associations, failed to cause the same indignation among public opinion, although it did cause some political inconvenience down the road. By agreeing to accept payment reductions that would save the government $155 billion over 10 years (an amount the hospitals could accept because of the additional revenue that expanded health insurance would bring), hospitals avoided more stringent cost-control measures. Democrats pledged that the coming legislation would be crafted so that the payment reductions were contingent on the expansion of coverage. Cost savings would come via reduced updates to Medicare rates. Republicans would portray this as cuts in Medicare, and use the deal as evidence that healthcare reform would hurt the elderly.[50]

With these deals in place, congressional discussions moved forward. Once the Senate Finance Committee had hammered out a basic legislative outline, the Health, Education, Labor, and Pensions Committee conducted 4 weeks of review, during which time 160 Republican amendments were accepted in the pursuit of bipartisanship.[51] This quest for Republican votes combined with the generally conservative outlook of Democratic reformers to yield a decidedly right-leaning bill. The general approach of the Democrats harkened back more closely with Nixon's proposals than with Ted Kennedy's; the notion of private insurance tax credits had been plucked from Republican proposals dating back to the 1940s and 1960s (when it had been offered as an alternative to Medicare); the individual mandate had come about in the 1990s as a conservative alternative to the Clinton healthcare reform effort, and had become the centerpiece of Republican governor of Massachusetts Mitt Romney's reformation of that state's healthcare system in the mid-2000s.[52]

This plethora of Republican ideas yielded essentially zero Republican support, as the opposition party moved with impressive uniformity to block all efforts at reform. This meant that Democrats were on their own and gave conservative Democrats (especially in the House) substantial influence over the legislative agenda. Thus, in seeking bipartisanship, the Democrats were pushed and pushed again to keep reforms as safe as possible for those already benefiting from the healthcare status quo.

Reform stalled as 2009 drew to a close, in both House and Senate. In the House, representative Waxman turned general attention away from healthcare and toward climate change. While his bill passed negotiations within the Energy and Commerce Committee and narrowly passed the House floor, it ultimately went nowhere in the Senate. This was one bill in a series that aggravated swing-district Democrats and chilled relations between the more progressive House and the more conservative Senate.

More seriously, a fight developed among Democrats over the "liberal" direction in which the House bill seemed to be moving. Blue Dog Democrats – the conservative wing of 58 representatives – bemoaned leftist amendments like a national health exchange where people could sign up for a public plan run by the Department of Health and Human Services or the mandate for employers to provide health insurance or contribute a percentage of an employee's average salaries toward purchase of insurance through a national exchange; they further insisted that reform cost less than $1 trillion over the next 10 years ($500 million less than the legislation then proposed). Inconveniently, eliminating the public option (and all the bargaining power that came with the state acting as one giant consumer) was a surefire way to increase healthcare costs, but that mattered little in the face of neoliberal orthodoxy. Eventually a compromise was worked out, whereby the public option would be maintained but payment rates were to be negotiated individually with insurers, rather than based on Medicare's existing rates.[53]

As intra-Democrat negotiations dragged on in the House and inter-party discussions went nowhere in the Senate, a reaction was brewing among conservative constituencies. Fueled by rumors of "Death Panels" (a deliberate misreading of a provision seeking to provide for physician end of life counseling), right-wing groups like Health Care Freedom Coalition organized mass protests against Democrats returning to their home districts at the end of the 2009 summer session of Congress. The virulence of the protests – with shouting matches making for regular YouTube viewing – caught many lawmakers off guard; and while counter protests were eventually waged by supporters of the gestating legislation, the perception remained that the public was intractably hostile to healthcare reform as the Democrats presented it. Progressives, moreover, were put off by news breaking of the deal struck between Democrats and Big Pharma, making them less keen on supporting a president that seemed increasingly run-of-the-mill, rather than the revolutionary they thought they had voted for.[54]

Addressing the slackening pace of reform and the decrease in public support, Obama delivered a speech to a joint session of Congress in September 2009. He quoted a letter from the recently deceased Senator Ted Kennedy – long a champion of healthcare reform – and implored his audience to embrace healthcare reform as past generations had embraced social security, appealing to what he thought of as the American national character:

I understand how difficult this health care debate has been. I know that many in this country are deeply skeptical that government is looking out for them. I understand that the politically safe move would be to kick the can further down the road – to defer reform one more year, or one more election, or one more term. But that's not what the moment calls for. That's not what we came here to do. We did not come to fear the future. We came here to shape it. I still believe we can act even when it's hard. I still believe we can replace acrimony with civility, and gridlock with progress. I still believe we can do great things, and that here and now we will meet history's test. Because that is who we are. That is our calling. That is our character.[55]

Obama further articulated some details of the legislation he would support: a subsidized and short-term high-risk pool to provide coverage for at least some of those denied due to pre-existing conditions (a stopgap measure while longer-term reforms in the insurance market took effect); a cost of $900 billion (which infuriated Pelosi and other Democrats, already smarting under the pressure to bring the legislation's cost down to the $1 trillion mark imposed upon them by conservative Democrats); no federal support for the healthcare of illegal immigrants (to which Republican representative Joe Wilson would shout "You lie!"). Despite the Republican breach of decorum and continued conservative criticism, the speech did have the effect of rejuvenating public support for healthcare reform, and Democrats returned to the uninspiring task of legislative sausage making.

The abortion issue now divided liberal and conservative Democrats. In 1976 the Hyde Amendment had barred the use of federal dollars to pay for abortions, except in cases of rape, incest, or a threat to the life of the mother. While Democrats mostly agreed that this precedent ought to be maintained, they differed on putting it into practice within the new legislation. Under existing law, private insurance plans could cover abortion, and many did. Most supporters of reproductive rights believed that private insurance plans offered through the proposed insurance exchanges should be able to continue to cover abortions as long as they segregated the federal subsidies they received from the private share of premiums, using only the private dollars to pay for abortions. Those in favor of government-mandated pregnancy, however, vehemently disagreed. The US Conference of Catholic Bishops regarded this separation of funds as a sham, asserting that if an insurance plan covered abortion and received federal subsidies, the federal government was thus promoting abortion.

Democratic House representative Stupak introduced an amendment reflecting this logic: it prohibited abortion coverage in the public insurance option and also precluded private insurance plans in the insurance exchange from covering abortion if their subscribers received *any* federal subsidy. Because many of those who would come to use the insurance exchanges would receive tax credits for part of the premiums, insurance plans in the exchange would not be able to cover abortions at all. The Stupak amendment did allow insurers to offer abortion coverage in an unsubsidized supplemental policy, but advocates of reproductive rights asserted that few would purchase abortion coverage by itself (which in turn would make it more expensive for the few who would come to buy it); that being the case, they further argued, insurers might not even choose to offer it. When compromise could not be reached, House speaker Pelosi agreed to the amendment in the House version of the bill, and on November 7, 2009 the healthcare bill passed the House (Stupak and all) by a vote of 220-215; 39 of 58 Blue Dog Democrats voted against the legislation.[56]

In the Senate the "public option" (i.e. a single federal insurance plan that would compete with private insurance companies) took center stage. Committee leaders, in the end, considered a bill unpassable (60 vote minimum) with the public option intact, largely as a result of resistance from senator Lieberman – who almost single-handedly held Senate Democrats hostage until the public option was extirpated from the bill. With that and a few other concessions, however, he added his vote to the "Yes" pile. The final votes on the Affordable Care Act were on straight party lines, 60 to 40, with not a single member of either party crossing the aisle. None could recall another omnibus bill so partisan in result or so acrimonious in debate.

In early 2010, Obama (seeking a more active line in the face of further congressional sluggishness) again reached out to Republicans to see if, in the process of reconciling the House and Senate bills, some sort of accommodation could be made and some aisle crossing be had. Again, his efforts were rebuffed. Despite abandoning the public option, moving further to the right, doing his best to draw the opposition into his arms, it came to naught.[57]

With further bipartisan efforts slowing down over the course of February, Obama turned instead to direct efforts to help Democrats pass reconciled legislation on their own. He worked tirelessly to corral votes, his staff penned op-eds in favor of the legislation, and operatives coordinated a $7.6 million PR campaign in 40 congressional districts. With further efforts on the part of Pelosi to garner the needed 216 House votes, a reconciled version of the bill passed both sections of Congress on March 21, 2010. Subsequent legislation that rounded out the reform effort passed on March 23, completing the legislative package.[58]

Collectively, the bills that passed by a razor's edge through a bitterly partisan Congress came to be known either as the Affordable Care Act or, with derision, Obamacare. They sought to expand the number of people covered and begin the work of restraining costs by building on the existing structure of private insurance. This market-based approach bore a clear resemblance to the leading Republican alternative to the old Clinton plan and counter proposals developed by the conservative Heritage Foundation, and to the 2006 legislation signed by Republican governor of Massachusetts Mitt Romney. Like in Massachusetts, the new reforms attempted to achieve (near) universal coverage via three main provisions: (1) Requiring insurers to provide coverage to all desirous of purchasing it, (2) mandating that everyone obtain health insurance, which broadened the risk pool by including the healthy and unhealthy alike, making it feasible for insurers (profitably) to offer coverage to people with existing medical conditions, and (3) subsidizing private insurance coverage for certain income levels so as to ensure that people could afford the now-required insurance coverage.

At the center of this trinity were to be the insurance exchanges: state-based marketplaces where, beginning in 2014, small businesses and people without employer-based insurance would be able to browse plans that met the law's new standards of coverage. Insurers would thereby have access to millions of new customers, provided they adhered to the new rules. The public option, treasured by Obama's progressive base, was nowhere to be found. It was markets all the way down.[59]

Crucially, the legislation spread out its effects across several years, with the bulk of the law gaining full force only in 2014 – years after its 2010 passage. Some of the key provisions were to be enacted as follows:

2010: Small business tax credit is introduced. People with pre-existing conditions are now able to obtain coverage as part of temporary "high-risk pools," and insurance companies are henceforth banned from refusing children with pre-existing conditions or from dropping people mid-coverage. Lifetime limits on coverage are made illegal. Children up to 26 can remain on their parents' coverage. A reinsurance program begins to help companies maintain coverage for people 55-64. A $250 rebate is issued for those in the Medicare Part D drug "doughnut hole" who purchase medication both too cheap and yet too expensive for Medicare to cover.

2011: Employers must now disclose the value of employer-provided health coverage on W2 forms. An annual fee on drug companies goes into effect. Restaurant chains of a certain size and vending machines must begin to disclose nutrition info. Discounts kick in for Medicare Part D drugs. Bonus payments begin to be issued for Medicare primary care doctors and general surgeons. Private Medicare Advantage plan payments are frozen at 2010 levels. States can now offer home- or community-based care for the disabled under their respective Medicaid programs.

2012: Payment rates for Medicare Advantage plans begin reduction. Centers for Medicare and Medicaid Services begin tracking hospital readmission rates and will use this data to establish financial incentives to reduce the rate of hospital readmissions.

2013: The threshold for claiming medical expenses on tax returns increases from 7.5 to 10 percent of income. Flexible spending accounts are now limited to $2500 per year; a 2.9 percent tax is imposed on the sale of medical devices. The Medicare payroll tax increases to 2.35 percent for individuals earning more than $200,000 and for married couples earning more than $250,000. A 3.8 percent tax is levied on investment income. Federal subsidies begin for brand-name prescriptions bought within the Medicare Part D "doughnut hole."

2014: Employers with 50 or more workers who do not offer coverage now face a fine of up to $2000 if any workers receive subsidized insurance in exchanges (the first 30 employees are not counted in the assessment of these fines). Insurance companies begin paying a fee based on their market share. State-based healthcare exchanges open. Premium credits and cost-sharing subsidies become available for those up to 400 percent of federal poverty level to buy coverage in these exchanges. Those with pre-existing conditions can no longer be refused coverage. Most people now need to buy insurance or pay a fine come tax season (the "individual mandate"). Medicaid will begin its expansion to all people younger than 65 who subsist at up to 133 percent of federal poverty level.

2015: Medicare creates a physician payment program aimed at rewarding quality over volume.

2018: An excise tax is levied on employer-provided plans that cost more than $10,200 for an individual or $27,500 for a family.[60]

This roadmap ensured a troubled rollout of the ACA's

provisions, for the very year it was passed also saw Republicans regain control of the House of Representatives, narrow the Democratic majority in the Senate, and sweep through many state governments. Now possessed of an even greater degree of counterweight, Republicans determined not just passively to block Obama and the Democrats but actively to proceed with efforts at dismantling what had so recently been written into law.

3.2.3 The Politics and Consequences of Reform

The Republican attack on the Affordable Care Act began the day it was signed into law. Attorneys general from 13 states initiated a legal challenge against the individual mandate; 26 states ultimately joined the lawsuit, which was not decided until 2012.

In the meantime, Republican legislators at the federal level introduced a number of bills seeking to repeal all or part of the ACA. Representative Steve King quickly introduced a discharge petition into Congress (based on repeal legislation he wrote but which went nowhere via normal channels) which demanded the repeal of "Obamacare." Had it garnered the necessary 218 signatures, it would have forced then-speaker of the House Nancy Pelosi to hold a vote, where King hoped a majority of the House would vote to repeal the law (a symbolic victory, since any repeal legislation would never have survived the Senate, let alone Obama's veto). Republicans then promised to refuse funding for the ACA, which would have made implementation impossible. Some, like representative Eric Cantor, pushed for partial repeal of the law, focusing particular attention on the individual mandate (forcing all adults to possess health insurance); senator Bob Corker admitted that he thought total repeal an impossibility, and so threw his political weight behind partial repeals as well.

After introducing two bills that sought to repeal the ACA, House Republicans then offered an alternative healthcare reform bill. This legislation went nowhere. Senators like Marco Rubio then attempted to salvage more popular sections of the ACA, like child coverage until the age of 26 or a ban on insurance discrimination based on pre-existing conditions, while stripping the individual mandate from the books. These efforts failed as well. Undaunted, Republicans proffered additional discharge petitions, attacked regulations as they came up for implementation, and stalled bureaucratic appointments – all before the year was out.

Once the Republican House majority took power in 2011, repeal activity picked up. Republicans drafted repeal legislation (the Repealing the Job-Killing Health Care Law Act) in January 2011, allowed a total of 7 hours of floor debate time, stifled Democratic efforts to amend the legislation, and passed the bill 245-189. The rushed legislative process stood in stark contrast to the myriad of opposition amendments incorporated into the original Obamacare legislation. Regardless, the bill did not pass the Senate, although it did set the tone for the months to come. Republicans declared known and expected government subsidies to be expense "bombshells" that none had known about when the law was passed; they told seniors that the full implementation of the ACA would destroy Medicare (a cynical claim, since many libertarians despised the closest thing to "socialized medicine" America has yet implemented); representative Steve King went so far as to claim that the Obama administration's decision to require new health insurance plans to cover birth control with no co-pays would signal the death of American civilization. In sum, Republicans knew a political cash cow when they saw one, and milked the unpopularity of various portions of the Affordable Care Act (and the president associated with the law) for all the political dairy they could (see also section 4.1.5.4).[61]

This Republican resistance impeded smooth implementation, and possibly damaged sections of the law (for instance, the temporary high-risk insurance pools), and yet the law remained substantially intact and on the books. Repeal efforts slackened in the face of this paucity of results, on the one hand, and a hope among Republicans that the looming Supreme Court case would soon spell doom for the ACA on the other.

In June 2012 the waiting ended and *National Federation of Independent Business et al. v. Sebelius, Secretary of Health and Human Services, et al.* passed from litigation to jurisprudence. The individual mandate, while not considered by the majority of the Supreme Court to fall under the Commerce Clause of the Constitution, was upheld as a "tax on those who do not buy [a] product" – i.e. health insurance – that fell within Congress's constitutional power to tax.[62] Although the individual mandate was upheld, the federally subsidized Medicaid expansion was not. The court majority took issue with section 1396c of the ACA, which indicated that, should a state refuse to expand its Medicaid program as stipulated by the bill, existing Medicaid funding could be withheld as a penalty. The court majority found that: "The threatened loss of over 10 percent of a State's overall budget is economic dragooning that leaves the States with no real option but to acquiesce in the Medicaid expansion."[63]

Justice Roberts wrote the majority opinion, but it is worth noting the dissent written by Ginsberg, the liberal darling of the court, for its defense of the ACA as written. She starts off with a welcomed rebuke of the conservatism of chief justice Roberts: "The Chief Justice's crabbed reading of the Commerce Clause harks back to the era in which the Court routinely thwarted Congress' efforts to regulate the national economy in the interest of those who labor to sustain it."[64]

From there, however, she paints a picture of American healthcare devoid of the corporate greed, business-friendly regulation, and outright fraud that accounts for so much of America's uniquely high healthcare costs. Instead, she emphasizes that billions of dollars in healthcare services go *unpaid*, as perhaps 50 million Americans sustain injury or illness and thus seek emergency room treatment or other health services; since almost all Americans involve themselves with healthcare at some point in their lives, and since businesses must recoup costs somehow, Ginsberg argues that prices must rise for those with insurance. She further asserts that state-level universal insurance (like that enacted by Massachusetts) would serve as a "bait to the needy and dependent elsewhere," resulting in a massive influx of out-of-state uninsured use of medical care, increased prices, and increased state taxes to meet the rising costs.[65] She then goes on to describe the federal solution to this thoroughly national problem: "Aware that a national solution was required, Congress could have taken over the health-insurance market by establishing a tax-and-spend federal program like social security. Such a program...would have left little, if any, room for private enterprise or the States. Instead of going this route, Congress enacted the ACA, a solution that retains a robust role for private insurers and state governments...Congress was able to achieve a practical, altogether reasonable, solution."[66]

Ginsberg's dissension encapsulates the extent to which neoliberalism has come to dominate the American mentality. She admits healthcare to be the domain of all – something often used in unpredictable, catastrophic circumstances – and yet despite this recognition, despite the implication that the perfect knowledge and cool rationality with which "Economic Man" makes their choices is utterly lacking in this context, she still believes there to be a place for private insurers, market competition, and financial profit. The public option is thus dismissed as detrimental to the marketplace, where (it seems) all things meet and mingle and find their destiny.

The *Sebelius* decision drastically impacted the effect Obamacare was to have on American healthcare, for now states could refuse to expand their Medicaid programs, precluding a major prop of the ACA's insurance coverage strategy from reaching its full potential. Indeed, as of 2017, 19 states continued in their refusal to expand their Medicaid systems, Republican controlled one and all.[67] In upholding the individual mandate but striking down the mandatory expansion of Medicaid, *Sebelius* gave complete victory to neither party, but did ensure the ACA would remain a fact of political life. Republicans continued to work toward excising the statute, usually by targeting specific pieces for dismantling (e.g. successfully repealing the individual mandate in 2018 within the paragraphs of a bill aimed at tax reform); they even came within a hair's breath, during Trump's first year in office, of repealing the law, but ultimately they failed to do so.

With most of the ACA still in place, we can now remove ourselves from the rumbling of political battle. What have been the results of implementation, such as it has been under Republican-imposed conditions?

The Obama White House stated:

President Obama promised that he would make quality, affordable health care not a privilege, but a right. After nearly 100 years of talk, and decades of trying by presidents of both parties, that's exactly what he did. Today, 20 million more adults gained access to health coverage. We've driven the uninsured rate below 10 percent – the lowest level since we started keeping records – and built stronger, healthier communities through advancements in public health, science, and innovation.[68]

Some of the many achievements listed by the Obama White House include: (1) improved access to care (particularly the removal of discrimination for pre-existing conditions and the expansion of Medicaid coverage); (2) more affordable coverage (via financial assistance, federal subsidies, employer wellness program incentives, no out-of-pocket fees for preventative services, and the phasing out of the Medicare "doughnut hole");

(3) improved accountability and efficiency of care (star ratings for hospitals, incentives for hospitals to avoid careless readmission, requiring drug and device makers to disclose the compensation they provide to doctors); and (4) additional funding to combat opioids and increase access to mental health services.[69]

From the research that has thus far been conducted, it does indeed seem as though insurance coverage has drastically improved and that less money is being spent on healthcare. The White House figure of 20 million more people covered is borne out by the available data. Of those 20 million, around half came from private coverage, augmented by the ACA's subsidies for plans purchased on the insurance exchanges, individual insurance market reforms, and the individual mandate. The other half of expanded coverage comes from the Medicaid expansion. These coverage gains, brought about by a combination of private and public insurance, have thus been shared across the socio-economic spectrum. Uninsured rates fell by a third or more for both the poor and the middle/upper income levels; and uninsured rates fell for all races, ages, and education levels.[70] It should be noted, however, that real disparities in coverage remain. As of 2017, those below the poverty line had an insurance coverage rate of 83 percent, compared to 95.7 percent of those at or above 400 percent of the poverty line.[71]

Reduced expenditures followed in the wake of expanded insurance coverage. When the ACA was passed, the Congressional Budget Office (CBO) predicted that overall healthcare expenditures would reach $4.14 trillion per year by 2017 (20.2 percent GDP); for 2017 alone the cost turned out to be $650 billion *less* than predicted (a mere 18 percent of GDP). Indeed, by the end of 2018 the CBO had reported that from 2010 to 2017 the ACA reduced healthcare spending by some $2.3 trillion.[72] While the precise reasoning for the slowdown in healthcare costs remains elusive, it could be argued that the ACA has had a considerable impact on costs. High-deductible plans might be encouraging people to refrain from using as many services and instead shop for care; physicians and hospitals might be influenced by new "value-based" payment metrics; waste and expense might have been reduced through the ACA's curbing of readmissions and encouragement of the efficient redesign of care; and the ACA's encouraging of the private sector (insurers and employers) to innovate their own payment reforms, such as reference pricing, to control costs might be stalling the upward cost trend as well.[73]

Reduced expenditures, of course, did not necessarily mean lower costs, just that not as much was being spent as had been predicted. Per capita US healthcare costs remained the highest in the developed world, standing at $10,209 in 2017 (compared to $6714 in 2009).[74] Individual costs continued to rise for three reasons: (1) Employers pushed more of the cost of health insurance onto employees, (2) drug prices have continued to climb, and (3) a larger number of Americans have enrolled in high-deductible health plans, which force enrollees to pay out thousands of dollars before insurance coverage begins to kick in. All of these factors can be traced to the structure of the economy more broadly (exemplified by the unequal distribution of the Great Recession's impact), and to the profit-centric model of healthcare delivery specifically.

Concerning the ratio of employer vs. employee health spending, the employee share of health premiums has risen 32 percent since 2012 while the employer portion rose only 14 percent. This is a direct result of the Great Recession, as companies have increasingly looked at divesting themselves from healthcare costs as a way to save money. This trend, as the continued climb of executive compensation illustrates, has not affected the upper echelons of the economic hierarchy.

Drug prices continue to rise. Despite no changes to its composition or the availability of its components, the price of insulin in the US has tripled over the last 10 years, with Eli Lilly's Humalog increasing from $93 to $275 per 10 milliliter vial. Similarly, the list price of a 1-month supply of Humira, an arthritis drug, rose from $2914 in 2014 to $5174 in 2019. This is not the fault of drug manufacturers merely. In yet another layer of profit making, intermediary parties called pharmacy benefit managers contract with insurers to write formularies – the list of drugs insurance will cover; drug makers, taking advantage of loopholes in federal law, pay these intermediaries for the privilege of formulary inclusion and that cost is passed on to consumers. Insurers also get a cut of the money made from the sale of many drugs.[75]

Insurance premiums and co-pays are commonplace; high-deductible plans constitute more and more of the insurance market. According to the Centers for Disease Control and Prevention (CDC), between 2007 and 2017, among adults aged 18–64 with employment-based coverage the percentage of those enrolled in high-deductible health plans with a health savings account (HSA) rose from 4.2 percent to 18.9 percent, while those enrolled in high-deductible plans lacking an HSA rose from 10.6 percent to 24.5 percent. Enrollment in traditional plans decreased from 85.1 percent to 56.6 percent over the same period.[76] Thus, even having insurance in America is no guarantee that coverage is affordable. It seems that the neoliberal solution to unaffordable healthcare (embodied by the ACA) is in fact *just don't use it*. There is a kind of logic to this: you do not pay too much for that which you never buy – regardless of how necessary something, like insulin, might be.

All of the complicated negotiations, tax breaks, and reliance upon market forces did little to grapple with the Opioid Crisis. Framed narrowly as a crisis in public health, the solution presented through Obama's reform efforts was incomplete: better *access* to care and more *funding* for treatment without addressing structural problems. The ACA made drug treatment one of the baseline aspects of health plans found on the healthcare marketplace and also required Medicaid to cover substance abuse treatment at least for some people. The Obama administration itself setup a new program at the Department of Health and Human Services, distributing tens of millions of dollars to individual states starting in 2015. Obama also signed congressional legislation – the 21st Century Cures Act – in 2016, which allotted $1 billion over the course of 2 years to deal with the crisis.[77] While funding for treating those currently addicted was a welcomed development, it did nothing to tackle the actual source of the crisis, which rests on the kind of behaviors our system of incentives promotes: violent conflict in pursuit of short-term profits heedless of public cost. With the profit motive continuing to dominate our medical decisions, another such crisis is, like another recession, only a matter of time.

3.2.4 Beyond Profit

In 1961 Ronald Reagan gave a radio address in which he attacked the proposal for federal health insurance for the elderly (what we now call Medicare) as socialized medicine, as a mere stepping stone on the road toward totalitarianism. To his mind, the two concepts of freedom and socialism were contraries, the latter to be fought against with all the brawn the Free World, the United States its beating heart, could muster. He said:

Now in our country under our free enterprise system, we have seen medicine reach the greatest heights that it has in any country in the world. Today, the relationship between patient and doctor in this country is something to be envied any place: the privacy, the care that is given to a person, the right to choose a doctor, the right to go from one doctor to the other...

[Under socialized medicine, t]he doctor begins to lose freedoms; it's like telling a lie, and one leads to another. First you decide that the doctor can have so many patients. They're equally divided among the various doctors by the government. But then the doctors aren't equally divided geographically, so a doctor decides he wants to practice in one town and the government has to say to him, "You can't live in that town. They already have enough doctors." You have to go someplace else. And from here it's only a short step to dictating where he will go.

This is a freedom that I wonder whether any of us have the right to take from any human being.

I know how I'd feel, if you, my fellow citizens, decided that to be an actor, I had to become a government employee and work in a national theater. Take it into your own occupation or that of your husband. All of us can see what happens: Once you establish the precedent that the government can determine a man's working place and his working methods, determine his employment, from here it's a short step to all the rest of socialism – to determining his pay, and pretty soon your son won't decide when he's in school, where he will go, or what they will do for a living. He will wait for the government to tell him where he will go to work and what he will do…

[If we do not act], this program, I promise you, will pass just as surely as the sun will come up tomorrow; and behind it will come other federal programs that will invade every area of freedom as we have known it in this country. Until, one day…we will awake to find that we have socialism.

And if you don't do this and if I don't do it, one of these days you and I are going to spend our sunset years telling our children, and our children's children, what it once was like in America when men were free.[78]

Humans are social creatures, political creatures: we think and act and feel in groups. Any conception of freedom must therefore start from that premise, must weigh the individual action against its effect on the group, and few things illustrate this better than healthcare. Illness precludes labor and places a burden on the community to care for the stricken; sickness spreads and infects others; the efforts required to ameliorate or cure are communal efforts, requiring the labor of mothers and fathers, doctors and nurses, technicians, drug manufacturers, researchers, construction workers, record keepers – practically the whole gambit of human effort. Such a communal need demands community rather than individuality.

The logic of Reagan is not the property of the Republican alone; Democrats have accepted the individualist position with nary a whiff of doubt. The acceptance of this orthodoxy affected Democratic efforts to reform the financial sector in the wake of the Great Recession and their efforts at redrawing the American healthcare constellation. In both cases, some symptoms were bandaged, the bleeding of the body politic slowed to one degree or another, but the disease – the false assumption that private greed will yield public good – persisted.

Moreover, Reagan's "free enterprise" has delivered precisely the adverse conditions he prophesied should socialism come to roost in the halls of American medicine. He praises the doctor/patient relationship, and yet doctors today are bound by company time, goaded to see as many patients in as little time as possible, cajoled into spending more time documenting billable conditions than in taking the time to get to know those in their care. He talks of being able to "choose" one's doctor or patient, and yet the vast majority of patients are tethered by prohibitive costs from venturing to any doctor that is outside their insurance network, and many doctors, now working for hospital conglomerates, have little choice in the patients that momentarily cross their clipboards.

He claimed that the lies of socialism would spread, and eventually one's education, residence, job would all be controlled by some central authority; and yet today so many of us are stymied by "market forces" into roles we would not have chosen for ourselves. "Housing markets" dictate that certain neighborhoods are worth more than others, keeping property values down, property taxes down, and thus denuding the children of those neighborhoods of a properly funded education.[79] "Healthcare markets" concentrate a dizzying array of specialists in rich areas that can afford all the plastic surgery and unnecessary testing money can buy; meanwhile, poor communities must rely on overburdened emergency rooms and little in the way of outpatient or primary care. Thus while the most severe ailments of the poor are often triaged successfully, the market gives little effort in providing the primary care doctors necessary to catch things before they get out of hand, keep people healthy, and nullify the need for a hospital visit in the first place. Again and again the market yields a kind of freedom – but one only available to those with money.

In a 1787 letter to George Washington, James Madison wrote: "The National government should be armed with positive and compleat authority in all cases which require uniformity such as the regulation of trade, including the right of taxing both exports and imports, the fixing [sic] the terms and forms of naturalization, etc. etc."[80] It strikes me that healthcare is a sector of life that, because it involves everyone and at times and places not of their choosing, requires uniformity; it falls under Madison's "etc. etc." This should not be a revolutionary proposition, for in a sense American healthcare is already a national endeavor. The government currently pays for 45 percent of US healthcare costs (via Medicare, Medicaid, the VA, Tricare, etc.).[81] Moreover, the suffering caused by the abusive practices of for-profit healthcare companies – exemplified in the lies and obfuscations of the Sackler family that placed business needs above medical ones – is nationalized as well: the public foots the bill for fixing the problems their business practices have caused. What this means is that we need more than government *involvement* in healthcare; we need *democratically transparent* and *publicly-minded* government involvement that prioritizes people, not profits. Whether this means a federally run "Medicare for All" program, something akin to Medicaid where the federal government collects and distributes funds that are then allocated and used on a state level, or some other policy initiative, we must come together to smash the profit-driven madness with which we currently cope.

Of course, access to quality care is only part of the solution to the problems of ill health. As the nineteenth century discovered, much sickness is the result of environment, whether the conditions of living, or work, or interpersonal relationships. The accumulation of money for its own sake has a deleterious effect on these factors as well. Universal health insurance on its own, therefore, will not yield a healthier society. As the ACA has shown, even giving millions more access to the *appearance* of care, without changing the fundamentals of how that care is structured and delivered, only means that healthcare profits are more publicly subsidized now than ever before, while many of the underlying causes of our cancer, mental breakdown, drug addiction, etc. remain unaddressed. Good public health policy, therefore, encompasses a foreign policy that does not send soldiers off to trauma-filled battlefields only to benefit the Few, an economic policy that promotes fulfilling and safe employment over corporate profits, a climate policy that safeguards the equilibrium necessary to human flourishing.

Nor should the opaque and domineering control over medical decisions doctors exercised during most of the twentieth century be recreated in the twenty-first. As was the case with transpeople desperate to please the capricious, arbitrary, often dismissive doctors they encountered in seeking surgical transition (see also section 4.3.2) or African Americans subjected to the unethical experiments of arrogant and racist doctors (see also section 4.1.5.2), we should not advocate for such an undemocratic delivery of healthcare that privileges the doctor's knowledge and sentiment to the exclusion of everything else. The specialized and expert knowledge possessed by doctors and other medical staff should both be held accountable to patients, and be given the liberty to deliver the best care possible, unbeholden to financial gain. Health, like all facets of life, will always be political (as the allocation of resources and the exercise of authority always is); its politics, therefore, should be democratic, transparent, and accountable to civic institutions rather than authoritarian, opaque, and beholden to business interests.

Chapter 4

On the Margins

History, based as it is on documents and testimonials, tends by necessity to privilege those with the resources to produce documentary evidence, the power to leave long-lasting testimonials, the authority to have their side of the story conveyed to posterity. This leaves out those living on the margins of power who might have a different view of events. In order to redress this imbalance, a chapter specifically privileging the margins of American society seems not only prudent but morally imperative. Three marginal groups merit especial attention during the time period covered here: African, gay, and trans Americans. The first group witnessed an unprecedented access to the halls of conventional political power, the second achieved historic levels of mainstream acceptance, and the third emerged from the shadows as a growing force in American culture and politics.

4.1 African Americans

To begin to talk about the current economic, cultural, or political status of African Americans, we must first recall their history. That we must remind ourselves of this history's importance, indeed its very existence – and of its special place within the larger context of US history – shows just how ill-informed contemporary discussions of race have become. Indeed, any mention of historical context is too often dismissed as an excuse for current problems that could be solved if only *they would just act right*, as if any group can function outside of its own past and the constraints those experiences have placed upon their freedom of action.

4.1.1 Our Profitable Institution

Of course, every American acknowledges that African Americans arrived here against their will. The African slave trade, wrinkled with age even in the seventeenth century, turned its attention to the Atlantic when Europeans found that their new colonies in the Americas required more labor than either the vanishing Indigenous populations or the indentured servants brought from Europe could provide. To meet the European demand first for more sugar, then more tobacco, and then most importantly more cotton, European slavers bargained or butchered their way down the African coast, exchanging whatever they could (often firearms) for as many Africans as possible. These they stuffed into ships and sailed across the Atlantic. The estimated death toll among the enslaved defies individual human experience: 4.5 percent died while awaiting transportation across the Atlantic, 12.5 percent died during the crossing of the Middle Passage between Africa and the New World, and 33 percent died during their first year laboring in bondage – their period of "seasoning." Between capture and the end of the first year of bondage, therefore, half of enslaved Africans perished.[1]

The Caribbean was, at first, the chief destination, and millions of Africans worked and expired under the brutal conditions imposed upon them by the masters of the sugar plantations of Jamaica, Haiti, and the like. American slavery, endemic to all the colonies by the mid-eighteenth century, grew most especially in areas where tobacco cultivation made up a large portion of economic activity. Cotton, as yet, had proven difficult to harvest on a mass scale.[2]

The founding generation could not make up its mind when it came to slavery. Some thought of it as an economic reality that could not be altered, others as necessary to the prosperity of the Union, others still as destined to die out as "free labor" (i.e. wage labor) took its place. Patrick "Give Me Liberty or Give Me Death" Henry's 1773 defense for his ownership of other human beings is typical: "Would any one believe that I am master of slaves of my own purchase? I am drawn along by the general inconvenience of living without them. I will not, I cannot, justify it."[3]

In the face of this divided opinion, the framers of the Constitution compromised by allowing all slaves to be counted in the national census as three-fifths of a person, giving the southern states (where most slaves were located) inflated federal representation and therefore inflated federal power. By the first decades of the nineteenth century, fearing the loss of their federal influence, southern politicians engineered the Missouri Compromise, in which every state admitted to the Union that outlawed slavery had to be followed by the creation of a slave-bearing state. This, the southerners hoped, would maintain the current makeup of federal representatives and therefore their dominance of the federal government.

Whether slavery in these United States would have ended on its own is a dubious proposition at best, but in the event it proved to be a moot point. The invention of the cotton gin at the beginning of the nineteenth century (which allowed easy separation of cotton fiber from seeds) completely changed the economic picture.[4] Suddenly cotton, which hitherto had been a difficult to grow luxury crop typically obtained from Indian or Chinese sources, could now be harvested in the climes of the southern states. This completely upended the nascent economy of the new federation. Speculators now looked for land to purchase, planters looked for land to buy and enslaved people to work it, politicians looked to satisfy these new demands of their enterprising constituents, and slavers suddenly found themselves with an unquenchable North American demand for their product.[5]

As the existing southern colonies retooled themselves for cotton production, the most forward thinking of entrepreneurs realized that the prime locations for cotton growing lay in the Louisiana territory. Cognizant of this fact, the federal government (dominated by the owners of enslaved people) promoted expansion into that region, purchasing vast quantities of land from the French, conquering land in Georgia and Florida, pushing the Indigenous peoples ever further west to make room for white settlers and their human chattel, and selling newly purchased or conquered land to prospective planters or speculators.

All this land required labor, of course, and in addition to the people still coming from Africa itself (a source of labor that would be made illegal early in the nineteenth century), these new southwestern forced labor camps (i.e. plantations) acquired their inmates from the camps of Virginia and the Carolinas. A vast exodus thus commenced, with hundreds of thousands of enslaved people making their way – in chained pairs or "coffles" – on foot the hundreds of miles south and west. These coffles made their way to New Orleans, which became the central hub of the internal slave trade. Whence went many to their doom.[6]

At the same time that enslaved people were erecting the nation's capital in Washington DC, eking out a somewhat stabilized existence in the Old South of Virginia and the Carolinas, or perhaps receiving the blessing of emancipation and second-class status in some northern state, many began the process of harvesting cotton for their new masters. This brutal endeavor is *the* commercial project that put America on the world economic stage. Slave-produced cotton accounted for 60 percent of US exports by the eve of the Civil War and about 60 percent of world cotton production.[7] The labor of enslaved Americans thus provided the vital and necessary fuel for the industrial revolutions taking place in England and (later) the American North. For indeed, the production of low-cost, mechanically made textiles is what, more than anything else, set England and then the West more broadly on a path to dominating the economics and politics of the entire world. And it was American cotton, produced by enslaved Americans, that provided the raw materials necessary for this shift to occur.[8] Because slave-produced cotton was the necessary fuel for the English and American industrial revolutions, it is also the indispensable foundation for our current standard of living.

Moreover, the incredible increases in productive capacity seen from 1800 to 1860 within the confines of the forced labor camps of the South were obtained not by the kind word of the genteel plantation owner, but rather through the innovative methods of torture brought to bear upon the bodies of black people by their white masters. In a very real way, therefore, our current economic prosperity has its foundation not only in theft, but in torture.[9] As the nineteenth century rolled on, a system of production developed among the slave states called the Pushing System, wherein slave "captains" set a pace of production for all the field slaves to match, severely punishing those that lagged behind. White overseers enforced final justice upon unproductive laborers, sometimes killing those who failed to keep up. This universal pace of work, coupled with all field hands living in the same place and all doing the same work, combined to increase at a drastic pace the productive capacities of the southern slave system, which by 1860 had nearly kept up with productivity increases among the industrializing textile factories of the American North (see also section 4.1.5.2).[10]

4.1.2 Emancipation

Resistance to slavery among the enchained accompanied the Atlantic Slave Trade from its inception. Some slaves chose suicide over enslavement.[11] Slave ships were often fortified against the prospect of slave revolt, with bastions ready to be locked and defended should the rest of the ship be overtaken by the African captives. Crewmen often tied their cutlasses to their persons so as to prevent a captive from using the blades against their captors.[12]

The successful slave revolt in Haiti at the beginning of the nineteenth century affected American slavery profoundly. It killed Napoleon's plans for his Louisiana territory and prompted him to sell it to Jefferson's government; many white Haitians fled to the United States, where they provided their knowledge and expertise to southern gentlemen; and its violence horrified white slave owners in America. Many a southern gentleman invested heavily in militias, surveillance, and other security measures to ensure that such a thing could never succeed in the new republic. Their efforts made the already difficult task of planning, organizing, arming, and carrying out a revolt among peoples of various languages, tribes, and locations exponentially more difficult and did much to blunt the organized revolts that did occur.[13]

The political compromises of the first generation of American politicians delayed a reckoning, but under the surface discontent simmered, each passing year seeing more bellicose bubbles quicken the pot to a boil. In economic terms, the North industrialized, using the cotton produced by slaves to fuel an explosion of textile mills and usher in the American chapter of the First Industrial Revolution. Ideologically, there arose in the North an outgrowth of a more general movement in the West to end the keeping of other human beings as property. Here was a true break between the tradition of Western thought and the thinkers of the Enlightenment. Not the august philosophers of antiquity, not the saints of the Middle Ages, not even most of the philosophers who led the charge against "barbarism" during the eighteenth century had seriously questioned the existence of slavery. Some, like Rousseau, might have wished for universal brotherhood, but few took the thought to its logical political and social conclusions. The French Revolution, however, saw a concerted attempt at real equality, and in the process the slaves under French dominion were momentarily freed. The vicissitudes of French politics meant that such freedom was inconsistently supported, but some colonies did indeed take their freedom at the point of a bayonet. Moreover, at the start of the nineteenth century, the British government responded to decades of lobbying and banned the slave trade as a first step to divesting itself of chatteled people altogether.

Now finally in America was this trend gaining traction, but only in the North, and primarily among evangelicals. The aristocratic South, formerly in agreement with their northern counterparts that slavery was an evil, albeit a necessary one, shifted gears in the face of more vocal and determined talk of abolition. They felt their very society threatened by the abolitionist movement, which they viewed as a deranged product of a North propped up by wage slavery, overreaching in its industrial expansion, and bent on the political domination of the South for its own profit. They also looked to the violent rebellion of Haiti against its white planters (recall that Haiti is the *only* nation in history to win its independence via slave rebellion) with alarm, and thus responded to any threat to their Peculiar Institution, be it Nat Turner's slave rebellion or Harriet Beecher Stowe's brilliant novel, with the same degree of focused wrath. Increasingly, they thought of leaving the Union altogether, rather than be subject to humiliation and the destruction of their civilization (what they themselves termed the trampling of their "rights").[14]

Tensions over slavery came to a head in Kansas, where settlers seeking to extend slavery clashed with those of more "free labor" sentiments. "Secession" was on the tip of many tongues across the South and in border states like Maryland and Kentucky. The notion of popular sovereignty was seized upon by men like Steven Douglas, who sought to bypass the general divide over slavery by leaving the answer to the individual states. He would not be the last politician to suggest such a fractured answer to a question of general significance. In his case, this was quite natural. There were few questions typically thought of as "of national significance," for indeed most did not recognize that there was such a nation as the United States. From the founding of the federal system, sovereignty had rested with the individual states. A national question, then, was a question to be dealt with by Pennsylvania, New Jersey, or Virginia. *Federal* questions were thought to be limited to commerce between these sovereignties, foreign affairs in general, the use of military force, and the coining of money. For Douglas, Secessionists, and the South in general, therefore, they considered any threat to their *national, sovereign right* to protect their property – up to and including other people – as an existential one, increasingly outside the ability of the federal arrangement to resolve. *Exeunt!* appeared to many to be the only logical solution.[15]

The Republicans, emerging in the 1850s, coalesced around a program not of abolition, but merely of the limitation of slavery to those states in which it had already entrenched itself. Much of the opposition to slavery arose not out of a profound disgust at the enchattelment of millions of human beings or the abuse of black bodies for the profitable ends of a few aristocrats, but rather from a far more mundane and economic consideration: African slaves were said to steal work from (more deserving) white people. How, Republicans asked, could an unemployed yeoman hope to compete with the uncompensated labor of the slave? Moreover, in his forced idleness, the unemployed white man was beset with moral decay, the inevitable result of a passive, purposeless existence. In order to strengthen the Anglo-Saxon stock in the emerging western states, therefore, Republicans thought it imperative that slavery spread no further.[16]

Signaling the paranoia of their mental state, the leaders of the South chose to secede from the Union after the hotly contested election to the presidency of a moderate Republican, Illinois lawyer Abraham Lincoln – a man who did not consider black people to be the intellectual equals of whites, who had advocated for the repatriating of black people to Africa, and who emphasized to the South that he had no interest whatsoever in dismantling their Peculiar Institution. Lincoln, however, made the fatal mistake of voicing even mild criticism of the institution of slavery, stating he would resist the expansion of slavery and on this point "hold firm, as with a chain of steel."[17] This made him anathema to the southern leadership. Considering Lincoln a harbinger of Republican domination of the federal government and, ultimately, a threat to their very way of life, politicians in South Carolina seceded from the Union. Seven states left the Union before Lincoln had even assumed the presidency. The rest of the South soon followed them.

None doubted at the time that slavery was the central issue of the war; only mythmaking by the defeated Confederates mystified the issue.[18] Consider South Carolina's *Declaration of the Immediate Causes which Induce and Justify the Secession...from the Federal Union*:

> We affirm that these ends for which this Government was instituted [the defense of property and contract] have been defeated, and the Government itself has been made destructive of them by the action of the non-slaveholding States. Those States have assumed the right of deciding upon the propriety of our domestic institutions; and have denied the rights of property established in 15 of the States and recognized by the Constitution; they have denounced as sinful the institution of Slavery...They have encouraged and assisted thousands of our slaves to leave their homes; and those who remain, have been incited by emissaries, books and pictures to servile insurrection.[19]

The Confederacy's constitution offers further proof. Within this foundational Confederate document slavery found explicit sanction within the realm of protected property rights. Article 1 Section 9(4) states: "No bill of attainder, ex post facto law, or any law denying or impairing the right of property in negro slaves shall be passed." Article IV Section 2(1) explicitly equates slaves to property: "The citizens of each State...shall have the right of transit and sojourn in any State of this Confederacy, with their slaves and other property; and the right of property in said slaves shall not be thereby impaired." Finally, Article IV Section 3(3) plans for the future by allowing the expansion of slavery into any prospective Confederate additions.[20]

At the onset, Lincoln (ever the shrewd politician) sought to ameliorate the concerns of the South that their property was threatened by declaring the Civil War nothing but an insurrection and thus his actions as the steps necessary to protect the Union. By the close of the war, Lincoln had discarded this conciliatory policy as no longer prudent. He issued the Emancipation Proclamation in 1863, which freed every slave in the recalcitrant states (notably, not loyal slave states like Maryland). This liberation threatened to undermine the labor system of the Confederacy and did much to turn international opinion thoroughly against the hypocrisies of the Southern System. The war then took on an overtly emancipatory character, becoming more than a war to preserve the Union; now it was to be a "new birth of freedom," a reinvigoration of the withered, indeed corrupted, tree of Liberty.

The victories of Grant and Sherman came, but only after years of defeat. The manpower of both sides was pushed to breaking point. The Confederacy turned to conscription in 1862, the North in 1863.[21] Moreover, as the war turned emancipatory and Lincoln feared antagonizing the South less and less, northern recruiters turned to black men, and by the war's end several hundred thousand would serve in the Union ranks (many distinguishing themselves in combat), while hundreds of thousands more labored to construct the trenches, fortifications, and supply depots necessary to win a modern war.[22]

After the war, people clamored to shape the new nationally conscious destiny. President Andrew Johnson, a stubborn southerner known hitherto as a rare Democratic supporter of the Union, attempted in 1866 and 1867 to allow the Confederate states to return to the Union with very little in the way of internal change. He wanted to avoid drama, had no interest in the plight of the black "freedmen," and sought no compromise with the Republicans. Once Congress returned to session and bore witness to the abuses of power in the South, to the unpunished return to authority of the very men that had led the land into the jaws of secession and death, a showdown became inevitable. Vetoes, overrides, and an impeachment controversy followed, and it was only when Johnson came within a single vote of being thrown out of office that he agreed to let the Republican Congress legislate unhindered.

Grant, hero of the war, succeeded the embattled and embittered Johnson. A good man and ardent general, he proved to be a tired president, although even with that criticism leveled at him Grant did more to defend black civil rights than any president until Lyndon Johnson. The Republican Congress, still reacting against Southern recalcitrance, the naked abuse of freedmen, and the resurrection of the planter aristocracy, bore down on the South with a volley of legislation aimed at curtailing the resurgent planter power. After the thirteenth amendment was passed, abolishing slavery except in the case of duly convicted criminals, the fourteenth amendment passed giving equal protection of the law to all, as did the fifteenth amendment outlawing voter discrimination based on race. The Republican Party, an alliance of radical abolitionists and northern business interests, hoped that giving black people the right to vote would keep the planters in check, while simultaneously providing the freedmen with the best tool to make something of their liberated lives.[23]

For a decade, then, a coalition of Southern allies (Scalawags), Northerners who moved to the South (Carpetbaggers), and newly-enfranchised blacks ruled the South. Many former slaves were elected to state office, even to state governorship, and a handful made it to federal office. A few black men held elected office in parts of the South into the 1890s. The white South reacted violently, with the KKK being the most organized and most infamous example. After incidents of butchery and intimidation became too numerous to ignore, Congress legislated against the domestic terrorists, and Grant enforced the anti-Klan law with federal troops. Within a few years they were (temporarily) extinguished as an organized force. Despite this victory, however, the South remained embattled, and as the years of Reconstruction dragged on, black people found it increasingly difficult to exercise their political rights.[24]

Enslaved Americans had never been compensated for their work, rarely were allowed an education, and only a minority could practice a trade or craft. When emancipation was thus at long last imposed by the necessities of combat upon the South, and the war concluded with a Union victory, the re-United States found itself with 4 million freedmen who had essentially no property, no money, and no education. The North, after fierce internal debate, satisfied itself with bequeathing to the freedmen the *legal* rights of the American citizen, neglecting to redress the economic imbalance. The question of how millions of destitute and illiterate people were expected successfully to exercise their rights without any kind of assistance was left to state governments to answer. The Reconstruction governments of the South sought to tackle these economic issues, but with the wave of white terrorism euphemistically referred to as Redemption, severe economic recession brought about by over speculation in railroads, and the subsequent return of former Confederates to political power, emancipated blacks found themselves incrementally stripped of their recently-won rights.[25]

Ultimately, the North abandoned the freedmen of the South in favor of being done with the whole agonizing business. The Republican Congress, so full of reforming zeal in 1866, had by the end of the 1870s little stomach for decisive action. Thus, the South was ultimately left to its own devices when it came to the integration of its former slave population. This local autonomy proved disastrous for many black people as they found themselves subject to laws and regulations designed to keep them from voting, from holding office, from getting ahead in society. In the generations after the Civil War, most southern blacks lived marginal lives barely distinguishable from the days of bondage. While slavery did not return in name, thousands of black people were arrested and convicted of petty crimes like vagrancy, forced back into the pool of coerced labor always so central to the American economy. Share-cropping, the system by which black people worked the land, purchased the necessities of life from white planters, and relied upon literate planters to settle the yearly accounting books, kept almost all in a state indistinguishable from slavery.

The twentieth century thus dawned on an American South in many ways identical to the antebellum situation, save that the world cotton market had shifted focus to places like Egypt and later India. The South no longer dominated cotton as it once had, so even as the former Confederacy settled back into familiar ways of cajoling productivity out of African Americans, the reduced demand for American cotton consigned the South to economic stagnation.

4.1.3 The Great Migration

A generation after liberty was won and lost, black people again found themselves tasked with fighting for their country (as they had done to decisive effect during the Civil War). They served with gallantry in the imperial wars of the early twentieth century – and were treated with contempt or dismissed out of hand by their white counterparts. For example, when a black battalion arrived at Fort Brown, Texas in 1906, to relieve a white contingent of soldiers, they were met with Jim Crow discrimination, one soldier was accused of raping a white woman, a gang of men roamed the nearby town that night shooting randomly, and the black soldiers were blamed for the subsequent damage to the town. Their guilt was presumed all the way up the chain of command, and president Theodore Roosevelt himself upheld the findings of the military on the matter. In all, 167 black soldiers were dishonorably discharged – denied back pay, allowances, benefits, ineligible for pensions, and disbarred from future employment in the armed or civil services. By any conventional standard these men deserved more from their government: six had won the Medal of Honor and 13 cited for bravery. Republicans delayed the public announcement of this mass dismissal so as to preclude any undue influence it might have had on the "colored vote."[26]

The black experience in World War One had an enormous impact on the remainder of the twentieth century. A total of 200,000 were sent to France during the war. African Americans returned from France and elsewhere dignified by the (comparatively) equal treatment they had received in Europe, and proud of their smart uniforms and military bearing. White Americans greeted them with scorn, violence, even death. Some whites reacted with such disgust to a black man in uniform that they resolved to lynching, and not a few black veterans were executed still wearing the evidence of their national service. Many African Americans reacted with bitter disappointment and began looking outside the South for hope and opportunity. The Great Migration had begun.[27]

Over the course of the next 60 years, upwards of 6 million African Americans would make their way north or west, seeking new economic opportunity and civic equality in the cities of Pennsylvania, New York, Michigan, Illinois, California. Many found work – often menial and always at a reduced pay compared to their white peers. Many found homes – in the worst buildings of the worst neighborhoods. All found a kind of racism they had not anticipated. In the South, Jim Crow was open and legal: statutes dictating where black people could sit on a train or where they might eat or what barriers they might need to hurdle in order to be able to vote were on the books and displayed on the signs of every southern town. In the North, discrimination came in the form of social taboos rather than legislation.[28]

The Great Migration produced hostile reactions from white communities that had grown accustomed to success at the expense of, or at least without the inclusion of, their fellow citizens of color. Labor unions in the North, reacting to the use by corporations of black labor as cheap scabs, sometimes fought viciously to keep black people out of their ranks, out of their factories, out of their neighborhoods. In order to secure southern Democrats' support in the 1930s, FDR and his administration consciously wrote New Deal legislation so as to exclude blacks, as for instance excluding farms workers (many of whom were black) from labor reforms. The most long-lasting instance of this was in federal housing policy. In order to promote home ownership, the federal government began guaranteeing mortgages, giving banks the security they felt necessary to lend to poorer people. This housing boom came to dominate the post-war American economic landscape (see also section 2.2). It also excluded non-white people. The federal government, designating which areas it would guarantee loans in (green signified guaranteed, red too risky), "redlined" majority black neighborhoods, making it impossible for black families to obtain government-backed mortgages. This exclusion, which continued well into the 1970s, meant that black communities were unable to participate in the federally-backed creation of wealth (equity) that many poor whites had access to.[29]

Coupled with federal housing discrimination was the flight of white people from communities "infected" by even a single black family. Since black neighborhoods were redlined, making them ineligible for federal assistance, banks looked askance at black families, realtors did too, and white families looking to maintain their newly-acquired equity were keen on keeping the value-depreciating southerners from living near them. When efforts by white communities failed to stop black people from moving in (typically to houses that they rented, since they were unable to obtain mortgages), whites responded by moving away. This is how the suburbs came to be.

So, in order to escape economic slavery and political tyranny in the South, blacks moved North. They worked long hours at jobs that paid more than they would have made in the South but less than whites would make doing the same work. Often both parents had to work in order to make ends meet, leaving children susceptible to the influences of already rundown and overcrowded neighborhoods. Is it any wonder that so many came under the dominion of crime and violence?[30]

Still, for all its problems most black people seem to have considered the North a real improvement over the legally sanctioned and violently enforced racism of the South. Indeed, their new-found pride in being treated with even a little dignity snowballed with their experiences in both world wars to produce an overwhelming feeling, by the 1950s, that enough was enough. Despair, humiliation, anger, pride churned within a growing number of the discontented and dispossessed African American population. The civil rights movement emerged from this breaking point of frustration and disappointment. As one black Alabaman who served during World War Two put it: "I spent four years in the Army to free a bunch of Dutchmen and Frenchmen, and I'm hanged if I'm going to let the Alabama version of the Germans kick me around when I get home. No sireebob! I went into the army a nigger; I'm coming out a man."[31]

4.1.4 Civil Rights vs. Law and Order

The federal government responded to black agitation in several ways. Under Truman, the military was desegregated (after much internal resistance). Eisenhower tried to ignore the civil rights movement, but after *Brown v. Board of Education* – and the shattering of the notion that separate institutions for African Americans could be equal in quality to those of whites – he belatedly sent federal troops to defend desegregation efforts in Little Rock, Arkansas (which he did not out of solidarity with the struggle for justice, but because the governor of Arkansas refused to honor federal law – a defiance Eisenhower could not brook).[32] By the early 1960s some reformist legislation had been passed, but federal law still did not do enough to protect black civil rights. The Kennedy administration talked a good talk, but did not make a priority of the black struggle; Kennedy, after all, was far more interested in foreign policy than anything on the domestic scene, having said to Nixon in 1961: "It really is true that foreign affairs is the only important issue for a President to handle, isn't it? I mean, who gives a shit if the minimum wage is $1.15 or $1.25...?"[33] After Kennedy's assassination, president Johnson, responding to increasingly large and fervent demonstrations by millions of blacks and their white allies across the country, reversed this emphasis and pushed strongly for domestic reform. In 1964 the strongest civil rights bill since Reconstruction passed Congress, and in 1965 the Voting Rights Act passed as well. Now federal eyes were looking at the abuses of the South, federal boots were marching in defense of black rights, and progress finally seemed at hand.

Crucially, this push for political reform did not occur in a vacuum. Martin Luther King Jr.'s non-violent marches (which often devolved into violence at the hands of brutal and determined policemen) swam in contentious currents. Opposition to the Vietnam War was growing – and would hit fever pitch by the early 1970s; levels of reported crime were on the rise; the migratory waves of millions of African Americans from the South to the North and West crested; and urban uprisings (notably that of Watts, a black Los Angeles neighborhood, in 1965) shook the foundations of polite society. Many whites, therefore, saw the civil rights movement in the context of national disintegration.[34]

Said representative John Bell Williams: "This exodus of Negroes from the South, and their influx into the great metropolitan centers of other areas of the Nation, has been accompanied by a wave of crime...What has civil rights accomplished for these areas?...Segregation is the only answer as most Americans – not the politicians – have realized for hundreds of years."[35]

FBI statistics did indeed show an increase in crime, especially as the civil rights movement gained momentum: reported street crime quadrupled and homicide rates nearly doubled.[36] Three things explain this rise. (1) Reforms in how crime was reported and tabulated: for instance, the number of recorded robberies and burglaries in New York City skyrocketed from a combined total of 48,000 in 1965 to 143,000 the following year, resulting not from an actual upsurge in crime, but from the crime reporting reforms of mayor John Lindsay.[37] (2) The reliance on the flawed FBI Uniform Crime rate: the agency, and the police departments from which it gleaned much information, were not impartial in their collection and dissemination of crime statistics; Johnson himself referred to their figures as "incomplete and unreliable."[38] Tellingly, the FBI tracked street crime via metrics like arrest rates, which relied upon an existing level of police presence – and police tended to patrol the streets of low-income neighborhoods more than they did corporate boardrooms (the FBI did not even bother to track rates of white collar crime).[39] The maturation of crime statistics at this time – in New York and elsewhere – correlated directly to rising crime reporting, which did skew perceptions of crime levels and violence.[40] (3) The explosive demographic growth of the Baby Boom generation: a spike occurred in the number of young men aged 15 to 24, the group historically responsible for most street crime. Incidentally, this surge occurred right as unemployment (a primary driver of criminal activity) for black men was rising sharply.[41]

Protests and riots continued even with the passage of reform legislation and so president Johnson took further action by declaring war on both poverty *and* on crime. To his mind, in the short-term crime had to be dealt with – and sternly – while long-term solutions to the causes of crime would include education, job training, and social outreach funded by federal dollars. As rioting continued throughout the latter 1960s, however, more and more middle-class whites came to view Johnson's anti-poverty programs as weak and misguided, mere handouts to the undeserving or ungrateful. Conservatives grabbed at this and, with Nixon's victory in 1968, took up the gauntlet of Johnson's War on Crime while leaving behind, as much as they could, his civil rights and anti-poverty initiatives. While Johnson, too, had called for the restoration of "Law and Order," it would be the conservatives (including notable opponents of desegregation like Democrat-turned-Republican senator Strom Thurmond) allied with Nixon that took those two words as the basis for much of their domestic policy. Congressional liberals went along with nary a murmur of complaint.[42]

In taking the lead on the bipartisan effort to combat crime, the Nixon administration went one step further. Seeking to curtail the political gains of the black community while at the same time pushing back against leftist political opposition (made noisily manifest in the aggressive protests against the Vietnam War), Nixon refocused the War on Crime onto illegal drug use. With thoroughgoing bipartisan support, his administration criminalized marijuana (associated with hippies) and heroin (associated with blacks), and inaugurated an extended period of growth for American prisons, the birth of the carceral state. Said former Nixon domestic policy chief John Ehrlichman:

> The Nixon campaign in 1968, and the Nixon White House after that, had two enemies: the antiwar left and black people... you understand what I'm saying? We knew we couldn't make it illegal to be either against the war or black, but by getting the public to associate the hippies with marijuana and blacks

with heroin, and then criminalizing both heavily, we could disrupt those communities. We could arrest their leaders, raid their homes, break up their meetings, and vilify them night after night on the evening news. Did we know we were lying about the drugs? Of course we did.[43]

Prison construction, too, saw huge upticks beginning in the 1970s, reversing the trend of the previous decade. The 1960s produced the single largest reduction in the population of federal and state prisoners in the nation's history, with 16,500 fewer inmates in 1969 than in 1950. Nixon requested the Federal Bureau of Prisons develop a strategy for housing the expected increase in prisoners he foresaw as a result of his crackdowns on behalf of law and order. The resulting "Long-Range Master Plan" touted four goals: (1) reduce overcrowding, (2) replace antiquated institutions, (3) establish more humane conditions, and (4) improve general security for staff and inmates alike.[44]

In pursuit of this Master Plan, federal money poured into prison construction, and the shift in federal funding priorities was felt by state governments increasingly reliant on block grants from the federal government. In 1969 states allocated 13.5 percent of their law enforcement block grant funding to corrections, doubling to 30 percent by 1970, with some spending upwards of half their grant funding on corrections. The Law Enforcement Assistance Agency (LEAA) spent $2 million for corrections and prison programs in 1969. Subsequent to the "Long-Range Master Plan" in 1970, that figure rose to $58 million. By 1971, federal funding had increased state spending to $178 million on corrections improvement programs (half via block grants, half via executive branch discretionary funding). By 1972, this number had reached nearly $250 million, a 12,400 percent increase in 3 years.[45] These policies had real consequences: American prisons confined a record 500,000 Americans by the end of the 1970s, reflecting an increase of more than 25 percent, or an additional 120,000 incarcerated people, over 1969.[46] And these increases affected people of color completely out of proportion to their population. In 1974 Pennsylvania's prisons contained 62 percent black citizens while they constituted only 10 percent of that state's population (in Philadelphia the proportion of black inmates had increased from 50 percent in 1970 to 95 percent by 1975). In Florida black people were 55 percent of prisoners and 15 percent of the population. In Alabama they made up 60 percent of prisoners and 26 percent of the population.[47]

Policymakers, police officials, and criminal justice scholars justified all this pouring of carceral concrete by citing the high rates of reported crime during the 1970s. Putting aside the overblown and flawed statistics cited at the time, incarceration rates had little relationship to actual crime rates – although they did correlate directly to the number of black residents and the extent of socio-economic inequality within a given state. Hawaii and Colorado presented high crime rates but relatively few black and Latino residents – and incarceration rates were low. States with higher populations of color actually had lower crime rates but kept larger numbers of citizens in prison and jail. Obsessed with population projections and assumptions about black criminality (and its basis in "culture"), federal planners ignored other factors (poverty, educational attainment, etc.) that fueled both crime and incarceration, using those same statistics as the basis for further projections and the subsequent expansion of the prison system.[48]

Reagan's administration made the antidrug efforts of the 1970s more official by declaring war on drugs. His administration presided over congressional legislation funneling more funds into fighting drugs. Reagan officials issued discretionary dollars to American police that militarized police forces all over the country while drastically expanding surveillance programs in poor urban areas (begun under Kennedy and Johnson, albeit with social services linked to police presence). The budgets of federal law enforcement agencies soared. Between 1980 and 1984, FBI antidrug funding increased from $8 million to $95 million. Department of Defense antidrug funding increased from $33 million in 1981 to $1.042 *billion* in 1991. Simultaneously, the Drug Enforcement Administration (DEA)'s antidrug spending grew from $86 million to $1.026 *billion*, while the FBI's antidrug allocations grew from $38 to $181 million.[49]

This war was waged at a time when deindustrialization shattered the economies of many communities, especially black ones where perhaps 70 percent of men relied on factory jobs for employment.[50] Recall that many African Americans had moved to northern and western cities to find jobs and a sense of freedom. Many of the jobs available, especially to the vast majority of blacks that lacked higher education, were factory or industrial jobs. As these jobs left American soil, black communities struggled, and with fewer legitimate opportunities to make a living, more turned to selling illicit drugs, notably crack-cocaine.

Crack, despite being almost identical to powder cocaine (it has been converted into a form that can be vaporized and inhaled for a more intense and ephemeral high while using less material but is not, therefore, more deadly or harmful), was framed at the time as an especially heinous drug requiring, not a concerted effort on the part of the nation's health infrastructure, but a draconian law enforcement response. The sensationalized media coverage of the "Crack Epidemic" helped siphon billions of federal dollars to *fighting* the drug, rather than *reconstructing* the communities so devastated as to resort to drug-selling in the first place. The year 1986 saw the passage of the Anti-Drug Abuse Act, which allocated $2 billion to combating drugs, required military aid in narcotics control efforts, allowed the death penalty for some drug-related offenses, authorized admission of some illegally obtained evidence in drug trials, and included mandatory minimum sentences for the distribution of cocaine, with much more severe sentencing mandated for the distribution of crack-cocaine. The Act's 1988 revision allowed public housing authorities to evict any tenant who allowed any form of drug-related activity to occur on or near public housing, eliminated many federal benefits (e.g. student loans) for convicted drug offenders, expanded the applicability of the death penalty for drug offenses, and imposed a 5-year mandatory minimum for simple possession of cocaine (with no evidence of intent to sell). Hitherto, one year had been the federal *maximum* for *possession* of *any amount of any drug*. Federal policymakers and legislators clearly took this war very seriously, and they were willing to cripple the lives of millions (disproportionately black and overwhelmingly poor) to win it.[51]

Despite the cost in dollars and lives, War on Drugs provisions remained overwhelmingly popular with large numbers of white voters, especially those resentful of the progress of the civil rights movement. Some black leaders, too, especially within the more socially conservative black churches, supported drug-fighting measures as *at least doing something* to stem the very real violence and social chaos that drugs brought to urban communities. Federal propaganda was so strong, and law enforcement so ensconced in social problems (thanks to the legacy of the liberal siblings: Great Society and War on Crime), that most accepted the inevitability of police involvement and the need to fight drugs, unable to conceive of any alternative (see also section 4.1.5.3).

Like Johnson before him, Clinton was a southern Democrat who did his level best to talk Tough on Crime™. During the 1992 election, he solidified his crime-fighting bona fides by attending the execution of a black criminal. When in office he did indeed deliver on his campaign promises. He endorsed a federal "Three strikes and you're out" policy in his 1994 State of the Union address (to enthusiastic, bipartisan applause); he signed into law a $30 billion crime bill that, among other things, created dozens of new federal capital crimes, mandated life sentences for some three-strike offenders, authorized more than $16 billion for state prison grants and the expansion of state and local police forces.[52]

In addition to fighting crime, Clinton also championed welfare reform and signed the Personal Responsibility and Work Opportunity Reconciliation Act into law. This ended Aid to Families with Dependent Children (AFDC) and replaced it with block grants to the states called Temporary Assistance to Needy Families; it also imposed a 5-year lifetime limit on welfare assistance and a permanent, lifetime ban on eligibility for welfare and food stamps for anyone convicted of a felony drug offense (including simple possession of marijuana). By 1996, the penal budget of the federal government had doubled the amount that had formerly been allocated to the AFDC. Money that had once gone to public housing now funded prison construction – with $17 billion slashed from public housing (a 61 percent reduction) and $19 billion bolstering corrections funding (a 171 percent increase). Prisons had become the federal government's public housing program, and drug offenders constituted the majority of those so housed. Drug arrests have tripled since 1980, with more than 31 million people having been arrested since the declaration of the drug war. As a direct consequence, more people are in prison or jail today for drug offenses than were incarcerated for *all reasons* in 1980.[53]

In 2000, there were seven states in which black people constituted 80 percent or more of incarcerated drug offenders. In at least 15 states, black people are admitted to prison on drug charges at a rate 20-57 times greater than whites. Nationwide, by 2000, the drug-related incarceration rate for black people had increased by more than 26 times its 1983 level, while the increase for whites stood at about eight times the 1983 level.[54] The disproportionate imprisonment of people of color did not reflect higher incidents of drug use among those populations. As of 2005, African Americans represented perhaps 12 percent of all drug users, but 34 percent of those arrested for drug offenses; and while the proportion of African Americans incarcerated for drug-related crimes declined to slightly less than 50 percent by the first decade of the twenty-first century, their numbers remain completely out of proportion to their representation in the general population.[55] The carceral state built on the back of the War on Crime and the War on Drugs affects poor people of all stripes, but it disproportionately impacts poor people of color.

It was within this combative context that Obama's presidency arrived; the black community, already enfeebled by decades of carceral policies, police surveillance, and economic stagnation, looked to the first black president with some hope that things would change, that economic disparities would be addressed, and that criminal justice policies would be reversed.

4.1.5 The Obama Presidency

When the worst waves of recessive devastation crashed into the shores of communities of color across the country, many minority voters saw the election of the first black president as a lifeboat amid the economic storm, even a way out of the neoliberalism that had brought them the devastating police violence of the War on Drugs. This was no mere accident. Obama courted this image of revolutionary change. During the campaign his rhetoric soared to such heights as:

> We've been asked to pause for a reality check. We've been warned against offering the people of this nation false hope. But in the unlikely story that is America, there has never been anything false about hope. For when we have faced down impossible odds, when we've been told we're not ready or that we shouldn't try or that we can't, generations of Americans have responded with a simple creed that sums up the spirit of a people: Yes, we can. Yes, we can. Yes, we can.

It was a creed written into the founding documents that declared the destiny of a nation: Yes, we can. It was whispered by slaves and abolitionists as they blazed a trail towards freedom through the darkest of nights: Yes, we can. It was sung by immigrants as they struck out from distant shores and pioneers who pushed westward against an unforgiving wilderness: Yes, we can. It was the call of workers who organized, women who reached for the ballot, a president who chose the moon as our new frontier, and a king who took us to the mountaintop and pointed the way to the promised land: Yes, we can, to justice and equality.

Yes, we can, to opportunity and prosperity. Yes, we can heal this nation. Yes, we can repair this world. Yes, we can.[56]

Once elected, however, Obama and his administration did indeed pause for reality – or at least a version of reality countenanced by those already benefiting from the status quo. Especially when it came to the poor and working class, his attitude morphed from "Yes We Can" into "Just Calm Down." His administration moved heaven and earth defending Wall Street and the auto companies, eagerly funded the military and continued talk about balanced federal budgets amid recession; it did precious little to keep the poor and the desperate in their homes, to reconstruct poor neighborhoods of color gutted by decades of economic neglect, or to curtail the abuses of a militarized police force.

4.1.5.1 Black Americans and the Great Recession

Economically, black America has always been somewhat removed from mainstream (white) financial and banking institutions. Communities already depressed economically necessitated banks that kept higher reserves for losses, which in turn meant higher operating costs than other banks, higher transaction costs (owing in part to a higher proportion of face-to-face retail customers), and an over-reliance on small, high-activity deposits. Black banking institutions also made fewer (and smaller) loans than their white counterparts, which further reduced their profitability, their ability to grow, and their ability to issue credit. Add to this financial weakness the history of redlining and thus the inability of many black people to acquire and grow equity, the lack of decent jobs in many black neighborhoods, and other trends of the neoliberal twenty-first century cityscape, and you have a national community particularly susceptible to the vicissitudes of economic fortune: in general, a recession in a white neighborhood means a depression in a black one.[57]

The history of "deregulation" also disproportionately damaged black communities. Congress (via the 1980 DIDMCA, the 1982 Garn-St. Germain Depository Institutions Act, and other deregulatory legislation) put into practice the belief that fewer government regulations would produce a healthier banking industry. This resulted in, for instance, the creation of adjustable-rate and subprime mortgages. This legislation was reinforced by the courts. In 1978 the Supreme Court ruled in *Marquette National Bank v. First of Omaha* that state usury laws were in effect null and void, peeling away another layer of consumer-oriented protection.[58] Combined, these federal policies paved the way for an explosion in subprime lending and financial exploitation in poor neighborhoods around the country.

The partner of deprivation is exploitation, for the former leads to desperation and allows victims to fall more readily into the maw of the latter. The old trend of ignoring black communities gave way, in the wake of deregulation, to an explosion of banking in black neighborhoods – high interest, adjustable-rate, subprime banking, predatory banking. Just as contract sellers (who rented houses to black families at cripplingly high rates) had exploited the credit-starved and the redlined in the mid twentieth century, high-priced lenders filled the banking void of the neoliberal years. Black borrowers were 150 percent more likely to get high-cost loans. Black people were targeted for subprime loans even when they could have qualified for prime loans. Countrywide and other such mortgage originators opened branches in inner cities to peddle as many subprime loans as possible. Most of the areas that were targeted for subprime lending were formerly redlined districts, like Chicago's black belt, the area with the most subprime loans between 2004 and 2006. Some lenders even zeroed in on elderly black homeowners to sell them fraudulent reverse mortgages that ultimately threw many into homelessness.[59]

The history of financial ostracism and fraud, combined with the legacy of slavery, Jim Crow, deindustrialization, and the drug war came together to ensure that the Great Recession wrecked the black economy. While general US unemployment at the height of the crash peaked around 10 percent, African Americans suffered through about 17 percent unemployment. The crash wiped out 53 percent of all black wealth, stripping millions of the meager material gains made over the previous generations of work and strife.[60]

The Obama administration, while emphasizing America's collective responsibility to bailout large financial institutions, championed individual responsibility regardless of social context when it came to the plight of the poor – and this included many African Americans. Emblematically, Treasury secretary Jack Lew emphasized the need for financial education over and above structural change, advising black people to forgo everyday expenses in favor of saving for retirement.[61] In reality, the ability of individuals to beat back the urge for the morning's cup of coffee had little to do with the disparity between white and black wealth: blacks save an average of 11 percent of their annual income while whites save 10 percent.[62] People of color cannot get ahead because those with power (whose interests president Obama worked judiciously to defend) do not wish to redistribute the resources hoarded via the exploitation of the poor to make the redress of this historically generated imbalance possible. The fundamental issue has little to do with individual choice on the part of the poor and everything to do with the individual choice of billionaires to hoard their wealth. Responsibility matters, but only in proportion to one's power within society. The rich, who occupy the positions of power, thus bear personal responsibility for their actions; the poor who labor just to survive very much less so.

While the financial crisis and ensuing Great Recession shattered the lives of millions – and made life most especially harder for poor Americans already suffering under the austere domestic policies of bipartisan origin – black communities and families, a disproportionately high percentage of the poor, were especially hard hit. Economic recovery, meanwhile, came more slowly to African Americans, if it came at all. The unemployment rate for black people stood at about 6 percent in 2017 (with places like Flint, Michigan upwards of 25 percent) while the general unemployment figure sat closer to 4 percent. The average net wealth of black families as of 2018 stood at $11,000, whereas for white families that figure was $141,900. A third of black families now have no assets at all.[63]

4.1.5.2 Black Americans and the Affordable Care Act

The history of black healthcare, and the socio-economic conditions that so profoundly influence health, is one of brutality, tyranny, and marginalization, the legacy of which stretches into the present day. Comparative rates of infant mortality between enslaved African Americans and free whites evince the harsh conditions in which African American slaves lived and worked. For all African Americans between 1820-1860, approximately 276 infants died per 1000 births; for nineteenth-century whites the infant death rate stood at an average of 162 deaths per 1000 births.[64] Slave punishment and the Pushing System provided black slaves with the "benefits" of white civilization, severely affecting their health and quality of life. Many planters and overseers whipped both their slowest and fastest pickers, seeking not just increased efficiency but mental control over their human property. For example, in 1840-41, Bennet Barrow (of West Feliciana Parish, Louisiana) kept a journal that he called his "Record of Punishment." Therein, Barrow jotted down the tortures he meted out in the name of good business. Three-quarters of these were directed at those who did not meet their picking objective. One October day he directed a "whipping frollick." He "whiped [sic] 8 or 10 for weight to day – those that pick least weights."[65]

Much ad hoc experimentation was visited upon the bodies of enslaved African Americans before the Civil War.[66] As the medical profession standardized its practices and systematized its research methods at the end of the nineteenth and into the twentieth centuries, this experimentation continued, now undergirded by a bastardized form of Darwinism that posited that the "Negro race," maladapted for civilized life in comparison to its white betters, was disease prone, vice ridden, criminal, and destined to die out now that emancipation had made these inherited disadvantages all the more prevalent.[67] This racist attitude focused most especially upon black sexuality and the assumption that this "southern race" possessed especially strong sexual appetites augmented by their more "emotional" brand of religious expression. While blacks were, said the bastard children of Darwin, not able to survive civilization on their own, their aggressive, uncontrolled sexuality did cause them to prey on white women – a pervasive theme in white discourse about black men at this time and a common reason cited for the lynching of black men and boys.[68]

Perhaps the most infamous example of this racially motivated, sexually charged medical research was the Tuskegee Syphilis study conducted from 1932 to 1972. Under the assumption that perhaps half of all "Negroes" were syphilitic, doctors sought to study syphilitic patients in Macon County, Alabama in an effort to assess the possibility of mass treatment. Their efforts were not to cure those they observed, but rather to engage in a "study in nature," letting the disease take its course (under the assumption that black people would not seek treatment in any case) so its etiology could be better understood.[69] The experiment comprised 600 black men (400 with syphilis and 200 uninfected that served as a control group). Reports were issued every few years over the course of 3 decades, regularly citing the deleterious effects syphilis had upon its subjects. In order to maintain the naturalness of the study, the investigators did their best to ensure the subjects did not receive syphilis treatment from other sources, trying in the 1930s to enlist the help of local black doctors in leaving the syphilis untreated, writing to the Alabama Health Department in the 1940s to keep its mobile VD unit from treating the Macon residents, etc.[70] By the 1950s some study subjects had managed to obtain penicillin (by that point recognized as the best treatment for syphilis) on their own, but most did not; indeed, many subjects were under the mistaken assumption that the federal doctors in their town, who provided some medical services but kept the syphilis deliberately untreated, were already caring for all their medical needs and thus did not seek outside treatment. They trusted the doctors, who rewarded that trust by continuing their "natural" study of syphilis.

By the late 1960s, most of the study's organizers in the government were still supportive of its continuation. While one doctor admitted in a 1969 memo: "Nothing learned will prevent, find, or cure a single case of infectious syphilis or bring us closer to our basic mission of controlling venereal disease in the United States," he ended by saying the study ought to continue "along its present lines."[71] Increased press coverage in the early 1970s brought the study into the spotlight, forcing the Department of Health, Education, and Welfare (HEW) to end it. The resulting criticism also prompted HEW to convene an Ad Hoc Advisory Panel to investigate. It faulted the study for failing to provide penicillin once that antibiotic had been verified as an effective treatment, although the panel failed to recognize that even in the 1930s treatments (like the use of arsenotherapy) existed; furthermore the panel, in focusing on the penicillin, failed to understand the racist intellectual underpinnings of the study as it had been formulated in 1932. When the study concluded, of the original 400 afflicted study subjects, 74 were still living and up to one hundred had died as a direct result of syphilitic lesions.[72]

Within the context of this medical experimentation and the racist philosophy that underpinned many of the views the medical community held about African Americans, liberal politicians made some efforts to broaden access to medical care. The Civil Rights Act of 1964 legislated to increase minority access to health services, although many hospitals resisted integration in various ways. It was not until the advent of Medicare and Medicaid, which conditioned receipt of payments on whether a hospital desegregated, that real desegregation began. Most hospitals could not afford to lose Medicare payments because many major private health insurance companies refused to pay for services to adults older than 65.[73]

A quarter century later, Congress passed the Disadvantaged Minority Health Improvement Act of 1990. The text of the legislation as originally proposed sought to: (1) boost support for campaigns aimed at promoting better health and alleviating diseases prevalent within minority communities, (2) provide the Office of Minority Health with the funding and authority commensurate with its responsibility and mandate, and (3) establish scholarships and loans to raise the number of minorities working in the health sector. Unable to pass a bill through Congress that dealt only with "minority" issues, the final bill was rewritten so as to include disadvantaged whites as well.[74]

These legislative solutions did expand medical coverage to some degree, but they failed to tackle the endemic racism within the medical profession or alleviate the material conditions in which most black people were forced to live and through which their health was so adversely affected. The Affordable Care Act continued this tradition of technocratic half-solutions. Its drastic expansion of Medicaid coverage, which by 2017 had come to include more than half the states in the Union, resulted in an additional 10 million Americans gaining health insurance of one sort or another. While this did have an impact in black communities across the country, many in the South (where Medicaid coverage has occurred less universally) remain uncovered. Moreover, even with the additional coverage taken into account disparities in health coverage remain between the races. In 2017, 93.7 percent of non-Hispanic whites had health insurance coverage, compared to 89.4 percent of blacks, 83.9 percent of Hispanics, and 92.7 percent of Asians.[75]

More importantly, the socio-economic conditions upon which so much of good health is predicated remained precarious for many African American communities. The tragedy in Flint, Michigan (one of the nation's poorest cities and a long-standing victim of pollution and abuse at the hands of the auto industry) exemplified this persistent fact. In 2011, citing Flint's $15 million deficit, Michigan's Republican governor Rick Snyder placed the city under emergency management. Unelected managers took over the city's budget, local law, and public sector union contracts.

One of these appointees, Darnell Earley, doubled residential water rates to twice the state average – twice that of New York, seven times that of Miami, and ten times that of Phoenix, Arizona. The managers opted to save another $20 million over 8 years by switching Flint off Detroit water. Earley, with approval from the Michigan Department of Environmental Quality, decided to source the heavily polluted Flint River instead of remaining on Detroit water until a new pipeline to Lake Huron could be completed. The Department of Environmental Quality advised Flint to follow protocol for treating water from the Flint River that was intended for new water systems, leaving out a crucial corrosion-control chemical (in use as a standard operating procedure across the country) that prevents lead from leaching out of older pipes.[76]

As the inadequately treated Flint River began to flow through the city's aging, lead-heavy plumbing, lead leeched into the water. Michigan's state government learned of the damage early, although they kept this knowledge from the public. In 2014 the General Motors plant in Flint, upon noticing its engine parts were rusting, obtained a variance to switch back to Detroit water, costing the state of Michigan $440,000 in operational costs and providing the first indicators that something was amiss. Emails as early as January 2015 evidence a state government so concerned about its own employees' safety that it took the precaution of having purified water delivered to Flint's state office building. This was done as repeated assurances to Flint residents that their water was safe to drink left the lips of Flint's administrators. Resident complaints grew louder as the year drew on, however. The Department of Environmental Quality officials responded by refusing to retest homes that scored high for lead and demanding owners of test homes flush their lines before water samplings, thus diluting readings. This bad faith response led Flint residents to contact the Virginia Tech team that discovered (and subsequently shared to the public at large) the extent of the crisis. Virginia Tech researchers tested 271 Flint homes for lead levels in their tap water, and found levels from 27 parts per billion (five times greater than concentrations considered safe, leading to cardiovascular problems, kidney damage, and neurological morbidity), to levels as high as over 5000 parts per billion, which the Environmental Protection Agency (EPA) itself refers to as "toxic waste."[77]

Later investigation by pediatrician Mona Hanna-Attisha and colleagues determined that the proportion of Flint infants and children with above-average levels of lead had doubled since 2014 and in some areas even tripled. In all likelihood, this increased exposure will result in lifelong impact on cognition and motor skills. Once the state admitted the extent of the damages and brought its own investigatory resources to bear, it announced a spike in Legionella bacterium in the water, with 87 reported infections, ten of them fatal.

Some aspects of this fiasco were unintended accident, some the result of negligence, some blatant cover up, but the chief structural culprit was neoliberalism, the marketization of all human interaction. Preceding Flint's water switch, the Detroit Water and Sewer Department offered Flint's appointed managers a deal that would have saved the emergency-managed city millions of dollars. Flint could have continued on the Detroit pipeline it had used for generations. The state rejected the offer because, insiders reported, governor Snyder was intent on breaking up the Detroit water system and privatizing its operations.[78]

Thus, whatever gains African Americans might have made in certain parts of the country in terms of access to some semblance of healthcare, these gains were limited in several important ways. Medicaid varies in quality from state to state, meaning the value of this coverage is uneven and sometimes quite miniscule; thanks to Republican efforts to stop Medicaid expansion it has not found its way across the entire country; and regardless of insurance coverage many black people still live in ostracized neighborhoods bereft of sustaining employment, polluted by the remnants of industrial development that left them behind decades ago, and utterly ignored by the machinations of the political class. Until the material conditions of their lives are improved, their health will remain precarious.

4.1.5.3 Increasingly Visible Police Violence

Police violence in general is nothing new. Recall the bloody history of American labor resistance to corporate abuse – and the integral role the first organized police departments played in crushing strikers. Nor is police violence against minorities new. Footage of the civil rights era protests – and the dogs, fire hoses, horses, and clubs with which the police answered that call for freedom and justice – ought to make that perfectly clear.

Policing and anti-poverty measures went hand in hand within the liberal policies of Kennedy (with his emphasis on delinquent youths) and Johnson (with his law and order pushback against protest).[79] Nixon, who promised on the campaign trail to "wage an effective war against this enemy within" and Ford built on the crime control measures of the Johnson years while neglecting anti-poverty initiatives.[80] They increased funding for undercover operations, more advanced equipment, and prison construction. And their focus was self-consciously low-income communities of color. In 1969 Nixon said to his chief of staff, "You have to face the fact that the whole problem is really the blacks. The key is to devise a system that recognizes this while not appearing to do so."[81]

To implement these policies, the federal government worked to fund state efforts to professionalize American police and modernize their equipment. The federal LEAA funded tuition for 50,000 officers enrolled in police science programs across the country in predominantly suburban communities; it incentivized the adoption and use of emerging technology like walkie-talkies and computerized criminal justice databanks.[82] In 1972 the federal government initiated a program called High Impact to provide additional federal funds to select cities (some with suspicious electoral importance to the Nixon campaign); the funding from this program allowed Baltimore to purchase walkie-talkies, helicopters, upgrades to their dispatch systems, create nine new special tactical units, and to increase its complement of foot patrolmen (to an ultimate goal of fivefold more officers by 1973). These efforts increased the number of police interactions in poor communities, and therefore the incidents of reported crime, but over time did not actually alleviate the problems of street crime. Despite this, the federal government continued to push funding away from the already inadequate welfare provisions and toward law enforcement.[83]

On the streets the police impact was brutal, violent, deadly. Officers were tasked with foot patrols, both in uniform and plainclothes (a shift away from the prevailing reliance on motor vehicles). What began under Johnson as an attempt to better integrate police officers into the communities they patrolled had evolved by the 1970s into a kind of military occupation. In Detroit, operation STRESS (Stop the Robberies, Enjoy Safe Streets) began in 1972 with additional grants from the LEAA. In just 2 years, STRESS made more than 6000 arrests and killed 18 civilians. Officers put themselves deliberately in peril so as to invite robbery – and these provocations could unsurprisingly end in violence. Emblematically, officer Peterson, who had compiled 1000 arrests and nine citizen complaints during the course of his previous decade on the force, was appointed a crew chief within the STRESS program in 1971; by 1973, having already killed two people since joining the program, Peterson killed a third and tried to frame the man by saying the victim had pulled a knife on the officer, forcing him to kill in self-defense. Forensic evidence exploded this cover up and the officer was removed from STRESS to face charges for second degree murder. The program was subsequently disbanded only after intense community outcry.[84]

These policies continued regardless of the party in power. The Carter administration placed crime control measures at the center of their urban policy, framing them as "security precautions" rather than control measures. During the neoliberal decades of the 1980s and 1990s, the War on Drugs brought to poor communities across the country, and therefore disproportionately to communities of color, the climax of this increased police presence, surveillance, nuisance, and violence.[85] Operation Pipeline, for example, began in 1984 to administer training to police officers in the large-scale use of pretextual traffic stops and consent searches. It taught officers how to: lengthen the time of a routine stop and leverage it into a search; obtain consent from a reluctant motorist; use drug sniffing dogs to obtain probable cause. Later estimates indicated 95 percent of stops made by those trained under Pipeline yielded no drugs.[86]

In addition to funding, the federal government provided training, intelligence, and additional support; the Pentagon began giving away military equipment as well. In 1997 perhaps 1.7 million pieces of military equipment were provided to local law enforcement.[87] This trend went into overdrive after George W. Bush redeclared the War on Terror. In addition to a plethora of assault rifles, grenade launchers, body armor, and armored vehicles being provided to police departments across the country, the technology used by the drone campaign to track metadata and impersonate cell towers eventually found its way into civilian law enforcement use as well. By 2016 almost 60 law enforcement agencies in 23 states possessed a Stingray or some form of cell-site simulator (see also section 1.3.6).[88]

Even with this history of policy, legislation, and incarceration, statistically quantifying the amount of violence inflicted upon African Americans by police has proven a difficult prospect, not least because until the issue came to national attention during Obama's second term, many precincts did not keep consistent data on their use of deadly force (let alone nonlethal force), and those that did often used proprietary methods of categorization that made comparison with other localities difficult. The limited data we currently possess is suggestive but not conclusive. According to the CDC, between 1999 and 2013, African Americans represented 27.6 percent of the 6338 recorded deaths at the hands of police, despite representing only 13.2 percent of the population. An estimate by Mapping Police Violence estimated that of the 1149 people killed by police in 2014, 26 percent were black. A third analysis, this time of 1316 police shootings across

12 police departments between 2000 and 2015, put the proportion of African Americans at 46 percent. This same analysis further indicated that, based on data from New York City's Stop-and-Frisk program (5 million encounters recorded between 2003 and 2013), blacks and Hispanics were 50 percent more likely to have force of some kind inflicted upon them by police.[89]

If this history has always been with us, why did it gain such attention in the second decade of this century? The election of a black man to the presidency may have played a role, prompting the mistreated to feel themselves less willing to take any more abuse. The prevalence of countervailing, compelling testimony made a difference as well. Hitherto, police violence – taking place largely in dark alleys, along lonely roadsides, or witnessed only by those marginalized individuals to whom mainstream society offers no sympathy, was downplayed, denied, or defended as justified by police. The offending officer's word routinely was taken as gospel even in the face of countervailing testimony, other police officers backed up whatever was said, and city officials had no incentive to look too deeply into claims contrary to what the police reported as fact. The advent of cell phone footage of increasing quality and ubiquity, however, changed that. For all that cell phone footage cannot do – too many videos lack enough context for determinations to be made on that evidence alone – it at least had the benefit of corroborating *enough* of what the marginalized said to make some in the mainstream more skeptical of police testimony.

The first few years of Obama's presidency were ones of anxious waiting and slowly receding hopes. The administration did nothing to address the drug war or the carceral state while it had a partisan majority in Congress. The 2010 Midterm victories for the Republican Party dimmed some hope among progressive activists that change would come – but they still held out for Obama to come through for them. In 2011, however, even many black progressives grew disenchanted after the president refused to intervene in the Georgia execution of Troy Davis. Widely believed to have been wrongfully convicted, activists had for years attempted to win his exoneration. Voices from around the world called on Obama to grant clemency – the governments of France and Germany, Amnesty International, even a former FBI director – and yet the president did nothing, said nary a word on the subject. While activist efforts in this case failed, a silver lining emerged: black activists and members of the Occupy movement found themselves working together on this cause – race and class coming together in common struggle.[90]

The year 2012 inaugurated a growing momentum within many black communities. The murder of Treyvon Martin by George Zimmerman, a trigger-happy neighborhood watchman, kicked off a national debate on police shootings and a national protest movement (inspired by the activism of the Occupy movement, which had demonstrated that street protests were still possible). Incidents like the Cleveland 137 shooting (where police shot into a car 137 times, killing two unarmed people) brought forth cries of outrage. Said one reporter: "The year 2012 was a major awakening point not just for me but also for other young black men and women across the country. We watched the Trayvon Martin shooting play out in real time in our Facebook pages and television screens. [Such stories as his and others] solidified the undeniable feeling in our hearts that their deaths and those of other young black men were not isolated."[91]

Protests erupted when Martin's killer was exonerated. Alicia Garza, in despair, responded by posting a hashtag on Facebook: #blacklivesmatter. She described the movement she would go on to co-found as: "an ideological and political intervention in a world where Black lives are systematically and intentionally targeted for demise. It is an affirmation of Black folks' contributions to this society, our humanity, and our resilience in the face of deadly oppression."[92] The slogan did not mean that only black lives mattered, simply that they mattered *as well* – a fact the American System has consistently chosen to ignore.

This skepticism of the system and frustration with the seemingly immovable status quo further erupted in 2014 with mass protests in Ferguson, Missouri. These began as an immediate response to the police shooting of Michael Brown, an unarmed black teenager, by Darren Wilson, a white police officer. Federal investigators concluded well after the fact that, based on credible witnesses augmented by forensic evidence, the shooting was in all probability justified. Brown had acted belligerently, attacking Wilson in his police cruiser, attempting to grab the officer's handgun, fleeing the scene, then turning around to charge the officer, at which point Wilson gunned him down.[93] What community members saw at the time, however, was that another young man had been killed, his body left to fester on the street for hours, the police deaf to calls for an investigation, acting as if they were unaccountable to those they sought to police. The particulars and the technicalities mattered little in such a charged context. Even if Brown's death could be explained away as a justified tragedy, members of the Ferguson community could recall countless other incidents of police brutality, cruelty, and indifference. The words of writer Charles Pierce encapsulated the feelings of many in the Ferguson community and beyond:

Dictators leave bodies in the street. Petty local satraps leave bodies in the street. Warlords leave bodies in the street. Those are the places where they leave bodies in the street, as object lessons, or to make a point, or because there isn't the money to take the bodies away and bury them, or because nobody gives a damn whether they are there or not.[94]

Nationally, the protests in Ferguson added fuel to the already heated discussion over race, policing, the War on Drugs, and the War on Terror. News footage of the protests proved stark viewing. Riot police met shouts and chants and angry looks with the rudiments and panoply of war; cotton-clad protestors arrayed themselves courageously against a wall of Kevlar. But police reaction was not limited to brandishing the niceties of the military industrial complex; they showed a penchant for disrespecting the protestors. A memorial for Michael Brown was desecrated by a canine unit that allowed one of its dogs to urinate on it. Flower arrangements left by Brown's family were run over by police cruisers. During one of the demonstrations, an officer pointed his AR-15 in the direction of a group of journalists, screaming, "I'm going to fucking kill you!" When asked for his name, the officer responded, "Go fuck yourself!"[95]

The Ferguson protests were a vivid manifestation of the lack of faith many now had with politics as usual. "I voted for Obama twice," Tef Poe, a local Ferguson activist, said, "And still got teargassed."[96] In 2016 co-founder of Black Lives Matter Aislinn Pulley refused an invitation by Obama for a private audience. When he scolded her that he was offering what any activist or community organizer ought to strive for, "a seat at the table," the activist replied in an open letter that the meeting was little more than a publicity stunt for an administration trying to placate the drive for fundamental change, another in a relentless cycle of vapid dialog sessions. She went on to write:

> If the administration is serious about addressing the issues of Black Lives Matter Chicago – and its sister organizations that go by different names across this nation – they can start by meeting the simple demands of families who want transparency, and who want police that kill Black people unjustly to be fired, indicted, and held accountable. A meeting arranged to carry this out is one that would be worthy of consideration. Until this begins to happen on a mass scale, any celebrations of Black history that go on inside the walls of the White House are hollow and ceremonial at best.

She criticized Rahm Emanuel – Obama's former chief of staff and then mayor of Chicago – for closing record numbers of public schools, half of Chicago's mental health clinics, shielding police and other public servants from justice. She ended her letter with a call to work beyond the stultifying confines of status quo politicking, beyond the milquetoast dithering of any self-appointed leadership class:

> ...we assert that true revolutionary and systemic change will ultimately only be brought forth by ordinary working people, students and youth – organizing, marching and taking power from the corrupt elites. No proponent of this system – Democrat or Republican – will upend the oppressive structures that maintain it. To hold the powerful accountable for their harmful and oppressive actions, we must continue to build power in the streets. We must act in concert and in coalition within our communities, because together, we have the power to uproot all oppression and systemic violence.[97]

The old guard of the black political class did not mesh well with this younger generation of protestors. Al Sharpton, who was appealing to the political establishment for his ability to organize protests focused on narrow issues or specific cases rather than any kind of systemic analysis, found himself somewhat out of the loop after 2014. Given his clout, Sharpton gave the eulogy at Michael Brown's funeral, but he used it as an opportunity to castigate the young black protestors in Ferguson and around the nation for giving up "the pursuit of excellence" in favor of wanting to "be a nigger and call your woman a ho," rather than to galvanize united action in the face of yet another tragedy.[98]

This culture war narrative of low pants and foul language being the cause of plight for communities of color reeked of the worst kinds of conservative racism, and conveniently ignored the system that condoned and encouraged the causes of poverty.

Of course, since Sharpton benefited from the status quo, he had little reason to criticize it. Condescending to the young played better with his liberal donors. Obama evinced similar limitations when, toward the end of his presidency, he grew confident enough to mention racial issues at some length.

Nevertheless, many young activists were having none of it. During a National Association for the Advancement of Colored People (NAACP) meeting, several turned their backs on the NAACP president while he gave a speech. Activist and hip-hop artist Tef Poe commented at the time, "This ain't your grandparents' civil rights movement."[99] Further differences between old and new could be seen among the leadership of these new protest movements. Women and queer folk threw their energy into the fray. This is likely a result of the War on Drugs, which saw millions of black men dragged from their homes and communities and shut off from the rest of society. Ferguson provided a stark example of this demographic reality: in 2015 the city had 1182 African American women between the ages of 25 and 34, only 577 men of the corresponding category resided there. Black and queer women sought to highlight the struggles of *all* people of color, not men merely. To do this, Black Lives Matter activists turned increasingly to a broader analysis, breaking free from the liberal/conservative talking points of the previous generation.[100]

Obama showed some public empathy for the black plight after the shooting of Trayvon Martin in 2012; after the not-guilty verdict of Martin's killer George Zimmerman in 2013, Obama gave an off the cuff speech in which he said, "Trayvon Martin could have been me thirty-five years ago," and this was his most extensive public recognition of systemic racism until 2015. But even this mild show of sympathy came with a political price, and the right skewered him. One commentator said: "[Obama] needlessly impl[ied] that it's dangerous being a black kid in America when white people with guns are around."[101]

But even when Ferguson was on the nightly news and the political conversation seemed ripe for soaring presidential words, Obama's tepid statements disappointed black activists and their allies. In the face of increased national focus on police violence, and recognizing that there might be some racial animus in some departments, Obama pushed for analysis rather than action, and federal investigators headed to Ferguson, Chicago, Baltimore, and Cleveland to review their police departments. Their observations regarding Chicago's police force are emblematic of all the departments investigated: "[Chicago PD] has engaged in a pattern or practice of unreasonable force in violation of the Fourth Amendment and...the deficiencies in CPD's training, supervision, accountability, and other systems have contributed to that pattern or practice." Among the various faults and failures, Chicago's police department: (1) did not provide officers with adequate guidance in the use of force or in the safe resolution of encounters with the public, (2) did not appropriately supervise officers so as to identify dangerous behavior, (3) did not review its use of force incidents to determine if they complied with either the law or internal policy, (4) did not review incidents to see whether the tactics used were safe or effective.[102]

To quote but one example of many cited in the report:

[A] man had been walking down a residential street with a friend when officers drove up, shined a light on him, and ordered him to freeze, because he had been fidgeting with his waistband. The man ran. Three officers gave chase and began shooting as they ran. In total, the officers fired 45 rounds, including 28 rifle rounds, toward the man. Several rounds struck the man, killing him. The officers claimed the man fired at them during the pursuit. Officers found no gun on the man. However, officers reported recovering a handgun nearly one block away. The gun recovered in the vicinity, however, was later determined to be fully-loaded and inoperable, and forensic testing determined there was no gunshot residue on the man's hands. IPRA [Chicago's Independent Police Review Authority] found the officers' actions were justified without addressing the efficacy of the pursuit or the number of shots fired.[103]

In addition to Justice Department investigations, Obama created the Task Force on 21st Century Policing in 2014 to investigate possible reforms and make recommendations. Based on that task force's observation that the data available in the field of police violence was sorely lacking, Obama launched the Police Data Initiative in 2015, which involved the participation of 21 departments across the country that all agreed to work with the federal government to standardize their methods and publicize their findings.[104] Obama also signed Executive Order 13688 at the beginning of 2015, establishing a Law Enforcement Equipment Working Group. Focusing specifically on the militarization of American police over the course of the wars on drugs and terrorism, this executive order did do more than previous administrations had done in recognizing that problems existed in how military equipment had historically been distributed to law enforcement agencies (LEAs). Rather than attempt to grapple with this issue root and branch by questioning the very idea that American police required military-grade hardware in the first place, this order asserted that: "These programs have assisted LEAs as they carry out their critical missions to keep the American people safe."[105] The order created a working group to study the issue, compile information on the kinds of equipment transferred to LEAs, and develop policy recommendations so as to ensure police had proper training in the use of such equipment and more thorough federal oversight so as to protect the civil liberties and rights of American citizens.

While the Obama administration, in ponderous reports and tepid legal diction, in speech after admonition after memorandum, was willing to admit the existence of police brutality and the need for some reform, Alicia Garza, a co-founder of BLM, wrote that these protests were about something far more fundamental to the American experience, something resistant to surface-level reform measures: the state-sanctioned violence, especially against racial minorities, that rests at the base of America's institutions:

> When we say Black Lives Matter, we are talking about the ways in which Black people are deprived of our basic human rights and dignity. It is an acknowledgment Black poverty and genocide is state violence. It is an acknowledgment that 1 million Black people are locked in cages in this country – one half of all people in prisons or jails – is an act of state violence. It is an acknowledgment that Black women continue to bear the burden of a relentless assault on our children and our families and that assault is an act of state violence. Black queer and trans folks bearing a unique burden in a hetero-patriarchal society that disposes of us like garbage and simultaneously fetishizes us and profits off of us is state violence...[106]

4.1.5.4 Race and Obama's Opponents

Obama's racial restraint may have mollified white liberals, but conservatives and white racists were quick to vilify Obama in any way they could. The energy that accompanied this backlash against the Obama presidency caught many liberals (and not a few mainstream conservatives) off guard. In hindsight, however, the euphoria of a black man's election to the presidency, especially within the context of the divisive Bush II years, hid the coming conflict from the predictions of many observers.[107]

Two pillars of racist resistance to Obama rose above any others: the Tea Party movement and the Birther Conspiracy. The former was only partially tainted by racial prejudice, the latter, however, was entirely beholden to that intellectual excrement.

Of course not all Tea Partiers were racist, and many no doubt held no conscious racial prejudice. It was an uncomfortable fact, however, that Small Government libertarianism often swam in the same waters as did white supremacy. Perhaps most infamously, the various newsletters published in the 1980s and 1990s under the banner of libertarian politician and presidential candidate Ron Paul contained, in and among their various invectives against the Federal Reserve and columns in support of the gold standard, a plethora of racist stereotypes, for instance claiming that the Rodney King riots only ended when it came time for those involved to collect their welfare checks. These references may or may not have reflected the author's personal beliefs, but they were a conscious attempt to engage in "outreach to rednecks" in a time before war and economic recession made government skepticism a broader sell.[108]

One especially egregious example of the Tea Party Caucus' conscious racism was Iowa representative Steve King. Although stripped by Republican leadership of his committee memberships in early 2019 (after blatantly defending White Nationalism), such bigotry had been part and parcel of his politics for nearly two decades. In the early 2000s he championed English as the official language of Iowa, introduced a bill to make it the official language of the United States, and sued Iowa's secretary of state for posting information in multiple languages. The presumption that English need be the *only* language allowed in a country whose history includes large populations of Germanic, Hispanic, East Asian, and Eastern European immigrants smacks of the deepest historical blindness. It also presupposes a nationalist definition of community so narrow and confining as to require the firm hand of state control in order to make real. His virulence towards immigrants did not stop at language. He claimed illegal immigrants were killing American citizens in a "slow-motion Holocaust," supported an electrified border wall that would deter illegal immigrants as one deters "livestock," and supported the profiling of Hispanic Americans in the search for illegal immigrants. His anxiety over the darkening hue of the American people spilled into his critique of the Affordable Care Act as well. In lambasting the law's coverage of contraception, King declared, "Preventing babies being born is not medicine. That's not constructive to our culture and our civilization. If we let our birthrate get down below the replacement rate, we're a dying civilization." Finally, he made the case that "western civilization," (a historically nebulous but politically useful term) has made the lion's share of contributions to humanity: "I would ask you to go back through history and figure out where are these contributions that have been made by these other categories of people you are talking about [African Americans and Mexicans]. Where did any other subgroup of people contribute more to civilization?"[109] Never mind that cultures, nations, communities of all sorts constantly intermingle with one another, sharing, trading, stealing, modifying, discarding each other's ideas, stories, practices, technologies, and institutions. Never mind that "Greek" philosophy was influenced by ideas from the Indian subcontinent and the kingdom of Egypt. Never mind that Muslim thinkers took up the ideas of Plato and Aristotle, made substantial modifications in areas like optics, and passed those ideas back across the Mediterranean to Medieval Christendom. In King's mind, culture is clad in iron, indivisible and immutable, and changes only to its own detriment.

In addition to conscious racial bias among at least some Tea Partiers, investigation of its members has found that self-identified Tea Party members often had stronger unconscious racial bias than did those of other political groups. This often expressed itself less via outright hostility toward other races than it did as a white defensiveness against being toppled from the peak of the socio-economic pyramid. Consider the context: not only was the United States wading its way through economic recession but the traditional racial dynamics were seemingly upended: the first non-white president in the country's history had just been elected and demographic trends consistently predicted a proportionally greater share of the population for so-called "minority" groups in comparison to whites. This triggered in a not insignificant sector of white America in general (and the Republican Party in particular) an anxiety that the status quo – in which whites sat atop a racial hierarchy – might be threatened.[110]

The Birther Conspiracy stood as the paramount example of racism (conscious or unconscious) infecting the political discourse – regardless of political party. It sought to establish that Barack Hussein Obama, not being a naturalized US citizen, was thus ineligible to be president. It originated within Obama's own party among several Hillary Clinton staffers during the Democratic primary campaign (although Clinton herself never pursued that angle of attack). It emerged onto the broader American scene alongside the Tea Party, claiming that Obama had been born in Kenya, not Hawaii, making him ineligible for the office of chief executive. Fox News' Sean Hannity and CNN's Lou Dobbs jumped on the issue. GOP representatives and pundits supported the inquiries, fanned the flames of doubt, and equivocated with "I think it's a fair question" platitudes, in turn.

In fact, Obama was born in the United States (August 4, 1961, in Honolulu, Hawaii). His mother, Dr. Stanley Ann Dunham, was a US citizen. Despite these facts, Birther Conspiracy theories persisted well after Obama proved his American citizenship. Obama twice addressed Birther claims with primary evidence of his US birth. He first did so on the campaign trail when he posted a scan of his certificate of live birth, supplied by the Hawaii Department of Health. Both Factcheck.org and PolitiFact concluded that the certificate of live birth was legitimate. Furthermore, the *Honolulu Advertiser* found "two separate newspaper announcements of the president's birth, one in the *Advertiser* on August 13, 1961, and another in the *Honolulu Star-*

Bulletin the next day. Both carried the words 'Mr. and Mrs. Barack H. Obama, 6085 Kalanianaole Highway, son, Aug. 4.'"[111] These facts, however, failed to move a sizable minority of white Americans, convinced that because Obama did not *look the part* of president (i.e. he was not white), he must somehow be ineligible for that role.

The Birther movement subsided for a time but resurfaced in 2011 with further allegations from business mogul Donald Trump, jumpstarting his political career. In April of that year the Obama administration responded directly to these renewed allegations by distributing copies of his original birth certificate to members of the press and posting a scan of the "long form" certificate on the White House website. Although the conspiracy theory subsided again after Obama's second electoral victory, many still believed it to be true. An NBC poll late in 2016, for instance, indicated that more than 70 percent of the Republicans surveyed doubted Obama's citizenship, with less than 20 percent of Democrats sharing their doubt.[112]

That racism rather than concerns over "citizenship" fueled this controversy is made plain by the comparative handling of Obama's 2008 Republican opponent's citizenship question. John McCain had been born in the US-controlled Panama Canal Zone, a US territory within American jurisdiction but whose connection to the United States as a whole was legally ambiguous. Congress addressed this gray area in 1937 by granting citizenship to people (past and future) born in US territories to parents who were already US citizens. McCain had been born in 1936; was he eligible to run for president? He had been granted citizenship retroactively but was not, technically, a "natural born citizen." The issue was never pursued with much interest. McCain, an old, white veteran, looked the part of president; there seemed no need to question *his* qualifications.[113]

Republicans and conservatives, hitting similar themes as the Birther movement, pushed further "inquiries" into the very

Americanness of Obama. For instance, Mark Williams, in *Taking Back American One Tea Party at a Time*, painted Obama as a race-baiting cult leader bent on dividing and destroying the nation: "He pits race against race, class against class, Americans against America."[114] Republican politicians showed only slightly less disdain for this most un-American, divisive chief executive. Former governor John Sununu wished that Obama would "learn how to be American." Former House Speaker Newt Gingrich said "[Obama] is the most dangerous president in modern American history."[115] These opinions of the commentariat filtered down into everyday conversation. Comments on *New York Times* and *Wall Street Journal* articles covering the Birther controversy included the following three examples:

> If Obama didn't act like an alien, nobody would question his birth place. But he is so un-American in words and actions, people look for an explanation. The Birthers are just one group of questioners;
>
> It is clear that Obama does not meet the "spirit" of the requirement that a president be a natural born citizen. Hawaii is pretty far from mainland US, Kenya is farther still and Indonesia still further;
>
> I believe these rumors about Barack Obama not being from America are true. I mean, who in this country would name their child Barack Husane [sic] Obama. Remember Saddam Hussane [sic]. Coincidence?[116]

Certainly some of this reaction had its roots in pure partisanship, yet to an unquantifiable but nevertheless palpable degree, racism played an important role. Pat Buchanan, long a staple of conservative commentary, encapsulated the racist tinge of American conservatism as he lamented Obama's 2012 electoral victory, painting one race as inherently superior to another, heedless of historical reality:

Of course that's what I'm saying [that White America died with the 2012 Obama victory]. Isn't it obvious? Anything worth doing on this Earth was first done by white people. Who landed on the moon? White people. Who climbed Mount Everest? White people. Who invented the transistor? White people. Who invented paper? White people. Who discovered algebra? White people. And don't give me all this nonsense about Martin Luther King and civil rights and all that. Who do you think freed the slaves? Abraham Lincoln. A white guy! But we're not led by Lincoln anymore, we're led by an affirmative-action mulatto who can't physically understand how great America once was. I cried last night...I cried for hours. It's over for all of us. The great White nation will never survive another four years of Obama's leadership...Of course I agree with half of what he does. He's half white! That's not the half I'm worried about.[117]

When not accusing Obama of being a foreigner or a faux-American, conservatives accused him of winning the presidency because he was an African American, nothing more. Said Rush Limbaugh (the second highest-paid radio host in America with perhaps 15 million listeners[118]) in 2010:

[Obama] wouldn't have been voted president if he weren't black. Somebody asked me over the weekend why does somebody earn a lot of money have a lot of money, because she's black. It was Oprah. No, it can't be. Yes, it is. There's a lot of guilt out there, show we're not racists, we'll make this person wealthy and big and famous and so forth...If Obama weren't black he'd be a tour guide in Honolulu or he'd be teaching Saul Alinsky constitutional law or lecturing on it in Chicago.[119]

By Obama's second term, the Republican Party seemed in large part to exist solely to thwart his agency. Their disparate wings – traditional conservatives, evangelicals, libertarians, Tea Partiers, and racial bigots – remained mostly united in the face of this singular point of political gravity, a black hole into which all of their effort was pulled. In the climate of political resistance, racist conspiracies, and vilification by talking heads and eager conservative authors, some resorted to more than words. Obama's life was threatened more than any other president. White terrorists targeted black people with increasing frequency. In addition to individual acts of wanton butchery (like Michael Dunn's murder of a 17-year-old student at a Florida gas station), in June 2015 Dylan Roof murdered nine black people as they worshiped within their Charleston, South Carolina church. Significance filled this act of terrorism, for to attack a black church was to attack the central institution of black America, the communal space wherein they historically have had the most control over their lives and bodies, wherein grievances were aired with candor, and prayers raised in the hope that a merciful God might see fit to deliver his worshipers from their plight.

Responding to the Charleston attack, Obama at first used more vigorous language, criticizing American society in terms rarely heard from presidential lips:

Perhaps this tragedy causes us to ask some tough questions about how we can permit so many of our children to live in poverty, or attend dilapidated schools, or grow up without prospects for a job or for a career. Perhaps it causes us to examine what we're doing to cause some of our children to hate...Maybe we now realize the way racial bias can infect us even when we don't realize it, so that we're guarding against not just racial slurs, but we're also guarding against the subtle impulse to call Johnny back for a job interview but not Jamal. So that we search our hearts when we consider laws to make it harder for some of our fellow citizens to vote...By recognizing our common humanity...treating every child as important...by [making] opportunity real for every American...we express God's grace.[120]

In subsequent speeches on race, however, Obama backed down somewhat. Instead of structural critique and an honest reckoning with racism, his audiences witnessed him falling back on well-worn themes like cops having dangerous jobs or focusing on early education as the primary answer to breaking the cycle of black poverty. Even so he did not back down entirely. Some speeches still managed mild criticism of America's racial status quo, and while no sweeping policy initiatives were introduced, Obama did begin accelerating the rate of presidential pardons for non-violent drug offenders, a belated recognition of the deep impact the War on Drugs has had on black people across the country. By the end of his second term Obama racked up 944 commutations in all, more than the past 11 presidents combined.[121]

4.2 Gay Rights

4.2.1 The Twentieth Century

For two thousand years homosexuality has been viewed as a sin in Western Christian countries. The Sin of Sodom, while more accurately characterized in the Bible as a lack of charity, was taken up by later Jewish commentators like Philo of Alexandria to have been sexual in nature, and Christians who followed in this intellectual wake linked that Biblical episode with the expression of same-sex love. "Sodomy" thus became synonymous with homosexual practices and thousands of men (and women, when lesbianism came on the radar periodically) were burned or otherwise killed or driven into hiding as a result.[122]

This cultural hostility is not inevitable or universal to the human experience. Depending on the city state, the ancient Greeks lauded same-sex relationships (as in the Sacred Band of elite Theban warriors), winked at them, or merely tolerated them. In Rome, homosexuality was not encouraged, but so long as a man was not on the receiving end of a dalliance, his reputation remained intact. Medieval and early modern Japan saw a long tradition of acquiescence, acceptance, and even encouragement at times. Two thousand years of Chinese history evinced (from a Western perspective) an astounding level of homosexual acceptance. Medieval Islam, perhaps surprisingly given some of the modern rhetoric, also often took a more relaxed approach to homosexuality.[123] There was an understanding in these societies, more so than in Christendom, that sexuality is about more than procreation merely, but about forging relationships between people, that it constitutes one facet of the myriad ways by which people relate to, bond with, and live among each other.

By the early twentieth century, homosexuality in America was still seen morally as a sin, but now also medically as a disease or pathology. The consensus medical view considered homosexuals sick or maldeveloped in some way. Doctors thus needed to find a way to cure them. Psychoanalysts tried intensive therapy of long duration in order to root out the childhood traumas that they thought distorted normal sexual development; psychiatrists attempted behaviorally to condition homosexual patients into a revulsion against their predilections, using electric shock or nausea-inducing drugs; later practitioners added social training components to this conversion therapy, providing assertiveness training and tips for asking women out. Investigators claimed success rates of better than 50 percent, although later studies suggested that even when homosexual inclinations were suppressed, conversion therapy did little to promote an alternative orientation.[124] Some in the medical community were less severe in their diagnoses. Famously, Sigismund Freud late in life wrote to a mother concerned that her child's sexuality was "inverted": "Homosexuality is assuredly no advantage, but it is nothing to be ashamed of, no vice, no degradation; it cannot be classified as an illness..."[125] This position remained marginal into the 1970s.

Laws reflected these beliefs, and "sodomy" was illegal in most states. Homosexuals were barred from government jobs due to the belief that they were more susceptible to blackmail or were otherwise morally corrupt – and this belief played into the paranoia of post-World War II America. In 1947 president Truman issued an executive order inaugurating an investigation into possible homosexuality within the State Department. By November 1950 at least 500 federal employees stationed across the country were fired or forced to resign; a simultaneous Senate subcommittee investigation into homosexuality found it to be a profound security risk, weakening the moral fiber and making one more easily susceptible to foreign agents.[126]

Homosexuals found great difficulty in uniting against this oppression. Being a rather disparate classification, comprised of people from various economic classes and racial backgrounds, the movement for homosexual rights was fraught with internal division almost from the start. What united gays and lesbians was their common enemy, nothing more.[127] This lack of internal cohesion would do much to trammel the fight for gay liberation up through the early 1990s.

The Mattachine society was formed in the 1950s and became one of the first organizations to push for mainstream acceptance of homosexuality. They focused their efforts on court cases against the Civil Service Commission, which at the time worked hard to snuff out possible homosexuals from its ranks. The military was also a target of homophile litigation, and the 1960s, 1970s, and 1980s saw several long, drawn out legal battles with various levels of success.

In the mainstream narrative of homosexual liberation, 1969 is seen as the pivotal year, for it was in the summer of that year that queer denizens of a local bar (the Stonewall) pushed back against a raid by vice cops and, after 3 nights of riots, made the first major dent in the taboo against homosexuality. Little attention was given to the Stonewall Riots by the mainstream press outside New York City, but homosexuals across the country came to see it as a beacon of hope that further resistance to injustice would meet with victory.[128]

From there, the 1970s saw the more visible presence of homosexuals protesting laws that unjustly targeted them for engaging in consensual acts that harmed no one. It was during this time that, in addition to the "suits" (lawyers, lobbyists, politicians) agitating for political reform and legal redress, the "streets" (direct activists) inaugurated a strategy of "zapping" recalcitrant public figures. These activists humiliated or embarrassed countless local officials, mayors, even Catholic clergymen in japes and protests.[129]

Conservative resistance soon coalesced around the singer Anita Bryant, who campaigned vigorously against homosexuality and the specific inclusion in local ordinances of legal protections for homosexuals. Her campaigning platformed and funded politicians and policies devoted to rolling back any progress in the struggle for gay liberation. Thanks in part to her efforts, civil ordinances defending homosexuals were repealed in Miami and Saint Paul. A Cincinnati ordinance extending "human rights" protections to the elderly and handicapped almost failed because it included protections for homosexuals – and the offensive sections were eventually excised in order to achieve passage.[130] These defeats pumped new energy into a faltering gay liberation movement, and Anita Bryant became the "devil" that helped unite many a disparate activist. She found her performances protested by militant gays and lesbians determined to end her career, which in large part they were successful in doing.[131]

At first activists invested too much energy into Bryant specifically; eventually they broadened their gaze and, with the help of more mainstream political figures like San Francisco's Harvey Milk, successfully defeated Proposition 6 in California, a proposed ban on homosexual teachers. Said one pastor during a debate on the matter, "Well, let me put it this way. I think Hitler was right about the homosexuals. I think we should find a humane way to kill them."[132] Language like that reinforced for the homosexual community the high stakes of this propositional fight and the doom planned for them should their conservative opponents gain too much political power.

The 1980s bludgeoned the optimism within the gay community that had been building throughout the 1970s. The AIDS virus, which had slowly been worming its way from Africa to the United States, took a brutal toll on gay men, as one method of its spreading was through sexual contact, prolific in a gay community that, fearful of discovery and barred from more conventionally monogamous relationships suiting their orientation, had turned to higher numbers of shorter affairs. Globally the majority of AIDS patients contracted the disease from heterosexual sex (67 percent of AIDS patients live in Sub-Saharan Africa, where heterosexual intercourse remains the driving factor in disease transmission), but in the United States the peculiar social circumstances of gay men made them especially vulnerable to the disease.[133] Thus in the public imagination AIDS became a gay plague.

The virus struck many gay men seemingly out of nowhere, health to horror in an instant. Fair weather family and friends deserted those with the disease. Hospital staff treated people with AIDS as pariahs. Patients often sat for days in emergency rooms. If they were finally admitted, orderlies would let them lie in their own shit and piss, too frightened to enter the room. Food trays piled up in the hallways. After death, a patient would be put in a black trash bag, but funeral parlors refused to handle the dead.[134]

Reacting to this gay plague, paleoconservative Pat Buchanan wrote in his newspaper column that AIDS was a sign that, "Nature is exacting retribution"; not only were homosexuals a "moral menace," they were a "public health menace," too. Buchanan reported that policemen were so worried about getting AIDS and bringing it home to their families that they wore masks and gloves when dealing with homosexual lawbreakers; he claimed that landlords were so worried about the spread of AIDS on their properties that they evicted infected homosexual tenets. Homosexual moral depravity also spread other diseases like hepatitis. He concluded from all this that homosexuals must not be allowed to work in restaurants or any job in which they handled food and that gay rights were a danger to heterosexual life.[135]

A vigorous federal response could have studied the virus, compiled information, and allayed a misinformed and panicked public about the realities of the situation. Neoliberalism, tying good public policy with good business and nothing more, could not countenance such an effort of government "intervention" in the healthcare market, nor could social conservatism be charitable to nontraditional human interaction. In 1984, with Ronald Reagan running for reelection, he told a group that kept tally of a "presidential Biblical scorecard" that his administration would continue to resist all attempts to "obtain any government endorsement of homosexuality."[136] Without saying it outright, this ban included federal support for AIDS patients. Neoliberalism combined with Evangelicalism to bring federal reaction to AIDS to a near standstill.

Arkansas provided an illuminating instance of the fear engendered by the AIDS epidemic, the lengths to which family members often went to ostracize their gay relatives, and, thankfully, the charity with which some Christians still act. While caring for a friend with cancer, then 25-year-old Ruth Burks, as she says 30 years later moved by a higher power, found herself compelled to enter a nearby door emblazoned with red. Inside she found a young man, less than 100 pounds, ignored by hospital staff and consigned to die alone. He pleaded with her that he wanted to see his mother again before he died; compelled by the inaction of the hospital staff, Burks called the young man's mother, but the woman absolutely refused to visit her son. She returned to the young man's room to find him delusional. He thought she was his mother, and she spent the last 13 hours of this young man's life at his side.

By a quirk of fate, Burks had inherited a cemetery of 262 plots. After confirming that the young man's mother did not want his remains, she had him cremated and interred at her cemetery, where her own relatives were buried. Over the course of the next several years, as word spread among the local gay community that they had an ally in this young woman, Burks would come to bury over 40 men whose families had abandoned them. As the local priests and preachers refused to assist her, Burks recited the funeral rites herself.

In addition to last rites and burial, Burks provided many AIDS patients with assistance in getting medication, navigating medical bureaucracy, paying rent, all with the financial assistance of local gay clubs, notably the Discovery club in Little Rock. "They would twirl up a drag show on Saturday night and here'd come the money. That's how we'd buy medicine, that's how we'd pay rent. If it hadn't been for the drag queens, I don't know what we would have done," recalled Burks.[137] This kind of local activism and solidarity could have been augmented by a more general government response. Without broader organizational effort backed by tax dollars, too many were left to the vicissitudes of fate and the random kindness of strangers.

Such external assistance as that provided by Ruth Burks was anomalous, meaning gays had to make do with their own often meager resources. The Gay Men's Health Crisis formed to try and aide those afflicted in New York City. AIDS Project LA and similar organizations in San Francisco mirrored these efforts. Lesbians, many of whom had considered their struggle separate from that of gay men, showed increasing solidarity; lesbian blood poured into donation centers (gay men were forbidden from donating), and lesbian charity succored many a lonely, dying AIDS patient.[138]

To this medical crisis, social isolation, and political disenfranchisement came legal defeat as well. In 1986, *Bowers v. Hardwick* went to the Supreme Court. Michael Hardwick had been caught by police (in his own home) having oral sex with another man, and in Georgia oral sex was considered "sodomy," and against the law. The majority of the Supreme Court justices, their poor opinion of gays bolstered by the popular perception of AIDS, upheld the right of states to continue outlawing homosexual sex. Chief justice Warren Burger (citing the eighteenth-century British jurist William Blackstone) went so far as to deem sodomy "a crime not fit to be named...the infamous crime against nature."[139]

The next year, 600,000 gay and lesbian people from across the country gathered in protest at the nation's capital. By that point more than 41,000 people had already died of the disease. A cure had yet to be found and federal efforts remained minimal. At sunrise on the day of the march, an AIDS quilt was unfurled at the Washington Mall – thousands of handmade panels, each in memory of a contemporary leper and carrying an embroidered message such as, "Dear God, I pray that soon this plague, too, shall pass. Be with us and those departed. Amen." Volunteers read the names of the dead aloud to the teeming and tear-laden crowd.[140]

Around this time, with mainstream avenues failing the gay community, several of its members formed ACT-UP to take matters into their own hands, zap officials, and spur federal action against AIDS. They invaded churches and television stations and tied up traffic, working to shake loose the cobwebs of indifference among the political class. A smaller team of ACT-UP-ers banded together to learn everything they could about AIDS treatment. The group included a film historian, a Harvard graduate who had wanted to be a writer but became a full-time AIDS activist instead, a theater arts major at Bennington who dropped out for AIDS activism, an ex-Wall Street bond trader, and a retired organic chemist who had studied the major AIDS drug AZT when it was being (unsuccessfully) tried on cancer patients. They called themselves the Treatment and Data Committee of ACT-UP.[141]

In 1990, ACT-UP gained the attention of Dr. Anthony Fauci at the National Institute of Health (NIH). They successfully convinced him that they knew what they were talking about and that more urgency was required of federal scientists and officials. The partnership between NIH and ACT-UP drastically altered how experimental drugs were handled, creating an Accelerated Approval process and more inclusion of activists from those communities affected by NIH policies. Big Pharma was also pressured via zaps to lower the prices of some of their anti-AIDS medications; AZT, for example, saw its price reduced from $8-10,000 a year down to $6400 as a result of a zap on Wall Street.

Before the plague was controlled, it killed millions worldwide and decimated gay America: by 1992 nearly 200,000 Americans had perished; this number would surpass 300,000 by 1995, 400,000 by 1998, and 500,000 by 2003 – more than the 400,000 Americans dead as a result of World War II, and dwarfed by the 20,000,000 AIDS deaths across the world as of 2001.[142] (Compare these numbers to those Americans killed by the Opioid Crisis so far, 400,000, and by the Global War on Terror, 17,000.)

The epidemic forced organizations such as the National Gay and Lesbian Task Force and the National Gay Rights Advocates to shift their focus away from civil rights and toward survival. Yet the plague also brought some unexpected dividends to the gay community. Gay men stared their mortality in the face, concluded that they had little to lose, that silence equaled death, and leapt collectively out of the closet. Many more were shoved out of the closet when they were discovered to have the disease. This mass coming out forced many a heterosexual to confront the sudden fact that a friend, family member, or other close associate was also a homosexual, and did much to begin the process of denuding homosexuality of its marginal social character. It also reunited many lesbian and gay activists that had wound separate struggles over the previous decade or more, concentrating political efforts in the years ahead.[143]

This increase in mainstream cache (and its limitations) was evident as early as 1992. Clinton courted homosexual voters and promised to allow gays to serve in the military, but in the face of severe conservative backlash, especially from the Joint Chiefs, he compromised with "Don't Ask, Don't Tell," a slightly less intrusive policy that still allowed any soldier to "tell" on their fellow, should homosexuality be suspected. Clinton's support for the homosexual community, such as it was, proved no shield against further homophobic legislation. The 1990s ended with the passage of the federal Defense of Marriage Act (DOMA) that precluded homosexuals from gaining many of the legal privileges that accompanied marriage. On the other hand all remaining US sodomy laws were repealed in a 2003 SCOTUS case. With each victory and defeat the fight continued.

4.2.2 The Obama Years

When it came to gay rights Obama emulated the campaign tactics of FDR and tried to please everyone all at once while remaining noncommittal on the level of policy. To that end he did not endorse gay marriage during the 2008 campaign. These efforts to balance the interests of the marginalized against those with power resulted, as they so often do, in bolstering the powerful at the expense of the marginal. Thus, as the campaign wore on Obama's rhetoric appealed more and more to the sexual status quo. His campaign tapped reverend McClurkin, an anti-gay black preacher, for a campaign event, which caused some degree of controversy.[144] He appeared at pastor Rick Warren's Saddleback Church in California trying to court evangelical voters; there he said, "I believe that marriage is the union between a man and a woman. Now, for me as a Christian...For me as a Christian, it's also a sacred union. Ya know, God's in the mix."[145]

Obama's ambivalence split gay voters in the Democratic primary. Those who favored Obama focused on Bill Clinton's record (compromising with DADT and signing DOMA into law) and Hillary's limited critique of the Defense of Marriage Act. Those who supported Hillary Clinton thought her desire to repeal only Section III of DOMA (preventing the federal government from recognizing same-sex unions) to be more politically realistic, since that would open the door to the compromise solution of "civil unions" for same-sex couples. Obama also supported civil unions, and most LGBT Americans seemed to accept the notion that the country was not yet ready to elect a candidate that supported same-sex marriage. For many, however, civil unions would not suffice; even if not the most important issue for many LGBTs, they recognized marriage as an institution through which society imbued certain relationships with legitimacy and legal privilege. Each candidate in their own way was thus a mixed bag at best.[146]

Obama's subsequent victory gained no immediate spoils for the gay community. John Berry's appointment to head the Office of Personnel Management (OPM) came the closest. OPM, formerly the US Civil Service Commission, was once responsible for scrubbing gays from the federal government. Now a gay man helmed the institution. Insiders cheered this progress while those further afield chafed at the lack of concrete policy action.[147] This meager progress, however, failed to counterbalance other initiatives of the young administration. It became known in June 2009 that the Obama Justice Department was in fact actively defending DOMA against legal challenge, and many in the gay community began to worry that they did not have a real ally in the White House. Responding to Obama's insufficient record thus far, LGBT activists marched on Washington in October 2009, trying to pressure Obama into further action.

Progress quickened in his second year. Internally, the Obama administration determined that DADT needed to come to an end, but, looking back on Clinton's mistakes that had led to DADT in the first place, did not wish to do so without the military's cooperation. In January, Obama made this policy shift public during his State of the Union. While defense secretary Gates felt "blindsided" by this announcement (perhaps done hastily in an effort to stay ahead of leaks), the president quickly worked to cooperate with Gates and the military, which meant going along with Gates' plan to survey opinion within the armed forces regarding the effect openly-serving homosexuals might have on combat effectiveness and morale. Preliminary survey results from September 2010 were positive – with only 30 percent of troops surveyed in opposition – but Gates was determined to complete this project before presenting a policy recommendation.[148]

Admiral Mike Mullen, chairman of the Joint Chiefs, pushed things along in February when he fully endorsed ending DADT:

Speaking for myself and myself only, it is my personal belief that allowing gays and lesbians to serve openly would be the right thing to do. No matter how I look at the issue, I cannot escape being troubled by the fact that we have in place a policy which forces young men and women to lie about who they are in order to defend their fellow citizens. For me personally it comes down to integrity – theirs as individuals and ours as an institution.[149]

Gates' survey was scheduled for release on December 1, 2010 – at the very end of the lame duck session of a Congress that was about to crimson itself with members of the Grand Old Party come the new year. This left very little time for Democrats to act on DADT once the results of the study were released. President Obama made no effort to hasten its completion, yielding the initiative entirely to the Department of Defense. Given the power of the Pentagon lobby, the administration had bargained that if they could not get military buy-in, they would never be able to get the votes for repeal.

The final month of the lame duck congressional session was an ambitious one, with tax cuts, the START nuclear arms reduction treaty with Russia, and DADT all on the agenda. On December 9, a defense reauthorization bill with DADT repeal tacked on failed in the Senate 57-40; senator Lieberman, the Senate champion of the repeal effort, remained undaunted, thinking that perhaps if he coupled DADT repeal with tax cuts he might be able to entice a few more senators to vote his way. When the House passed a standalone repeal bill, further pressure was placed on the Senate to act. The budget bill (tax cuts and all) went down in flames, which had the unintended benefit of leaving a sliver of time in which to pass DADT repeal. Finally, on December 18, 2010, the Senate voted 66-33 for cloture on the repeal bill, allowing it to go to a general vote where it passed 65-31.[150]

In a December 21, 2010 interview, Obama said of this legislative victory: "This is one of those issues where you know individual people directly that are going to be impacted and you know it helps shift attitudes in a direction of greater fairness over the long term. I think when people look back 20 years from now, they'll say this [DADT repeal] was one of the more important things I've gotten done since I've been president."[151]

The administration made other progressive moves as well. On April 15, 2010, Obama announced expanded federal benefits for homosexuals. Hospital visitation rights now became available to same-sex couples in any hospital that took Medicare or Medicaid. As the year came to a close, Obama signaled that he was *evolving* on the question of gay marriage, while still reiterating his strong support of civil unions. In October he said, "But I also think you're right that attitudes evolve, including mine. And I think that it is an issue that I wrestle with and think about because I have a whole host of friends who are in gay partnerships."[152]

By this point, Obama's Justice Department had also curtailed its courtroom defense of the Clinton-era Defense of Marriage Act. In attorney general Eric Holder's letter informing Congress that the Justice Department would no longer defend the law, he made the case for using a higher standard of review. "The President and I have concluded that classifications based on sexual orientation warrant heightened scrutiny and that, as applied to same-sex couples legally married under state law, Section 3 of DOMA is unconstitutional."[153]

As the 2012 election approached, the question arose: would Obama openly endorse gay marriage? Some thought such an endorsement political suicide; it would alienate independent voters and religious black voters. This logic was hard to shake, as it arose from the very public political drubbing LGBT Americans had been subject to over the past decade. In Washington, even at the beginning of 2011, conventional wisdom still viewed homosexuality as a political liability on the national level. DADT repeal was viewed as both a miracle and a fluke by many Washington political operatives.[154]

Polls, however, shifted amid this conventional political wisdom. By 2012, 65 percent of Democrats and 51 percent of Independents supported same-sex marriage (up from 50 and 44 percent in 2008).[155] Obama and his advisors had watched and waited as this trend played itself out, rather than working to accelerate its pace. While they led the vigorous defense of Wall Street and haphazardly championed a modicum of healthcare reform, other progressive causes like gay marriage met with little presidential leadership, as the deferential effort to end DADT makes plain. Lack of real progressive action on LGBT issues was one member among a growing chorus of Progressive concern: why had Wall Street received trillions while millions of families faced foreclosure and unemployment, why had the public option been excised from reform legislation, why did the military's budget continue to predominate federal priorities? As these questions grew louder, they drowned out memories of the inspired rhetoric of 2008, and Obama's authenticity suffered as a result.

Obama attempted to regain the political initiative by bypassing Congress. In April 2012, he announced his We Can't Wait campaign in which he promised to turn to executive orders to circumvent congressional deadlock that had long stifled his legislative goals. Billions were given to startups, the FDA directed to work on preventing drug shortages, the EPA to set its sights on higher mpg standards for new cars and light trucks, etc. And yet the presidential pen remained dormant concerning protections for the LGBT community.[156]

Seeking to defend the administration's LGBT record, Joe Biden went on *Meet the Press* on May 4, 2012 to do damage control. When asked if he was comfortable with same-sex marriage, Biden said, "I am absolutely comfortable with the fact that men marrying men, women marrying women, and heterosexual men marrying women are entitled to the same exact rights. All the civil rights, all the civil liberties." Biden then rambled for a while but eventually came back to emphasizing the love felt in same-sex relationships. The White House press corps worked to reiterate that Biden had not actually endorsed same-sex marriage as such; then, a few days later, secretary of education Arne Duncan said he supported gay marriage on *Morning Joe* on MSNBC, and it became increasingly clear that Obama was surrounded by people ahead of him on this issue.[157]

Obama's evolution continued. On May 9, in an ABC interview, the president said:

When I think about members of my own staff who are

incredibly committed, in monogamous relationships, same-sex relationships, who are raising kids together. When I think about those soldiers or airmen or marines or sailors – who are out there fighting on my behalf – and yet, feel constrained, even now that "don't ask, don't tell" is gone because they're not able to commit themselves in a marriage. At a certain point, I've just concluded that – for me personally, it is important for me to go ahead and affirm that – I think same-sex couples should be able to get married.[158]

His evolution now complete, Obama declared his change of stance at the 2012 Democratic National Convention: "We, the people, declare today that the most evident of truths – that all of us are created equal – is the star that guides us still; just as it guided our forebears through Seneca Falls, and Selma, and Stonewall. It is now our generation's task to carry on what those pioneers began. [Our journey as a nation will not be complete] until our gay brothers and sisters are treated like anyone else under the law – for if we are truly created equal, then surely the love we commit to one another must be equal as well."[159] As it turned out, this endorsement did not cost Obama the election.

His second term added to the list of executive orders defending the legal equality of homosexuals. In July of 2014, Obama issued an executive order that prohibited federal contractors from discriminating against LGBT employees. The president also strengthened protections for transgender workers in the federal government via executive order in his second term, an action that built upon his 2010 addition of transgender workers to the federal government's Equal Employment Opportunity policies (see also section 4.3.3).[160]

Outside the executive branch a legal battle was under way. On August 4, 2010, California federal judge Vaughn Walker ruled against the validity of Proposition 8, which had defined California marriage in purely heterosexual terms. Walker drew heavily from Supreme Court justice Kennedy's opinions in *Romer v. Evans* (1996, annulling a state ban on protective language specific to homosexuality and bisexuality) and *Lawrence v. Texas* (2003, rendering unconstitutional all bans on homosexual activity between consenting adults). California was but one example of an escalating clash at the state level over the definition of marriage. Indeed, by 2013 nine states plus the District of Columbia had legalized same-sex marriage.

Federally, the 2012 Supreme Court case *Windsor v. United States* overturned a critical section of the Defense of Marriage Act and unleashed a domino effect of court rulings in its wake. The number of states that legalized gay marriage grew to 36 by 2015. The final nail in the coffin of hetero-dominated marriage came in a second Supreme Court case, 2015's *Obergefell v. Hodges*. President Obama's Justice Department had by this point fully supported the legal effort to defend same-sex marriage and filed a "friend of the court" brief arguing for the right of same-sex couples to marry in all 50 states. The decision in *Obergefell*, issued on June 26, 2015, struck down gay marriage bans nationwide.[161] Wrote justice Kennedy for the majority of the court:

As some of the petitioners in these cases demonstrate, marriage embodies a love that may endure even past death. It would misunderstand these men and women to say they disrespect the idea of marriage. Their plea is that they do respect it, respect it so deeply that they seek to find its fulfillment for themselves. Their hope is not to be condemned to live in loneliness, excluded from one of civilization's oldest institutions. They ask for equal dignity in the eyes of the law. The Constitution grants them that right.[162]

Conservative opinion came out firmly against the Supreme Court decision. David French at *National Review* bemoaned the triumph of mushy feelings over solid constitutional scholarship, which he saw as opening up rhetorical and religious liberty to subsequent attack by this "secular theology of self-actualization" by making well-meaning Christians vulnerable to giving up their ideals in the quest to be seen as "the 'nicest' or 'most loving' people in their communities."[163] 2016 presidential hopefuls waffled between disagreeing with the decision but promising to "abide by the law" (Jeb Bush, Marco Rubio) to prophesying a coming assault on "religious liberty" (Bobby Jindal).[164]

This emphasis on religious liberty framed much of the subsequent conservative rhetoric and reaction to the legal gains made by mainstream homosexuals. The countermovement, spearheaded by the Family Research Council and other groups of the Religious Right, sought to impose limitations on the "sexual radicals" they saw as running rampant across the American political and legal landscape. Such efforts had been building for years. In the 1990s Congress sought to clarify the constitutional protections concerning religion by passing the Religious Freedom Restoration Act (RFRA). The law stated that the government "should not substantially burden religious exercise without compelling justification," only doing so if it furthers a compelling governmental interest in the least restrictive way possible. While not problematic in itself, the law was made so by the 2014 US Supreme Court decision in *Burwell v. Hobby Lobby*. By treating two private corporations – Hobby Lobby and Conestoga Wood Specialties – like individuals with the right to the free exercise of religion, the ruling allowed the religious beliefs of the company owners to override those of their employees.[165] In the wake of the *Hobby Lobby* and *Obergefell* decisions, social conservatives moved their campaign for religious freedom into high gear. The Family Research Council claimed after *Obergefell* that radicals had declared war on "[Y]our values. Your family. Your religious beliefs and freedom." They responded with a legislative strategy, which they characterized as: "a 'Government Nondiscrimination Act' that can be customized to every state. After the Supreme Court's ruling this summer, the pressure to approve of same-sex marriage is bearing down on every Christian. The Government Nondiscrimination Act would bar state governments from penalizing individuals and entities for their moral or religious beliefs that marriage is the union of one man and one woman."[166]

Religious Freedom bills predated this recommendation, but picked up steam in 2016. Such bills sought to bring the Supreme Court's interpretation of religious freedom down to the state level, thus allowing businesses run by conservative Christians the ability to discriminate against LGBT applicants and employees who did not meet their "religious" values heedless of existing state laws to the contrary. Hundreds of such bills were introduced in state legislatures across the country in 2015 and 2016. One example came in March 2016 when then-governor Mike Pence signed Indiana Senate Bill 101 (the Religious Freedom Restoration Act) into law; according to the state government's website the bill attempts to protect the "exercise of religion" except in cases where the government can prove that barring a religious practice furthers a "compelling government interest" and that said restriction is the "least restrictive means" of furthering that government interest. The law also prohibits "an applicant, employee, or former employee from pursuing certain causes of action against a private employer," meaning that, should an employer choose to discriminate based on religious grounds – by firing a gay man, for instance – the employee may have no legal recourse.[167]

While the conservative interpretation of the RFRA has been used by the Trump administration to roll back many of Obama's executive orders upholding the legal equality of LGBT Americans, same-sex marriage has enjoyed continued mainstream acceptance. Thousands of marriages have been issued since full legalization – bringing with them a level of civic buy-in that would be hard for state and local governments to reverse. Moreover, the long-standing trend toward acceptance of same-sex marriage has continued: Pew Research indicated that support rose from 55 percent in 2015 to 62 percent in 2017, with a shrinking minority (32 percent) of Americans opposing gay marriage as of 2017.[168]

On the other end of the political spectrum, progressives and leftists questioned the unalloyed nature of this kind of mainstream progress. Homosexuals could now serve in the US military without hindrance; but what good did serving the imperialist war machine do for those so recently marginalized? Same-sex marriage had been legalized; but how often was monogamy merely a societal imposition that reinforced existing relations of power, precluding individual freedom or other kinds of communities from forming? After all, marriage imposes a certain distribution of public and private wealth. Law professor Ruthann Robson noted: "A regime of marriage allows the state to privatize problems of economic and other inequalities: the solution to a person not having medical care, for example, is not a government policy of universal health care but the individual becoming married to someone whose employer provides good health insurance."[169] It seemed to these critics, therefore, that this much-touted progress, while it made the lives of some marginalized people easier, left the oppressive systems of control – legal, military, political, economic – very much in place.

4.3 Transpeople and Their Emergence into the Mainstream

4.3.1 Preliminary Considerations

Language is always in flux – words come and go, change meaning within different political, legal, social, and economic contexts; this is especially true when a new concept invades a hitherto comfortable or established realm of the intellectual life. Consider, for instance, the drastic change in the use of existing language as the Roman Empire shifted from a pagan culture to one dominated by Christianity. *Ecclesia,* which had denoted the Athenian general assembly of citizens that busied itself with political concerns, morphed into the dual notion of a local Christian community and the Church Universal; the Christian clergy took its name from *Kleros,* which had carried with it a technical judicial meaning related to an allotted share of an inherited estate – which Christians modified to reference the portion of the Christian community God had allotted to himself to be used specifically as his professional clergy.[170] The recently popularized discussion of transpeople, and its attendant linguistic difficulties, are merely another example of the thorny process of accommodating existing language to new concepts. In order to make discussion of this topic easier, a preliminary understanding of some key terms is necessary.

Sex: In the popular imagination genitals constitute biological sex; some writers include chromosomes and secondary characteristics as well. To a biologist, however, the definition of sex comes down solely to gametes: *"'male' means making small gametes, and 'female' means making large gametes.* Period! By definition, the smaller of the two gametes is called a sperm, and the larger an egg. Beyond gamete size, biologists don't recognize any other universal difference between male and female."[171] Indirect markers of gamete size exist in some species. Male mammals, for instance, usually have a Y chromosome. Still, whether an individual is male or not comes down to making sperm, and even some mammalian sperm makers lack a Y chromosome. In birds, reptiles, and amphibians the Y chromosome does not occur. Amid all of nature's diversity, the gamete-size-based definition is as close to universal as biological science can provide.

Intersex: This is estimated to affect 1 in 2000 people and describes those who fall outside the typical binary of human development, whether as a result of chromosomes combining in uncommon ways (such as XXY or XO), glandular conditions shifting development while in the womb or after birth, or certain genetic anomalies. Sometimes these have the effect of producing a body that is genetically XY (typically male) to look typically female at birth. Some bodies are born with genitals that look like a mixture of typically male and typically female shapes. Some genetically female bodies (typically XX) are born without vaginas, wombs, or ovaries.[172] It is necessary to recall the existence of intersex people because, historically, the medical profession has decided their gender expression for them, imposing from the outside a set of social assumptions, for instance that all people should be either men capable of injecting seed or women capable of bearing offspring.

Gender: This is a term still very much under construction, the field of gender theory being still in its infancy. In the previous century people often conflated gender and sex; today we commonly associate sex with biology and gender with behavior that expresses biological reality: hence we use the words *man* and *woman* to refer to gender just as *male* and *female* are used to refer to sex. Even in the commonly accepted understanding, therefore, we are born one or the other sex but are not born a certain gender, a certain set of cultural markers that indicate biological sex. Gender could therefore be thought of as the social organization of bodies into different categories of people.

In the contemporary United States, this sorting into categories is based on sex. For instance, a biologist might define gender as: "*the appearance, behavior, and life history of a sexed body*. A body becomes 'sexed' when classified with respect to the size of the gametes produced. Thus, gender is appearance plus action, how an organism uses morphology, including color and shape, plus behavior to carry out a sexual role."[173]

But historically and across cultures there have been various social systems of organizing people into genders not necessarily tied directly to biology. Cultures from areas in the Indian subcontinent and pre-Columbian America possessed more than two genders, defined in terms of the work people did rather than to the bodies that did that work. In Western antiquity eunuchs occupied a third gender role outside either biological men or biological women. Gender can therefore instead be thought of as historical, i.e. changing over time, varying from place to place and culture to culture; it can also be thought of as contingent, depending on many different and seemingly unrelated things coming together in a particular way.[174]

Not everything in human existence revolves around power relations, but much of social life is taken up by such considerations. Gender falls under this aegis, insofar as the activities allowed to people have been heavily controlled through the regulation of gender roles. Based on the presupposition that gender expression must conform rigidly to biological sex, elements of American society have sought to justify the segregation of men and women into distinct and rigid roles within a gendered hierarchy of power. The shorthand for this state of affairs is the Patriarchy, which refers to the conservative articulation of a Good Society as that in which, everyone being in their natural and fitting place, men lead in political and economic life, with women supporting them with a clean house, a good meal, and a disciplined progeny. Given the traditional justification for this state of affairs – which trammels individual choice, funnels freedom toward those few privileged with biological maleness and in so doing benefits some and subjugates others – a trans critique of sex and gender, building upon those critiques already levied against the Patriarchy made by feminist thinkers in the twentieth century, challenges the Political Order.

The trans emphasis on human diversity and variability is political precisely because it contradicts the belief that whether a person is a man or a woman in the social sense is fundamentally determined by a self-evident bodily sex, unambiguously perceived. The categorization of people has never been a politically neutral act; certain categories possess more wealth and more power than others, so who gets to do the sorting can be quite lucrative and self-serving.[175] This creation of gender, moreover, evinces the kind of nature-dominating ethos that has led Western civilization to the brink of climate collapse. Thus, in seeking to undermine this mindset, trans philosophy may prove critical in the fight against global warming (see also section 6.1.2).[176]

Transgender: This is a word of recent vintage, still under construction. In order to cover a wide basis, I use it here referring to people-in-movement: those detaching from the gender they were assigned at birth, transversing the constructed and constraining boundaries their culture uses to categorize them. Whether initiated because they feel strongly that they belong to another gender, because they want to strike out toward some new location, some new and undiscovered social space, or because they simply feel the need to challenge the conventional expectations bound up with the gender that was initially put upon them, it is this movement across a socially imposed boundary (and away from a place not of their choosing), that I want to emphasize, not a specific destination (e.g. from woman to man) or mode of transition (e.g. surgery).

This notion of transgender is in keeping with my personal view of human nature, which emphases evolution. Whether we concern ourselves with the course of all human biology, the developing modes of social interaction, or keep within the purview of a single lifetime, we can see clearly that adaptation to changing external and internal circumstance (a shifting climate, a mutated gene, the machinations of another nation, the loss of a first love) is a constant of human existence.

I am reminded of a quote from Karl Marx which encapsulates the role of individual choice within the milieu of unchosen historical circumstance: "Men make their own history, but they do not make it as they please; they do not make it under self-selected circumstances, but under circumstances existing already, given and transmitted from the past. The tradition of all dead generations weighs like a nightmare on the brains of the living."[177]

To sum up, sex is not tied to genitals, chromosomes, or secondary characteristics but rather to gamete size; the sexual binary of sperm-producing "man" and egg-producing "woman" is made insufficient by the mere existence of those, like the intersexed, who exist outside this system of categorization; gender need not be a social category tied to biological sex but rather can be thought of in broader terms like one's work or role in the community; and transpeople are seeking out identities within which they might find comfort and shelter amid circumstances not of their choosing. In their own way, they, like so many in the contemporary world, are looking for a home.

4.3.2 A Brief Survey of Trans American History

The first recorded European settler one could consider trans was Thomas / Thomasine Hall, an indentured servant in the Virginia colony in the 1620s, who claimed to be both a man and a woman and, at different times, adopted the traditional roles and clothing of men and women, changing their name accordingly. Unable to establish Hall's gender to their satisfaction, in spite of repeated physical examinations, and unsure of whether to punish them for wearing men's or women's clothing, local citizens asked the court at Jamestown to resolve the issue. The court split the difference, ordering Hall in 1629 to wear both a man's breeches and a woman's apron and cap, perhaps indicating Hall was in fact intersex and thus beyond the sexed binary conventional wisdom expected.[178]

Other examples of European stock abound. Deborah Sampson enlisted in the revolutionary army as a man. Joseph Lobdell, though christened Lucy Ann, in adulthood lived as a male author in New York circa 1800; he was reputed an excellent shot with a rifle, advocated for marriage reform, and for his trouble was deemed psychiatrically ill and incarcerated for the remainder of his life. During the Civil War, one Loreta Janeta Velazquez enlisted in the Confederate armed forces under the name Harry Buford.

Indirect evidence for the existence of transgressive Americans comes from laws against what we today would label "trans" behavior. Massachusetts passed an ordinance in the 1690s forbidding cross-dressing, the first known example in the Thirteen Colonies. We can surmise that the colonial legislators were reacting to behavior they did not condone, which presumes the existence of transpeople who acted thusly. In literature, *The Knickerbocker* published "The Man Who Thought Himself a Woman," a short story, in 1857, evincing further indirect evidence for such behavior.[179]

Contrasting with European American society, many Indigenous communities fostered transpeople in their midst. Spanish conquistador Cabeza de Vaca recorded one of the earliest known descriptions of non-binary genders in an Indigenous society. Writing in the 1530s, he described the Coahuiltecan people in modern-day Texas as including "effeminate, impotent men" who were married to other men and, "go about covered-up like women [doing] the work of women, and [yet drawing] the bow and [carrying a] very heavy load."[180] European conquistadors, explorers, missionaries, or traders, whose worldviews were shaped by Christian doctrines espousing adherence to strict gender roles and condemning any expressions of sexuality outside of married male-female relationships, penned the majority of these accounts. Their reactions to instances of non-binary genders thus erred toward incredulity, dismay, disgust, and sometimes violence.

In an example of the kind of anti-trans violence we still see today, Vasco Núñez de Balboa, trekking across the Isthmus of Panama in 1513, set his troop's dogs on 40 members of the

Cuevas people for being "sodomites," as they had assumed the roles of women. Another conquistador, Nuño de Guzmán, while traveling through Mexico in the 1530s, burned to death a male-assigned individual who presented as female because he considered the person to be a male prostitute.[181]

The ways that the Indigenous societies that accepted gender diversity characterized non-binary genders varied culturally and temporally. Male- and female-assigned individuals who assumed different genders in most of these cultures were not considered to be women or men. Instead, they constituted separate genders that combined female and male elements. This fact is reflected in the words that Indigenous communities developed to describe these additional genders. The terms for male-assigned individuals who took on female roles used by the Cheyenne (*heemaneh*), the Ojibwa (*agokwa*), and the Yuki (*i-wa-musp*) translate as "half men, half women" or "men-women." Other groups referred to male-assigned individuals who "dress as a woman," "act like a woman," "imitate a woman," or were a "would-be woman." Similarly, the Zuni called a female-assigned individual who took on male roles a *katsotse*, or "boy-girl."[182]

Limited data, especially regarding female-assigned individuals who presented as male, makes an exact count of Indigenous communities with additional gender roles difficult to tabulate, and scholars differ on what should count as gender diversity. Figures range from 113 Indigenous groups in North America that had female roles for male-assigned individuals and 30 that had male roles for female-assigned individuals to 131 and 63, respectively.[183]

We must resist the urge to over-generalize the transpeople within these Indigenous communities as holding positions of esteem. From the evidence available, most Native American societies in which they have been known to exist accepted transpeople, but the details differed with the community. Some

Indigenous cultures considered them to possess supernatural powers and afforded them special ceremonial roles; in other cultures, they were less revered and viewed more secularly. In these societies, the status of individuals who assumed different genders seems to have reflected their gender role, rather than a special gender status. If women predominated in particular occupations, such as being healers, shamans, and handcrafters, then male-assigned individuals who took on female roles engaged in the same professions. In a similar way, the female-assigned individuals who took on male roles became hunters and warriors. A few communities denigrated or openly despised their trans members, as for instance among certain communities within the Incan Empire where male-assigned individuals presenting as female were forced to be the sexual subordinates of local lords.[184]

Without comparable institutional roles in their own societies, Europeans labeled the aspects that seemed familiar to them: male-assigned individuals engaged in same-sex sexual behavior they called "sodomites"; individuals that combined male and female elements they termed "hermaphrodites." Anthropologists and historians in the twentieth century continued this tradition, interpreting these individuals as "homosexuals" or "transvestites," or as "berdaches," a French adaptation of the Arabic word for a male prostitute or a young male slave used for sexual purposes.[185] Indigenous transpeople, like their counterparts in communities of European ancestry, were not grappled with on their own terms.

After the Civil War, incidences of documented transpeople increased drastically in response to the social upheaval of the Second Industrial Revolution. Urban dwelling skyrocketed, families broke apart or moved to find work in factories, and traditional mores, even regarding gender, felt the strain of economic change. Able to take advantage of the anonymity afforded by new surroundings, these migrants had greater opportunities to fashion their own lives, which included engaging in same-sex relationships and presenting as a gender different from the one assigned to them at birth.[186] For example, adapting the existing tradition of costume balls, people who would variously be referred to today as gay men, transpeople, and female-presenting cross dressers started to organize drags in large cities. One of the earliest known drags took place in Washington, DC, New Year's Eve 1885. A participant, "Miss Maud," was arrested while returning home the following morning, prompting a local paper to find the event coverage worthy. Dressed in "a pink dress trimmed with white lace, with stockings and undergarments to match," the male-assigned, 30-year-old African American defendant was charged with vagrancy and sentenced to 3 months in jail. The paper could not help but add that the judge "admired [Maud's] stylish appearance."[187]

Female-assigned individuals who presented as male lacked the publicity of their male-assigned counterparts, but they were not absent. Some performed as male impersonators, others cross dressed both on and off stage but did not desire to be read as men. An exemplar of the latter group was Gladys Bentley, a Black blues singer and pianist who gained notoriety during the Harlem Renaissance of the 1920s. Bentley, an open lesbian, performed in a white tuxedo and top hat in some of Harlem's most popular bars and regularly wore "men's" clothing out in public with her female partner.[188]

The uptick in trans activity that accompanied the Second Industrial Revolution in the reunited States prompted a reaction. Municipal ordinances against what we would now consider trans activities like cross-dressing spread across the continent. Columbus, Ohio started the trend in 1848, with six more cities passing similar legislation before the outbreak of the Civil War. The pattern gained steam with Appomattox, and by 1929 an additional 25 such ordinances had been passed in various parts of the country. San Francisco's 1863 statute is exemplary:

> If any person shall appear in a public place in a state of nudity, or in a dress not belonging to his or her sex, or in an indecent or lewd dress, or shall make any indecent exposure of his or her person, or be guilty of any lewd or indecent act or behavior, or shall exhibit or perform any indecent or immoral or lewd play, or other representation, he should be guilty of a misdemeanor, and on conviction, shall pay a fine not exceeding five hundred dollars [about $9700 in 2017 dollars]."[189]

While gendered behavior was increasingly policed as the twentieth century dawned, so too was gender under more and more scientific scrutiny. Often these research endeavors were used to bolster existing modes of control, as when psychiatric professionals transformed homosexuality (very much tied at the time to trans activities like cross-dressing) from a sin into a sickness, allowing the hospital to become a primary controlling structure of queer life.

This trend continued during and after the world wars. For example, under the direction of Karl Bowman, a former president of the American Psychiatric Association, the Langley Porter Clinic became a major center of research on variant sexuality and gender after World War Two. During the war, Bowman conducted research on homosexuality in the military, using as test subjects gay men whose sexuality had been discovered while in uniform and who were being held in a military psychiatric prison at the Treasure Island Naval Base in San Francisco Bay. After the war, he was the principal investigator for a statewide project funded by the California Sex Deviates Research Act of 1950 to discover the "causes and cures" of homosexuality. A part of this research involved castrating male sex offenders in California prisons and experimenting on them to see how their sexual behavior might be affected. This included the administering of Metrazol, insulin shock or electro shock treatment, hormonal injections, sterilization, group therapy, and sometimes frontal lobotomy. As the clinical literature of the time admitted, none of these efforts proved effective in reducing "uncontrolled desires."[190]

Sometimes, though, as in the case of Dr. Magnus Hirschfeld, scientists proved able champions of an emerging understanding of trans and queer reality. In 1897 he cofounded the Scientific-Humanitarian Committee – perhaps the first organization effectively to push for social reform on behalf of sexual minorities. He wrote *The Transvestites* in 1910, the first book-length treatment of transgender phenomena. He worked with the Berlin police to end harassment against transpeople there. In 1919 he founded the Institute for Sexual Science, where he compiled a vast literature on human sexuality. He also arranged the first genital transformation surgery in 1931. His advocacy for the marginalized did not conform to National Socialist designs, and before the decade ended the new rulers of Germany forced him to flee, the flames of his now burning library licking his heels.[191]

Networks of transpeople developed in this context of medical research and literary output, banding together to seek access to newly developed surgical procedures. By the late 1940s and early 1950s, however, such procedures were becoming increasingly difficult to procure inside the United States, owing to the pall cast over such efforts by the 1949 decision of California Attorney General Pat Brown to characterize such surgeries as medical "mayhem" i.e. the willful destruction of healthy tissue. This opinion opened up the possibility of exposing the surgeon performing the operation to criminal prosecution. Since much transgender research was being performed in San Francisco, and researchers elsewhere took their cue from Californian trends, Brown's decision repercussed nationwide.[192]

While not widely available in the United States, sexual transition surgery was becoming somewhat more accessible in Europe; hence, a young ex-GI ended up receiving her reassignment surgery in Denmark, returning to the United States as Christine Jorgensen in 1952-53, causing a media sensation on par with Sputnik. The hoopla evidenced the post-war feelings of both fear and admiration for the power of human technology also found in the various reactions to the atomic bomb and the exploration of outer space.[193]

The interest of the mainstream media faded by the early sixties, but medical professionals continued to study the "transsexual phenomenon." A tension developed in these years between doctors (by turns sympathetic, curious, repulsed, intrigued at a surgical challenge) and prospective patients who, whether they considered themselves really "sick" or not, desired surgical services in order to achieve some degree of self-actualization. This idea of making the core self whole, of progressive individual transformation via the consumption of a product or a service, came to dominate much of the American attitude to life, then as now, and transpeople were not immune to its allure. To attain what they wanted, some transpeople essentially told the doctors what they wanted to hear. Enough transpeople were versed in the existing literature on transsexuals, notably the work of Dr. Walter Benjamin, and knew that his narrative of the symptoms and antecedents of transsexualism would be relied upon by many American practitioners, that they were able to regurgitate boilerplate life histories so as to obtain the sexual transformation surgery they desired. When medical practitioners began to realize that some of their patients were less than forthright in narrating the events of their lives, relations between transpeople and the medical establishment became all the more fraught. Hitherto, if a transperson did not adhere to the standard narrative, their pain, desire, goals were dismissed out of hand; now this mainstream medical dismissal spread further to trans narratives more broadly.[194]

While attempting to navigate the medical scene, many transpeople (unwilling or unable to fit themselves into the rigid gender roles required for most employment) had to live and work on the margins. Reacting to a lack of job opportunities – and the desperation that not being able to earn a living entails – transpeople joined in the struggle for "gay liberation," pushing back against aggressive and sometimes sadistic police harassment. Indeed, the 1966 riot at Compton's Cafeteria in San Francisco by a number of transpeople resisting police brutality predates the Stonewall Riots by several years. While fundamental issues remained at large, the riot did result in "dressing female" being legalized in San Francisco, a small but heartening victory.[195]

Transpeople played a pivotal role in the Stonewall Riots as well; trans street prostitutes were the first to stand up to police aggression as the bar was raided, and continued to be on the front lines while the riots continued. As the 1970s progressed and gay liberation moved more into the mainstream, the leaders of the liberation movement turned away from radicalism and toward "seat at the table" politics. In so doing, they pushed to the margins those who they thought might preclude a compromise with the establishment, which meant the militant lesbian and gay people, but also many transpeople as well. Moreover, a number of feminist thinkers at the time considered transpeople to be antithetical to the objectives of Women's Liberation. Janice Raymond sounded the clarion call in her book *The Transsexual Empire*, wherein she claimed men who transitioned into female bodies raped "real females" by attempting to dominate their spaces, were part of a patriarchal medical conspiracy reminiscent of the experiments of Nazi Germany, and recommended that transpeople be "morally mandat[ed] out of existence."[196]

Forgotten in the public imagination, marginalized out of mainstream liberation movements, and attacked even by some left-wing intellectuals as a kind of Manchurian Candidate assault on womanhood itself, transpeople entered the twilight of the twentieth century in something of a nadir. In the 1990s this began to change; an intellectual movement developed seeking to push back against what would later be termed transexclusionary radical feminists (TERFs) like Raymond. This intellectual ferment was accompanied by a limited revival in the public eye, with several Hollywood films depicting the trans experience – albeit through the lens of white, male directors.

The renewed attention of Hollywood exemplified the limits of neoliberal progressivism. Transpeople were increasingly accepted to the extent that they could be commodified – made into a product that could be sold and a demographic that could be sold to. The flourishing of transgender movements for social change in the 1990s and beyond thus has to be understood as part of a broader shift in how society and the state sought to manage various communities vying for recognition and political clout. Some greater freedom for some transgender people became possible precisely because the changes they needed and worked for also served other ends for other forms of power.[197]

During the first decade of the new millennium, trans scholarship gained further confidence, with several works emerging that grappled with the history of transpeople in America and elsewhere. Lively, sometimes heated, debates continued regarding the philosophical ideas of sexuality and political power, personhood and identity, the very idea of what it meant to be an embodied consciousness. Language itself came under the critical gaze, with even some of the littlest linguistic actors – pronouns – finding themselves under investigation for their role in communication and therefore the maintenance of existing social (power) relations. Intellectual confidence helped push trans activists back into the realm of politics, where clamors began for increased legal protections for transpeople – for instance adding clauses to existing hate crime legislation addressing the deliberate attacking of transpeople.

4.3.3 Transpeople in the Obama Years

The Obama administration began promisingly for many transpeople. On October 28, 2009 president Barack Obama signed into law the Matthew Shepard and James Byrd, Jr. Hate Crimes Prevention Act, which expanded on previous legislation to include gender identity among the other "protected categories." The Act was the first federal law to extend the legal language of protection to transpeople. It gave federal authorities greater ability to pursue hate crime enhancements for bias-motivated violent crime and also required the FBI to collect data on hate crimes perpetrated against transpeople. It was a major victory for mainstream trans activism, which sought political goals similar to those of their counterparts in the most politically influential gay liberation groups, i.e. status quo recognition and the benefits advertised therein. Such legislation was framed as at least a symbolic declaration of socio-political inclusion that worked to increase the good press of transpeople and bring them into the social fabric of normalcy.

This was a real victory: trans activists had pressured receptive politicians and they had reacted by making some accommodation to this vocal and newly confident constituency. It had real limitations as well. This kind of legislation legally articulated the value of transgender people's lives as being worth protecting. This articulation, however, came at the price of trans lives, for the law was reacting to very real transphobic violence to which it was a wholly inadequate response. At the same time, hate crimes legislation in general contributed to a broader biopolitical imperative to manage poor people and people of color (the disproportionate victims of anti-trans violence), for it legally codified people's bodies into medically-backed categories (transsexual as defined by the psychiatric bible, aka the DSM-V), and channeled them into the legal system, which for people of color almost certainly meant the Prison Industrial Complex.[198]

This political success augured a further edging into the mainstream. The two most well-known transpeople to emerge from this period were Chelsea Manning and Caitlyn Jenner, the former for attempting to hold the powerful accountable, the latter for being an example of the eccentricities that were said to accompany inordinate wealth.

Beginning on February 3, 2010, a soldier we now know as Chelsea Manning transmitted hundreds of thousands of classified and sensitive documents, videos, and cables about US operations to WikiLeaks. Several major international papers made the documents a worldwide sensation. This massive and unprecedented leak contributed to the global geopolitical upheavals already underway as a result of the financial crisis and was credited with lighting the fire of the Arab Spring protests in Tunisia. Manning's professed goal in leaking the material was "revealing the true nature of 21st century asymmetric warfare," because, "without information, you cannot make informed decisions as a public."[199]

Authorities arrested Manning in May 2010 and kept them in isolation for weeks in Kuwait, then moved them to a 6 foot by 8 foot cell in Virginia for 9 months; they were eventually court marshaled in 2013 and sentenced under the Espionage Act to 35 years in prison. Desirous of transitioning from their assigned male gender toward a female gender, their transition was haltingly and arbitrarily granted by the authorities. Transgender reading material Manning had been allowed to read in prison was later used as evidence to extend the time before they would be eligible for parole. Two suicide attempts landed them in solitary confinement. More than 100,000 petitioned for clemency, as their treatment had been harsher than comparable whistle blower cases in which no US personnel had been harmed and no leaked documents marked "Top Secret." At the very end of his presidency and after years of harsh jail time for Manning,

Obama commuted Manning's sentence and ordered them to be released by May 2017 (see also section 1.3.6).[200]

The other trans celebrity to emerge, this time higher up the social ladder and decidedly less radical in their politics, did so in a June 2015 article in *Vanity Fair*. The article presented one-time star athlete Bruce Jenner in their self-actualized form: Caitlyn Jenner. This figure hogged more of the pop culture oxygen than did Manning and did much to further the growing mainstream discussion (and to a degree acceptance) of transpeople.[201] Their conservative politics, however, up to and including a vote for billionaire Donald Trump in 2016 in an attempt to "shake the system up," calls their commitment to other transpeople into question, for it is under the especially harsh version of neoliberalism championed by conservatives that most transpeople suffer today.[202]

As Congress grew increasingly hostile, Obama's turn to executive orders later in his presidency also benefited transpeople in some small but still affecting ways. The federal government amended the requirements for changing name and gender on identity documents, including passports. It forbade discrimination against LGBT people in federal employment and contracts involving federal funds (something religious liberty bills would seek to challenge). It lifted the ban on transpeople serving openly in the military, allowing the Veterans Administration to provide medical and psychological services to trans veterans.[203]

Obama also appointed transpeople to government positions, including Amanda Simpson as deputy assistant secretary of the Department of Defense; others, like Raffi Freedman-Gurspan, were hired for White House positions, in their case as an outreach and recruitment director for the personnel office. The administration had gender neutral toilets installed in the White House – a symbolic gesture of note. Touchingly, the National Parks Service also issued *LGBTQ America*, a 1200-page study of places of historical significance to the queer community, including a section on transgender history. The Stonewall Inn became the first National Historic Site to be landmarked for its role in LGBT history.[204]

Moreover, the advancement of gay and lesbian rights during the Obama presidency had the added effect of mending the hitherto fraught relationship between many gay activists and their trans compeers. Mainstream groups like the Human Rights Campaign that had hitherto pushed transpeople into the margins suddenly developed, after the series of legal wins like the repeal of DADT and legalization of gay marriage, a keen interest in the topic. The Palm Center (instrumental in overturning DADT) shifted attention to trans military policy. At the same time, a host of new trans focused and community-based groups arose across the country, becoming more insistent on addressing specifically trans needs. Existing groups like the National Center for Transgender Equality took advantage of the improving political climate and expanded their operations.[205]

This rapprochement, coupled with a more involved and robust trans politics, signaled a strong push to mainstream transpeople. Pop culture, whether in the fascination with Caitlyn Jenner or with the appearance of trans characters (often played by trans actors, moreover) in shows like Netflix's *Orange is the New Black* and *Sense8*, seemed to evince a wave of social progress for transpeople. The election of Donald Trump to the presidency, however, would give political clout to the strong and growing anti-trans reaction, and many of the executive-order-backed legal gains made by the trans community during the Obama presidency would, only a few years later, largely be undone.

Despite these gains, the Obama administration continued other policies that harmed many a trans life. Its furtherance of neoliberalism, by which the private accumulation of wealth was backstopped by the public subsidizing of risk (e.g. bailing out banks that were Too Big to Fail), continued to wreak havoc on the lower class, the lower class of color more especially, and the trans lower class of color most especially. This combined with the Obama administration's continued waging of the War on Terror to hamper trans freedom. For an example that illustrates both, consider the Real ID Act. Enacted in 2005, this law sought to secure the nation's identification documentation by imposing federal standards upon state governments. One result of this legislation has been to enlarge the bureaucracy imposed upon those seeking to change key aspects about themselves, and therefore their identifying documentation. Bureaucracy means time and it means fees, and those are things that many marginalized people (paid low wages and trapped in abusive jobs) have great difficulty surmounting.[206] As we have seen, the Obama administration did nothing to question the need or reason for this level of state control, opting instead to continue the fight and its curtailment of civil liberties. Transpeople felt these oppressive policies all the more acutely. Existing at this intersection of oppression has had a profoundly deleterious impact on the health of many transpeople, with perhaps 10 percent reporting a recent suicide attempt in 2014.[207]

Here as elsewhere, the gains made for trans Americans under Obama's watch were real, they were narrowly confined, and they were dangerously ephemeral. Transpeople found some degree of representation within the administration; several executive orders made their lives appreciably easier in the labor market and the military, but such gains did little to chip away at the fundamental assumptions in the broader society in the very areas that trans identity focused: personhood and its relation to the self and the broader social fabric. Instead, the mainstream narrative of trans identity as a disease in need of a cure was generally accepted, the binaries of the status quo affirmed.

4.4 The Limits of Political Reform
As will be discussed in more depth later on, capitalist economics

and its attendant political and social institutions necessitate a division between the core of a country and its periphery (see also Chapter 6). Markets have winners and losers: the sick and the healthy, housed and homeless, employed and unemployed. The surplus, controlled by the few, is distributed based on their preferences. Government attempts to alleviate the conditions of our historically marginalized populations have never come to grips with this fundamental reality, and thus always have fallen short of producing real equality, whether in legal, economic, or political terms.

Black people, their uncompensated and unfree labor used for centuries to enrich white America, were emancipated, left to fend for themselves, and quickly subsumed once again in exploitative labor arrangements. They survived their second-class status, made great strides in their own education and a precious few did eke out a degree of success despite the colossal odds stacked against them. Better organized and increasingly discontent after generations of Jim Crow, African Americans made a concerted attempt to better their lot. The limited legal equality garnered during the civil rights era, while it did improve many lives, did not reach into the economic sphere. This meant that communities of color, already living in far less stable conditions than most of their white peers, were once again left to their own devices, while many white people still benefited from the economic legacy of slavery.

Gay and trans people, too, have felt the Invisible Hand of economic marginalization and its hideous social costs. Success in a capitalist world has historically been tied to "manly" virtues and institutions: market competition, heterosexual marriage (and progeny), a patriarchal breadwinner, etc. Alternative modes of living – an emphasis on sexual intercourse as a way to bond with another human so as to better cooperate and survive, or looking at gender as something that evolves over time based on changing conditions rather than some fixed quality – were degraded and demeaned, leaving such people unable to live with dignity within the confines of an enforced status quo.

President Obama self-consciously viewed himself as part of the generation able to enjoy the fruits of the civil rights era while also continuing its fight for equality. His vision of that struggle was limited to a legalistic understanding. He looked to the legacy of the Voting Rights Act, not Dr. King's attempt to organize the nation's poor to seek better working conditions and a redistribution of wealth. Obama's reform efforts, whether pushing for existing institutions to be more inclusive, modifying existing laws to encompass more people, or appointing people from marginalized communities into government positions, sought to broaden the status quo rather than fundamentally change it. The essential economic division of exploited class (who create economic surplus) and exploiting class (who control the economic surplus), and its attendant socio-political division of society into the margin and the core, remained untouched.

In judging his accomplishments we must, therefore, understand what we would have liked to happen in conjunction with what he wanted to do and what was actually possible. Obama wanted to push liberal reform measures: more inclusion in government, in the military, in social institutions, in the Free Market. In that capacity, he had some real success, including government posts going to people of color and members of the LGBT community, repeal of DADT and the legalization of gay marriage, a drastic, though still unequal, increase of marginalized communities gaining health insurance.

Even when judged by his own liberal criteria, however, Obama fell far short in alleviating the economic precarity of marginal groups. His economic recovery did almost nothing for those facing the foreclosure of their home, those trapped in the economic isolation of the ghetto, those wading through the deindustrialized ruins of America's great urban centers. He had options in this regard – mainstream ones, at that. For example, he could have chosen to assist African Americans by backing legislation that would have provided some reparations to the descendants of slaves (people never compensated for their labor, whose children had to grow up in conditions that often precluded their full flowering, and whose children's children thus still feel the weight of this economic legacy). Legislation of this kind has been discussed intermittently since the 1970s and, while surely coming with steep political costs, would not have required a fundamental retooling of the economy. But he did not. Instead, he used his large cache of initial political capital to save the banks, bolster the insurance companies, and defend the Free Market. By the time his executive actions made some slight changes, the possibility for legislative (and therefore long term) change had been lost in the wake of 2010's red tide.

Chapter 5

The Anthropocene Age

5.1 Brief History of a Theory

5.1.1 First Steps

The idea that the earth's climate can and does change – and that this change might fundamentally impact human life – is nothing new. Aristotle observed that:

> In the time of the Trojan wars the Argive land was marshy and could only support a small population, whereas the land in Mycenae was in good condition (and for this reason Mycenae was the superior). But now the opposite is the case...Now the same process that has taken place in this small district must be supposed to be going on over whole countries and on a large scale.[1]

As the Modern Era dawned, people continued to comment on the effects of a changing climate – even of humanity's impact on it. Cotton Mather, for instance, noted in 1721: "our cold is much moderated since the opening and clearing of our woods, and the winds do not blow roughly as in the days of our fathers, when water, cast up into the air, would...be turned into ice before it came to the ground."[2] In and among his voluminous writings, Edward Gibbon managed to find space for an observation on climatic variation in the first volume of his *Decline and Fall of the Roman Empire* (published in 1776), noting that Germanic barbarians were once able to "without apprehension or danger, [transport] their numerous armies, their cavalry, and their heavy wagons, over a vast and solid [Danube or Rhine]. Modern ages have not presented an instance of a like phenomenon."[3]

In the nineteenth century, science began its separation from philosophy to become its own branch of thought and study. In this century came the notions that "carbonic acid" might affect the climate. In 1827, Joseph Fourier tried to understand the various components of the earth's temperature, ultimately asserting that there was no way the earth could maintain its current habitable temperature via the sun alone; moreover, he theorized various earth-bound factors that contributed to the earth's temperature, including the "movements of the air and the waters, the extent of the seas, the elevation and the form of the surface, the effects of human industry and all the accidental changes to the terrestrial surface."[4] John Tyndall, while mountain climbing in 1860, studied the movement of glaciers and the effect of heat upon them.[5] He also attempted to understand better the relationship between temperature and the earth's atmosphere, concentrating especially on the effects of water vapor.[6]

At the end of the century, Svante Arrhenius put much of this previous scientific work together, but shifted the focus away from water vapor. He theorized that "carbonic acid" (aka carbon dioxide, CO_2) warmed the planet. He wrote that the air retains heat either in its diffusion through the air or through its absorption by atmospheric gases. He noted, among other things, that these two ways of storing heat impacted light of different wavelengths, with the light rays most responsible for heating the earth being affected by atmospheric gases.[7] This theory met with understandable skepticism at the time and did not receive mainstream adoption. Further observation, data collection, and study was required.

In 1938 Guy Stewart Callender revived and expanded on this theory of carbonic acid, correlating increases in measured temperatures over the previous century with measured increases in CO_2 concentration. He concluded that over the previous century the concentration of carbon dioxide had increased by about 10 percent and that this increase explained the warming of the earth's temperature. His ideas met with initial skepticism as well, but by the time of his death in the 1960s his advocacy had had a real impact on the emerging field of climate science. It should be noted, moreover, that he was not alarmist in his global warming advocacy; in fact he thought a continued increase in CO_2 concentrations – and the accompanying increases in global temperature – would stave off another ice age.[8]

In the late 1950s Roger Revelle, with substantial funding from the US Navy's Office of Naval Research, delved deeply into the mysteries of ocean chemistry. Working with men like Hans Suess, his institute looked into the effects of carbon and calcium compounds, the effects nuclear testing had on tsunamis, the intricacies of ocean mixing and ocean circulation, and eventually the specific impact of CO_2 on the ocean. In 1957 he co-authored a paper concluding that most CO_2 emitted since the Industrial Revolution had been absorbed by the oceans (contrary to the then-prevailing theory). While the paper admitted the paucity of contemporary evidence linking the greenhouse effect to warming temperatures, it pointed out that continued human emissions of CO_2 might impact the climate as time went on: "human beings are now carrying out a large-scale geophysical experiment of a kind that could not have happened in the past nor be reproduced in the future."[9]

5.1.2 Debate and Consensus

Climate science matured in the 1970s. Up-to-date estimates of global temperature were finally being maintained, and they were accompanied by ongoing atmospheric CO_2 measurements, which had only started in 1958. The first punch-card-driven computer models of the earth's climate system were being developed, giving researchers new tools to analyze questions about the physical processes of the earth's atmosphere. A rudimentary understanding of how the sunlight-reflecting aerosol particles behaved in the atmosphere also coalesced at this time. Amid this maturation, fossil fuel use increased dramatically, but temperature increases had actually slowed – a trend that had begun in the 1940s and would only be broken at the end of the 1970s. Two factors caused this slowdown: the post-WW2 surge in aerosol emissions (increasing particulates in the atmosphere and therefore earth albedo, its ability to reflect sunlight) and the cool phase of a Pacific Ocean cycle related to the strength of the trade winds.[10]

Scientists, noting these trends, had yet to determine which factor would gain the upper hand in the long term: the cooling of the aerosols or the warming of CO_2. A 1971 paper, for instance, predicted a drastic increase in the rate of human injection of particulates into the atmosphere, raising global background opacity, and thus cooling the earth. This opinion proved to be the minority view. A 1975 US National Academy of Sciences paper called for further research, but summarized the field as leaning toward CO_2 as the more powerful actor, and indeed scientists at the time published far more studies predicting a warmer future than a cooler one.[11]

In 1978, cautiously recognizing the need for further study, president Carter signed the National Climate Act into law, which provided the legal authority for additional federal study into the matter. While the infusion of federal dollars into the research effort was important, this theme of "needs more study" would hamper an active political response from then on.[12]

By the early 1980s, even the petroleum industry had begun to take an interest in the growing consensus among climate scientists. In 1986 Shell's Health, Safety and Environment Division (part of its Environmental Affairs section) commissioned a Greenhouse Effect Working Group to report on the current state of scientific literature. It summarized the current greenhouse theory (but did not dispute it):

Man-made carbon dioxide, released into and accumulated in

the atmosphere, is believed to warm the earth through the so-called greenhouse effect. The gas acts like the transparent walls of a greenhouse and traps heat in the atmosphere that would normally be radiated back into space. Mainly due to fossil fuel burning and deforestation, the atmospheric CO_2 concentration has increased some 15% in the present century to a level of about 340 ppm [parts per million]. If this trend continues, the concentration will be doubled by the third quarter of the next century. The most sophisticated geophysical computer models predict that such a doubling could increase the global mean temperature by 1.3-3.3 ºC.

The report admitted the scientific consensus while also warning that further study was critical so the problem could be better understood and addressed as needed:

There is reasonable scientific agreement that increased levels of greenhouse gases would cause a global warming. However, there's no consensus about the degree of warming and no very good understanding what the effects of warming might be. But as long as man continues to release greenhouse gases into the atmosphere, participation in such a global "experiment" [note the reference to Revelle's framing] is guaranteed. Many scientists believe that a real increase in the global temperature will be detectable toward the end of this century or early next century...By the time the global warming becomes detectable it could be too late to take effective countermeasures to reduce the effects or even to stabilise the situation.

The likely timescale of possible change does not necessitate immediate remedial action. However, the potential impacts are sufficiently serious for research to be directed more to the analysis of policy and energy options than to studies of what we will be facing exactly.[13]

Presciently, the report also underscored the difficulties to be found in the politics of dealing with global warming:

> It is estimated that any climatic change relatable to CO_2 would not be detectable before the end of the century. With the very long time scales involved, it would be tempting for society to wait until then before doing anything. The potential implications for the world are, however, so large that policy options need to be considered much earlier. And the energy industry needs to consider how it should play its part.[14]

In the late 1980s global warming transitioned from the ivory of science to the muck of politics. Prominent geophysicist Gordon MacDonald testified before Congress in 1987: "observations have been duplicated in various parts of the world over shorter periods of time. In all sets of observations, the exponential increase is clear…The exponential growth in atmospheric CO_2 concentration correlates with the release of CO_2 by the burning of oil, coal, gas, and wood." In 1988, James Hansen (from NASA's Goddard Institute for Space Studies) asserted vociferously that the connection between greenhouse gas emissions and the warming of the planet was robust.[15]

The UN responded to this uptick in public declarations by creating the Intergovernmental Panel on Climate Change (IPCC) to combine and distill world scientific opinion on the matter. Despite a reputation among climate deniers as a bastion of climate "alarmism," the IPCC did not start its life belching the fire and brimstone of a looming apocalypse. Indeed, over a generation of study and analysis they have had to be convinced first that humans had any impact on the discernible warming of the planet and second that our industrial actions contributed decisively.

The IPCC has issued five reports since its inception. The first IPCC report, issued in 1990, concluded that human influence on climate had not been detected, although it was possible that our impact might not be observable for another decade. In 1995 they issued their second report, concluding that "the balance of evidence suggests a discernible human influence on climate." The third IPCC report was released in 2001 and strengthened this conclusion, stating, "most of the observed warming over the last 50 years is likely to have been due to the increase of greenhouse gas concentrations." The fourth IPCC report went still further, indicating in 2007 that: "Most of the observed increase in global average temperatures since the mid-twentieth century is very likely due to the observed increase in anthropogenic greenhouse gas concentrations." The fifth and most recent IPCC report, issued in 2014, stated firmly: "It is extremely likely that more than half of the observed increase in global average surface temperature from 1951 to 2010 was caused by the anthropogenic increase in greenhouse gas concentrations and other anthropogenic forcings together."[16]

Furthermore, we can see the lack of alarmism in the language used within the federal government's fourth National Climate Assessment (2019). "Virtually certain" appears 10 times in the text, "very high confidence" appears 145 times, "medium confidence" appears 127 times, "low confidence" appears 35 times, and "uncertain" 441 times. Every chapter ends with a list of key findings, a review of the evidence upon which the findings are based, and a review of any uncertainties (and they are sometimes myriad) regarding a given topic. For example, some key findings of Chapter 11 include: "Annual average near-surface air temperatures across Alaska and the Arctic have increased over the last 50 years at a rate more than twice as fast as the global average temperature (*very high confidence*)," and, "Rising Alaskan permafrost temperatures are causing permafrost to thaw and become more discontinuous; this process releases additional carbon dioxide and methane, resulting in an amplifying feedback and additional warming (*high confidence*)."

The evidence base is described as "observational evidence from ground-based observing stations, satellites, and data-model temperature analyses from multiple sources and independent analysis techniques," and seven studies are cited. The major uncertainties include: "The lack of high quality and restricted spatial resolution of surface and ground temperature data over many arctic land regions and essentially no measurements over the Central Arctic Ocean," which hampers their ability to refine the rate of warming and restricts their ability "to quantify and detect regional trends, especially over sea ice."[17] The conclusion is provided, evidence cited, and remaining uncertainties admitted – all in a cool, methodical, thoroughly unalarmed way. This indicates in the scientists who penned the 400+ page report a skeptical confidence in their findings – not the dogmatic blindness so often attributed to climatologists by their political enemies.

The issues of climate change in general and human-induced global warming in particular have been studied over the course of generations in all their complexity and murk; the consensus has thus been reached after much observation, calculation, and debate – and comes, therefore, dearly bought by the hard labor of thousands all over the world. It should not be discounted lightly, however profitable in media circles it might be to pretend a scientific debate over the fundamentals of the issue remains. The blithering talking heads of the American commentariat remain the last bastion of such debate. Taking them seriously while ignoring the work of the great mass of climate scientists, technicians, analysts, and researchers is analogous to forming an opinion on the theory of evolution based on the circumlocutions of the Scopes Monkey Trial over and above the actual work of Charles Darwin and the many biologists who came before and after him. You might still arrive at the correct conclusion (as Clarence Darrow, the lawyer defending the teaching of evolution in schools did), but it will be based on the partisan, second-hand, half-understood utterances of people who are paid to win rather than to seek the truth.

5.1.3 The Scientific Consensus

Trends in globally averaged temperature provide consistent evidence of a warming planet. Surface air temperature has increased by approximately 1.8°F (1.0°C) over the past century. Four data sets – (1) the UK's University of East Anglia Climatic Research Unit working with the Met Office Hadley Centre, (2) America's National Oceanic and Atmospheric Administration, (3) NASA's Goddard Institute for Space Sciences, and (4) Japan's Meteorological Agency – constitute our record of the earth's surface temperatures. Although this data is drawn from thousands of thermometers around the world, gaps in temperature data from remote areas of the world remain, and differences in how each dataset works around such gaps lead to slight variation among the four groups. Despite this, each shows a consistent warming trend over the last 130 years.[18]

Surface temperature readings are then compared to satellite data, which goes back to 1979. Satellites augment surface-level data, collecting information about the lower troposphere, which is impacted by weather events differently than the earth's surface and thus shows slightly different measurements. Even so, a warming trend exists over the last 30 years here as well. Finally, longer-term climate records over past centuries and millennia bolster these contemporary measurements. Climatologists have woven together a broader context for contemporary warming trends by combining proxy measurements such as tree ring widths, coral growth trends, variations in isotopes found within ice cores, ocean and lake sediments, and glacier length records. This context indicates that the warming currently detected has occurred much more rapidly than at any time in the last 1700 years or more.[19]

Granted temperatures are rising across the globe; what

processes work to construct this temperature? It is determined, first, by the amounts of incoming and outgoing radiation (i.e. sunlight). The more radiation that bombards us, the warmer we will be; the more radiation remains trapped inside the earth's atmosphere, the warmer we will be. This means that the more radiation we reflect or allow to dissipate back into space, the cooler things become. Greenhouse gases, by absorbing infrared energy radiated from the earth's surface, trap the heat of that energy which leads to the warming of the surface and atmosphere. Taken together, this intermingling of incoming sunlight and the earth's ability to reflect, absorb, and trap it, control the equilibrium ("radiative balance") of the earth's temperature.[20]

Anthropogenic (human-born) activities have changed the earth's radiative balance and its albedo (its ability to reflect sunlight back into space) by adding greenhouse gases, aerosols (reflective particles), and aircraft contrails to the atmosphere, and also through changes in land use like deforestation. Changes in the radiative balance (the various factors of which are known as "forcings") produce changes in temperature, precipitation, etc. via a mixture of processes, many of which are coupled. These changes, in turn, trigger additional (feedback) processes which can further amplify and/or dampen the adjustments in radiative balance.[21] Understanding the proportional importance of these "forcings" is a critical component of climate science, for successfully doing so can tell us what elements are most important, which trends will continue (warming or cooling), and therefore what policies might need to be implemented – if any.

Carbon dioxide (CO_2), methane (CH_4), and nitrous oxide (N_2O) constitute the principal greenhouse gases, i.e. those gases that contribute most substantially to the trapping of heat and thus planetary warming. The abundance within the atmosphere (and associated "radiative forcings," i.e. proportional importance) of these primary greenhouse gases have increased substantially over the industrial era. Critically, fossil fuel combustion (coal, gas, oil), cement manufacturing, and land use (e.g. deforestation) have exploded human CO_2 emissions. While not the most efficient or effective greenhouse gas, CO_2 is the most important due to its atmospheric life, which can last for centuries. Other more effective heat-trapping gases maintain themselves in the atmosphere for far shorter durations, thus making them less important in determining long-term climatic trends.[22]

The global average CO_2 concentration has risen by 40 percent over the industrial era, increasing from 278 parts per million (ppm) in 1750 to 390 ppm in 2011; it now exceeds 400 ppm (as of 2016). Methane (a stronger greenhouse gas than CO_2 for the same emission mass, with a shorter atmospheric lifetime of about 12 years) has increased by a factor of about 2.5 over the industrial era.[23] Thus while climate scientists stress the general importance of CO_2 in the ongoing process of global warming, it is not the only way in which humans are having an effect.

In addition to the principal gases (CO_2, methane, and nitrous oxide), water vapor in the atmosphere acts as a powerful natural greenhouse gas, raising the earth's equilibrium temperature. In the stratosphere, water vapor levels are controlled by transport from the troposphere and from oxidation of methane. Increases in methane from human activities thus boost stratospheric water vapor, increasing its proportional importance in the interrelated processes of global warming. As increases in greenhouse gas concentrations warm the atmosphere, tropospheric water vapor concentrations increase, thereby amplifying their warming effect.[24] This is an example of a positive feedback loop, whereby a change in one variable (rising levels of CH_4) impacts another variable (increasing levels of water vapor) that augments the effects of the first variable (both contribute to global warming).

Clouds complicate our understanding of the climate significantly and remain the chief source of uncertainty. This is so because clouds have various and contradictory effects. An increase in cloudiness has two direct impacts on temperature: first, it increases the scattering of sunlight, which increases the earth's albedo and cools the surface (the shortwave cloud radiative effect); second, it increases the trapping of infrared radiation, which warms the surface (the longwave cloud radiative effect). A decrease in cloud cover will have the opposite effects.[25]

The earth's albedo is constituted primarily of snow and ice, which are highly efficient at reflecting sunlight. Loss of snow cover, glaciers, ice sheets, or sea ice resulting from warming temperatures thus lowers the earth's surface albedo. These losses create the snow-albedo feedback loop whereby subsequent increases in absorbed solar radiation (sunlight) lead to further warming as well as changes in the fluctuations of surface temperature. Changes in sea ice can also influence Arctic cloudiness: Arctic clouds have responded to sea ice loss in fall but not summer. This has important implications for future climate change, as an increase in summer clouds could offset a portion of the amplifying surface-albedo feedback, slowing down the rate of Arctic warming. This provides a good example of the complexities involved in adducing what exactly occurs throughout the earth's climate and the regional variations to be found amid the global trends.[26]

The ocean plays a significant role in climate change. It is critical in controlling the amount of greenhouse gases (including CO_2, water vapor, and N_2O) and heat in the atmosphere. At base, a warmer ocean absorbs less CO_2. Ocean warming and climate-driven changes in ocean stratification (the different layers of the ocean, based on salt content i.e. salinity, water density, temperature, etc.) and circulation (the movement of ocean water) modify more than ocean temperature, however; these processes also impact oceanic biological productivity. In one example, changes in ocean temperature, circulation, and stratification driven by climate change reduce the amount of phytoplankton by hampering its reproduction; absorption of CO_2 by the ocean also increases its acidity, which further reduces phytoplankton. Since phytoplankton (like trees) absorb CO_2, its reduction diminishes the ability of the ocean to absorb greenhouse gases. Increased ocean temperatures also accelerate ice sheet melt, particularly for the Antarctic Ice Sheet. This has contributed substantially to a rise in the global average sea level, which has increased about 8 inches in the last century (half of this growth having taken place since 1993). Not only do these changes in the rate of ice sheet melting decrease the earth's albedo, they also alter the amount of cold and fresh water flowing into the ocean. This, in turn, changes salt levels, fluxes temperatures, and thus rearranges the various layers of ocean water, affecting ocean circulation and its ability to absorb additional greenhouse gases.[27]

The effect of land use (deforestation, agriculture, urbanization, etc.) on the climate depends primarily on the type of land cover present in a given area. For instance, replacing existing rainforest with crops lessens the transpiration that occurs (i.e. the evaporation of water from leaves), which in turn warms the local climate. Conversely, irrigating farmland yields an increase in the water that is transpired and evaporated from moist soils, cooling and moistening the local atmosphere. More transpiration can also affect local levels of precipitation and cloudiness. In snowy areas, reforestation (planting trees in a depleted forest) or afforestation (creating a forest where none previously existed) decreases snow cover, reducing local albedo levels, meaning the land reflects less sunlight and absorbs more heat. This, despite the increased ability of the area to absorb CO_2 via photosynthesis, results in an overall warmer climate. Urbanization also tends to warm local temperatures. More people living in densely populated areas and the high concentration of construction materials like pavement and roofing materials that absorb more sunlight than they reflect combine to produce the "urban heat island" effect, whereby urban temperatures tend to be higher than the surrounding areas.[28]

Permafrost and methane hydrates store large quantities of methane and (for permafrost) carbon in the form of organic materials. With global warming, this organic material is now beginning to thaw, making previously frozen organic matter available for microbial decomposition, which releases CO_2 and methane into the atmosphere, thus providing yet another variable in the climate change equation (another "radiative forcing") and accelerating the warming process. This "permafrost–carbon feedback" will likely increase carbon emissions between 2 and 11 percent by 2100. Critically, once initiated, this process will continue for an extended period because emissions from decomposition occur slowly over decades. Over the next generation or so, enhanced plant growth at high latitudes and its associated CO_2 absorption are expected partially to offset the increased emissions from permafrost thaw but thereafter, the decomposition of previously trapped plant matter will predominate and the permafrost–carbon feedback will again contribute more to warming than cooling.[29]

Most climate scientists predict global warming will continue well into the twenty-first century and beyond, but the magnitude of the change beyond the next few decades will depend mostly on the amount of greenhouse (heat-trapping) gases emitted globally and on the remaining uncertainty in the sensitivity of the earth's climate to those emissions. With significant reductions in the emissions of greenhouse gases, the global annually averaged temperature rise could be limited to 3.6°F (2°C) or less. Without major reductions in these emissions, the increase in annual average global temperatures relative to pre-industrial times could reach 9°F (5°C) or more by the end of the twenty-first century. We will have to deal with the consequences of a warmed climate whether we address the issue or not; the critical question is whether we will work as a species to quell the warming trend and thus mitigate future impacts.[30]

What makes these changes in the climate so problematic and potentially catastrophic is the speed at which they are occurring compared to the pace of the natural variations in climate that have happened across time. Such rapid climate change leaves precious little time for plants and animals – including humans – to adapt to changing conditions of life. The 2020 wildfires in Australia provide a good example of this. Wildfires require four things to blaze: (1) available fuel, (2) that fuel to be dry, (3) weather conducive to its spread, and (4) an ignition source. Flawed fire management policy contributed to the accumulation of fuel, and the ignition source of many of the fires remains under investigation. The warmer, dryer climate, however, brought about by global warming augmented factors two and four, acting like a "force multiplier" such that these fires grew to record-breaking levels. The wildfires have, as of early 2020, affected more than 10 million hectares, caused substantial air pollution, emitted perhaps 400 million tons of CO_2, and killed more than one *billion* animals across the continent – an apocalypse from which many species may not survive.[31]

Australia serves as an example of a trend. The frequency, the intensity of extreme heat and heavy precipitation events are worsening around much of the world. These trends are consistent with expected physical responses to a warming climate. Climate model studies are also consistent with these trends, although models tend to underestimate the observed trends, especially for the increase in extreme precipitation events. In addition to these immediate effects, the frequency and intensity of extreme high temperature events are virtually certain to increase in the future as global temperature increases, and extreme precipitation events will very likely continue to increase in frequency and intensity across the globe. Observed and projected trends for some other types of extreme events (floods, droughts, and severe storms) vary more by region, making generalization impossible, at least for now.

5.1.4 How Is Humanity Responsible?

The planet has warmed substantially over the last century or so, but is humanity responsible? Perhaps the sun, more than greenhouse gas levels or reduced earth albedo, could account for the rise in global temperatures. Most climatologists have investigated such alternative theories and found them insufficient to account for what they observe. The consensus is that humanity dominates the processes behind this changing climate. This has been confirmed across a myriad of evidentiary threads, and predictions based on a human-centered warming process have been borne out by observed data: between 1951 and 2010 the observed global mean surface temperature warming correlated to the middle of the range of what human actions had been predicted to contribute. No convincing evidence that natural variability predominates the process of global warming over the industrial era exists. Indeed, shifts in solar energy output and the internal variability of the earth's climate can only contribute marginally to the swift and drastic climatic changes observed over the last century.[32]

Deniers of the scientific consensus, rather than cohering around an alternative theory, have instead assaulted the consensus view with various, often mutually contradictory propositions, with little effort made to produce a consistent thesis. For instance, at the panels devoted to climate science setup at the fossil-fuel-funded Heartland Institute's International Conference on Climate Change in 2011, the Australian geologist Bob Carter questioned whether warming occurred at all; astrophysicist Willie Soon acknowledged some warming had occurred, but blamed fluctuations in the sun instead; Patrick Michaels (of the Cato Institute) contradicted both by conceding that CO_2 increased temperatures, but insisted the impacts were so minor as to necessitate no policy action. These mutually contradictory theories sparked no debate among the deniers in attendance. None made any attempt to defend one position over another or arrive at some general denier theory. Speakers opined, the audience mumbled general agreement that climate scientists, in *some way*, were wrong, and people moved on. Heartland did not want a competing theory with which to understand the intricacies of the earth's climate; it sought only to poke holes in the existing theory so as to strengthen their argument for continuing business as usual.[33]

What exactly are humans doing to yield such drastic changes to the climate? Ordered from least to most important, humans (1) have drastically increased in population during the industrial age; (2) altered considerably the use of land across the globe; and (3) continued to expand the extracting and burning of fossil fuels to encompass practically all facets of modern life.

Since 1970 the global population has doubled. While more people means an increase in the consumption of resources, this population increase is of least importance in terms of global warming because the majority of per capita pollution still occurs in the developed parts of the world, whereas population has predominantly risen in less developed sections of the globe.[34] China, while it is the highest overall contributor of greenhouse gases (over 9000 metric gigatons of CO_2 emitted in 2016 compared to the US's #2 contribution of 4800 metric gigatons), only ranks #12 in per capita terms (6.4 metric tons per capita in 2016 versus America's #3 contribution of 15 metric tons, Australia's #2 contribution of 16.2 metric tons, and Saudi Arabia's #1 contribution of 16.3 metric tons).[35]

Contemporary land use can be divided between that related to agriculture and that related to resource extraction, with the pace and ferocity of the latter far outstripping the trend in population growth. While the global population has doubled, the global extraction of natural resources has increased even more so. Human industry extracted some 27 billion tons of materials from the earth in 1970; by 2017 that yearly tonnage had tripled.[36] Most of these emissions accumulate over developing countries (especially middle-income nations like China and India), and for two reasons: (1) these nations are building new infrastructure at a tremendous rate, and (2) it is in these poorer countries that the resources extracted for use in the economies of the developed world originate.[37]

Developing countries commit themselves to agricultural or extractive activities that take a heavy toll on the environment so as to satisfy the demands of rich countries. In this sense, richer countries are responsible for the land-use related emissions produced by poorer countries. In Brazil, for instance, 2970 square miles of rainforest were felled in the first 9 months of 2019, the downed trees then burned to produce ash to fertilize future grass for future cows to eat – beef that would then be exported abroad.[38]

Most damaging of all, the lives of an ever-multiplying humanity, and the economic activities engaged in by many of these people predominantly in the developed world, rely upon the burning of fossil fuels. Fossil fuels are the largest source of anthropogenic greenhouse gas emissions in the world. Over the course of the industrial age fossil fuels have comprised about 70 percent of all anthropogenic greenhouse gas emissions.[39] While individual consumption and habits of life are not irrelevant, the dominant source of emissions is corporate in origin: 100 corporations are responsible for 71 percent of the world's emissions (this includes both investor-owned entities like ExxonMobil, Shell, British Petroleum (BP), and state-owned companies like Saudi Aramco, Gazprom, and China National Coal Group).[40]

Although China has contributed the vast majority of greenhouse gas emissions since 1988 (14 percent via coal extraction alone),[41] the US has historically been the main driver of emissions, continues to rely on fossil fuels for its energy needs, and remains the second highest emitter globally. In 2017 America consumed some 7.28 billion barrels of oil.[42] That year,

CO_2 emissions from burning fossil fuels for energy equaled perhaps 76 percent of America's human-made greenhouse gas emissions.[43] Government policy drastically impacts these emissions. Domestically, as will be detailed in the next section, state and federal governments have a great say in where companies can send pipelines, sink wells, or fell forests. Foreign affairs plays a decisive role as well. In order to wage the Global War on Terror, for instance, the US military emitted 766 million metric tons of greenhouse gases into the atmosphere between 2001 and 2017 (an average of about 48 million metric tons per year, which for comparison is slightly more than Hong Kong's annual output of about 43 million metric tons). When all US military emissions during that same period are accounted for, the estimate rises to 1212 million metric tons (about 76 million metric tons per year, slightly more than Peru).[44] And our use of fossil fuels has not abated; US oil consumption rose about 3 percent in 2018 to 7.5 billion barrels.[45]

5.2 The Politics of Climate Change

5.2.1 Initial Political Responses

Two environmental issues preceded global warming on the political stage: the hole in the ozone layer and the phenomenon of acid rain. The former was dealt with by a general ban on the underlying cause, the latter via a market-based incentive program aimed at reducing the activity causing the problem. Both solutions would serve as possible precedents in dealing with global warming.

By the 1970s scientists had detected a considerable depletion of ozone particles above the Antarctic. The layer of ozone in our atmosphere acts essentially as the earth's sunscreen, shielding us from 95 percent of the UV radiation that bombards the planet. A breach of this protection thus posed a serious threat. By 2000 this hole in the ozone layer encompassed 11 million square miles, and a thinning ozone layer covered most of the globe below 40ºS. In the 1990s a second hole appeared, this time above the Arctic, and over the tropics ozone concentration had diminished by 7 percent.[46] The long-term consequences for people living under a depleted ozone, even after mitigating policies were put in place, remain considerable. Skin cancer rates in populations nearer the holes have skyrocketed: 66 percent in Punta Arenas, for instance. Even further afield rates have increased: in America the skin cancer rate went from 1 in 250 around 1970 to 1 in 84 by the turn of the century. Incidents of UV-related eye damage have increased. Vulnerable populations like the Inuit have seen deleterious effects on their immune systems related to increased UV exposure.[47]

Investigators traced the cause of this ozone depletion to a single category of molecules: fluorocarbons (CFCs and HFCs), hitherto used in refrigeration, the making of Styrofoam, spray can propellants, and air conditioning units. Their molecular stability, which made them so useful, also meant that they remained in the atmosphere over long periods, and it turned out that over time the chlorine from these CFCs eviscerated ozone, a consequence made all the more severe at extremely cold temperatures.

In 1987, responding to the scientific consensus, the world's governments signed on to the Montreal Protocol, pledging to phase out the offending chemicals. Incrementally over the next 20 years, the countries obliged to change their industrial practices did so, and the effects have been substantial. By 2004 the Antarctic hole had been reduced by some 20 percent.[48] In 2019 NASA reported that, although the hole would not return to its pre-1980 concentration until the 2070s, it was the smallest it had ever been since measurements began in 1982.[49]

When George Bush I ascended to the presidency in the late 1980s, he promised (among other things) that he would tackle the problem of acid rain. This phenomena had come about as a result of a drastic increase in aerosols (tiny particles) in the earth's atmosphere after a century of human industrial activity. The primary aerosol was sulfur dioxide (SO_2) pumped upwards by coal burning power plants.[50] Carbon scrubbers were forced on power plants starting in the 1970s, which had reduced the issue somewhat by the next decade, but acid rain was still denuding trees of their needles and lakes of their aquatic denizens. Bush I's response was not, as had occurred with Montreal, the banning or curtailment of sulfur dioxide producers but a market regime whereby a nationwide cap would be set for sulfur dioxide, under which emitters could either pay other companies to make reductions for them, purchase allowances permitting them to pollute, or make a profit by selling the permits they did not use.[51] This "cap-and-trade" arrangement, legislated under a 1990 amendment to the Clean Air Act, yielded a 40 percent reduction in SO_2 emissions between 1980 and 2004. Comparatively, the more conventional regulation of SO_2 by the European Union (e.g. setting a binding ceiling on the SO_2 emissions of each member state, setting emissions standards for existing and new power plants, and establishing standardized ambient air pollution levels) yielded a 77 percent drop.[52]

Preliminary discussions for grappling with global warming were held in 1985 and 1988, but it was not until 1992, during the Rio Earth Summit, that political action was taken. A total of 155 nations pledged themselves to the UN Framework Convention on Climate Change and reducing their CO_2 emissions to 1990 levels by the year 2000. In 1997 these signatories came together again to sign the Kyoto Protocol, which established: (1) the assignment of greenhouse emission targets to developed countries; and (2) mechanisms for emissions trading of the six principal greenhouse gases. Taking their cue from the (very profitable) national market on sulfur dioxides, American negotiators at Kyoto insisted on a similar regime for carbon dioxide.[53] It was hoped that the creation of a market for carbon (most especially) would allow a cost-effective way for industries to reduce emissions by establishing in essence a "carbon dollar."

Ratification of the treaty among its signatories, however, proved sluggish, and it was not until 2004 that enough nations had done so that it could be said to be anything but a dead letter.[54] Although the US had done much to shape the final form of the Protocols (especially its emphasis on carbon markets), Bush II pulled America from the treaty early in his presidency, leaving its implementation severely hampered. Nevertheless, from 2005 to 2010 the various global carbon markets witnessed perhaps $500 billion in trades, with some seven thousand projects across the globe generating carbon credits by 2014. The environmental efficacy of these projects is often dubious at best. For example, oil companies operating in the Niger Delta that practice "flaring" (setting fire to the natural gas released in the oil drilling process because capturing and using the potent greenhouse gas is more expensive) have argued that they should be paid if they stop the practice. Some are already registered to receive carbon credits under the UN system for doing so, this despite the fact that gas flaring has been illegal in Nigeria for decades. So now an extremely dirty facility that installs a piece of equipment to keep a greenhouse gas out of the atmosphere can qualify as "green development" under UN rules. Adding insult to injury, this "green" project can be used as an offset justifying a more carbon intensive project elsewhere in the world.[55]

While the administration of Bush I made some (albeit market-oriented) efforts to safeguard the environment, Bush II's administration worked hard to undermine existing regulations and push domestic fossil fuel production to new and profitable heights. The relationship between the administration and the hydraulic fracturing industry is illustrative of the trend. Hydraulic fracturing ("fracking") attempts to use high pressure water to break up coal seams in order to obtain the methane trapped therein. In 1997 the US eleventh Circuit Court of

Appeals ordered that the EPA regulate the fracking industry under the Safe Drinking Water Act. In 2000 the EPA initiated a study of the threats to water supplies attendant to fracturing processes. In 2001, before this study had even been completed, vice president Dick Cheney (recently the CEO of Halliburton) convened a special task force on energy policy and recommended to Congress that they exempt hydraulic fracturing from this regulation. In 2004 Bush II's EPA completed this study of fracking and determined that little or no threat to drinking water existed and no further study was necessary. Later evidence suggested that EPA administrators (mirroring the intelligence team of Bush II's administration when dealing with Iraq) omitted potentially damaging counter evidence and deleted countervailing opinions from the 2004 report.[56] In 2005 Congress acted on the EPA's recommendations and exempted fracking from the purview of the Safe Drinking Water Act. This ensured that companies did not have to report any of the chemicals they injected underground (in the process of exploding natural gas pockets) to the EPA, thus shielding them from unwanted oversight and keeping the public blind as to the possible risks involved in the fracturing of their communities.[57]

In his 8 years as president, Bush II mentioned climate change only twice. In his 2007 State of the Union address he admitted the need to diversify US energy sources, reduce gasoline use, and restrict oil production for the protection of the environment. Again in 2007, he said:

Energy security and climate change are two of the great challenges of our time. The United States takes these challenges seriously…Our guiding principle is clear: We must lead the world to produce fewer greenhouse gas emissions, and we must do it in a way that does not undermine economic growth or prevent nations from delivering greater prosperity for their people.[58]

With his administration full of oil men, however, this was little more than empty rhetoric.

Throughout this period lobbying and corporate political funding undergirded many of the political decisions being made, and the funding advantage rested decisively with the interests of the fossil fuels industry. The American media often portrays the "debate" between believers and deniers of global warming to be one of equally well-funded, well-researched, well-matched opponents. This distorts the reality, however, which we can illustrate through a few numbers that give us a sense of proportion between those claiming climate change is real (and human caused) and those denying its existence or its human origins.

Between 2009 and 2016, lobbyists for various environmental groups and causes spent $148,829,103 to push for their pet policies and legislation. They spent an average of $18,603,637 per year.[59] Meanwhile, the budget of the much maligned IPCC has averaged about $5.3 million over the course of the last 30 years.[60] Siding with those denying some facet of the climate change consensus, oil and gas lobbying between 2009 and 2016 totaled $1,151,971,454, with an average spending of $143,996,431.[61] Outside the lobbyists, climate denial has evolved in the United States into a vast industry: between 2003 and 2010, 140 foundations made a total of 5299 grants totaling $558 million to 91 organizations; broken down, this spending averaged $69,750,000 per year or $766,483 per organization per year.[62]

The funding, and therefore the power, of American politics stacked against the prospect of reform on the climate change front. The question remained as to whether president-elect Obama would be willing and able to surmount this difficult lobbying landscape and marshal the American political system against climate doom.

5.2.2 The Obama Administration and Climate Change

After 8 years of Republican government, many environmental activists thought they had an ally in the newly elected Democrat. Obama's words bolstered this hope. On January 26, 2009, Obama stated: "Year after year, decade after decade, we've chosen delay over decisive action. Rigid ideology has overruled sound science. Special interests have overshadowed common sense... For the sake of our security, our economy, and our planet, we must have the courage and commitment to change."[63]

Addressing the UN General Assembly in September 2009, Obama emphasized the responsibility of the richer nations, including the US, to take the lead against global warming.[64] Yet progress on this front would prove difficult. Obama and his administration would need to surmount at least four hurdles in order to pass legislative action on global warming.

(1) The growing partisan divide made environmentalism and climate change all the more ideological. The environment had once been an issue on which many Republicans and Democrats could unite. Recall that Nixon had called clean air an "American birthright."[65] Bush I had taken the 1992 Rio Earth Summit at least somewhat seriously, signing the US to the agreement once the conditions were made voluntary. In 2008 Republican former speaker of the House Newt Gingrich and current Democratic speaker Nancy Pelosi went on TV pledging to fight climate change together.[66]

As the years wore on into the Obama presidency, however, the hostility exemplified by radio host and cigar aficionado Rush Limbaugh came to predominate in Republican circles:

Now, the bottom line is, the whole man-made global warming movement is a fraud. It is a hoax. Its [sic] made-up lies. I have known this since the beginning of the movement. I'm the one who said that militant environmentalism is the home of displaced communists after the Berlin Wall came down.

Now, scientists cannot rely on common sense. So the anti-global warmers have to go out there and get their own science to counter the science that the pro-global warming crowd is using, and they're making it up.[67]

(2) Business interests and conservatives have traditionally been critical of environmental regulations and the "financial burden" these impose upon the private sector. Powerful interests, therefore, would array themselves against any legislation they might find onerous. The lobbyist funding brought to bear by the fossil fuels industry (more than a billion dollars spent between 2009 and 2016, ten times that spent by the environmental lobby) makes this point quite clear.

(3) The existing "green" groups that lobby on behalf of environmental policy constrain change in their own way, reluctant to adapt to new policy challenges such as climate change and keen on protecting their own vested interests in the political status quo. In the late 1980s the Earth Defense Fund put its weight behind the market-based solution to acid rain over the more straightforward direct regulation of sulfur dioxide; the Nature Conservancy (which includes officers on its business council from BP America, Chevron, and Shell) sunk its own oil well on land it had purported to protect from extraction; the Conservation Fund receives money from Shell, BP, and American Electric Power (a coal utility); the World Wildlife Fund maintains a long-standing relationship with Shell.[68]

(4) The very nature of the climate change problem itself, a "wicked problem" that works on transhuman timescales beyond those within which traditional environmental problems like water and air pollution have operated, bedevils normal political solutions.[69] It requires a holistic approach that pulls from political science, psychology, economics, engineering, sociology, anthropology. It requires action at all levels of government, national and international. This would be no easy

task for any administration in any context, and proved utterly impossible for a liberal president attempting to tackle global war, economic crisis, and abysmal healthcare at the same time as global warming – all through the lens of a dogmatic capitalist.

The first major international action after Obama came to power occurred at Copenhagen in 2009, resulting in a set of Accords bearing that city's name. The conference began with optimism over America's reengagement in environmental concerns, although this did not necessarily translate into results. While president Obama's passion for climate action was a welcome change, there were tough issues to work through – most especially the shivering of nations into the categories of "developed" and "developing."

From the perspective of US negotiators, a major reason the 1997 Kyoto Protocol had failed was that it adhered to the "polluter pays" principle, through which those nations that polluted the most (i.e. industrialized first) would bear the brunt of the burden in cleaning up the mess. Kyoto required much more from the United States and other developed nations and essentially nothing from developing countries, including major emitters like China and India. Even in 1997 China was already the world's number two polluter, and though China promised it would undertake serious efforts, by 2009 it had yet to pledge itself to even nonbinding emissions reductions. From the American perspective, everyone had to contribute, regardless of the volume of any one nation's gaseous responsibility.[70]

Obama's negotiating team had hoped a deal would be in hand by the time the president arrived at Copenhagen. Instead, he arrived to find China and the G77 (the 77 "developing" nations of the world) unwilling, as the Americans saw it, to do their part. Rushing from meeting to meeting, Obama leaned hard into personal diplomacy, even going so far as to interrupt a meeting between the leaders of China, India, Brazil, and South Africa. Eventually he succeeded in convincing his counterparts to come together around a list of principles, which coalesced into the Copenhagen Accord. It was not the agreement he had wanted, but it was a start.[71]

While many dismissed Copenhagen as a failure, it did achieve two things: (1) The world's major economies – developed and developing alike – agreed to make national commitments to reduce pollution. (2) They agreed to be transparent in their emissions reductions. Like the Kyoto Protocols before it, international politicians hoped Copenhagen would be the start of a growing momentum of action. And this time, the US was on board.

Domestically, in his first 2 years in office, Obama pushed for green and renewable funding to be included in recession recovery legislation, which succeeded in passing. The Recovery Act invested some $25 billion into the generation of green energy and $90 billion in tax incentives for all manner of green projects. This directly funded 180 "advanced energy manufacturing projects," such as the Saft America facility in Florida (which makes batteries).When we include tax incentives and loans, these funds subsidized some 100,000 projects, including large-scale wind and solar farms. Said the Obama White House: "Since 2008, solar electricity generation has increased over 30 times and wind generation has increased over three times. In fact, renewable energy accounted for more than half of new installed power sector capacity in 2015."[72]

Obama also advocated for a free-market based approach to carbon emissions reduction, so-called "cap-and-trade," similar to the regulatory structure surrounding the sulfur dioxide (SO_2) that caused acid rain. This approach evidenced both his neoliberalism (a belief that markets are naturally efficient and can solve most problems) and his overriding desire to achieve bipartisanship (cap-and-trade had originated among Republicans). The Great Recession, however, made abundantly clear the biggest problem with this approach: carbon markets fluctuate as all markets do and care little for any overarching political objectives. In Europe – where a carbon market already exists –companies and countries had been incentivized to join the market by the distribution of a huge number of cheap carbon permits. When the 2007 economic crisis spread to Europe in 2009, it caused production and consumption to contract, reducing emissions. The European emissions market was now awash in excess permits, which in turn caused the price of carbon to drop dramatically. Little incentive remained to shift away from fossil fuels or to buy carbon credits. So while the European Commission might boast that its market-oriented policies have reduced EU greenhouse gas emissions by 23 percent between 1990 and 2018, these figures are impermanent and subject to market-based fluctuations that care more about short-term profit than they do long-term survival.[73] In a sobering example of this kind of about-face, in 2012 coal's share of electricity production in the UK rose by more than 30 percent in response to the lack of profit found in the recession-era carbon market.[74]

Having used much of his political capital on economic recovery and healthcare, however, Obama found his other legislative initiatives stalled amid congressional morass and his proposal for carbon cap-and-trade went nowhere. In the context of the European experience with carbon trading, however, the failure of Congress to pass climate legislation in 2009 should not be seen as a defeat. Instead, by avoiding an ineffectual (but massively profitable) market-based non-solution, America actually left itself open to more radical (and effective) initiatives.

After 2010, when the Republicans regained control of the House, several attempts emerged to roll back climate change progress – for instance the Energy Tax Prevention Action of 2011 (supported by Tea Party Republicans and oil/coal Democrats). This proposed legislation sought to deny EPA the ability to regulate CO_2 emissions (despite a 2007 Supreme Court ruling giving them that authority). While such bills died in legislative limbo, it signaled to Obama that he could no longer count on Congress for action. He thus turned increasingly toward executive orders: stricter codes for clean air, action on greenhouse gas emissions, protection for endangered species, and higher fuel efficiency standards all came into effect via this method.[75]

The Obama administration made several proposals during its first term, such as the Biden/Obama energy plan in 2009 and the Blue Print for Secure Energy Future in 2011 – each seeking drastic increases in renewable energy production within the United States. Neither, however, made much impact within policy circles. Upon achieving victory in the 2012 election, Obama again signaled to Congress his desire to see climate change legislation enacted but found no cooperation there. Failing action on their part, he turned once more to executive prerogative, issuing the President's Climate Change Action Plan in 2013 which talked of the moral obligation to future generations to fight climate change, reiterated the commitment to reduce US greenhouse gases, pledged the administration to work globally to achieve responses to climate change, set out proposals for innovating in renewable energy and green technology, and set efficiency targets for vehicles, among other proposals.[76]

In 2014 Obama's EPA unveiled its most ambitious policy blueprint yet, the Clean Power Plan (CPP). The executive branch launched the finalized version on August 3, 2015. The White House spoke of the plan as an example of continued US leadership on climate change. The EPA echoed this line, arguing that the plan "is an historic and important step in reducing carbon pollution from power plants that takes action on climate change…[It] shows the world that the United States is committed to leading global efforts to address climate change."[77]

Among its many pages, the CPP articulated the first ever set of national standards addressing carbon emissions from American power plants. It made central a commitment to reduce carbon emissions specifically from power plants by 32 percent below

2005 levels by 2030. It partnered the EPA and the states: the EPA set targets for each state with implementation to be administered locally based on the context of each state. Troublingly, however, the plan still allowed an important role for fossil fuels, notably natural gas, within the American energy matrix of the future.[78]

During Obama's remaining presidency the Plan became mired in legal disputes and never achieved the status of active policy. Twenty-four entities – state governments, power producers, trade associations, and coal companies – filed suits against the EPA in October 2015 seeking to delay the implementation of the CPP. In February 2016 the Supreme Court (5-4 majority) upheld the delay pending judicial review, and upon succeeding to the office of the presidency, Obama's Republican successor issued an executive order attempting to rescind the plan, which met with its own legal challenges from environmental groups.[79]

The administration had designed the plan as a principal part of the US commitment to the United Nations Framework Convention on Climate Change (UNFCCC) – scheduled to be held in Paris in December of 2015. The administration also emphasized renewed cooperation with China, reflecting the Obama administration's tendency in foreign affairs to reorient away from the Middle East and toward East Asia. As secretary of state, John Kerry committed himself to bringing the US and the world's other major polluter into closer cooperation on the matter of climate change. Copenhagen had proven this would be no easy task, but starting in 2013 the State Department pushed ahead. In February 2014, Kerry announced in the Chinese capital Beijing that the two nations would cooperate, beginning the process of removing the "real roadblocks we had hit for decades," and in so doing set the stage for a fruitful UNFCCC conference.[80]

Within this context of increased US-China cooperation, negotiations in Paris started in earnest. Unsurprisingly, negotiations stalled, devolving once again into a debate over whether developed and developing countries should have different emissions requirements. Developing nations voiced their outrage that they were paying the price for the reckless industrialization of developed nations, adding that richer nations were perfectly capable of bearing more of the burden if they chose to do so. To these developing nations, the US emphasized that "common but differentiated" responsibility meant giving teeth to the limitations to be imposed upon the nations that had already caused the problem. Negotiating continued as Kerry and others tried to build consensus by emphasizing that everyone had a shared burden, that the only way a global agreement would pass muster in the developed countries would be to emphasize this fact. Eventually, the negotiators worked through their differences, hammered out an agreement, and adopted it.[81]

The text of the Paris Accords contained three broad aims: (1) to keep global temperature increases below 2ºC from pre-industrial levels and to pursue efforts to keep it below 1.5ºC; (2) to review every 5 years the climate change commitments of the nations of the world at the Paris summit (the initial review would be in 2018); (3) to support developing nations in the adoption of renewable and clean technologies. Developed nations pledged $100 billion dollars each year by 2020, although this amounted to 8 percent of total declared military spending across the globe, underscoring the priority given to fighting the phantoms of national security hawks rather than the far more consequential antagonist of global warming.[82]

Obama hailed the "ambitious" and "historic" agreement: "Together we have shown what is possible when the world stands as one." He recognized the imperfections, but said it was "the best chance to save the one planet we have."[83] Indeed, the Paris Accord was the first time all the nations of the world agreed to tackle climate change. Secretary of state Kerry hoped (in a typically neoliberal framing) that this universal recognition of the problem would galvanize the private sector to action. In his memoirs, the former secretary of state championed private innovation and technological solutions, as if the cause of climate change were not in fact capitalist production and its need for eternal growth heedless of external costs:

> The real importance of our achievement was the message we were sending to the world's private sector that 196 nations were now committed to moving in the same direction on energy policy. That message, we hoped, would unleash a torrent of investment into sustainable, alternative and renewable energy...We were betting on the genius of the entrepreneur to recognize that public policy was reinforcing the largest market the world has ever known, a market today of four to five billion energy users worth multitrillions of dollars, which would be growing over the next thirty years to nine billion users and worth multiples of those trillions. No burden was placed by government on anyone. It was an invitation to the marketplace to get the job done and make money doing it. That was the real success of the Paris Agreement. Paris was inviting the private sector to save us from ourselves.[84]

Obama's environmental legacy was an improvement over his predecessors, but as the vital inclusion of natural gas in his CPP made abundantly clear, he could not say "No" to the fossil fuel industry, and given fossil fuels' intimate relationship with human-caused global warming, this was a critical flaw in Obama's push to address that problem. His understanding of America's energy needs tried to compromise between two mutually exclusive understandings of energy: (1) national security and (2) environmental conservation. If viewed through a national security lens, it mattered less what kind of energy was used to power the American economy and the American war machine so much as the source of that energy – domestic was better because it was more secure. An environmentalist view of energy, contrariwise, cared less about the geopolitical source of energy so much as the environmental impact of its extraction and use. In seeking a compromise between these two extremes, Obama sought less dependence on foreign oil while also promoting green technologies. In January 2009 he articulated this compromise position, stating:

> At a time of such great challenge for America, no single issue is as fundamental to our future as energy. America's dependence on oil is one of the most serious threats that our Nation has faced. It bankrolls dictators, pays for nuclear proliferation, and funds both sides of our struggle against terrorism.
>
> These urgent dangers to our national and economic security are compounded by the long-term threat of climate change, which if left unchecked could result in violent conflict, terrible storms, shrinking coastlines, and irreversible catastrophe.[85]

Seeking a more secure domestic source of energy, the Obama administration continued the policies of Bush II, opening up more and more territory to exploration and extraction. Speaking to a college audience in March of 2012, Obama detailed his efforts:

> Over the last 3 years, my administration has opened millions of acres of land in 23 different States for oil and gas exploration. Offshore, I've directed my administration to open up more than 75 percent of our potential oil resources. That includes an area in the Gulf of Mexico we opened up a few months ago that could produce more than 400 million barrels of oil.
>
> So do not tell me that we're not drilling. We're drilling all over this country...We are drilling at a record pace, but we're

doing so in a way that protects the health and safety and the natural resources of the American people.[86]

The facts back up his words. US domestic crude oil production experienced an 88 percent increase from 2008 to 2016, a result of the shale oil boom in the United States and the Tar Sands boom in Canada.[87] The number of US rail cars carrying oil increased by more than 4000 percent between 2008 and 2013, from 9500 cars to an estimated 400,000.[88] With this acceleration came new sites of extraction, new oil pipelines, and new battles between private firms backed by government power and locals (including Indigenous peoples) none too keen on allowing their land to be obliterated (see also section 6.2.2).

Other fossil fuels boomed as well. Natural gas, already given a regulatory opening under Bush II, saw further success under Obama's presidency. While natural gas is often given credit for a 12 percent drop in US carbon dioxide emissions since 2007, this statistic fails to include the fact that US methane emissions are very likely underestimated (the EPA does a poor job measuring them). Any climate gains from this will continue to be undercut not only by the increased emission of methane, but also by the tendency of cheap natural gas to displace or delay the adoption of wind and solar power. The natural gas boom has deleterious consequences globally as well. Reacting to coal generation being displaced by natural gas in the US, American coal companies have begun exporting their product abroad, likely more than offsetting the domestic emissions savings from natural gas since 2007 with an increase in foreign coal burning.[89]

To lower emissions as rapidly and as deeply as required, America (and the world) must keep large – and still profitable – concentrations of carbon in the ground, resources that fossil fuel companies are working hard to extract heedless of environmental cost. Obama's neoliberalism had convinced him that there was something inherently wrong with telling corporations how to run their business – indeed, that corporations possessed something called "their business" in the first place, that somehow they operated outside and beyond the communities from which they extracted resources, in which their workers lived, and to which they sold their goods and services.

Obama himself articulated the hollowness of his legacy in the fight against global warming. In November 2018, while speaking off the cuff at Rice University, he said: "Now, I know we're in oil country. And we need American energy and – by the way – American energy production…it went up every year I was president…And that whole, 'suddenly America's, like, the biggest oil producer and the biggest gas,' that was me, people [laughter and applause]. I just wanted you to know that."[90]

Chapter 6

Indigenous Resistance and the Intersectionality of American History

6.1 A Violent Development

6.1.1 Capitalism and Empire

Consider capitalism as a contradictory social totality, comprised of various forms of domination, subordination, and exploitation that combine, conflict, and reproduce each other: hierarchies of state and private power, domestic and colonial extraction of resources and labor, ideologies of racism and patriarchy, they all reverberate throughout the history of the last 400 years. The sum total of this equation of social relations and processes results in the systematic reproduction of the capital relation (money is power).[1]

Typically capitalism is thought of as emerging around 1780 with the advent of the Industrial Revolution. But the first inklings of this new mode of production appeared centuries earlier, during the so-called Age of Exploration. This first phase of capitalist development, characterized by the slavery and expropriation of Indigenous peoples, that is to say the imperial expansion, armed trade, and assertion of sovereignty over people and land by entrepreneurs who were backed by national power, we might call War Capitalism. Instead of the machines and the wage laborers of later Industrial Capitalism, War Capitalism flourished on the fields of battle and of agriculture, was labor-intensive, and land hungry.[2] From this violence came the great wealth and new knowledge that further strengthened European institutions and states, and it was this strength that proved the crucial precondition for Europe's astonishing economic and political domination over the course of the nineteenth and twentieth centuries (see also section 4.1.1).[3]

This economic expansion fueled and was fueled by a drastic increase in military-centered production among certain European polities that were still emerging from the energetic experimentation of the Middle Ages to become modern nation states. For example, in the first half of the sixteenth century, perhaps 16,000 workers were employed at the state-run Venetian Arsenal where they worked as wage laborers building galleys of standardized design via an assembly line production method. This Arsenal also employed managerial and accounting methods, practices reminiscent of how such things are done today. This "hybrid organization," fusing capitalist and pre-capitalist forms of labor, was but one example of the interlocking processes that brought about capitalism's full development. In another, ship yards in Amsterdam, working to build up the Dutch navy so necessary for imperial trade and conquest, pioneered the use of economies of scale we take for granted today by using wage labor, strictly managed labor processes, and the thoroughgoing employment of science to develop labor-saving technologies.[4]

Ships, not guns, proved the decisive technology of the War Capitalist era. Not only was it via ship that Europeans were able to move their goods, ideas, troops, and diseases across the globe, but their prolonged use allowed for the space and opportunity to master the employment of firearms. Originally invented by the Chinese and in use by Christians and Muslims in Europe since the Late Middle Ages, by the sixteenth-century experience with their use on land had taught Western gunsmiths enough to enable their application in naval warfare, where their bulk, weight, and inaccuracy were of less consequence. Their firepower proved far more valuable against other large and slow vessels densely packed with soldiers than against the fast moving cavalry of the Eurasian step. Cannon-centered naval combat provided endless opportunities to innovate further in the tactical use of guns, take that experience back to the gunsmiths, and further refine the manufacture of firearms.[5] Thus in ships we see the intermixing of warfare, economic production, and global trade in the steady accumulation of power among certain nations of western Europe.

The resources, lands, and commercial relationships formed under War Capitalism were essential to the later success of Industrial Capitalism and the Western dominance of that economic transformation. The vicissitudes of that mode of production – the tendency of firms to monopolize sectors of the economy over time, organized labor pushing back against abusive working conditions, colonial peoples revolting against imperial exploitation, the capture of government regulation by business interests, etc. – yielded by the 1970s another shift in capitalism, this time into the Post-Industrial (or Rentier) Capitalism we see today. This is characterized by the financialization of the economy, making money from existing assets rather than creating new goods and services. Corporations increasingly offshored industrial production to countries with lower labor standards and less environmental regulation; resource extraction increased as new markets were found for existing products; innovation emphasized the abuse or circumvention of laws, the gaming of existing systems in order to perpetuate the growth seen as necessary to continued corporate health.

It was amid these various capitalist processes that Indigenous peoples in America and around the globe acted and reacted. Their success varied over time and space but tended toward defeat or accommodation. Perhaps in the contemporary world that trend is starting to change.

6.1.2 Extractivism

The capitalist mindset is an atomistic one. People are individuals radically divorced from one another, consigned to make rational economic choice devoid of essential social connection. The environment (the land, other living organisms, and the climate) is divorced from humanity, becoming instead this mythical place we call Nature.[6] From the "natural world," of which humanity has no part, we extract the resources necessary for our productive enterprises. This Extractivism is in a nonreciprocal, dominance-based relationship with the earth, one in which all is taken and nothing given back. Its foil is stewardship, i.e. taking but also taking care that regeneration and future life continue. Extractivism is the reduction of life into objects for humanity's sole use; living complex ecosystems become "natural resources," mountains become "overburden." Humanity itself becomes "human resources," something to extract and exploit, jail, and deport, something profitable. Extractivists (and the economy they foster) ignore the interconnections among these various objectified components of life and heed not the consequences wrought from severing the world from itself.

Extractivism also separates the human world into two collections of atoms: the core and the periphery. The former benefits from the extraction of resources and the exploitation of labor, the latter becomes a "sacrifice zone" from which prosperity is leeched.[7] This arrangement is not unique to capitalism, as slaves throughout the history of human civilization can attest, but under this contemporary form of economic organization the dichotomy has reached new heights of refinement. Fossil fuels are a prime example of this sacrificial relationship, for they always require sacrifice zones, be it the black lungs of coal miners or the poisoned waterways surrounding oil pipelines.

In articulating the capitalist relationship with land, labor, and society, it is helpful to contrast it with something different, lest we think that capitalist reality is the only reality. Many (perhaps most) Indigenous societies related to the land as part of a broader understanding of reality which underpinned the whole of native life. Perhaps the most basic element of this understanding was the belief in what we might call sacred power, the proposition that everything in the universe is interconnected, possessing a spiritual energy that can shape the lives of all living things.

In this mental milieu, attaining power and the aid of powerful spirits was vital, since success in hunting, in farming, in health, in family, and in battle was a holistic affair with each part energetically connected to all the others.[8]

Developments in history and sociology, in biology and atmospheric science over the course of the twentieth century have exploded the atomistic view of the world. Fossil fuels did not free us from our relations with the rest of reality, they merely delayed our reckoning with it. Global warming now looms, pledging to repay our every chemical reaction burn for burn. Hope lies not in some fanciful return to nature or some miraculous technology but in renewing the bonds of matrimony between humanity and the rest of existence, recognizing the interconnectedness of all things, and planning our economic activities with reciprocity, regeneration, and balance first in mind. The histories of Indigenous peoples in the context of European empires gives some precedent for this – and the descendants of these struggles, who continue to resist and persevere, give hope for our collective future.

6.2 Indigenous Reaction and Resistance to Empire

6.2.1 Indigenous Resistance in American History

Justice cannot be done in so small a space to the long history of interaction between Europeans and Indigenous Americans – the first contacts (both friendly and hostile), the Columbian Exchange of ideas, trade goods, diseases, and bodies, the wars and treaties and betrayals and massacres, the ultimate subjugation, eradication, or eviction of nation upon Indigenous nation. Still, some sense of time and scale is necessary, if only in outline form.

During the Colonial Era, the English Crown vacillated in its active policy toward the natives, but did at least pay lip service to attempting to keep them free from white encroachment.

Unfortunately, the English government ran into the same problem that the Spanish had a century earlier in trying to enforce any sort of Indigenous protection: distance. Each English law or proclamation, decreed across the vast abyss of the Atlantic Ocean, were but dead letters, unenforceable in the face of such distance and in the face of such colonial determination to exploit and conquer. More importantly, enough of the people within the government (of both the colonies and the mother country) recognized the connection between brutality toward the natives; private accumulation by determined colonials of land, labor, and wealth (in the Thirteen Colonies, the Caribbean, and India); and the state revenues generated by the cycle of imperial expansion, domestic manufacturing, and foreign export that – whatever their personal moral qualms – they were willing to allow colonial cruelty if it meant economic success.[9]

Differing methods of colonization – whether focused more on trade or on settlement – produced a varied reaction from Indigenous communities. Groups living near Puritan settlements in seventeenth-century New England attempted to live with the newcomers, and found some success before the brutal Pequot War late in the seventeenth century, which, through a level of violence no Indigenous person had expected, all but broke native direct resistance in that area.[10] Communities that participated in the fur trade – the first large-scale transatlantic trade in North America – did not find themselves immediately subjugated; nevertheless the long-term effects of their commercial contact with Europeans was profound. First, the fur trade (and European contact generally) brought contagious disease that did much to weaken Indigenous communities. Second, the metal tools and weapons Europeans traded for furs did more than alter the lives of those who acquired them: they affected enemies and neighbors as well, now at a comparative disadvantage and thus pushed by circumstance to seek their own sources of European goods in order to feed and defend their people. This cascaded throughout the interconnected Indigenous communities and their calculated, ritually maintained relationships, plunging more and more peoples into a desperate quest for trade.

Once enmeshed in this network, it was almost impossible to go back. Hunting for furs interrupted the normal cycle of subsistence activities and led to an erosion of the skills needed to make necessities – such as cooking pots – for which the fur trade offered a ready European alternative. From being self-sufficient farmers or hunter-gatherers functioning with an admirable degree of equilibrium with their surroundings, Indigenous people shifted into specialist producers in a transatlantic economy that could only exist by taking more from them than it gave back. The immense profits of the fur trade resulted from the difference between what a merchant paid for furs in America and what they got for them in Europe; although most Indigenous traders likely never saw it in these terms, every transaction ultimately undermined their own position, siphoning ever more wealth (and therefore power) from the New World to the Old.[11]

Europeans were not ignorant of the kind of dependent relationship engaging in trade might engender between Europeans with manufactured goods (including guns and alcohol) and natives with an abundance of raw material. Wrote one fur trader circa 1750:

...I am convinced they must be ruled with a rod of Iron to bring and keep them in a proper state of subordination, and the most certain way to effect this is by letting them feel their dependence upon us...In the woods and northern barren grounds this measure ought to be pursued rigidly next year if they do not improve, and no credit, not so much as a load of ammunition, given them until they exhibit an inclination to renew their habits of industry. In the plains, however, this system will not do, as they can live independent of us, and by withholding ammunition, tobacco and spirits, the Staple articles of Trade, for one year, they will recover the use of their Bows and spears, and lose sight of their smoking and drinking habits...[12]

The networking of European traders, the settlement of European colonists, the spread of European goods, and the infiltration of European diseases had a profoundly deleterious effect upon the 7 million natives inhabiting North America, over and above the obvious destruction caused directly by European invasion and conquest.[13] Indeed, the devastation caused by small pox in particular did not escape the notice of contemporary Europeans. Wrote one Pilgrim: "Thus farre hath the good hand of God favoured our beginnings...In sweeping away great multitudes of the natives..., a little more before we went thither, that he might make room for us there."[14]

Emptiness became a common colonial theme. Already inhabited land was considered empty by Europeans if the inhabitance failed to "improve" it with productive enterprises – irrigation, farmland, manufacturing (known in legal theory as the doctrine of *vacuum domicilium*). Land could also be considered retroactively empty if the people previously living there had been decimated by disease, driven off by bands of colonists, or (once the US was established) officially resettled by government fiat.[15] This perceived or concocted emptiness fooled many Americans into assuming that the entire continent, rather than already teeming with life and culture, had been, in one telling metaphor, "virginal" territory ripe for the plucking. Despite the myth of emptiness, Indigenous communities have continued to exist across the continent, whether white historians choose to acknowledge them or not.[16]

By the eighteenth century, Europeans had established themselves firmly in the New World and were a reality of life for all Indigenous nations. Throughout the vicissitudes of the previous 200 years of contact, the natives had been forced to change more than their interlopers. We can see this in the words of the Delaware shaman Neolin, who inspired Pontiac's 1763 war against European settlers. Neolin was a prophet who believed that Indigenous peoples had brought the disaster of European domination on themselves by embracing aspects of European culture and neglecting the spiritual roots of their own power. He counseled that only by rejecting alcohol, Christianity, and other pollutants introduced by whites, and returning to the rituals and ceremonies of tradition, could natives find the strength needed to repel the invader. This dichotomy between European and Native (uniting previously disparate Indigenous nations under one categorical banner) was in fact a new development, resulting from the need to meet a common enemy and from the importation of a kind of racial attitude from the Europeans – although it emphasized culture rather than blood, thus lacking much of the biological essentialism that would come to dominate white intellectual discourse. Neolin's views also reflected an awareness of the dependence that had developed among Indigenous nations for European goods and the competition this had engendered among various communities all vying for a spot in the international fur trade. This new "nativist" mindset would prove far more durable than the previous system of ad hoc alliances found among the Indigenous nations of the eastern and Great Lakes regions.[17]

While Pontiac's war ended in defeat, the fighting continued elsewhere. In 1814 war broke out between the US and the Red Sticks, ending in Indigenous defeat. The Treaty of Horseshoe Bend resulted, surrendering 23 million acres of Indigenous land as "compensation" for American troubles; much of this land actually came from Indigenous people allied to the US during the war. This catastrophe taught the Muskogee nation and their neighbors that the fundamental principles which, from the Indigenous point of view, governed relations between societies had broken down. They had hitherto viewed the universe as reciprocal, wherein a policy of political submission and voluntary land cessions on their part should have brought protection from the United States; or low levels of warfare against their white foe should have deterred further American aggression. Yet both accommodation and resistance seemed only to accelerate the influx of settlers and the loss of Indigenous land. Even the nativism that arose in the late eighteenth century, while finally recognizing that Europeans would never agree to live reciprocally with Indigenous peoples, had failed to bring them victory.[18]

So the Cherokee tried a new tactic: become as the European. In 1820 the Cherokee nation formally became a republic, with a police force, European style judicial system, written language, farmsteads replacing stockade towns, and even entrepreneurship (and slaveholding) among some Cherokee elite. One Cherokee, Elias Boudinot, wrote in his *Address to the Whites* (1826):

What is an Indian? Is he not formed of the same materials with yourself?...Though it be true that he is ignorant, that he is a heathen, that he is a savage; yet he is no more than all others have been under similar circumstances. Eighteen centuries ago what were the inhabitants of Great Britain?

You here behold an Indian, my kindred are Indians, and my fathers sleeping in the wilderness grave – they too were Indians. But I am not as my fathers were...I have had greater advantages than most of my race; and I now stand before you delegated by my native country to seek her interest...and by my public efforts to assist in raising her to an equal standing with other nations of the earth...

...There is, in Indian history, something very melancholy... We have seen everywhere the poor aborigines melt away before the white population. I merely speak of the fact, without at all referring to the cause. We have seen, I say, one family after another, one tribe after another, nation after nation, pass away; until only a few solitary creatures are left to tell the sad story of extinction.

Shall this precedent be followed? I ask you, shall red men live, or shall they be swept from the earth? With you and this public at large, the decision chiefly rests.[19]

This appeal to common humanity and a modern culture that could be shared across nations fell on deaf ears. President Andrew Jackson initiated an aggressive "Indian removal" policy, culminating in the infamous Trail of Tears. Americans forced the resettlement of these Cherokees, regardless of how much they Europeanized, onto "Indian Territory" far to the west. Said a Confederate veteran about his earlier work against the Cherokee: "I fought through the civil war and have seen men shot to pieces and slaughtered by the thousands, but the Cherokee removal was the cruellest [sic] work I ever knew."[20] Removal to the west, however, proved no safeguard for the remaining Indigenous peoples. It was only a matter of time before Manifest Destiny brought White and Red into conflict yet again.

Victory in the Mexican American War delivered Indigenous communities (hitherto under the Spanish yoke) to star-spangled subjugation. The US conquest of the Southwest ushered in a very different era indeed. Unlike Spain, the United States had little interest either in native labor or the salvation of native souls. They coveted native land, upon which they wanted to build new Anglo-American communities.[21]

The 1848 Gold Rush carried whites to the California coast in droves, inaugurating perhaps the single most destructive episode in the whole history of Native/Euro-American relations. The miners flocked, by and large, not to the existing Hispanic settlements along the coast but to the mountains and forests of the interior which, since the arrival of the Spanish, had become almost exclusively Indigenous territory. Native groups had no time to adapt and nowhere to escape to as, sometimes within a matter of days, their lands were completely overrun.[22]

The Civil War brought its own profound repercussions for those on the "frontier." In 1862 the Union forces sent to occupy New Mexico turned their attention to pacifying the bands of Navajo and Apache who were raiding local settlements. The Mimbreno Apache leader Mangas Colorado was captured under a flag of truce and murdered; in a relentless war of attrition, the Mescaleros were finally forced to surrender and accept a reservation at Bosque Redondo, an arid area chosen "for the concentration and maintenance of all captive Indian from the New Mexico territory." This was only one instance in a frontier war that escalated until the massacre at Wounded Knee in 1890, by which point organized Indigenous resistance had been broken by the repeating rifle, the telegraph, and the railroad.[23]

An increasingly hostile and contemptuous view of Indigenous people undergirded this nineteenth-century onslaught. As a point of contrast, consider the 1789 writing of David Ramsay, a rather typical Enlightenment-era Carolina gentleman and politician, chronicling the discovery of the New World:

The country thus discovered...was possessed by numerous tribes or nations of people...Of the various principles on which a right to soil has been founded, there is none superior to immemorial occupancy...In this state no European prince could derive a title to the soil from discovery, because that can give a right only to lands and things which either have never been owned or possessed,...[or] have been voluntarily deserted...

The blinded superstition of the times regarded the Deity as the partial God of christians, and not as the common father of saints and savages...

By tacit consent [Europeans] adopted as a new law of nations, that the countries which each explored should be the absolute property of the discoverer...[European governments] so far adopted the fanciful distinction between the rights of heathens and the rights of christians, as to make it the foundation of their respective grants.[24]

Compare this relatively honest picture of early Indigenous interactions with Europeans, one that treats the Indigenous nations as fully part of the human race, to one Father Geronimo Boscana, a Franciscan priest who wrote voluminous observations about native culture and customs during his stay at Mission San Juan Capistrano from 1812 until 1826: "Indians of California may be compared to a species of monkey." Or the 1849 comments of Samuel Upham concerning Indigenous Californians: "Like his brother, the gorilla, he is a vegetarian and subsists principally on wild berries and acorns, occasionally luxuriating on snails and grasshoppers."[25] Finally, in the words of the commissioner of Indian Affairs, Ely S. Parker, we see Indigenous nationhood being stripped away. He proclaimed in 1869:

The Indian tribes of the United States are not sovereign nations, capable of making treaties, as none of them have an organized government of such inherent strength as would secure a faithful obedience of its people in the observance of compacts of this character. They are held to be wards of the government, and the only title the law concedes them to the lands they occupy or claim is a mere possessory one. But because treaties have been made with them, generally for the extinguishment of their supposed absolute title to land inhabited by them, or over which they roam, they have become falsely impressed with the notion of national independence. It is time that this idea should be dispelled, and the government cease the cruel farce of thus dealing with its helpless and ignorant wards...[26]

This notion that Indigenous people no longer held sovereign

independence would dominate the underlying assumptions of a great deal of America's future "Indian" policy.

The early twentieth century brought a white campaign to wipe out the last vestiges of Indigenous culture, "killing the Indian to save the man," as the saying went. Reformers abducted Indigenous children to raise them within a white "School System" that forbade them from dressing, speaking, or acting "Indian," instead teaching them English and the rudiments of Anglo-American culture. The Allotment System strove to break up remaining Indigenous communities by allotting communal native land to individual "fit Indians," although much land ended up stolen by whites in the process.[27]

The New Deal attempted to rectify some of these past atrocities via the actions of John Collier as Commissioner of Indian Affairs. This "Indian New Deal" achieved some remarkable results. During his 11 years in office Collier halted the process of Native American land loss, indeed reversing it (probably for the first time in history). The total area of Indigenous lands in the continental US rose from perhaps 47 million to 51 million acres, where it has stayed ever since. He gave back some semblance of empowerment to Indigenous communities: during his administration, the government lent the tribes a total of $12 million, fueling an explosion of economic activity. Native American beef herds, for instance, increased by 105 percent, their yield of animal products by 2300 percent, and their total agricultural income from $1.85 million to $49 million. A significant minority of Indigenous communities remained, however, outside the purview of even these haltingly positive policies. Moreover, in loaning money to natives that was then paid back with interest, there remained in the government's mindset the notion that Indigenous people were not deserving of compensation (no strings attached) for centuries of brutality and injustice.[28]

In 1946, back in more conservatives hands, "Indian policy"

shifted again. The US Indian Claims Commission was established to address all outstanding claims and settle things once and for all. With Eisenhower came a new policy, "Termination," best summarized by HCR (House Concurrent Resolution) 108, adopted in August 1953. This declared Congress's intention to make Indigenous peoples "subject to the same laws and entitled to the same privileges and responsibilities as...other citizens of the United States" by "freeing" them from "all Federal supervision and control." From 1954 to 1960 some 14 recognized tribes with reservations were terminated, often without their consent. Most were small, impoverished communities possessed of little inkling of what was being done to them. Others, like the Menominee of Wisconsin and the Klamath of Oregon, larger and wealthier and owning considerable natural resources, fought the government's decision to denude them of tribal status.[29] Despite the government's best efforts, many natives did not wish to be assimilated out of existence; they remained proud of their independent existence (however economically dependent they remained upon a federal government that had driven many tribes onto inhospitable, arid, unproductive land). Said Ben Nighthorse Campbell, a Colorado senator, criticizing the policy of termination and forced assimilation:

In Washington's infinite wisdom, it was decided that tribes should no longer be tribes, never mind that they had been tribes for thousands of years. It is analogous to the federal government mandating that black Americans can no longer be black. Many tribes are still trying after years of work to be reinstated as a federally recognized entity. The reason is that the federal government has a contractual obligation through treaties to perform 'trust responsibility' to tribes – not individuals – rather an ingenious manner of avoiding responsibility. If we get rid of "tribes," we can avoid responsibility to individual Indians and save lots of money.[30]

In the 1970s Indigenous activism picked up as many Indians pushed back against government attempts to assimilate them into oblivion. The year 1971 saw Indigenous activists from the American Indian Movement (AIM) occupy Alcatraz Island for several days, bringing national attention to "Indian issues" for the first time in generations. This was followed up in 1972 with AIM's Trail of Broken Treaties campaign to Washington DC: marchers took possession of the Bureau of Indian Affairs office for 6 days, at which point the government agreed to "investigate" the demands of the protestors. 1973 witnessed the high-water mark of late-twentieth century Indigenous activism when AIM occupied Wounded Knee for 71 days. Activists exchanged gunfire with police and national guardsmen; two activists were killed and one police officer seriously wounded.[31]

In addition to protest, some Indigenous people turned to the court system, hoping that the Western rhetoric of impartial justice and due process really meant something. In 1980, the legal fighting reached a climax with the Supreme Court case *United States v. Sioux Nations of Indians*. The case revolved around the Fort Laramie Treaty of April 29, 1868, which dictated that the Great Sioux Reservation, including the Black Hills, would be "set apart for the absolute and undisturbed use and occupation of the Indians." General George Custer and a plethora of white settlers violated the treaty in the 1870s in the search for gold. After the Sioux resisted these encroachments, up to and including the destruction of Custer and his band of soldiers, the US government declared the Sioux hostile and conquered their remaining territory. The court recognized the historic injustice. Instead of returning the stolen land to the tribes, however, the court focused on the fact that no just compensation had been given to the natives for their land at the time; by way of recompense, therefore, they decreed a cash payment be dispensed to settle the issue. The Native Americans, who had never desired to sell their land in the first place, refused this payment outright, characterizing it as a betrayal of their heritage. The payment has continued to accrue interest since it was first refused and stood at over a billion dollars by the early twenty-first century.[32]

This legacy of forceful assimilation, termination of tribal status, protests, and incomplete legal victory set the stage for the Indigenous struggles of the twenty-first century.

6.2.2 Blockadia

The contemporary fight against extractivist enterprises – the heirs of the imperialism and colonialism of old – has been referred to as "Blockadia," a roaming battlespace flaring up wherever extractive projects seek to pierce mines into the black, fracture gas into the air, or lay pipes into the distance. Rather than being led by the Big Green groups of old, so vulnerable to fossil fuel infiltration and the self-serving compromise of their core principles, these contemporary struggles are led by local activists who are united in preventing the sacrifice of their communities upon the altar of cheap energy. So committed are these people to defending themselves that many are reaching across historical divisions to unite against a common enemy, as, for example, ranchers and Indigenous peoples in places like North Dakota and Montana coalitioning against extractivist enterprises.[33]

The increasingly widespread conviction that contemporary extractive efforts pose significantly higher risks than conventional methods bolsters Blockadia resistance. Tar Sands oil, more disruptive and damaging to local ecosystems than conventional crude, more dangerous to transport, and harder to clean up once spilled, is one example. Activists voiced similar concerns over the shift from conventional to fracked oil and gas, from shallow to deep-water drilling, and from warm water to Arctic drilling.

The 2010 BP disaster in the Gulf of Mexico solidified for many the soundness of their fossil fuel skepticism, and catapulted them into political action. In what became the largest accidental marine oil spill in history, a state-of-the-art offshore oil rig exploded, killing 11 workers, while oil gushed from the ruptured wellhead more than a mile below the water's surface. BP evinced an utter lack of preparedness for a blowout at such depths, with their immediate hot fixes proving woefully inadequate. Government regulators, meanwhile, showed a willful cluelessness and indecisiveness. They had taken BP at its word about the safety of the operation and were so ill-equipped for the disaster that they allowed BP itself to be in charge of the cleanup operations. This explosive example of profit-driven disaster and regulatory capture opened the eyes of many to the need for broad-based resistance and systemic change.[34]

The environmental consequences of this oil spill, in which 4.9 million barrels poured into the Gulf of Mexico, were myriad. Massive levels of polycyclic aromatic hydrocarbons blanketed the affected area, producing a variety of deleterious effects upon marine life (inability to intake oxygen, cardiac arrests, organ deformities). Perhaps 1 million coastal birds died directly as a result of the spill, with another million dying due to subsequent environmental effects. Ten times the number of dead dolphin infants were discovered washed up along the Gulf shore after the spill than in previous years. Mutated fish appeared with increasing frequency, from 0.1 percent of observed Gulf fish prior to the spill to between 20 and 50 percent (depending on location). In cleaning up the mess, unprecedented quantities of Corexit were used to break up the oil into tiny droplets that could more easily be consumed by microbes; this had the effect of permeating oil throughout the local food chain – and chemicals from the oil and cleanup efforts were found in migratory birds as far away as Minnesota.[35] While subsequent investigations placed the blame squarely on BP (and its corporate partners) for the errors, omissions, and deliberate actions that led to the disaster, none were sentenced to any prison time.[36]

The aggression of fossil fuel companies also had the

unintended effect of bringing disparate elements of surviving Indigenous communities together. Their political and social bonds shattered by the locomotion of white conquest, the seven nations of Dakota-, Nakota-, and Lakota-speaking peoples had been separate for more than a century. Once spanning territory from the western shores of Lake Superior to the Bighorn Mountains, *Oceti Sakowin* (the Seven Council Fires, aka the Great Sioux Nation) had once united in times of celebration, for annual sun dances, large trading fairs, and buffalo hunts. The last such unification had occurred in the nineteenth century in response to invasion. More than one hundred years later, they found themselves forced once again to unite in the face of threats to their land, *He Sapa* ("the heart of everything that is"), and their water, *Mni Sosa* ("roiling water," the active life flowing through the heart of everything).[37]

In resisting imperialism, capitalism, and settler colonialism, Indigenous people stand at the intersection of contemporary struggle. They fight against the national hubris we have witnessed in the War on Terror, the private greed (backed by public dollars) of the Great Recession, and the rapacity mirrored in American healthcare. Their struggles are related to – though distinct from – the struggles of African Americans: poverty, social collapse, and marginalization all enforced by systems of control and domination (police brutality, rigged justice systems, living space deliberately separated from affluent society). Moreover, much contemporary Indigenous struggle is led by LGBT people, i.e. those possessed of "two spirits." And of course, in combating the interlocking sectors of hegemony, Indigenous peoples are the tip of the spear in the fight against global warming, itself an unintended consequence of the unhindered, for-profit resource extraction amid stolen land.

Of the many Blockadia campaigns waged during Obama's presidency, two stand out for the amount of national attention they received. Both involved thwarting the construction of oil pipelines, one crossing the international border between the US and Canada, the other crossing between the contested boundary separating the United States from an Indian Reservation.

6.2.2.1 The Keystone XL Pipeline

The Keystone XL pipeline, meant to bring Canadian crude from the Tar Sands into the US for processing and export, began construction in 2010. Despite rhetoric that he would fight climate change, Obama did nothing to halt this expansion of fossil fuel infrastructure. Indeed, his administration did much to encourage new, more volatile methods of extracting dirty fuels – fracking, deep-water drilling, etc. – as part of its plan for diversifying US energy, strengthening energy security, and (hopefully but not as a matter of first priority) fighting climate change. As more than 9 million US families – many of them poor and people of color – faced home foreclosures, Indigenous people were once again set to be sacrificed on the altar of cheap energy and eternal economic growth. Like the Occupy movement of 2010, resistance against Keystone emerged from an atmosphere of increasing frustration with the status quo and a sense that only militant action could accomplish that which mainstream politics, exemplified by the decidedly ordinary presidency of Barack Obama, failed to do.[38]

In 2012 Obama fast-tracked the construction of the pipeline's southern leg from Cushing, Oklahoma, to the Gulf Coast, promising, "As long as I'm president, we're going to keep on encouraging oil development and infrastructure, and we're going to do it in a way that protects the health and safety of American people."[39] Troublingly, this mention of health and safety seemed to disregard the deleterious effects climate change is sure to have upon the American people. Nevertheless, crews completed Phases I through III by the middle of Obama's second term in office.

Blockadia resistance coalesced against Phase IV of the pipeline, the northern section known as Keystone XL. One group, Tar Sands Blockade, organized an 86-day tree blockade in August 2012 challenging a portion of pipeline construction in East Texas. Local activism such as this combined with large-scale urban protest, with the February 2013 protest of over 40,000 people outside the White House being the largest climate movement protest up to that point. Responding to this pressure from below, Obama denied the required presidential permit for Keystone's northern section in December 2015.[40]

President Trump rescinded this denial on January 24, 2017. His State Department declared the pipeline to be in the "national interest" in March, and Trump granted a permit for TransCanada to build the XL section that same month. Court battles followed this presidential permission, but failed to stop the regulatory process from continuing apace – although construction has yet to commence as of early 2020. Ominously, however, a South Dakota section of the pipeline leaked 210,000 gallons in November 2017, prophesying the kind of environmental impact the new section of pipeline is sure to have.[41]

6.2.2.2 The Dakota Access Pipeline (DAPL)

Keystone XL had crossed an international border and thus required State Department review and presidential approval. Announced in June 2014, the Dakota Access Pipeline (DAPL) was a domestic project weaving its way from northwest North Dakota into South Dakota, Iowa, and terminating in Illinois. It relied on the Army Corps of Engineers to assess the pipeline according to Nationwide Permit 12, encompassing individual construction sites rather than cumulative negative impacts on entire nations of people, ecosystems, or the climate. This bypassed environmental review under the Clean Water Act and the National Environmental Policy Act. It also avoided the kind of public scrutiny received by Keystone XL and significantly undermined the ability of impacted communities to mobilize in opposition.[42]

The Sioux couched their resistance to DAPL in terms of national sovereignty. Viewing the conflict through a tribal rather than individual lens, they still recognized the borders set by the 1868 Fort Laramie Treaty, which established the Great Sioux Reservation, its ownership of the Black Hills, and set aside additional unceded "Indian territory" in areas of South Dakota, Wyoming, Nebraska, and possibly Montana (depending on the treaty's interpretation). While the federal government broke the treaty, warred on the natives, and annexed the land in 1877, the Sioux had never recognized the legality of this seizure, and refused the government's 1980 attempt to compensate them for the land as "a sellout of the Lakota nation, religion and culture."[43] From the Sioux perspective, then, DAPL was more than an interstate concern; it was international.

The chief environmental objection to the pipeline involved water. As planned, the pipeline would travel underneath the Missouri River, the primary drinking water source for the Standing Rock Sioux, about 10,000 people living on a reservation more than twice the size of Rhode Island and straddling the central portions of North and South Dakota. While the builders insisted that they had taken extraordinary measures to safeguard against disaster, opposition groups pointed out that all pipelines can (and do) leak. Indeed, the Pipeline and Hazardous Materials Safety Administration reported more than 3300 incidents of leaks and ruptures at oil and gas pipelines between 2010 and 2016.[44] Even a small rupture could damage the drinking water supply.

The Standing Rock Sioux further argued that the pipeline traversed sacred land. Although the land being used for the pipeline was not on its reservation, the reservation borders had been drawn at the convenience of white politicians and had never taken into consideration things like the location of the Sioux dead. Tribal leaders tried to work within the system, arguing that the federal government did not adequately follow federal law and engage the Standing Rock Sioux during the permitting process.[45]

Indigenous scholar Nick Estes summarized the struggle as follows:

> #NoDAPL was also a struggle over the meaning of land. For the Oceti Sakowin, history is the land itself: the earth cradles the bones of the ancestors. As Tasunka Witko, Crazy Horse, once said, "My land is where my dead lie buried." For others, however, the earth had to be tamed and dominated by a plow or drilled for profit. Because Native people remain barriers to capitalist development, their bodies needed to be removed – both from beneath and atop the soil – therefore eliminating their rightful relationship with the land.[46]

In 2016, billionaire Kelcy Warren, the CEO of Energy Transfer Partners (of which Dakota Access is a subsidiary), disagreed that the Standing Rock Sioux had not been adequately consulted, saying: "I really wish for the Standing Rock Sioux that they had engaged in discussions way before they did. We could have changed the route. It could have been done, but it's too late."[47] In point of fact, Standing Rock had passed a resolution in 2012 opposing all new pipelines and declaring a moratorium on hydraulic fracturing on its land; in September 2014 the tribal council had met with Energy Transfer representatives and indicated their opposition to the project.[48] Indeed, local opposition (among various groups) had been voiced since the first community meetings regarding the project were held in 2014, but state governments (always short on cash and thus understandably desirous of any and all development projects) overwhelmingly supported the endeavor, and by 2015 the Army Corps of Engineers was on board as well, drafting a plan for the pipeline to go under the Missouri River. In April 2016 the Army Corps of Engineers determined that no historic properties would be affected by the pipeline crossing, although it did note that some cultural sites were in the area and that the Standing Rock Sioux had requested further surveying be done. After some additional internal debate, the corps officially approved the crossing at the Lake Oahe reservoir in July 2016, stating plainly, "No significant comments remain unresolved."[49]

In August Standing Rock responded by issuing a suit against the Army Corps of Engineers, alleging a failure adequately to consult the tribe. The suit further argued that the Army Corps of Engineers, lacking any provision in their plan to protect against the destruction of culturally important sites near the construction route, violated the National Historic Preservation Act. Dakota Access countersued in response to protests on the ground that the activists had illegally halted construction activities. In September the tribe's historic preservation officer asserted: "I surveyed this land and we confirmed multiple graves and specific prayer sites. Portions, and possibly complete sites, have [already] been taken out entirely [by bulldozer crews along a 2-mile area near Lake Oahe]."[50]

The legal battle raged concurrently with clashes between protestors (known as "water protectors") and security forces onsite. Beginning in the summer of 2016, Indigenous communities came together under the aegis of mostly young people to protest construction (with notable participation from Indigenous transpeople). Initially, corporate security guards made up the ranks of antagonism. Local law enforcement joined the fray soon thereafter. On September 6, 2016 a US District Judge temporarily halted construction pending a full decision of the Sioux's pending lawsuit. Two days later North Dakota's governor, Jack Dalrymple, activated the National Guard. By early December some 500 guardspeople had been deployed to the area.[51]

Police, clad in riot gear that echoed Ferguson, Missouri, confronted the unarmed protestors. Nick Estes, chronicling one encounter, paints the following picture:

They dragged half-naked elders from ceremonial sweat lodges, tasered a man in the face, doused people with CS gas and tear gas, and blasted adults and youth with deafening LRAD sound cannons. The 142 arrests were marked with a number in black permanent marker on their forearm, led onto buses, and kept overnight in dog kennels. To add insult to injury, personal belongings – including ceremonial items like pipes and eagle feathers, as well as jackets and tents – confiscated by the police during the raid were returned soaked in urine.[52]

Indeed, Governor Dalrymple ultimately marshaled the largest armed response in the state since 1890: 76 law enforcement jurisdictions were deployed alongside National Guard and corporate mercenaries like those employed by the company TigerSwan. These officers were, like their counterparts around the country stifling other marginalized protests, augmented by the War on Terror via the Department of Defense's 1033 Program that provided surplus military equipment to law enforcement agencies nationwide. For example, between 2006 and 2015 the South Dakota Highway Patrol obtained military equipment, including dozens of assault rifles and five armored vehicles, worth some $2 million. Lake County Sheriff's Office in northwestern Indiana (which sent four deputies to the DAPL protests) received 100 assault rifles and two armored trucks, valued at $1.5 million.[53]

The police and National Guard response was couched in the language of law and order, upholding an impartial and neutral justice. But the timing refutes this claim: the pipeline's legality was still very much up in the air in the fall of 2016. A federal judge had halted construction. Lawsuits were pending. The officers and soldiers on the ground had no legal ruling as yet to defend. They proceeded under the assumption that the company was in the right, the Indigenous community in the wrong, and executed their own brand of legal interpretation; the brutality that ensued echoed that of Wounded Knee or Sandy Creek.

In early November, months after construction had begun, protests had erupted, and hundreds of arrests had been made, Obama at long last spoke publicly on the matter. He emphasized that he wanted to respect native sacred lands and was open to a possible reroute, but would remain aloof for the time being and "let it play out for several more weeks." He admonished "both sides" to remain civil: "There's an obligation for protestors to be peaceful and there's an obligation for authorities to show restraint." Of course this middle ground approach made no one happy, but, as is typical, inaction supports the status quo, and so the lack of federal involvement on behalf of the Sioux allowed the continuation of police abuse against the water protectors resisting the pipeline.[54]

Finally, on December 4, 2016, as a group of 4000 war veterans arrived to lend their weight to the force of protestors, the Army Corps denied the permit for DAPL to cross the Missouri River, citing the need for an additional environmental impact study to be done before construction could resume. By this point 832 arrests had been made.[55] On January 24, 2017, Trump signed an executive memorandum expediting the review process; and in February the water crossing was allowed to continue, with the Army Corps of Engineers rescinding its commitment to an environmental impact assessment. Standing Rock attempted further legal maneuvers but ultimately failed to stop construction of the pipeline.

During its first year of operation, the arguments of economic development and the pipeline's safety and stability when compared to other transportation methods (notably by train) prevailed. Between June 2017, when the pipeline went operational, and June 2018 it transported about 182.5 million barrels of oil. Still, despite its relative safety, leaks occurred – at least five in the first six months of service, amounting to several hundred gallons in all. Even so, industry allies argued that thicker pipe walls, rigorous testing of the pipeline's welds during construction, and the especially deep depth of the pipeline's route all protected the local water supply.[56]

They may be correct, and the *local* environmental impact might remain well within reasonable bounds. This narrow mindset forgets the broader issues: the continued violation of Indigenous sovereignty in the pursuit of natural resources, the continued burning of fossil fuels (however safely extracted) that warm the planet and deform the earth, our economy's reliance on violent police action and captured politicians to push corporate projects to their profitable fruition. So long as these structures of power and processes of control remain in place, democracy will remain a dream, the environment will wither, and the rich – perhaps including former president Obama, whose net worth stands at $40 million[57] – will continue to rule. Or, should things degrade to the point of environmental apocalypse, the rich may elect to abandon the fruits of their labor and follow the billionaire prophet Elon Musk to the stars, there to build new Martian chateaus away from the wasteland they left here on *He Sapa*.[58]

Perhaps there is no alternative but to flee to another world, there to be dominated once again by the rapacious, the ruthless, the callous, and the sociopathic. But if there is a chance for something better – something more transparent, democratic, and accountable – then I think we ought to fight for that better future, however remote its possibility. William James echoes in my mind: "as the essence of courage is to stake one's life on a possibility, so the essence of faith is to believe that the possibility exists."[59]

Conclusion

He was our man in Washington. How many thought this to be the case during the Obama presidency? Mainstream Progressives thought this to be the case early in Obama's first term, as he wrote an executive order to close Guantanamo Bay and talked of a public option for healthcare. Liberals, looking at the Clinton-era appointees to Obama's cabinet and his subsequent slight regulation of the financial and healthcare sectors of the economy, certainly thought so. Conservatives made much public ballyhoo over Obama's perceived socialism, but quietly acquiesced to much of his foreign policy, from his massive military budgets, to his drone strikes and continued surveillance of American civilians in the name of national security. The financial institutions and corporations that donated to his campaigns (regardless of partisan affiliation) most assuredly found in him an ally and champion.

On the policy level, legitimate criticism of president Barack Obama abounds, although perhaps not from the direction we might expect given the typical liberal/conservative political spectrum foisted upon US politics. From a liberal perspective (and therefore, at least economically, from a conservative perspective as well) Obama did rather well, and his faults and the imperfections of his policies can be chalked up more often than not to a recalcitrant opposition party fueled to an uncomfortable but unsurprising degree by racist animosity. For social conservatives, upset at even the slightest inclusion of marginal groups into mainstream society, his presidency was of course an abject failure. From a progressive or socialist perspective, Obama's presidency was more of the same, and therefore fairs poorly. The wars continued, the economy remained weighted toward the rich and dedicated to endless growth regardless of externalities, healthcare remained the domain of the profit-seeker at the expense of both the patient and the practitioner, the marginalized largely remained so, and all of this combined to prophesy no end to human-made global warming.

How did Obama do by his own standards? By way of goalposts, we might look to the vision he laid out in his first inaugural address, given on January 21, 2009. Concerning the War on Terror, he said:

> We will begin to responsibly leave Iraq to its people and forge a hard-earned peace in Afghanistan. With old friends and former foes, we will work tirelessly to lessen the nuclear threat and roll back the specter of a warming planet. We will not apologize for our way of life, nor will we waver in its defense. And for those who seek to advance their aims by inducing terror and slaughtering innocents, we say to you now that our spirit is stronger and cannot be broken. You cannot outlast us, and we will defeat you.

On the economy, healthcare, and the environment, he proclaimed:

> The state of the economy calls for action, bold and swift, and we will act not only to create new jobs but to lay a new foundation for growth. We will build the roads and bridges, the electric grids and digital lines that feed our commerce and bind us together. We will restore science to its rightful place and wield technology's wonders to raise health care's quality and lower its cost. We will harness the sun and the winds and the soil to fuel our cars and run our factories...All this we can do. All this we will do.[1]

Based on these criteria, the administration missed many marks: Iraq remained a country in which America had much direct involvement, Afghanistan saw no peace, and the specter of global warming haunts us still; America's economy is still overly reliant on the ephemeral efforts of the financial sector, our infrastructure remains rusted and inadequate, healthcare is not affordable for most people, and our economic activities still rely predominantly on fossil fuels. On the other hand, in helping a bruised status quo back into the ring, Obama fulfilled his promise not to apologize for the American Way of Life – and all the costs that go along with it; indeed, he continued to marshal the resources of the federal government to defend it. Obama himself, citing the fanatical resistance he faced on many issues, might with justice claim that he would have gotten far closer to achieving these goals with a more cooperative opposition party. With that in mind, he himself might view his efforts ultimately as a noble, though perhaps Sisyphean, crack at being chief executive.

Popular opinion of Obama, always mixed during his time in office, surged after he left office. Retrospective polling from 2018 put Obama's approval rating at 63 percent (Reagan stood at 72 percent, Clinton 62 percent, Bush II 53 percent, Nixon 28 percent in the same poll).[2] This post-presidency popularity of Obama stems more from a comparison with his successor than from any new-found love for his policies. His charm, his willingness to dialog, his attention to issues of legality and ethics, made Obama seem all the better when compared to the Trump administration.

In an indirect way, however, Obama's popularity in comparison to Trump did result from his presidential policies. The compromises of his actual presidency combined with the soaring campaign rhetoric of 2008 to set the stage for the dramatic occurrences and incredible upset of the 2016 presidential election. Without Obama there would have been no Bernie Sanders to challenge Clinton's presumed leadership of the Democratic ticket; without Obama there would have been no Donald Trump. Many had voted for Obama because they hoped he would change the system and address its many injustices – whether never-ending foreign wars, unconscionable economic inequality, maldistributed healthcare, continued marginalization of historically oppressed groups, the destruction of a human-friendly climate. Of course he could never have changed things by himself, but he did not even try to lead a movement for fundamental transformation. He abandoned the progressivism of the campaign trail as soon as the day was won.

The sense of betrayal that followed soured many to the prospect of mainstream political action. Thus when new challengers to the status quo, whether self-described socialists like Vermont senator Bernie Sanders or those pretending to outsider status like Donald Trump, came onto the political scene many voters turned to them rather than establishment candidates. Trump specifically framed himself as an outsider seeking to *Drain the Swamp®*, and too many either took him at his word or ignored politics altogether and did not vote. The prospect of "more of the same" presented by Hillary Clinton energized too few.

Now Americans are dealing with the vicissitudes of a Trump presidency. For the first time since Richard Nixon, the chief executive mirrors the ugliness of the policies being carried out in the name of the American electorate. I submit to you that the solution to this quandary is not another Obama, another nice guy that does mean things behind closed doors for the benefit of his corporate allies. The answer involves electoral politics, for we surely need politicians not beholden to corporate interests, but it lies beyond elections as well: in local action, mutual aid, and rabble rousing.

There are signs that some Americans are taking up the gauntlet of this political challenge. In the wake of Trump's victory – and the seething conservatism unleashed therewith –leftist groups have grown in size and scope. The Democratic Socialist of America, for instance, blossomed from about 5000 members in 2016 to more than 30,000 in 2017 and 49,000 before the close of 2018, becoming the largest socialist political association this country has seen in a century.[3] Standard bearers of this socialist wave, like House representative Alexandria Ocasio-Cortez and Vermont senator Bernie Sanders, have garnered sustained national news coverage, and have begun to challenge mainstream Democratic politicians across the country. Let us hope this leftward surge of energy and action continues.

No one is an island; we are a continental species; and as Thomas Paine wrote in 1776: "There is something absurd in supposing a Continent to be perpetually governed by an island."[4] Obama's presidency sought to bolster the foundations of that island of power that is a business-dominated federal government. In that fundamental sense, he was a servant of the status quo. Regardless of one's conscious political affiliation, his legacy should thus be judged based on one's opinion of this current state of affairs. If you support things more or less as they are, then you might consider Obama to have been a somewhat positive force in American politics. If, like me, you see more bad than good in the structure of our contemporary economic and political world, then Obama comes across far more negatively.

Writing in the early nineteenth century, at the dawn of what he labeled a democratic age, French politician and historian Alexis de Tocqueville opined that the written word is "an arsenal open to all, from which the weak and the poor [come] each day to seek arms."[5] If this be true, then I hope this book will arm the reader with some appreciation for what happened under Obama, why it happened, and of what significance it all was within the larger context of American history. So armed, those desirous of fundamental change might then, in addition to the bare minimum of voting in "the lesser of two evils," devote their energies to laboring outside the crippling compromises inherent in American electoral politics.

Left to their own devices, politicians working within our undemocratic system inevitably favor the rich and the defenders of the rich. Without a Mass Movement shoving him along, Obama did just that. It is only after the voices of the oppressed rise to a howling roar and exert irresistible pressure from below – the street protest, the industrial strike, the student walk out, the draft refusal, the riot – that those in power turn their ear away from the sweet whispers of their peers, forced instead to listen to the cries of everyone else.

Endnotes

Introduction

1. Barack Obama, *2004 Democratic National Convention Keynote Address*, accessed November 11, 2019, https://tinyurl.com/s48au8u

2. Obama, *A More Perfect Union*, accessed November 27, 2019, https://tinyurl.com/v8prcfx

3. Obama, *Address to the People of Berlin*, accessed November 27, 2019, https://tinyurl.com/rojwryk

4. Obama, *Barack Obama's Pennsylvania Primary Speech*, April 22, 2008, https://tinyurl.com/wtt64nj

5. Gabriel Schoenfeld, *The Case for Impeaching Barack Obama*, last modified December 10, 2018, https://tinyurl.com/ydxqud45

6. Robert Ehrlich, *A Retrospective on the Obama Years*, last modified January 26, 2016, https://tinyurl.com/saoay58

7. Ross Douthat, *The Obama Legacy*, last modified January 18, 2017, https://tinyurl.com/wvpppyb

8. Ta-Nehisi Coates, *We Were Eight Years in Power: An American Tragedy* (New York: One World Publishing, 2017), 295.

9. Coates, *We Were Eight Years in Power*, 299.

10. Ibid., 302-303.

11. Cornel West, *Obama has failed victims of racism and police brutality*, last modified July 14, 2016, https://tinyurl.com/zq7zp9c

12. For evolutionary biology, see Roughgarden, *Evolution's Rainbow*. For the debate over competition vs. cooperation in human history, contrast Thomas Hobbes' *Leviathan* with Peter Kropotkin's *Conquest of Bread*.

13. Howard Zinn, *A People's History of the United States* (New York: HarperCollins, 2015), 10.

14. Hans Gadamer, *Truth and Method* (New York: Continuum,

2006), 300.

15. Larry Schweikary, Michael Allen. *A Patriot's History of the United States: From Columbus's Great Discovery to the War on Terror* (New York: Sentinel, 2004), 5. The authors assert that "What is most amazing and refreshing is that the past usually speaks for itself." Whether this statement is the result of hubris, ignorance of historical method, or the deliberate obfuscation of the impact of bias in even the most judicious scholarship, I will leave up to the reader's judgment.

Chapter 1: The Forever War

1. Daniel Immerwahr, *How to Hide an Empire: A History of the Greater United States* (New York: Farrar, Straus and Giroux, 2019), 226.

2. Ibid., numbers 232-233, Truman quote 234.

3. James T. Patterson, *Grand Expectations: The United States, 1945-1974* (New York: Oxford University Press, 1996), 187-188, 204-205, 209-210.

4. Daniel Yergin, *The Prize: The Epic Quest for Oil, Money and Power* (New York: Free Press, 2009), 466-480.

5. Ibid., 479.

6. Rachel Schmidt, *Global Arms Exports to Iraq, 1960-1990* (Santa Monica: RAND, 1991), 7.

7. Andrew J. Bacevich, *War for the Greater Middle East: A Military History* (New York: Random House, 2016), 32.

8. Bacevich, *War for the Greater Middle East*, 64-76.

9. Ibid., 94-95; David Crist, *The Twilight War: The Secret History of America's 30 Year Conflict with Iran* (New York: Penguin Press, 2012), 47, 176.

10. Bacevich, *War for the Greater Middle East*, 140.

11. CIA, *Iraq Economic Data (1989-2003)*, last modified April 23, 2007, https://tinyurl.com/7b73v6t

12. Jeremy M. Sharp, *CRS Report for Congress: US Foreign Aid*

to Israel (Washington DC: Congressional Research Service, 2007), 11, 16.

13. Louise Richardson, *What Terrorists Want: Understanding the Enemy, Containing the Threat* (New York: Random House, 2007), 23: this work cites the zealots and the Thugi. For examples of KKK terrorism, see WEB Du Bois, *Black Reconstruction in America 1860-1880* (New York: The Free Press, 1998), 674-675.

14. Richardson, *What Terrorists Want*, 64-66.

15. Immerwahr, *How to Hide an Empire*, 373.

16. Ibid., 380.

17. Richardson, *What Terrorists Want*, 137.

18. Ibid., 44.

19. James L. Gelvin, *The Modern Middle East: A History* (New York: Oxford University Press, 2011), 281-282, 315.

20. Jean Edward Smith, *Bush* (New York: Simon and Schuster, 2016), 339.

21. Bacevich, *War for the Greater Middle East*, 218.

22. Smith, *Bush*, 247.

23. Noam Chomsky, *Who Rules the World?* (New York: The New Press, 2002), 249-250.

24. Richardson, *What Terrorists Want*, 92.

25. Ibid., 93.

26. Kevin M. Kruse and Julian E. Zelizer, *Fault Lines: A History of the United States Since 1974* (New York: W.W. Norton & Company, 2019), 256-257.

27. Dara Lind, *Everyone's heard of the Patriot Act. Here's what it actually does*, last modified June 2, 2015. https://tinyurl.com/y8q58th6

28. Charlie Savage, *Power Wars: The Relentless Rise of Presidential Authority and Secrecy* (New York: Back Bay Books, 2017), 185, 190-192.

29. Ibid., 173, 212-213.

30. Smith, *Bush*, 607.

31. Brian Glyn Williams, *Counter Jihad: America's Military Experience in Afghanistan, Iraq, and Syria* (Philadelphia: University of Pennsylvania Press, 2017), 94-95.

32. Bacevich, *War for the Greater Middle East,* 222 (Rumsfeld quote), 240 (Bush's reasons for war).

33. Williams, *Counter Jihad,* 102-130.

34. Ibid., 153.

35. Smith, *Bush,* 340.

36. Kruse and Zelizer, *Fault Lines,* 264.

37. Williams, *Counter Jihad,* 181-184.

38. Ibid., 201.

39. Ibid., 186.

40. Ibid., 187-188.

41. Pew Research Center, *Mapping the Global Muslim Population,* last modified October 7, 2009, https://tinyurl.com/y49kadm7; Gelvin, *Modern Middle East,* 18-19.

42. Williams, *Counter Jihad,* 193.

43. Bacevich, *War for the Greater Middle East,* 276.

44. Andrew Hosken, *Empire of Fear: Inside the Islamic State* (London: Oneworld, 2015), 45-47.

45. *The National Security Strategy of the United States of America* (Washington DC: White House, 2002), 21.

46. Savage, *Power Wars,* 39-40.

47. Ibid., 336-338.

48. Ibid., 51.

49. Ibid., 14.

50. Ibid., 104-105.

51. Ibid., 12.

52. Ibid., 86, 95-96.

53. Ibid., 554.

54. Robert Gates, *Duty: Memoirs of a Secretary at War* (New York: Alfred A. Knopf, 2014), 336.

55. Gates, *Duty,* 349-356, 362-369.

56. Bacevich, *War for the Greater Middle East,* 308.

57. Ibid., 309.

58. Ibid., 309-311.

59. Gates, *Duty*, 487-488, 491.

60. Ian S. Livingston and Michael O'Hanlon, *Afghanistan Index, Also including selected data on Pakistan* (Brookings Institute, 2017), 4, https://tinyurl.com/vnzgkdt

61. The Guardian, *US embassy cables: US complains about Karzai's release of prisoners*, last updated December 2, 2010, https://tinyurl.com/vnpjyf4

62. Bacevich, *War for the Greater Middle East*, 318.

63. Ibid., 59.

64. Gates, *Duty*, 372.

65. Bacevich, *War for the Greater Middle East*, 335.

66. Ibid., 333.

67. Williams, *Counter Jihad*, 226-227.

68. Ibid., 229.

69. Leon Panetta and Jim Newton, *Worthy Fights: A Memoir of Leadership in War and Peace* (New York: Penguin Press, 2014), 252.

70. Williams, *Counter Jihad*, 229-230.

71. Panetta and Newton, *Worthy Fights*, 245-246.

72. Jeremy Scahill, *The Assassination Complex: Inside the Government's Secret Drone Warfare Program* (New York: Simon & Schuster, 2016), 43.

73. Ibid., 81.

74. Ibid., 101.

75. Ibid., 10.

76. Eric Holder, *Letter to Patrick J. Leahy*, (May 22, 2013), 2, https://tinyurl.com/w8gtwr6

77. Scahill, *The Assassination Complex*, 186.

78. Ibid., 57.

79. Panetta and Newton, *Worthy Fights*, 307.

80. Gates, *Duty*, 539-543.

81. Panetta and Newton, *Worthy Fights*, 318-326.

82. Bacevich, *War for the Greater Middle East*, 325-327.

83. Ash Carter, *Inside the Five-Sided Box: Lessons from a Lifetime of Leadership in the Pentagon* (New York: Dutton, 2019), 227.

84. Ibid., 228.

85. Michael E. O'Hanlon and Ian Livingston, *Iraq Index: Tracking Variables of Reconstruction and Security in Iraq* (Brookings Institute, 2013), 4.

86. Thomas C. Frohlich, *Saudi Arabia buys the most weapons from the US government. See what other countries top list*, last modified March 26, 2019, https://tinyurl.com/rsurzum

87. Edward Daileg, *Iraqi Army receives last shipment of Abrams tanks*, last modified September 6, 2011, https://tinyurl.com/w4kn58q

88. Williams, *Counter Jihad*, 264-267.

89. Ibid., 270.

90. Hosken, *Empire of Fear*, 163-165.

91. Ibid., 199-205.

92. Ibid., 178.

93. Williams, *Counter Jihad*, 284-285.

94. Hosken, *Empire of Fear*, 183-195.

95. Williams, *Counter Jihad*, 296.

96. Carter, *Inside the Five-Sided Box*, 229.

97. Williams, *Counter Jihad*, 276.

98. Tim Lister, Ray Sanchez, Mark Bixler, Sean O'Key, Michael Hogenmiller and Mohammed Tawfeeq, *ISIS goes global: 143 attacks in 29 countries have killed 2,043*, last modified February 12, 2018, https://tinyurl.com/y76q9g9q

99. Williams, *Counter Jihad*, 313-317; BBC, *Battle for Mosul: Iraq PM Abadi formally declares victory*, last modified July 10, 2017, https://tinyurl.com/w4mvfhl

100. Bacevich, *War for the Greater Middle East*, 351.

101. Ben Rhodes, *The World as It Is: A Memoir of the Obama White House* (New York: Random House, 2018), 115.

102. Savage, *Power Wars*, 61.

103. UN Meetings Coverage, *Security Council Approves 'No-Fly Zone' over Libya, Authorizing 'All Necessary Measures' to Protect Civilians, by Vote of 10 in Favour with 5 Abstentions*, last modified March 17, 2011, https://tinyurl.com/skznbax

104. Obama, "Remarks on the Situation in Libya From Brasilia," in *Public Papers of the Presidents of the United States: Barack Obama 2011 Book I – January 1 to June 30, 2011* (Washington, DC: United States Government Publishing Office, 2014), 259.

105. Obama, "Remarks to the United Nations General Assembly in New York City," in *Public Papers of the Presidents of the United States: Barack Obama 2011 Book II – July 1 to December 31, 2011* (Washington, DC: United States Government Publishing Office, 2015), 292.

106. Christopher S. Chivvis and Jeffrey Martini, *Libya After Qaddafi* (RAND Corporation, 2014), 22-23.

107. Ibid., 38.

108. Chris Stephen, *War in Libya – the Guardian briefing*, last modified August 29, 2014, https://tinyurl.com/v6slkcx; Ahmed Elumami, *Libya's self-declared National Salvation government stepping down*, last modified April 5, 2016, https://tinyurl.com/vu3ut8b

109. Ibid.

110. Chivvis and Martini, *Libya After Qaddafi*, 25-26.

111. Nick Turse, *Tomorrow's Battlefield: US Proxy Wars and Secret Ops in Africa* (Chicago: Haymarket Books, 2015), 27.

112. Angelique Chrisafis and Afua Hirsch, *Mali: French troops in direct combat with insurgents 'within hours'*, last modified January 16, 2013, https://tinyurl.com/v42n2ss

113. Ann Pujot-Mazzini, *How Mali Is Pursuing Justice for a War That Never Really Ended*, last modified November 26, 2019, https://tinyurl.com/r2u9zo8

114. Turse, *Tomorrow's Battlefield*, 47, 113-114.

115. Ibid., 74.

116. Louis Jacobson and Amy Sherman, *PolitiFact Sheet: Military Spending under Obama and Congress,* last modified December 14, 2015, https://tinyurl.com/quzlhr3

117. Kimberly Amadeo, *US Military Budget, Its Components, Challenges, and Growth,* last modified December 7, 2019, https://tinyurl.com/y7zusoem

118. Washington Post, *NSA slides explain the PRISM data-collection program,* last modified July 10, 2013, https://tinyurl.com/w274432

119. Edward Jay Epstein, *How America Lost its Secrets: Edward Snowden, the Man and the Theft,* (New York: Alfred A. Knopf, 2017), 124; Savage, *Power Wars,* 169, 214-215.

120. Jared Newman, *NSA spied on World of Warcraft, Xbox Live, and Second Life gamers,* last modified December 9, 2013, https://tinyurl.com/yx4qaoba

121. Gregory Ferenstein, *Report: NSA Considered Revealing Porn Habits to Discredit Radicals,* last modified November 27, 2013, https://tinyurl.com/yd4omkk4

122. Kia Pfaffenbach, *From Merkel to Tymoshenko: NSA spied on 122 world leaders, Snowden docs reveal,* last modified March 29, 2014, https://tinyurl.com/qunadks

123. Spencer Ackerman, *Snowden Disclosures helped reduce use of Patriot Act provision to acquire email records,* last modified September 29, 2016, https://tinyurl.com/zjqfgtx

124. T.C. Sottek and Janus Kopfstein, *Everything you need to know about PRISM,* last modified July 17, 2013, https://tinyurl.com/yc59tfxt

125. Epstein. *How America Lost its Secrets,* 304.

126. Ash Carter, *Inside the Five-Sided Box,* 338-339.

127. Savage, *Power Wars,* 364-366.

128. Ibid., 377.

129. CIA Policy and Procedures, *Signals Intelligence Activities,* 2, https://tinyurl.com/t2w8blf

130. Savage, *Power Wars,* 196.

131. Rhodes, *The World as It Is,* 225.

132. These numbers are based on my review of the Global Terrorism Database's list of attacks in the United States. Raw datasets can be found here: https://tinyurl.com/uzc34d6

133. US Department of State Bureau of Counterterrorism, *Foreign Terrorist Organizations,* accessed February 2, 2019, https://tinyurl.com/hutjwk4

134. Jeanne Park, *Europe's Migration Crisis,* last modified September 23, 2015, https://tinyurl.com/yafvukbu

135. Physicians for Social Responsibility, *Body Count: Casualty Figures after 10 Years of the "War on Terror"* (Washington, DC: IPPNW, 2015), 15.

136. Syrian Observatory for Human Rights, *More than 570 thousand people were killed on the Syrian territory within 8 years of revolution,* last modified March 15, 2019, https://tinyurl.com/y3e95ejp

137. Samy Magdy, *Database says 91,600 killed in Yemen fighting since 2015,* last modified June 19, 2019, https://tinyurl.com/wl24vvt

138. These numbers have been especially contested and not very deeply studied in western media. Estimates for the 2011 civil war range from 1000 to 30,000: https://tinyurl.com/yd347mbn; for the post 2014 conflict perhaps 6000: https://tinyurl.com/sm5tjjs

139. Neta C. Crawford, *Human Cost of the Post-9/11 Wars: Lethality and the Need for Transparency* (Providence: Watson Institute of International and Public Affairs, 2018), 1.

140. Wikipedia, *Motor vehicle fatality rate in US by year,* last modified November 14, 2019, https://tinyurl.com/yxr3gejq

141. Arnold J. Toynbee, *A Study of History: Abridgment of Volumes I-VI,* abridged by D.C. Somervell (New York: Oxford University Press, 1947), 109, 149-150; Will Durant, *Caesar and Christ: A History of Roman Civilization and of Christianity from their beginnings to A.D. 325* (New York: Simon and

Schuster, 1944), 88, 108.

142. Richardson, *What Terrorists Want*, 84-85.

143. Estimates on these numbers vary, since much of Saudi influence is murky and indirect, done via charity contributions that end up in terrorist coffers, etc. For one estimate, see Paul Vallely, *Wahhabism: A deadly scripture*, last modified November 1, 2007, https://tinyurl.com/yx793nnk

144. Dore Gold, *Hatred's Kingdom: How Saudi Arabia Supports the New Global Terrorism* (Washington DC: Regnery Publishing Inc., 2003), 126; Youssef Michel Ibrahim, *The Mideast Threat That's Hard to Define*, last modified August 11, 2002, https://tinyurl.com/s655yho

145. Gates, *Duty*, 272.

146. Gates perceived Obama to be less "committed" to the US mission in Afghanistan than Bush II. Ibid., 298-299.

Chapter 2: Economy in Crisis

1. Richard D. Wolff and Stephen A. Resnick, *Contending Economic Theories: Neoclassical, Keynesian, and Marxian* (Cambridge, MA: MIT Press, 2012), 15, 59.

2. Ibid., 53.

3. Ibid., 106.

4. Ibid., 152.

5. Ibid., 133, 137.

6. Ibid., 146-147.

7. Ibid., 23, 262-263.

8. Joseph Stiglitz, *The Price of Inequality: How Today's Divided Society Endangers Our Future* (New York: W.W. Norton & Company, 2012), 41, 48-49, 107.

9. Wolff and Resnick, *Contending Economic Theories*, 21-23, 64-65, 337, 341.

10. Kruse and Zelizer, *Fault Lines*, 234.

11. Dylan Matthews, *You're not imagining it: the rich really are hoarding economic growth*, last modified August 8, 2017,

https://tinyurl.com/ya38nxlu

12. Jean Jacques Rousseau, "The State of War," *The Social Contract and other later political writings* (New York: Cambridge University Press, 2007), 162.

13. Edward E. Baptist, *The Half Has Never Been Told: Slavery and the Making of American Capitalism* (New York: Basic Books, 2014), 234-235, 247-248, 270.

14. Quentin R. Skrabec Jr., *The 100 Most Important American Financial Crises: An Encyclopedia of the Lowest Points in American Economic History* (Denver: Greenwood, 2015), 82.

15. Zinn, *A People's History of the United States*, 227-228; Baptist, *The Half Has Never Been Told*, 387.

16. Adam Smith, *The Wealth of Nations*, Book III, Chapter IV, 437.

17. Wolff and Resnick, *Contending Economic Theories*, 266-267; Stiglitz, *The Price of Inequality*, 44-48.

18. Eric Foner, *Give Me Liberty!: An American History*, Vol 2 (New York: W.W. Norton & Company, 2013), 624-626.

19. Ibid., 619-620.

20. Skrabec, *The 100 Most Important American Financial Crises*, 90-92.

21. Foner, *Give Me Liberty!* Vol 2, 637.

22. Internal Revenue Service, *Statistics of Income from Returns of Net Income for 1920* (Washington: Government Printing Office, 1922), 7, https://tinyurl.com/sluyqqz; Zinn, *A People's History of the United States*, 382.

23. Zinn, *A People's History of the United States*, 386.

24. Barry Eichengreen, *Hall of Mirrors: The Great Depression, the Great Recession, and the Uses – and Misuses – of History* (New York: Oxford University Press, 2015), 155-158.

25. Ibid., 232.

26. Ibid., 266.

27. Neil Irwin, *What Is Glass-Steagall? The 82-Year-Old Banking Law That Stirred the Debate*, last modified October 14, 2015,

https://tinyurl.com/rksc34o

28. Kenneth S. Davis, *FDR: Into The Storm 1937-1940, A History* (New York: Random House, 1993), 9; Eichengreen, *Hall of Mirrors*, 269-270.

29. Eichengreen, *Hall of Mirrors*, 233.

30. Foner, *Give Me Liberty!* Vol 2, 847.

31. Office of Soviet Analysis, *A Comparison of the US and Soviet Economies: Evaluating the Performance of the Soviet System* (Directorate of Intelligence, 1985), 5.

32. Doug Henwood, *Paul Volcker Was a Hero of the Ruling Class*, last modified December 9, 2019, https://tinyurl.com/t32tqk9

33. Kruse and Zelizer, *Fault Lines*, 30.

34. Ibid., 38.

35. Henwood, *Paul Volcker Was a Hero of the Ruling Class*.

36. Foner, *Give Me Liberty!* Vol 2, 1034.

37. Kenneth J. Robinson, *Savings and Loan Crisis, 1980-1989*, last modified November 22, 2013, https://tinyurl.com/sonxb9n

38. Eichengreen, *Hall of Mirrors*, 65-68.

39. Wikipedia, *Savings and loan crisis*, last modified November 9, 2019, https://tinyurl.com/prbapl7

40. Ibid.

41. Foner, *Give Me Liberty!* Vol 2, 1037.

42. Ibid., 1053.

43. Eichengreen, *Hall of Mirrors*, 19-20.

44. Kruse and Zelizer, *Fault Lines*, 238.

45. David Kleinbard, *The $1.7 trillion dot.com lesson*, last modified November 9, 2000, https://tinyurl.com/yxytglb7

46. Foner, *Give Me Liberty!* Vol 2, 1059.

47. Eichengreen, *Hall of Mirrors*, 68.

48. Ibid., 70.

49. Ibid.

50. The Financial Crisis Inquiry Commission, *The Financial Crisis Inquiry Report: The Final Report of the National Commission on the Causes of the Financial and Economic Crisis in the United*

States (Washington DC: US Government Printing Office, 2011), 19, 59, 62-63.

51. Eichengreen, *Hall of Mirrors*, 73; Financial Crisis Inquiry Commission, *Inquiry Report*, 18.

52. Andrew Sorkin, *Too Big to Fail: The Inside Story of how Wall Street and Washington Fought to Save the Financial System – and Themselves* (New York: Viking Press, 2009), 5.

53. Eichengreen, *Hall of Mirrors*, 75-76.

54. Sorkin, *Too Big to Fail*, 157.

55. Peter J. Wallison and Arthur F. Burns, "Dissenting Statement of Peter J. Wallison and Arthur F. Burns," in *The Financial Crisis Inquiry Report*, 473.

56. Mehrsa Baradaran, *Color of Money: Black Banks and the Racial Wealth Gap* (Cambridge, MA: the Belknap Press of Harvard University Press, 2017), 256-257; Adam Tooze, *Crashed: How a Decade of Financial Crises Changed the World* (New York: Viking, 2018), 47-48.

57. Financial Crisis Inquiry Commission, *Inquiry Report*, 34.

58. Tooze, *Crashed*, 6-7, 43.

59. Financial Crisis Inquiry Commission, *Inquiry Report*, 82-83.

60. Ibid., 192.

61. Michael D'antonio, *A Consequential Presidency: The Legacy of Barack Obama* (New York: St Martin's Press, 2016), 65.

62. Tooze, *Crashed*, 195.

63. Sorkin, *Too Big to Fail*, 504; Tooze, *Crashed*, 199-201.

64. Timothy Geithner, *Stress Test: Reflections on Financial Crisis* (New York: Crown Publishers, 2014), 8-15.

65. Financial Crisis Inquiry Commission, *Inquiry Report*, 67.

66. Ibid., 68.

67. Ibid., 210, 212.

68. Ibid., 338-339.

69. Geithner, *Stress Test*, 314; Sorkin, *Too Big to Fail*, 419.

70. Geithner, *Stress Test*, 11.

71. Financial Crisis Inquiry Commission, *Inquiry Report*, 404.

72. Stiglitz, *The Price of Inequality*, 180. (Combined $140 billion spent on Temporary Assistance to Needy Families / Assistance and Aid to Families with Dependent Children programs from 1990 to 2006.)

73. Geithner, *Stress Test*, 316.

74. Ibid., 338-339.

75. Ibid., 352.

76. Eichengreen, *Hall of Mirrors*, 247.

77. Tooze, *Crashed*, 279.

78. Ibid., 279.

79. D'antonio, *A Consequential Presidency*, 45.

80. Geithner, *Stress Test*, 382.

81. Tooze, *Crashed*, 281; US Census Bureau, *Historical Families Tables*, last modified November 2019, https://tinyurl.com/ycsodvv8 (specifically Table FM-1).

82. Center for Responsive Politics, *Barack Obama (D) Contributions by Industry, 2008 Cycle*, accessed December 14, 2009, https://tinyurl.com/vmphju6

83. Obama, "Remarks Following a Meeting with Economic Advisers," in *Public Papers of the Presidents of the United States: Barack Obama 2009 Book I – January 20 to June 30, 2009* (Washington, DC: United States Government Publishing Office, 2010), 18.

84. Obama, "Remarks Following a Meeting with Economic Advisers," in *Barack Obama 2009 Book I*, 155.

85. Ron Suskind, *Confidence Men: Wall Street, Washington, and the Education of a President* (New York: Harper Perennial, 2011), 235, 242, respectively.

86. Geithner, *Stress Test*, 389-390.

87. Eichengreen, *Hall of Mirrors*, 11.

88. Geithner, *Stress Test*, 399-400.

89. Suskind, *Confidence Men*, 459.

90. Geithner, *Stress Test*, 408.

91. Ibid., 418.

92. Obama, "Remarks on Signing the Dodd-Frank Wall Street Reform and Consumer Protection Act," in *Public Papers of the Presidents of the United States: Barack Obama 2010 Book II – July 1 to December 31, 2010* (Washington, DC: United States Government Publishing Office, 2013), 101-102.

93. Tooze, *Crashed*, 302.

94. Ibid., 305.

95. Steve Eder, Jessica Silver-Greenberg, and Stacy Cowley, *Republicans Want to Sideline This Regulator. But It May Be Too Popular*, last modified August 31, 2017, https://tinyurl.com/y9lglzga

96. Davis Polk Regulatory Tracker, *Dodd-Frank Progress Report* (Davis Polk Portal, 2016), https://tinyurl.com/ycovbwpx

97. John Carney, *America Lost $10.2 trillion in 2008*, last modified February 3, 2009, https://tinyurl.com/qmgskt9

98. Based on the more comprehensive supplementary poverty rate: J. Semega, K.R. Fontenot, and M.A Kollar, *What is the current poverty rate in the United States?*, last modified October 15, 2018, https://tinyurl.com/yd37vz3k

99. Paul Kiel and Dan Nguyen, *Bailout Tracker: Tracking Every Dollar and Every Recipient*, last modified October 2, 2019, https://tinyurl.com/lpxhfc8

100. US Department of the Treasury, *The Dodd-Frank Act: Reforming Wall Street and Protecting Main Street* (The White House: 2017), https://tinyurl.com/rgm38oz

101. Matt Philips, *The chart Obama-haters love most – and the truth behind it*, last modified November 4, 2014, https://tinyurl.com/jo9uxrq

102. Lawrence F. Katz and Alan B. Krueger, *The Rise and Nature of Alternative Work Arrangements in the United States, 1995-2015* (Cambridge: NBER, 2016), 2, 15.

103. Semega, Fontenot, and Kollar, *poverty rate in the United States*, https://tinyurl.com/yd37vz3k

104. Jesse Colombo, *US Household Wealth is Experiencing an*

Unsustainable Bubble, last modified August 24, 2018, https://tinyurl.com/qta3s5h

105. Ibid.

106. Treasury, *The Dodd-Frank Act*, https://tinyurl.com/rgm38oz

107. Tooze, *Crashed*, 316; Laura Layden, *Banks fell in the Great Recession, but they're stronger now*, last modified February 9, 2018, https://tinyurl.com/tfrmsrq

108. Baradaran, *Color of Money*, 268-269; Layden, *Banks fell in the Great Recession*.

109. Tooze, *Crashed*, 460-461.

110. Trevor Hunnicutt, *Rich get richer, everyone else not so much in record US expansion*, last modified July 12, 2019, https://tinyurl.com/y5zlacym

111. Diana Hembree, *CEO Pay Skyrockets To 361 Times That of The Average Worker*, last modified May 22, 2018, https://tinyurl.com/wnsxbtj

112. Wikipedia, *List of Occupy movement protest locations in the United States*, last modified December 12, 2019, https://tinyurl.com/tp9tgtd

113. Michael Levitin, *The Triumph of Occupy Wall Street*, last modified June 10, 2015, https://tinyurl.com/zbz2xyt

114. Michael Hastings, *Exclusive: Homeland Security Kept Tabs on Occupy Wall Street*, last modified February 28, 2012, https://tinyurl.com/qvx53ot

115. Partnership for Civil Justice Fund, *FBI Documents Reveal Secret Nationwide Occupy Monitoring*, accessed December 19, 2019, https://tinyurl.com/nnbjlt8

116. Matthew W. Hughey and Gregory S. Parks, *Wrongs of the Right: Language, Race, and the Republican Party in the Age of Obama*, (New York: New York University Press, 2014), 33-34.

117. Wikipedia, *Electoral history of the Tea Party movement*, last modified December 6, 2019, https://tinyurl.com/gvemuek

118. Jeremy W. Peters, *The Tea Party Didn't Get What It Wanted*,

but It Did Unleash the Politics of Anger, last modified August 30, 2019, https://tinyurl.com/qv5m3cb

119. Paul H. Jossey, *How We Killed the Tea Party*, last modified August 14, 2016, https://tinyurl.com/rwdprce

120. *Silence, A Thirteenth-Century French Romance* (East Lansing: Michigan State University Press, 2007), 5.

Chapter 3: Healthcare Reform

1. Paul Starr, *Social Transformation of American Medicine: The rise of a sovereign profession and the making of a vast industry* (New York: Basic Books Inc., 1982), 47, 73, 185.

2. Robert Chernomas and Ian Hudson, *To Live and Die in America: Class, Power, Health, and Healthcare* (New York: St. Martin's Press, 2013), 11-13.

3. Foner, *Give Me Liberty!* Vol 2, 595.

4. Zinn, *A People's History of the United States*, 257.

5. Chernomas and Hudson, *To Live and Die in America*, 57-58.

6. Zinn, *A People's History of the United States*, 267.

7. Ibid.

8. Chernomas and Hudson, *To Live and Die in America*, 72-74.

9. Starr, *Social Transformation of American Medicine*, 181.

10. Ibid., 173.

11. Paul Starr, *Remedy and Reaction: The Peculiar American Struggle Over Health Care Reform* (New Haven: Yale University Press, 2011), 33-34.

12. Ibid., 35-41.

13. Starr, *Social Transformation of American Medicine*, 310.

14. Starr, *Remedy and Reaction*, 42.

15. Starr, *Social Transformation of American Medicine*, 341-343.

16. Elisabeth Rosenthal, *An American Sickness: How Healthcare Became Big Business and How You Can Take It Back* (New York: Random House Large Print, 2017), 23.

17. Jonathan Engel, *Unaffordable: American Healthcare from Johnson to Trump* (Madison: University of Wisconsin Press,

2018), 12-13.

18. Starr, *Social Transformation of American Medicine*, 378.

19. Engel, *Unaffordable*, 12.

20. Ibid., 13-14.

21. Starr, *Remedy and Reaction*, 54-55.

22. Ibid., 56-58.

23. Engel, *Unaffordable*, 129; Starr, *Social Transformation of American Medicine*, 417, 428.

24. Starr, *Remedy and Reaction*, 122-123.

25. Washington Post, *Landmark: The Inside Story of America's New Health-Care Law and What it Means for Us All* (New York: Public Affairs, 2010), 67.

26. Rosenthal, *An American Sickness*, 30-31.

27. Harris Meyes, *Hospitals vary in publishing CMS chargemaster prices*, last modified January 7, 2019, https://tinyurl.com/rkgh35u

28. Rosenthal, *An American Sickness*, 55-56.

29. Ibid., 293-294.

30. Ibid., 41.

31. Ibid., 64-65.

32. Ibid., 77.

33. Brian O'Connell, *How Much Do Doctors Make in 2018?*, last modified November 13, 2018, https://tinyurl.com/vz5wnyx

34. Rosenthal, *An American Sickness*, 77.

35. Diane M. Dewar, *The Economics of US Health Reform: A Global Perspective* (New York: Routledge, 2018), 20-21.

36. Rosenthal, *An American Sickness*, 90, 105-107.

37. Chernomas and Hudson, *To Live and Die in America*, 148.

38. Rosenthal, *An American Sickness*, 186-188.

39. Ibid., 194.

40. Ibid., 169.

41. Ibid., 148.

42. Ibid., 140-141.

43. Joanna Walters, *Meet the Sacklers: the family feuding over*

blame for the opioid crisis, last modified February 13, 2018, https://tinyurl.com/yctfg843

44. Jan Hoffman and Danny Hakim, *Purdue Pharma Payments to Sackler Family Soared Amid Opioid Crisis*, last modified December 16, 2019, https://tinyurl.com/qmlkfc2

45. National Institute on Drug Abuse, *Opioid Overdose Crisis*, last modified January 2019, https://tinyurl.com/y2esed4e

46. Laura Strickler, *Purdue Pharma offers $10-12 billion to settle opioid claims*, last modified August 17, 2019, https://tinyurl.com/yxh6fcsn

47. Daniel E. Dawes, *150 Years of ObamaCare* (Baltimore: Johns Hopkins University Press, 2016), 92, 95.

48. Starr, *Remedy and Reaction*, 198-199.

49. Ibid., 237.

50. Ibid., 205.

51. Purva H. Rawal, *The Affordable Care Act: Examining the Facts* (Santa Barbara: ABC-CLIO, 2016), 6-7.

52. Starr, *Remedy and Reaction*, 202-203.

53. Ibid., 208-209.

54. Dawes, *150 Years of ObamaCare*, 125-126.

55. Obama, "Address Before a Joint Session of the Congress on Health Care Reform," in *Public Papers of the Presidents of the United States: Barack Obama 2009 Book II – July 1 to December 31, 2009* (Washington, DC: United States Government Publishing Office, 2013), 365-366.

56. Starr, *Remedy and Reaction*, 224-225.

57. Washington Post, *Landmark*, 54-55.

58. Ibid., *58, 62;* Dawes, *150 Years of ObamaCare*, 155-156.

59. Washington Post, *Landmark*, 68-69.

60. Ibid., 70-71.

61. Igor Volsky, *Blow by Blow: A Comprehensive Timeline of the GOP's 4-Year Battle to Kill Obamacare*, last modified March 23, 2014, https://tinyurl.com/qvr7jsc

62. *National Federation of Independent Business et al v. Sebelius,*

Secretary of Health and Human Services, et al, 567 US 7 (2012), 3.

63. Ibid., 5.

64. Ibid., 67.

65. Ibid., 72.

66. Ibid., 73-74.

67. Edward R. Berchick, Emily Hood, and Jessica C. Barnett, "Health Insurance Coverage in the United States: 2017," *Current Population Reports, P60-264* (Washington, DC: US Government Printing Office, 2018), 18.

68. Obama White House, *The Record: President Obama on Health*, https://tinyurl.com/vs2c62t, 1.

69. Ibid., 2-7.

70. *Accomplishments of Affordable Care Act* (Center on Budget and Policy Priorities, 2019), 3.

71. Berchick, Hood, and Barnett. *Health Insurance Coverage*, 12.

72. Ezekiel J. Emanuel, *Name the much-criticized federal program that has saved the US $2.3 trillion. Hint: it starts with Affordable*, last modified March 22, 2019, https://tinyurl.com/y6fehfyd

73. Ibid.

74. Tanza Loudenback, *The average cost of healthcare in 21 different countries*, last modified March 7, 2019, https://tinyurl.com/y5a9xz69

75. Rachel Gillet and Shayanne Gal, *One chart reveals how the cost of insulin has skyrocketed in the US, even though nothing about it has changed*, last modified September 18, 2019, https://tinyurl.com/tyxgqy5; Lisa L. Gill, *The Shocking Rise of Prescription Drug Prices*, last modified November 26, 2019, https://tinyurl.com/yx72yzdc

76. Robin A. Cohen and Emily P. Zammatti, *High-deductible Health Plan Enrollment Among Adults Aged 18-64 With Employment-based Insurance Coverage*, last modified August 9, 2018, https://tinyurl.com/uxtwzan

77. Stephen Barlas, *US and States Ramp Up Response to Opioid*

Crisis: Regulatory, Legislative, and Legal Tools Brought to Bear, last modified September 2017, https://tinyurl.com/to2bjfz

78. Ronald Reagan, *Radio Address on Socialized Medicine*, last modified March 8, 2017, https://tinyurl.com/w8238je
79. Financial Crisis Inquiry Commission, *Inquiry Report*, 33.
80. John Robert Irelan, *History of the Life, Administration and Times of James Madison, Fourth President of the United States: Struggle for Constitutional Government and Second War with England* (Chicago: Fairbanks & Palmer, 1886), 82.
81. Dewar, *The Economics of US Health Reform*, 19.

Chapter 4: On the Margins
1. Noel Rae, *The Great Stain: Witnessing American Slavery* (New York: the Overlook Press, 2018), 123.
2. Eric Foner, *Give Me Liberty!: An American History* Vol 1 (New York: W.W. Norton & Company, 2012), 99-100.
3. Moses Coit Tyler, *Patrick Henry* (New York: Houghton Mifflin Company, 1898), 389.
4. Baptist, *The Half Has Never Been Told*, 82.
5. Ibid.
6. Ibid., 27.
7. Ibid., 114.
8. Sven Beckert, *Empire of Cotton: A Global History* (New York: Alfred A. Knopf, 2015), xv-xvi; 33; 48-49; 150-155.
9. Baptist, *The Half Has Never Been Told*, 113, 140.
10. Ibid., 117-119, 140.
11. Rae, The Great Stain, 75.
12. Ibid., 129-130.
13. Baptist, *The Half Has Never Been Told*, 65; 148-155.
14. Frances Fitzgerald, *The Evangelicals: The Struggle to Shape America* (New York: Simon and Schuster, 2017), 40, 55; Foner, *Give Me Liberty!* Vol 1, 382-383, 450.
15. Foner, *Give Me Liberty!* Vol 1, 259, 500.
16. Nancy Isenberg, *White Trash: The 400 Year Untold History of*

Class in America (New York: Penguin Books, 2016), 147.

17. Foner, *Give Me Liberty!* Vol 1, 505.

18. Charles B. Dew, *Apostles of Disunion: The Southern Secession Commissioners and the Causes of the Civil War* (Charlottesville: University of Virginia Press, 2001), 14-15.

19. *Declaration of the Immediate Causes Which Induce and Justify the Secession of South Carolina from the Federal Union; and the Ordinance of Secession*, 9, https://tinyurl.com/ujrgl23

20. Du Bois, *Black Reconstruction in America*, 50; *Constitution of the Confederate States; March 11, 1861*, accessed October 15, 2019, https://tinyurl.com/upv38lx

21. Foner, *Give Me Liberty!* Vol 1, 512, 514, 539.

22. Du Bois, *Black Reconstruction in America*, 57-58, 103-104, 106-111.

23. Foner, *Give Me Liberty!* Vol 2, 564-569.

24. Ibid., 576-581.

25. Du Bois, *Black Reconstruction in America*, 674, 677-678, 681-682.

26. Jack Foner, *Blacks and the Military in American History* (New York: Praeger Publishers, 1974), 98.

27. Isabel Wilkerson, *The Warmth of Other Suns: The Epic Story of America's Great Migration* (New York: Random House, 2010), 57; Foner, *Blacks and the Military*, 126.

28. Ibid., 57, 232, 387.

29. Patterson, *Grand Expectations*, 27.

30. Wilkerson, *The Warmth of Other Suns* 232.

31. Robert L. Fleegler "Theodore G. Bilbo and the Decline of Public Racism 1938-1947," *Mississippi Journal of History* 68, no 1, (2006), 3.

32. Maurice Isserman and Michael Kazin, *America Divided: The Civil War of the 1960s* (New York: Oxford University Press, 2000), 32.

33. Ibid., 47.

34. Elizabeth Hinton, *From the War on Poverty to the War on Crime:*

The Making of Mass Incarceration in America (Cambridge, MA: Harvard University Press, 2016), 56; Isserman and Kazin, *America Divided*, 199-203.

35. Michelle Alexander, *The New Jim Crow: Mass Incarceration in the Age of Colorblindness* (New York: the New Press, 2012), 40-41.

36. Alexander, *The New Jim Crow*, 41.

37. Hinton, *From the War on Poverty*, 6.

38. Ibid., 93-94.

39. Ibid., 24.

40. Ibid., 6.

41. Alexander, *The New Jim Crow*, 41.

42. Hinton, *From the War on Poverty*, 56-57; 134; 136-137.

43. Dan Baum, *Legalize It All: How to win the war on drugs*, accessed April 27, 2019, https://tinyurl.com/z65kdd2

44. Hinton, *From the War on Poverty*, 166-167.

45. Ibid., 173.

46. Ibid., 163.

47. Ibid., 173-174.

48. Ibid., 175-176.

49. Alexander, *The New Jim Crow*, 49.

50. Ibid., 50-51.

51. Ibid., 53-54.

52. Ibid., 56-57.

53. Ibid., 57, 60.

54. Ibid., 98.

55. Marc Mauer, *The Changing Racial Dynamics of the War on Drugs* (Washington DC: The Sentencing Project, 2009), 6-7.

56. Keeanga-Yamahtta Taylor, *From #BlackLivesMatter to Black Liberation* (Chicago: Haymarket Books, 2016), 90-91.

57. Baradaran, *Color of Money*, 4, 22, 41-46, 51, 95, 141-142.

58. Ibid., 237.

59. Ibid., 258-259.

60. Andre M. Perry, *Black workers are being left behind by full*

employment, last modified June 26, 2019, https://tinyurl. com/yyxzhro2; Baradaran, *Color of Money*, 253-254.

61. Baradaran, *Color of Money*, 253.

62. Ibid.

63. Perry, *Black workers are being left behind*, https://tinyurl.com/ yyxzhro2; Baradaran, *Color of Money*, 249.

64. The number for African Americans is averaged from 256 girls and 296 boys dying per 1000 births: Baptist, *The Half Has Never Been Told*, 123.

65. Ibid., 140.

66. C. Riley Snorton, *Black on Both Sides: A Racial History of Trans Identity* (Minneapolis: University of Minnesota Press, 2017), Chapter 1.

67. Allan M. Brandt, "Racism and research: The case of the Tuskegee Syphilis study," The Hastings Center Report 8(6): 21-29, 2.

68. *Racial Lynchings in America – Interactive Map*, accessed October 28, 2019, https://tinyurl.com/y77qzc5g69

69. Brandt, "Racism and research," 3.

70. Ibid., 6.

71. Ibid., 7.

72. Ibid., 2.

73. Dawes, *150 Years of ObamaCare*, 28.

74. Ibid., 37-38.

75. Berchick, Hood, and Barnett, "Health Insurance Coverage in the United States: 2017," 15.

76. Howard Waitzkin and the Working Group on Health beyond Capitalism, *Healthcare Under the Knife: Moving Beyond Capitalism for our Health*, (New York: Monthly Review Press, 2018), 229-230.

77. Ibid., 229-231.

78. Ibid., 231.

79. Hinton, *From the War on Poverty*, 30, 64-65.

80. Ibid., 134, 162.

81. Ibid., 141-142.
82. Ibid., 145-147.
83. Ibid., 160-162.
84. Ibid., 191-194.
85. Ibid., 4.
86. Alexander, *The New Jim Crow*, 71.
87. Ibid., 74.
88. This number is likely higher than reported since police often use asset forfeiture (confiscating assets supposedly related to a crime) in addition to government subsidies to fund the purchase of this equipment, making it hard to track: Scahill, *The Assassination Complex*, 127.
89. Amnesty International, *Deadly Force: Police Use of Lethal Force in the United States* (New York: Amnesty International Publications, 2015), 13; Ronald G. Fryer Jr., *An Empirical Analysis of Racial Differences in Police Use of Force* (Cambridge: National Bureau of Economic Research, 2016), 4-6.
90. Taylor, *From #BlackLivesMatter to Black Liberation*, 95-96.
91. Wesley Lowery, *They Can't Kill Us All: Ferguson, Baltimore, and a New Era in America's Racial Justice Movement* (New York: Little, Brown and Company, 2016), 84-85.
92. Taylor, *From #BlackLivesMatter to Black Liberation*, 99.
93. United States Department of Justice, *Federal Report on Police Killings* (Brooklyn: Melville House, 2017), 10, 16-18, 24-28, 35-45, 97-99.
94. Taylor, *From #BlackLivesMatter to Black Liberation*, 100.
95. Ibid., 101.
96. Lowery, *They Can't Kill Us All*, 101.
97. Aislinn Pulley, *Black Struggle is Not a Sound Bite: Why I Refused to Meet with President Obama*, last modified February 18, 2016, https://tinyurl.com/wqz66jb
98. Taylor, *From #BlackLivesMatter to Black Liberation*, 104.
99. Ibid.
100. Ibid., 107.

101. Michael Eric Dyson, *The Black Presidency: Barack Obama and the Politics of Race in America* (Boston: Mariner Books, 2016), 187.

102. Department of Justice, *Federal Report on Police Killings*, 413.

103. Ibid., 416.

104. Megan Smith and Roy L. Austin, Jr., *Launching the Police Data Initiative*, last modified May 18, 2015, https://tinyurl.com/rd88vmy

105. Obama. Executive Order. "Federal Support for Local Law Enforcement Equipment Acquisition, Executive Order 13688 of January 16, 2015", *Federal Registrar* 80, no. 14 (January 22, 2015): 3451, https://tinyurl.com/sgdbq3l

106. Alicia Garza, *A Herstory of the #BlackLivesMatter Movement*, last modified October 7, 2014, https://tinyurl.com/y36ttplk

107. Coates, *We Were Eight Years in Power*, 62.

108. Michael Brendan Dougherty, *The Story Behind Ron Paul's Racist Newsletters*, last modified December 21, 2011, https://tinyurl.com/wm9yuhv

109. Trip Gabriel, *A Timeline of Steve King's Racist Remarks and Divisive Actions*, last modified January 15, 2019, https://tinyurl.com/y82agemp

110. Robb Willer, Matthew Feinberg, and Rachel Wetts, *Threats to Racial Status Promote Tea Party Support among White Americans* (Stanford: Stanford Business School, 2016), 2, 7, 9-10, 12, 16.

111. Hughey and Parks, *Wrongs of the Right*, 44-45.

112. Josh Clinton and Carrie Roush, *Poll: Persistent Partisan Divide Over 'Birther' Question*, last modified August 10, 2016, https://tinyurl.com/teufz5v

113. Immerwahr, *How to Hide an Empire*, 395.

114. Hughey and Parks, *Wrongs of the Right*, 47-48.

115. Dyson, *The Black Presidency*, 135.

116. Hughey and Parks, *Wrongs of the Right*, 49.

117. Ibid., 154-155.

118. Talkers, *Top Talk Audiences*, accessed January 15, 2020, https://tinyurl.com/v2xzs8v; Hayley C. Cuccinelli, *The World's Highest-Paid Radio Hosts of 2017*, last modified October 5, 2017, https://tinyurl.com/u63q76x

119. Hughey and Parks, *Wrongs of the Right*, 79.

120. Dyson, *The Black Presidency*, 265.

121. Coates, *We Were Eight Years in Power*, 302-303.

122. Louis Crompton, *Homosexuality and Civilization* (Cambridge: Belknap Press of Harvard University Press, 2003), 35, 37, 111-112; Ronald Bayer, *Homosexuality and American Psychiatry* (Princeton: Princeton University Press, 1987), 16-17.

123. Crompton, *Homosexuality and Civilization*, 7-8, 29, 61-62, 74 (Greece); 80, 97 (Rome); 413 (Japan); 213, 218, 238 (China); 161 (Islam).

124. Douglas C. Halderman, "Sexual Orientation Conversion Therapy for Gay Men and Lesbians: A Scientific Examination," in *Homosexuality: Research Implications for Public Policy*, edited by John C. Gonsiorek and James D. Weinrich (Newbury Park: SAGE, 1991), 2-5.

125. Sigmund Freud, "Letter 277 to Anonymous," in *The Letters of Sigmund Freud*, edited by Ernst L. Freud (New York: Basic Books, Inc, 1975), 423.

126. Lillian Faderman, *The Gay Revolution: The Story of the Struggle* (New York: Simon and Schuster, 2015), 21-22.

127. Ibid., 132.

128. Ibid., 172-187.

129. Ibid., 223-225; 334-335.

130. Ibid., 359.

131. Ibid., 361-363.

132. Ibid., 374.

133. UNAIDS, *Status of the Global HIV Epidemic: 2008 Report on the Global AIDS Epidemic* (Geneva: UNAIDS, 2008) 34, 45.

134. Faderman, *The Gay Revolution*, 419.

135. Ibid., 416.

136. Ibid., 418.

137. David Koon, *Ruth Coker Burks, the cemetery angel*, last modified January 8, 2015, https://tinyurl.com/w75y6md

138. Faderman, *The Gay Revolution*, 419-420.

139. Ibid., 428-429.

140. Ibid., 429-430.

141. Ibid., 436.

142. Foundation for AIDS Research, *Thirty Years of HIV/AIDS: Snapshots of an Epidemic*, accessed December 10, 2019, https://tinyurl.com/y3pdx57s; Patterson, *Grand Expectations*, 4, fn; UNAIDS, *Report on the global HIV/AIDS epidemic 2002* (Geneva: UNAIDS, 2002), 23.

143. Faderman, *The Gay Revolution*, 440.

144. Kerry Eleveld, *Don't Tell Me to Wait: How the Fight for Gay Rights Changed America and Transformed Obama's Presidency* (New York: Basic Books, 2015), 10-12.

145. Ibid., xi.

146. Ibid., 21.

147. Ibid., 51.

148. Gates, *Duty*, 433, 436, 441.

149. Eleveld, *Don't Tell Me to Wait*, 120.

150. Ibid., 166-182.

151. Ibid., 211.

152. Ibid., 189; 163.

153. Ibid., 220.

154. Ibid., 216.

155. Pew Research Center, *Two-thirds of Democrats Now Support Gay Marriage*, last modified July 31, 2012, https://tinyurl.com/ulaqdms

156. Eleveld, *Don't Tell Me to Wait*, 249.

157. Ibid., 252-254.

158. Ibid., 257.

159. Ibid., 262.

160. Ibid., 267.

161. Ibid., 266.

162. David French, *The Supreme Court Ratifies a New Civic Religion That Is Incompatible with Christianity*, last modified June 26, 2015, https://tinyurl.com/vwyzqzo

163. Ibid.

164. Amita Kelly, *'Abide by the Law': Campaign Trail Responds to Same-Sex-Marriage Ruling*, last modified June 26, 2015, https://tinyurl.com/rgffe4r

165. Emily London and Maggie Siddiqi, *Religious Liberty Should Do No Harm*, last modified April 11, 2019, https://tinyurl.com/t53u3gx

166. People for the American Way Foundation, *Who is Weaponizing Religious Liberty?* Accessed November 11, 2019, https://tinyurl.com/rok8jjy

167. *Senate Bill 101 Digest*, accessed November 11, 2019, https://tinyurl.com/nb97vgl

168. Walter Olson, *Gay Marriage Is Here to Stay, Even With a Conservative Court*, last modified July 8, 2018, https://tinyurl.com/w5okbga

169. Ruthann Robson, "Reinscribing Normality?: The Law and Politics of Transgender Marriage," in *Transgender Studies Reader 2*, edited by Susan Stryker and Aren Z. Aizura (New York: Routledge, 2013), 627-628.

170. Arnold J. Toynbee, *A Study of History: Abridgment of Volumes VII-X*, abridged by D.C. Somervell (New York: Oxford University Press, 1957), 109-110.

171. Joan Roughgarden, *Evolution's Rainbow: Diversity, Gender, and Sexuality in Nature and People* (Berkley: University of California Press, 2013), 23-24.

172. Susan Stryker, *Transgender History: The Roots of Today's Revolution* (New York: Seal Press, 2017), 28-29.

173. Roughgarden, *Evolution's Rainbow*, 27.

174. Stryker, *Transgender History*, 14-15.

175. Ibid., 16.

176. Susan Stryker, "My Words to Victor Frankenstein above the Village of Chamounix: Performing Transgender Rage," in *Transgender Studies Reader*, edited by Susan Stryker and Stephen Whittle (New York: Routledge, 2006), 246.

177. Karl Marx, *The Eighteenth Brumaire of Louis Bonaparte*, accessed October 23, 2019, https://tinyurl.com/phpxqn6; this sentiment is echoed in, of all places, the Hillsdale College *American Heritage* reader: The Hillsdale College History Faculty, *American Heritage: a Reader* (Acton, MA: Tapestry Press, Ltd, 2001), xi.

178. Genny Beemyn, "Transgender History in the United States," in *Trans Bodies, Trans Selves: A Resource for the Transgender Community*, edited by Laura Erickson-Schroth (New York: Oxford University Press, 2014), 2.

179. Author Unknown, *The Man Who Thought Himself A Woman*, The Knickerbocker, December 1857, https://tinyurl.com/tw67s88

180. Beemyn, "Transgender History in the United States," 6.

181. Ibid.

182. Ibid., 7.

183. Ibid.

184. Ibid., 8.

185. Ibid., 6.

186. Stryker, *Transgender History*, 48.

187. Beemyn, "Transgender History in the United States," 9.

188. Giovanni Russonello, Gladys Bentley, "A gender-bending blues performer who became 1920s Harlem royalty," accessed December 11, 2019, https://tinyurl.com/yc4va5bo

189. Stryker, *Transgender History*, 47.

190. Estelle B. Freedman, "'Uncontrolled Desires': The Response to the Sexual Psychopath, 1920-1960," *The Journal of American History* 74, No 1 (1987): 83-106, 18.

191. Stryker, *Transgender History*, 55-56.

192. Ibid., 62.

193. Susan Stryker, "Kaming Mga Talyada (We Who Are Sexy): The Transsexual Whiteness of Christine Jorgensen in the (Post)colonial Philippines," in *Transgender Studies Reader 2*, 545.

194. Dean Spade, "Mutilating Gender," in *Transgender Studies Reader*, 319-320.

195. Che Gossett, "Silhouettes of Defiance: Memorializing Historical Sites of Queer and Transgender Resistance in an Age of Neoliberal Inclusivity," in *Transgender Studies Reader 2*, 585.

196. Janice G. Raymond, "Sappho by Surgery: The Transsexually Constructed Lesbian-Feminist," in *Transgender Studies Reader*, 134; Stryker, *Transgender History*, 133-135.

197. Stryker, *Transgender History*, 184-185.

198. C. Riley Snorton and Jin Haritaworn, "Trans Necropolitics: A Transnational Reflection on Violence, Death, and the trans of Color Afterlife," in *Transgender Studies Reader 2*, 68; José Esteban Muñoz, "'The White to Be Angry': Vaginal Davis's Terrorist Drag," in *Transgender Studies Reader 2*, 81.

199. Stryker, *Transgender History*, 206.

200. Ibid., 207-208.

201. Buzz Bissinger, *Caitlyn Jenner: The Full Story*, last modified June 25, 2015, https://tinyurl.com/y7unr3qj

202. Frank Pallotta, *Caitlyn Jenner, Laverne Cox condemn Trump's transgender military ban*, last modified July 26, 2017, https://tinyurl.com/qmmgs4o

203. Stryker, *Transgender History*, 219-220.

204. Ibid., 220-221.

205. Ibid., 185-187.

206. Toby Beauchamp, "Artful Concealment and Strategic Visibility: Transgender Bodies and US State Surveillance after 9/11," in *Transgender Studies Reader 2*, 47-51.

207. Centre for Suicide Prevention, *Transgender people and suicide*,

accessed January 21, 2020, https://tinyurl.com/ra8qe5k

Chapter 5: The Anthropocene Age

1. Aristotle, "Meteorology Book II," *The Complete Works of Aristotle* Vol 1, edited by Jonathan Barnes (Princeton: Princeton University Press, 1984), 573-574.

2. Glen Sussman and Byron W. Daynes, *US Politics and Climate Change: Science Confronts Policy* (Boulder: Lynne Reinner Publishers, 2013), 2.

3. Edward Gibbon, *History of the Decline and Fall of the Roman Empire*, last modified April 14, 2019, https://tinyurl.com/swtq56o, Volume I, Chapter IX, Part I.

4. Joseph Fourier, *Memoir on the Temperature of the Earth and Planetary Spaces*, last modified July 2, 2004, https://tinyurl.com/yx2v34uf

5. John Tyndall, *The Glaciers of the Alps. Being a Narrative of Excursions and Ascents, an Account of the Origin and Phenomena of Glaciers and an Exposition of the Physical Principles to Which They Are Related* (New York: Longmans, Green, and Co., 1896), 422-425, https://tinyurl.com/vnnjcwa

6. John Tyndall, *Heat Considered as Mode of Motion* (New York: D. Appleton, 1869), 408, https://tinyurl.com/u6es4lf

7. Svante Arrhenius, "On the Influence of Carbonic Acid in the Air upon the Temperature of the Ground," in *The London, Edinburgh, and Dublin Philosophical Magazine and Journal of Science* series 5, Vol 41 (April, 1896), 2, https://tinyurl.com/y5kr87as

8. *The Discovery of Global Warming: The Carbon Dioxide Greenhouse Effect*, last modified February 2019, accessed October 29, 2019, https://tinyurl.com/qmu7sbq

9. Sussman and Daynes, *US Politics and Climate Change*, 27-28.

10. Scott K. Johnson, *That '70s myth – did climate science really call for a "coming ice age?"*, last modified June 7, 2016, https://tinyurl.com/wcdpnhs

11. Ibid.
12. Sussman and Daynes, *US Politics and Climate Change*, 28-29.
13. Greenhouse Effect Working Group, *The Greenhouse Effect*, 1, https://tinyurl.com/yb88h4e5
14. Ibid., 6.
15. Sussman and Daynes, *US Politics and Climate Change*, 29.
16. USGCRP, 2017, *Climate Science Special Report: Fourth National Climate Assessment, Volume I*, edited by D.J. Wuebbles, D.W. Fahey, K.A. Hibbard, D.J. Dokken, B.C. Stewart, and T.K. Maycock (Washington, DC: US Global Change Research Program, 2017), 122-123.
17. Ibid., 322.
18. Ibid., 16; Roz Pidcock, *Explainer, How do scientists measure global temperature?*, last modified January 16, 2015, https://tinyurl.com/gspky7m
19. USGCRP, 2017, *Climate Science Special Report Vol 1*, 42.
20. Ibid., 80-81.
21. Ibid., 81.
22. Ibid., 86-87.
23. Ibid., 88-89.
24. Ibid., 90-91.
25. Ibid., 96.
26. Ibid., 97.
27. Ibid., 16, 99-100.
28. Environmental Literacy Council, *Land Use Changes & Climate*, accessed December 9, 2019, https://tinyurl.com/w53kf65
29. USGCRP, 2017, *Climate Science Special Report Vol 1*, 101.
30. Ibid., 41.
31. Daisy Dunne, Josh Gabbatiss, Robert McSweeney, *Media reaction: Australia's bushfires and climate change*, last modified January 7, 2020, https://tinyurl.com/yx5jrxj7
32. USGCRP, 2017, *Climate Science Special Report Vol 1*, 41.
33. Naomi Klein, *This Changes Everything: Capitalism vs. The*

Climate (New York: Simon & Schuster, 2014), 33.

34. International Resource Panel 2019, *Global Resources Outlook 2019: Natural Resources for the Future We Want* (Nairobi, Kenya: United Nations Environment Programme, 2019), 9-10, 42.

35. Union of Concerned Scientists, *Each County's Share of CO_2 Emissions*, last modified October 2019, https://tinyurl.com/yyxgukld

36. International Resource Panel 2019, *Global Resources Outlook 2019*, 9.

37. The Environmental Literacy Council claims 18% of emissions result from land use changes: Environmental Literacy Council, *Land Use Changes & Climate*, accessed December 9, 2019, https://tinyurl.com/w53kf65; according to the Guardian, the emission level is 26%: Jonathan Watts, *Resource Extraction responsible for half world's carbon emissions*, last modified March 12, 2019, https://tinyurl.com/yxqb3x54

38. Sue Branford and Mauricio Torres, *As 2019 Amazon fires die down, Brazilian deforestation roars ahead*, last modified October 23, 2019, https://tinyurl.com/txzq7mg

39. Paul Griffin, *The Carbon Majors Database: CDP Carbon Majors Report 2017* (London: CDP, 2017), 7.

40. Ibid., 8.

41. Ibid., 14.

42. American Geosciences Institute, *How much oil is consumed in the United States?*, accessed January 11, 2020, https://tinyurl.com/y3apr4aq

43. US Energy Information Administration, *Energy and the environment explained: Where greenhouse gases come from*, last modified June 19, 2019, https://tinyurl.com/y39wlws8

44. Neta C. Crawford, *Pentagon Fuel Use, Climate Change, and the Costs of War* (Boston: Watson Institute, 2019), 2; Hannah Ritchie and Max Roser, *CO2 and Greenhouse Gas Emissions:*

Annual CO2 emissions, last modified December 2019, https://tinyurl.com/yy4p4w34

45. US Energy Information Administration, *FAQ*, last modified May 31, 2019, https://tinyurl.com/yxjvwqvq

46. Tim Flannery, *The Weather Makers: How Man is Changing the Climate and What it Means for Life on Earth* (New York: Atlantic Monthly Press, 2005), 214-215.

47. Ibid., 218.

48. Ibid., 220.

49. NASA, *2019 Ozone Hole is the Smallest on Record Since Its Discovery*, last modified October 21, 2019, https://tinyurl.com/y58zzdng

50. Flannery, *The Weather Makers*, 158-159.

51. Klein, *This Changes Everything*, 208.

52. Milieu Ltd., *Comparison of the EU and US Approaches Towards Acidification, Eutrophication, and Ground Level Ozone* (DG Environment, 2004), 9, 37.

53. Klein, *This Changes Everything*, 219.

54. Flannery, *The Weather Makers*, 224.

55. Klein, *This Changes Everything*, 219.

56. Earthworks, *The Halliburton Loophole*, accessed November 3, 2019, https://tinyurl.com/vcv4pb4

57. Klein, *This Changes Everything*, 328.

58. Sussman and Daynes, *US Politics and Climate Change*, 91.

59. Center for Responsive Politics, *Industry Profile: Environment*, accessed September 7, 2019, https://tinyurl.com/ujq5soz

60. Secretary of the IPCC, *IPCC Trust Fund Programme and Budget* (Kyoto: IPCC Secretariat, 2019), 7.

61. Center for Responsive Politics, *Industry Profile: Oil & Gas*, accessed September 7, 2019, https://tinyurl.com/vbspl4u

62. Robert J. Brulle, *Institutionalizing delay: foundation funding and the creation of US climate change counter-movement organizations* (Dordrecht: Springer Science and Business Media, 2013), 4.

63. Hugh Atkinson, *The Politics of Climate Change under President Obama* (New York: Routledge, 2018), 24.

64. Ibid., 2.

65. Sussman and Daynes, *US Politics and Climate Change*, 81.

66. Klein, *This Changes Everything*, 35.

67. Sussman and Daynes, *US Politics and Climate Change*, 11.

68. Klein, *This Changes Everything*, 195-196; 208.

69. Atkinson, *The Politics of Climate Change*, 13.

70. John Kerry, *Every Day Is Extra* (New York: Simon and Schuster, 2018), 559-560.

71. Ibid., 560.

72. Office of the Press Secretary, *FACT SHEET: The Recovery Act Made the Largest Single Investment in Clean Energy In History, Driving The Development Of Clean Energy, Promoting Energy Efficiency, And Supporting Manufacturing*, last modified February 25, 2016, https://tinyurl.com/qkm689j

73. European Commission, *Progress made in cutting emissions*, accessed January 21, 2020, https://tinyurl.com/reqf22o

74. Klein, *This Changes Everything*, 224.

75. Atkinson, *The Politics of Climate Change*, 27.

76. Ibid., 28-29.

77. Ibid., 31.

78. Ibid.

79. Ibid., 32-33.

80. Kerry, *Every Day Is Extra*, 564.

81. Ibid., 569-570.

82. Atkinson, *The Politics of Climate Change*, 35.

83. Ibid., 36.

84. Kerry, *Every Day Is Extra*, 571-572.

85. Obama, "Remarks on Energy," in *Barack Obama 2009 Book I*, 15.

86. Obama, "Remarks at Prince George's Community College in Largo, Maryland," in *Public Papers of the Presidents of the United States: Barack Obama 2012 Book I – January 1 to*

June 30, 2012 (Washington, DC: United States Government Publishing Office, 2016), 306.

87. Nick Estes, *Our History Is the Future: Standing Rock versus the Dakota Access Pipeline, and the Long Tradition of Indigenous Resistance* (New York: Verso, 2019), 29.

88. Klein, *This Changes Everything*, 311.

89. Ibid., 144, fn.

90. Fox News Insider, *'That Was Me, People': Obama Takes Credit for Oil Production Boom*, uploaded November 29, 2018, https://tinyurl.com/ru8wlo8

Chapter 6: Indigenous Resistance and the Intersectionality of American History

1. Alexander Anievas and Kerem Nisancioglu, *How the West Came to Rule: The Geopolitical Origins of Capitalism* (London: Pluto Press, 2015), 8-9.

2. Beckert, *Empire of Cotton*, xv.

3. Ibid., xv-xvi.

4. Anievas and Nisancioglu, *How the West Came to Rule*, 29.

5. Kenneth Chase, *Firearms: A Global History to 1700* (Cambridge: Cambridge University Press, 2003), 72.

6. Timothy Morton, *Hyperobjects: Philosophy and Ecology after the End of the World* (Minneapolis: University of Minnesota Press, 2013), 112-113.

7. Klein, *This Changes Everything*, 169-170.

8. James Wilson, *The Earth Shall Weep: A History of Native America* (New York: Atlantic Monthly Press, 1999), 23-24.

9. Priva Satia, *Empire of Guns: The Violent Making of the Industrial Revolution* (New York: Penguin Press, 2018), 6-7, 167, 173, 175, 179-180.

10. Wilson, *The Earth Shall Weep*, 92.

11. Ibid., 58-59.

12. Ibid., 59-60.

13. Ibid., 20.

14. Ibid., 77.

15. Ibid., 84.

16. Isenberg, *White Trash*, 19; Wilson, *The Earth Shall Weep*, 77.

17. Wilson, *The Earth Shall Weep*, 149-150.

18. Ibid., 157.

19. Ibid., 161.

20. Ibid., 170.

21. Ibid., 213.

22. Ibid., 228.

23. Ibid., 269; Chase, *Firearms: A Global History to 1700*, 81-82.

24. David Ramsay, *History of the American Revolution* Vol 1, edited by Lester H. Cohen (Indianapolis: Liberty Fund, 1990), 4-5.

25. Deborah A. Miranda, "Extermination of the Joyas: Gendercide in Spanish California," in *Transgender Reader 2*, 361.

26. Wilson, *The Earth Shall Weep*, 278-279.

27. Ibid., 295, 298; 303-304.

28. Ibid., 354-55.

29. Ibid., 362.

30. Ben Nighthorse Campbell, "Opening Keynote Address: Activating Indians into National Politics," in *American Indian Nations: Yesterday, Today, and Tomorrow*, edited by George P. Horse Capture, Duane Champagne, and Chandler C. Jackson (New York: Altamira Press, 2007), 2-3.

31. Wilson, *The Earth Shall Weep*, 396-405.

32. Tom LeGro, *Why the Sioux Are Refusing $1.3 Billion*, last modified August 24, 2011, https://tinyurl.com/ya8tptac

33. Klein, *This Changes Everything*, 294-295, 299.

34. Ibid., 324, 330.

35. Wikipedia, *Deepwater Horizon Oil Spill*, last modified December 5, 2019, https://tinyurl.com/vcje88q

36. James Gill, *Disaster prosecution is, well, a disaster*, last modified March 12, 2016, https://tinyurl.com/tgrptwg

37. Estes, *Our History Is the Future*, 2-3, 8-9.

38. Ibid., 29.

39. Obama, "Remarks at the TransCanada Pipe Storage Yard in Stillwater, Oklahoma," in *Barack Obama 2012 Book I*, 339.

40. Klein, *This Changes Everything*, 302-303; Estes, *Our History Is the Future*, 33-34, 40.

41. Mayra Cuevas and Steve Almasy, *Keystone Pipeline leaks 210,000 gallons of oil in South Dakota*, last modified November 17, 2017, https://tinyurl.com/yclflpqv

42. Estes, *Our History Is the Future*, 42-43.

43. Frederic Frommer, *Black Hills Are Beyond Price to Sioux; Culture: Despite economic hardship, tribe resists US efforts to dissolve an 1868 treaty for $570 million*, last modified November 11, 2014, https://tinyurl.com/rhklzgv

44. Justin Worland, *What to Know About the Dakota Access Pipeline Protests*, last modified October 28, 2016. https://tinyurl.com/rysoq84

45. Ibid.

46. Estes, *Our History Is the Future*, 47.

47. Ibid., 47.

48. Steven Mufson, *A Dakota Pipeline's Last Stand*, last modified November 25, 2016, https://tinyurl.com/hyp5ejm

49. Rebecca Hersher, *Key Moments in the Dakota Access Pipeline Fight*, last modified February 22, 2017, https://tinyurl.com/y3krpx24

50. Ibid.

51. Ibid.

52. Estes, *Our History Is the Future*, 53-54.

53. Ibid., 54.

54. Ibid.

55. Ibid., 64.

56. Brigham A. McCown, *What Ever Happened to the Dakota Access Pipeline?*, last modified June 4, 2018, https://tinyurl.com/vmapjpz; Alleen Brown, *Five Spills, Six Months in*

Operation: Dakota Access Track Record Highlights Unavoidable Reality – Pipelines Leak, last modified January 9 2018, https://tinyurl.com/yb4l4mva

57. Michael B. Sauter and Grant Suneson, *The Net Worth of the American Presidents: Washington to Trump,* last modified February 26, 2019, https://tinyurl.com/v5kydrl

58. L.M. Sacasas, *Elon Musk: Prophet of Cosmic Manifest Destiny,* last modified October 11, 2014, https://tinyurl.com/seq8622

59. He is actually quoting a friend of his: F.O. Matthiessen, *The James Family, Including Selections from the Writings of Henry James Senior, William, Henry, and Alice James* (New York: Alfred A. Knopf, 1947), 231.

Conclusion

1. Obama, "Inaugural Address," in *Barack Obama 2009 Book I,* 2.

2. Jeffrey M. Jones, *Obama's First Retrospective Job Approval Rating is 63%,* last modified February 15, 2018, https://tinyurl.com/y799azka

3. Theresa Alt, *DSA Finances 2017 Fiscal Year and January – June 2018 Budget Report to the Membership,* accessed January 16, 2020, https://tinyurl.com/v2q585y

4. Thomas Paine, *Common Sense,* last modified June 24, 2017, https://tinyurl.com/yx3tp992

5. Alexis de Tocqueville, *Democracy in America,* translated and edited by Harvey C. Mansfield and Delba Winthrop (Chicago: University of Chicago Press, 2002), 5.

Bibliography of Major Works

Background

Anievas, Alexander and Nisancioglu, Karen. *How the West Came to Rule: The Geopolitical Origins of Capitalism*. London: Pluto Press, 2015.

Beckert, Sven. *Empire of Cotton: A Global History*. New York: Alfred A. Knopf, 2015.

Chase, Kenneth. *Firearms: A Global History to 1700*. Cambridge: Cambridge University Press, 2003.

D'antonio, Michael. *A Consequential Presidency: the Legacy of Barack Obama*. New York: St. Martin's Press, 2016.

Durant, Will and Ariel Durant. *The Story of Civilization*. 11 vols. New York: Simon and Schuster, 1954-1975.

Roberts, J.M. and Odd Arne Westad. *The Penguin History of the World*. 6th ed. New York: Penguin Group, 2014.

Satia, Priya. *Empire of Guns: The Violent Making of the Industrial Revolution*. New York: Penguin Press, 2018.

Yergin, Daniel. *The Prize: the Epic Quest for Oil, Money & Power*. New York: Free Press, 2009.

Surveys of US History

Fitzgerald, Frances. *The Evangelicals: the Struggle to Shape America*. New York: Simon and Schuster, 2017.

Foner, Eric. *Give Me Liberty! An American History*. Vol 1. 3rd ed. New York: W.W. Norton & Company, 2012.

—. *Give Me Liberty!: An American History*. Vol. 2. 4th ed. New York: W.W. Norton & Company, 2013.

Immerwahr, Daniel. *How to Hide an Empire: A History of the Greater United States*. New York: Farrar, Straus, and Giroux, 2019.

Isenberg, Nancy. *White Trash: The 400 Year Untold History of Class in America*. New York: Penguin Books, 2016.

Isserman, Maurice and Michael Kazin. *America Divided: The Civil*

War of the 1960s. New York: Oxford University Press, 2000.

Kruse, Kevin M. and Julian E. Zelizer. *Fault Lines: A History of the United States since 1974*. New York: W.W. Norton & Company, 2019.

Patterson, James. *Grand Expectations: The United States, 1945-1974*. New York: Oxford University Press, 1996.

Scott, Shaun. *Millennials and the Moments that Made Us: A Cultural History of the U.S. from 1982 – Present*. Washington: Zero Books, 2018.

Zinn, Howard. *A People's History of the United States*. New York: HarperCollins, 2015.

Contemporary Political Memoirs

Carter, Ash. *Inside the Five-Sided Box: Lessons from a Lifetime of Leadership in the Pentagon*. New York: Dutton, 2019.

Gates, Robert. *Duty: Memoirs of a Secretary at War*. New York: Alfred A. Knopf, 2014.

Geithner, Timothy. *Stress Test: Reflections on Financial Crisis*. New York: Crown Publishers, 2014.

Kerry, John. *Every Day is Extra*. New York: Simon and Schuster, 2018.

Panetta, Leon, and Jim Newton. *Worthy Fights: A Memoir of Leadership in War and Peace*. New York: Penguin Press, 2014.

Rhodes, Ben. *The World as It Is: A Memoir of the Obama White House*. New York: Random House, 2018.

Chapter 1: The Forever War

Bacevich, Andrew. *America's War for the Greater Middle East: A Military History*. New York: Random House, 2016.

Chomsky, Noam. *Who Rules the World?* New York: Henry Holt and Company, 2016.

Crist, David. *The Twilight War: The Secret History of America's 30 Year Conflict with Iran*. New York: Penguin Press, 2012.

Epstein, Edward, Jay. *How America Lost its Secrets: Edward*

Snowden, the Man and the Theft. New York: Alfred A Knopf, 2017.

Gelvin, James L. *The Modern Middle East: A History*. New York: Oxford University Press, 2011.

Gold, Dore. *Hatred's Kingdom: How Saudi Arabia Supports the New Global Terrorism*. Washington DC: Regnery Publishing Inc., 2003.

Hosken, Andrew. *Empire of Fear: Inside the Islamic State*. London: Oneworld, 2015.

National Commission on Terrorist Attacks upon the United States. *9/11 Commission Report: Final Report of the National Commission on Terrorist Attacks Upon the United States*. New York: W.W. Norton & Company Inc, 2004.

Richardson, Louise. *What Terrorists Want: Understanding the Enemy, Containing the Threat*. New York: Random House, 2007.

Savage, Charlie. *Power Wars: The Relentless Rise of Presidential Authority and Secrecy*. New York: Back Bay Books, 2017.

Scahill, Jeremy. *The Assassination Complex: Inside the Government's Secret Drone Warfare Program*. New York: Simon & Schuster, 2016.

Smith, Jean Edward. *Bush*. New York: Simon and Schuster, 2016.

Turse, Nick. *Tomorrow's Battlefield: US Proxy Wars and Secret Ops in Africa*. Chicago: Haymarket Books, 2015.

Williams, Brian Glyn. *Counter Jihad: America's Military Experience in Afghanistan, Iraq, and Syria*. Philadelphia: University of Pennsylvania Press, 2017.

Chapter 2: Economy in Crisis

Davis, Kenneth S. *FDR: Into the Storm, 1937-1940*. New York: Random House, 1993.

Eichengreen, Barry. *Hall of Mirrors: The Great Depression, the Great Recession, and the Uses – and Misuses – of History*. New York: Oxford University Press, 2015.

Financial Crisis Inquiry Commission. *The Financial Crisis Inquiry*

Report: The Final Report of the National Commission on the Causes of the Financial and Economic Crisis in the United States. Washington DC: US Government Printing Office, 2011.

Neoliberalism: A Critical Reader. Edited by Filho-Saad, Alfredo and Deborah Johnston. Ann Arbor, MI: Pluto Press, 2005.

Sorkin, Andrew. *Too Big to Fail: The Inside Story of how Wall Street and Washington Fought to Save the Financial System – and Themselves.* New York: Viking Press, 2009.

Stiglitz, Joseph. *The Price of Inequality: How Today's Divided Society Endangers Our Future.* New York: W.W. Norton & Company, 2012.

Suskind, Ron. *Confidence Men: Wall Street, Washington, and the Education of a President.* New York: Harper Perennial, 2011.

Tooze, Adam. *Crashed: How a Decade of Financial Crisis Changed the World.* New York: Viking, 2018.

Wolff, Richard D., and Stephen A. Resnick. *Contending Economic Theories: Neoclassical, Keynesian, and Marxian.* Cambridge, MA: MIT Press, 2012.

Chapter 3: Healthcare Reform

Berchick, Edward R., Emily Hood, and Jessica C. Barnett. "Health Insurance Coverage in the United States: 2017," *Current Population Reports, P60-264.* Washington, DC: US Government Printing Office, 2018.

Dawes, Daniel. *150 Years of ObamaCare.* Baltimore: Johns Hopkins University Press, 2016.

Dewar, Diane M. *The Economics of US Health Reform: A Global Perspective.* New York: Routledge, 2018.

Engel, Jonathan. *Unaffordable: American Healthcare from Johnson to Trump.* Madison: University of Wisconsin Press, 2018.

Hudson, Ian and Robert Chernomas. *To Live and Die in America: Class, Power, Health, and Healthcare.* New York: St Martin's Press, 2013.

International Profiles of Health Care Systems. Edited by Elias

Mossialos, Ana Djordjevic, Robin Osborn, and Dana Sarnak. The Commonwealth Fund, May 2017. https://tinyurl.com/y2nwch78

Kominski, Gerald F., Narissa J. Nonzee, and Andrea Sorensen. "The Affordable Care Act's Impacts on Access to Insurance and Health Care for Low-Income Populations." *The Annual Review of Public Health* 38 (2017): 489-505.

Kowalski, Amanda E. "The Early Impact of the Affordable Care Act, State by State."*Brookings Papers on Economic Activity* (Fall 2014), https://tinyurl.com/wae7t2o

Okorno, Catherine A., Guixiang Zhao, Jared B. Fox, et al. "Surveillance for Health Care Access and Health Services Use, Adults Aged 18-64 – Behavioral Risk Factor Surveillance System, United States, 2014."*MMWR Surveillance Summary* 66, no 7 (2017).

Rawal, Purva H. *The Affordable Care Act: Examining the Facts.* Santa Barbara: ABC-CLIO, 2016.

Rosenthal, Elisabeth. *An American Sickness: How Healthcare Became Big Business and How You Can Take It Back*. New York: Random House Large Print, 2017.

Starr, Paul. *Remedy and Reaction: The Peculiar American Struggle Over Health Care Reform.* New Haven: Yale University Press, 2011.

—. *The Social Transformation of American Medicine: The rise of a sovereign profession and the making of a vast industry.* New York: Basic Books Inc., 1982.

Washington Post. *Landmark: The Inside Story of America's New Health-Care Law and What it Means for Us All.* New York: Public Affairs, 2010.

Waitzkin, Howard and the Working Group on Health beyond Capitalism. *Healthcare Under the Knife: Moving Beyond Capitalism for Our Health.* New York: Monthly Review Press, 2018.

Waitzkin, Howard. *Medicine and Public Health at the End of Empire.*

Boulder: Paradigm Publishers, 2011.

Chapter 4: On the Margins: African Americans

Alexander, Michelle. *The New Jim Crow: Mass Incarceration in the Age of Colorblindness*. New York: the New Press, 2012.

Baptist, Edward E. *The Half Has Never Been Told: Slavery and the Making of American Capitalism*. New York: Basic Books, 2014.

Baradaran, Mehrsa. *The Color of Money: Black Banks and the Racial Wealth Gap*. Cambridge, MA: the Belknap Press of Harvard University Press, 2017.

Berman, Ari. *Give us the Ballot: The Modern Struggle for Voting Rights in America*. New York: Farrar, Straus and Giroux, 2015.

Coates, Ta-Nehisi. *We Were Eight Years in Power: An American Tragedy*. New York: One World Publishing, 2017.

Dew, Charles B. *Apostles of Disunion: Southern Secessionist Commissioners and the Causes of the Civil War*. Charlottesville: University of Virginia Press, 2001.

DuBois, WEB. *Black Reconstruction in America: 1860-1880*. New York: The Free Press, 1998.

Dyson, Michael Eric. *The Black Presidency: Barack Obama and the Politics of Race in America*. Boston: Mariner Books, 2016.

Fleegler, Robert L. "Theodore G. Bilbo and the Decline of Public Racism 1938-1947,"*Mississippi Journal of History* 68, no 1, (2006). https://tinyurl.com/v3uv8d2

Foner, Eric. *A Short History of Reconstruction: 1863-1877*. New York: Harper and Row, 1990.

Foner, Jack. *Blacks and the Military in American History*. New York: Praeger Publishers, 1974.

Hinton, Elizabeth. *From the War on Poverty to the War on Crime: The Making of Mass Incarceration in America*. Cambridge, MA: Harvard University Press, 2016.

Hughley, Matthew and Gregory Parks. *The Wrongs of the Right: Language, Race and the Republican Party in the Age of Obama*. New York: New York University Press, 2014.

Johannsen, Robert W., and Wendy Hamand Venet. *Union in Crisis: 1850-1870*. Acton, MA: Copley Publishing Group, 2003.

Lowery, Wesley. *They Can't Kill Us All: Ferguson, Baltimore, and a New Era in America's Racial Justice Movement*. New York: Little, Brown and Company, 2016.

Rae, Noel. *The Great Stain: Witnessing American Slavery*. New York: the Overlook Press, 2018.

Smedley, Audrey. *Race in North America: Origin and Evolution of a Worldview*. 3rd ed. Boulder, CO: Westview Press, 2007.

Taylor, Keeanga-Yamahtta. *From #Blacklivesmatter to Black Liberation*. Chicago: Haymarket Books, 2016.

Wilkerson, Isabel. *The Warmth of Other Suns: The Epic Story of America's Great Migration*. New York: Random House, 2010.

US Department of Justice. *Federal Report on Police Killings*. Brooklyn, NY: Melville House, 2017.

Chapter 4: On the Margins: LGBT

Bayer, Ronald. *Homosexuality and American Psychiatry: The Politics of Diagnosis*. Princeton: Princeton University Press, 1987.

Crompton, Louis. *Homosexuality & Civilization*. Cambridge: Belknap Press of Harvard University Press, 2003.

Dowbiggin, Ian Robert. *Keeping America Sane: Psychiatry and Eugenics in the United States and Canada, 1880-1940*. Ithaca: Cornell University Press, 1997.

Eleveld, Kerry. *Don't Tell Me to Wait: How the Fight for Gay Rights Changed America and Transformed Obama's Presidency*. New York: Basic Books, 2015.

Faderman, Lillian. *The Gay Revolution: The Story of the Struggle*. New York: Simon and Schuster, 2015.

Roughgarden, Joan. *Evolution's Rainbow: Diversity, Gender, and Sexuality in Nature and People*. Berkley: University of California Press, 2013.

Snorton, C. Riley. *Black on Both Sides: A Racial History of Trans Identity*. Minneapolis: University of Minnesota Press, 2017.

Stryker, Susan. *Transgender History: The Roots of Today's Revolution*. New York: Seal Press, 2017.

The Transgender Studies Reader. Edited by Susan Stryker and Stephen Whittle. New York: Routledge, 2006.

The Transgender Studies Reader 2. Edited by Susan Stryker and Aren Z., Aizura. New York: Routledge, 2013.

Chapter 5: The Anthropocene Age

Atkinson, Hugh. *The Politics of Climate Change under President Obama*. New York: Routledge, 2018.

Flannery, Tim. *The Weathermakers: How Man is Changing the Climate and What It Means for Life on Earth*. New York: Atlantic Monthly Press, 2005.

Giddens, Anthony. *The Politics of Climate Change*. Malden: Polity Press, 2009.

Hoffman, Andrew. *How Culture Shapes the Climate Change Debate*. Stanford: Stanford University Press, 2015.

Intergovernmental Panel on Climate Change. *Climate Change 2014: Synthesis Report-Contribution of Working Groups I, II and III to the Fifth Assessment Report of the Intergovernmental Panel on Climate Change*. Edited by R.K. Pachauri and L.A. Meyer. Geneva, Switzerland: IPCC, 2014.

Klein, Naomi. *This Changes Everything: Capitalism vs. The Climate*. New York: Simon & Schuster, 2014.

Morton, Timothy. *Hyperobjects: Philosophy and Ecology after the End of the World*. Minneapolis: University of Minnesota Press, 2013.

Oreskes, Naomi, and Erik M. Conway. *Merchants of Doubt: How a Handful of Scientists Obscured the Truth on Issues from Tobacco Smoke to Global Warming*. New York: Bloomsbury, 2011.

Outwater, Alice. *Wild at Heart: America's Turbulent Relationship with Nature, from Exploitation to Redemption*. New York: St. Martin's Press, 2019.

Sussman, Glen and Byron Daynes. *US Politics and Climate Change:*

Science Confronts Policy. Boulder: Lynne Reinner Publishers, 2013.

USGCRP, 2017. *Climate Science Special Report: Fourth National Climate Assessment, Volume* I. Edited by D.J. Wuebbles, D.W. Fahey, K.A. Hibbard, D.J. Dokken, B.C. Stewart, and T.K. Maycock. Washington, DC: US Global Change Research Program, 2017.

Chapter 6: Indigenous Resistance and the Intersectionality of American History

Brown, Dee. *Bury My Heart at Wounded Knee: An Indian History of the American West*. New York: Holt, Rinehart & Winston, 1970.

Estes, Nick. *Our History Is the Future: Standing Rock versus the Dakota Access Pipeline, and the Long Tradition of Indigenous Resistance*. New York: Verso, 2019.

Vaughan, Alden T. *New England Frontier: Puritans and Indians 1620-1675*. Boston: Little Brown and Company, 1965.

Wilson, James. *The Earth Shall Weep: A History of Native America*. New York: Atlantic Monthly Press, 1999.

Author Biography

Owen grew up in Scranton, Pa, and spent his childhood buried in science fiction and history. He attended Hillsdale College, receiving a BA in history and meeting his future wife. After college, he spent several years as a psychiatric technician in a for-profit hospital, transitioned to retail (selling and repairing computers), and then tech support at a call center. Dissatisfaction at work coupled with an increasing political awareness prompted him to turn to writing history full time. He lives in Michigan.

CULTURE, SOCIETY & POLITICS

The modern world is at an impasse. Disasters scroll across our smartphone screens and we're invited to like, follow or upvote, but critical thinking is harder and harder to find. Rather than connecting us in common struggle and debate, the internet has sped up and deepened a long-standing process of alienation and atomization. Zer0 Books wants to work against this trend.
With critical theory as our jumping off point, we aim to publish books that make our readers uncomfortable. We want to move beyond received opinions.
Zer0 Books is on the left and wants to reinvent the left. We are sick of the injustice, the suffering, and the stupidity that defines both our political and cultural world, and we aim to find a new foundation for a new struggle.

If this book has helped you to clarify an idea, solve a problem or extend your knowledge, you may want to check out our online content as well. Look for Zer0 Books: Advancing Conversations in the iTunes directory and for our Zer0 Books YouTube channel.

Popular videos include:
Žižek and the Double Blackmain
The Intellectual Dark Web is a Bad Sign
Can there be an Anti-SJW Left?
Answering Jordan Peterson on Marxism

Follow us on Facebook
at https://www.facebook.com/ZeroBooks and Twitter at https://twitter.com/Zer0Books

Bestsellers from Zer0 Books include:

Give Them an Argument
Logic for the Left
Ben Burgis
Many serious leftists have learned to distrust talk of logic. This is a serious mistake.
Paperback: 978-1-78904-210-8 ebook: 978-1-78904-211-5

Poor but Sexy
Culture Clashes in Europe East and West
Agata Pyzik
How the East stayed East and the West stayed West.
Paperback: 978-1-78099-394-2 ebook: 978-1-78099-395-9

An Anthropology of Nothing in Particular
Martin Demant Frederiksen
A journey into the social lives of meaninglessness.
Paperback: 978-1-78535-699-5 ebook: 978-1-78535-700-8

In the Dust of This Planet
Horror of Philosophy vol. 1
Eugene Thacker
In the first of a series of three books on the Horror of Philosophy, *In the Dust of This Planet* offers the genre of horror as a way of thinking about the unthinkable.
Paperback: 978-1-84694-676-9 ebook: 978-1-78099-010-1

The End of Oulipo?
An Attempt to Exhaust a Movement
Lauren Elkin, Veronica Esposito
Paperback: 978-1-78099-655-4 ebook: 978-1-78099-656-1

Capitalist Realism
Is There No Alternative?
Mark Fisher
An analysis of the ways in which capitalism has presented itself
as the only realistic political-economic system.
Paperback: 978-1-84694-317-1 ebook: 978-1-78099-734-6

Rebel Rebel
Chris O'Leary
David Bowie: every single song. Everything you want to know,
everything you didn't know.
Paperback: 978-1-78099-244-0 ebook: 978-1-78099-713-1

Kill All Normies
Angela Nagle
Online culture wars from 4chan and Tumblr to Trump.
Paperback: 978-1- 78535-543-1 ebook: 978-1-78535-544-8

Cartographies of the Absolute
Alberto Toscano, Jeff Kinkle
An aesthetics of the economy for the twenty-first century.
Paperback: 978-1-78099-275-4 ebook: 978-1-78279-973-3

Babbling Corpse
Vaporwave and the Commodification of Ghosts
Grafton Tanner
Paperback: 978-1-78279-759-3 ebook: 978-1-78279-760-9

New Work New Culture
Work we want and a culture that strengthens us
Frithjoff Bergmann
A serious alternative for mankind and the planet.
Paperback: 978-1-78904-064-7 ebook: 978-1-78904-065-4

Malign Velocities
Accelerationism and Capitalism
Benjamin Noys
Long listed for the Bread and Roses Prize 2015, *Malign Velocities*
argues against the need for speed, tracking acceleration
as the symptom of the ongoing crises of capitalism.
Paperback: 978-1-78279-300-7 ebook: 978-1-78279-299-4

Meat Market
Female Flesh under Capitalism
Laurie Penny
A feminist dissection of women's bodies as the fleshy fulcrum of
capitalist cannibalism, whereby women are both consumers and
consumed.
Paperback: 978-1-84694-521-2 ebook: 978-1-84694-782-7

Romeo and Juliet in Palestine
Teaching Under Occupation
Tom Sperlinger
Life in the West Bank, the nature of pedagogy and the role of a
university under occupation.
Paperback: 978-1-78279-637-4 ebook: 978-1-78279-636-7

Ghosts of My Life
Writings on Depression, Hauntology and Lost Futures
Mark Fisher
Paperback: 978-1-78099-226-6 ebook: 978-1-78279-624-4

Why Are We The Good Guys?
Reclaiming your Mind from the Delusions of Propaganda
David Cromwell
A provocative challenge to the standard ideology that Western
power is a benevolent force in the world.
Paperback: 978-1-78099-365-2 ebook: 978-1-78099-366-9

Sweetening the Pill
or How We Got Hooked on Hormonal Birth Control
Holly Grigg-Spall
Has contraception liberated or oppressed women?
Sweetening the Pill breaks the silence on the dark side of hormonal
contraception.
Paperback: 978-1-78099-607-3 ebook: 978-1-78099-608-0

The Writing on the Wall
On the Decomposition of Capitalism and its Critics
Anselm Jappe, Alastair Hemmens
A new approach to the meaning of social emancipation.
Paperback: 978-1-78535-581-3 ebook: 978-1-78535-582-0

How to Dismantle the NHS in 10 Easy Steps (Second Edition)
Youssef El-Gingihy
The story of how your NHS was sold off and why you will have
to buy private health insurance soon. A new expanded second
edition with chapters on junior doctors' strikes and government
blueprints for US-style healthcare.
Paperback: 978-1-78904-178-1 ebook: 978-1-78904-179-8

Most titles are published in paperback and as an ebook.
Paperbacks are available in traditional bookshops. Both print and
ebook formats are available online.
Follow us on Facebook
at https://www.facebook.com/ZeroBooks
and Twitter at https://twitter.com/Zer0Books